COLDITZ

Colditz Castle at night

P. R. REID, M.B.E., M.C.

COLDITZ

The two classic escape stories
in one volume—"The Colditz
Story" and "The Latter Days"

Illustrated by
JOHN WATTON

BOOK CLUB ASSOCIATES
LONDON

This edition published 1972 by
Book Club Associates
by arrangement with Hodder and Stoughton Ltd

Reprinted 1973
Reprinted 1974

Printed in Great Britain by
Richard Clay (The Chaucer Press), Ltd, Bungay, Suffolk

APOLOGIA

ESCAPE books are sometimes said to make escaping more difficult for the future, but the escape stories of the First World War made the majority of POWs in the Second World War escape-conscious. In the First World War escapers were an uncommon breed of men. A spirit was created by the early books which throve and bore fruit.

Minor escape techniques may have been made public by these early books, but they are never criticised for that by the escapers of the Second World War. Besides, much was left unsaid, and that applies even more to the stories of today—thanks to the authors who have deliberately omitted many details of enthralling interest. The different conditions of life in Germany were what our generation was really up against: the Gestapo, the Allied bombing and the Hitler Youth. Big Bertha cannot be compared to Allied air bombardment, nor can Allied air bombardment be compared to guided, stratospheric, atomic warhead rocket missiles. It will be the new conditions which will be the obstacles in the future, not escape books. The inspiration of escape books lives in men's memories and serves to keep alive the spirit of adventure.

CONTENTS

LIST OF ILLUSTRATIONS

[1] Reproduced by courtesy of the Falcon Press.
[2] Reproduced by courtesy of the *Illustrated London News*.

THE COLDITZ STORY

TO MY WIFE
JANEY

ACKNOWLEDGMENTS

THIS book, written ten years after the events it portrays, would not have materialised without the help of many friends. They are, one and all, former Colditz POWs, including the artist who has contributed the illustrations.

John Watton used to send drawings to England from Colditz. They were published in the *Illustrated London News* and gave to many anxious relatives, as well as to a wide and sympathetic public, a vivid insight into the life of that fortress prison. A few of those illustrations are to be found in this book and, for the permission to reproduce them, my thanks are due to the proprietors of that illustrious journal. The majority of the pictures, however, are new creations from Watton's talented hand. I have been fortunate in having the collaboration of a man who lived the story of Colditz and who has the talent to conjure into life again the atmosphere and the detail of those days and events.

Other officers, former Colditz inmates, who have helped me are: Flight Lieut. H. D. Wardle, Lieut-Comdr. W. L. Stephens, Major P. Storie Pugh, Lieut-Col. A. Neave, Capt. K. Lockwood, Capt. R. Howe, Col. G. German, Major H. A. V. Elliott, Major R. R. F. T. Barry and Capt. A. M. Allan. Major Elliott's many contributions and unstinted help have been of especial value, and I am grateful to Captain Allan for his correction of the German in the text.

I have been fortunate, too, in finding the whereabouts, on the Continent, of several ex-Colditz POWs of the Allied armies: Dutch, French, and Polish. Lieut.-General C. Giebel, Major P. Mairesse Lebrun and Lieut. F. Jablonowski (in the U.K.), in particular, have kindly given me their assistance.

Lastly, to my wife I owe much, for her comments and for her untiring help in the preparation of the material of the book.

PROLOGUE

WHEN I was a boy at school, I read with avidity three of the greatest escape books of the First World War. They were: *The Road to Endor* by E. H. Jones, *The Escape Club* by A. J. Evans, and *Within Four Walls* by H. A. Cartwright and M. C. C. Harrison. All of them, as exciting reading, are as fresh today as when they were first published. These three epics lived long in my memory, so that when the fortunes of war found me a prisoner in an enemy land the spirit enshrined in them urged me to follow the example of their authors.

A. J. Evans said that escaping is the greatest sport in the world. In my early twenties I thought that to ride in the Grand National Steeplechase at Aintree would be the epitome of sporting excitement—more so even than big-game hunting. I longed to do both. Since the war and my experiences as an escaper, my one-time ambitions have died a natural death. I feel I have quaffed deeply of the intoxicating cup of excitement and can retire to contemplate those 'unforgettable moments' of the past. I can think of no sport that is the peer of escape, where freedom, life, and loved ones are the prize of victory, and death the possible though by no means inevitable price of failure.

The Second World War had just come to a close when A. J. Evans wrote some further memoirs in a book he called *Escape and Liberation, 1940-1945*. In it he wrote:

> The whole story of Colditz will, no doubt, one day be told, and it will make an enthralling story; but it must be written by one of the men who was there.

This book is the story of Colditz. I was one of the men imprisoned there.

We called Colditz 'the bad boys' camp'; the Germans called it the *Straflager*. An officer had to pass an entrance exam. before being admitted through its sacred—the

French would say its *sacré*—portals. The qualifying or passing-out test was the performance of at least one escape from any one of the many 'Prep.-school' camps that were dotted all over Germany. Naturally, the qualifying escape exam. was not set by the Germans, nor were 'full marks' a guarantee of entry—in fact, the contrary, for the hundred per cent. candidate was never available to take up his vacancy. He was out of bounds and, happily for him, 'expelled' for good!

Unfortunately, the nearer the applicant's marking came to a hundred without actually attaining it, the more certain he was of finding a wooden trestle bed and straw palliasse awaiting him in Colditz.

You, my reader, I feel, would also like to qualify before entering Colditz. You should run the gauntlet as hundreds of us did and pass the exam. So, in order to get you into training, you will, I hope, forgive me if you do not reach Colditz until Chapter IV. If you have read many escape books and are an old-timer, you may skip the early chapters if you wish. But at least in my qualifying exam. I escaped as a woman—almost the only feminine interest in the book, I am sorry to say—so it might be worth your while. . . .

When you eventually arrive at Colditz, I shall not waste your time with details that every escaper knows. All the other inhabitants are professionals, and professionals do not demean themselves with the lesser problems. In fact, there will not be time to go into all the details, for that was Colditz.

It was supposed to be impregnable and certainly looked like it for a long time. It was the German fortress from which there was no escape. It had been escape-proof in the 1914–1918 War and was to be so again in this war, according to the Germans.

The garrison manning the camp outnumbered the prisoners at all times. The Castle was floodlit at night from every angle, in spite of the blackout. Notwithstanding the clear drops of a hundred feet or so on the outside from barred windows, there were sentries all round the camp, within a palisade of barbed wire. Beyond the palisade were precipices of varying depth. A detailed description of the plan and elevations of the Castle is impossible, but the above outline gives an indication of what we were up against.

But the Germans overlooked the fact that successful escapes depend mostly on the accumulation of escape technique, and they gathered together in one place, in Colditz, all the escape technicians of the Allied forces from all over the world. Together with this, they concentrated in Colditz the highest morale it is possible to imagine.

To cite an example, let me mention 'Never-a-dull-moment' Paddon—Squadron Leader B. Paddon, R.A.F., in other words. He earned his title well, for he was never out of trouble. Time after time his escape preparations were discovered, or he was caught red-handed by the German 'snoops' wielding a contraband file or saw. He earned months of solitary confinement for himself and others, as well as the stopping of 'privileges' for the whole prisoner contingent. Colditz was proud of Paddon long before he escaped successfully. It was ironical that the opportunity for his last escape should have been provided by a court-martial charge earned by him in earlier days when he was busy qualifying for Colditz.

'Never a dull moment' might well have been the motto on the Castle's armorial bearings. If there were not three hundred and sixty-five escape attempts in a year at Colditz, there were not far short of that number in the four and a half years of its war history.

If you feel in a mood to launch into the feverish underground activity of a camp full of diehards, read on. But remember, as I said before, a little preliminary training may be of advantage. It was at Laufen that not a few of the Colditz escapers began their studies, myself among them.

LE VESINET,   P. R. REID.
NEAR PARIS.
   September, 1951.

I

Apprentice

ESCAPE RECONNAISSANCE

IT was June 5th, 1940. We arrived at Laufen, about eighteen miles north-east of Salzburg, on the tenth day of my captivity. It was our final destination and we disembarked. My first impression was of a charming village on the banks of a murmuring river, the Salzach. The inhabitants lined the road and watched in silence as we marched by. The Salzach separates Bavaria from Austria at this point. We saw beside the river an enormous block-like building which looked a little like a mediæval Schloss and a great deal like a huge asylum. It was the ancient palace of the Archbishop of Salzburg, sentimentally revered as the place where Mozart composed and played many of his works. To us, it was remarkable, on first inspection, only for the amazing number of windows it possessed; in one wall-face alone I counted over sixty. This was to be our permanent home.

We were the first arrivals. Everything was prepared for us in the way of barbed wire and guards falling over each other. We were paraded while the Commandant made an appearance, surrounded by his hierarchy, and delivered a speech. For the first time, we were searched individually and thoroughly. Our heads were shaven under riotous protest, and we were each given a small aluminium disc with a number upon it. Our photos were taken and we were let loose into a small compound as duly recognised prisoners-of-war. Captain Patrick Reid, R.A.S.C., had become *Kriegsgefangenennummer* 257. The prison was Oflag VII C.

*   *   *   *

June 12th brought two hundred more arrivals, making our total four hundred. We were told that when the camp was full it would hold fifteen hundred officers. Many of the newcomers were allotted to our room, No. 66, and among them was Captain Rupert Barry of the 52nd Light Infantry. From the moment of our first meeting we talked escape.

He was sitting on a bench in front of a long kitchen-type table, playing patience with a pack of cards which he had made out of pieces of paper, when I came into the room.

I sat opposite him in silence for a long time, my chin in my hands. My mind wandered hundreds of miles away to a home in England.

The man in front of me continued his game, deliberately, carefully smoothing out and adjusting his pieces of paper. Occasionally he twirled his large guardee moustache with a slow controlled movement of his long fingers. My thoughts switched to him.

"Control. Yes, the man in front of me has certainly taught himself control. Maybe he has need of it. Still waters run deep," I mused.

He looked up from his game. His dark eyes smouldered, but withal there was kindliness somewhere within and his smile was pleasant.

"I'm determined to get out of this place within three months," I said, wondering in the next instant why I had confided in him.

"You're an optimist. Why the hurry?"

"I've got a date for Christmas which I don't want to miss. If I leave early in September, I could hope to get a sailing from Gibraltar or Lisbon in time."

"I wouldn't mind joining you," Rupert Barry said. "My wife will never forgive me if I don't escape from here. She'll accuse me of not caring for her any more."

"She sounds as if she's rather a strong personality."

"That's one of the things I like about her," he said, and added: "You're obviously not married."

"No, I'm a bachelor and what little eligibility I ever possessed is fading rapidly with every day that passes here."

"How about a systematic reconnaissance of the premises?"

"Good, let's start."

* * * * *

Rupert was twenty-nine, about five feet eleven inches tall, and well-proportioned. Considering the circumstances, he was dressed smartly and was an imposing personality with his handsome, rather sallow-complexioned face set off by the big dark guardee moustache and a large chin. Straight-nosed, brown-eyed, with dark-brown hair (after it

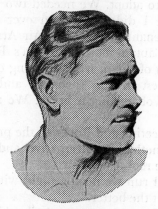

The Author

had grown again!); a man who could play havoc with the female sex but, in fact, lived only for his wife 'Dodo' and his two children. He was a professional soldier and had been educated at King's School, Canterbury.

For several days we scoured the camp together on our reconnaissance tour. We examined all the possibilities of passing the barbed-wire entanglements in the compounds, discussed the pros and cons of rushing the gates, and argued over wall-climbs blatantly suicidal. When the flood-lights were switched on at night, we judged the depths and positions of shadows, timed sentries on their beats, and stayed up for hours on end peering cautiously through windows to see if the guards became lazy or changed their habits in the early hours, giving us a possible opening. In the end we found ourselves concentrating on one particular corner of a tall building in the inner quadrangle, and our ideas filtered down to two opposing schemes.

The first, Rupert's idea, was simply a tunnel; the second, mine, involved a long roof-climb and a rope-descent. These were the embryos from which the first escape attempt from Laufen developed. Rupert's plan involved tedious work for months on end. Mine was a 'blitz.' We agreed it was worth making an experiment on my scheme before deciding what plan to adopt. We needed two helpers to act as observers while I did a trial run over the roofs. Sailor Nealy, a Lieutenant of the Fleet Air Arm, and Kenneth Lockwood, a Captain of the Queen's Royal Regiment, joined us. Both of them, without being over curious, had expressed interest in our 'snooping' and had told us of their intention of making a break. We all four lived in room 66.

We held a meeting and I opened the proceedings. I told Nealy and Kenneth of the alternatives and of our intention to start with the roof. I went on:

"For the trial run we need a night with no moon—the darker the night the better."

"Yes, but you don't want rain," said Nealy. "You'll career off the roof like a toboggan, and you'll have to wear gym. shoes anyway."

"A wind wouldn't matter. In fact, it should help," said Kenneth.

"You see the idea. We need all these conditions if possible. Rupert is the strongest of us, so I suggest he lets me down on the sheet-rope to the flat inter-connecting roof."

"We'll need at least two sheets; better have three for the twelve-foot drop," put in Kenneth.

"I'll drop and then carry on to the main roof. Kenneth, you'll have to watch my whole journey and check for visibility, shadows and noise. Sailor, you'd better keep your eye on each sentry in turn as I come into his line of vision and area of responsibility, and watch for reactions."

"The idea," said Rupert, "is that Pat will go to the far end of the long roof and see if it is practicable to make a sheet-descent outside the prison. There's a sentry in the roadway round the corner, but we don't know how much he can see. Pat can check on that too. A lot depends on the depth of shadow in which the descent will be made."

"The moon will be nearly gone on June 30th. That's a Sunday," I went on, "and the guards should have drunk some beer and may be more sleepy than usual. I suggest we agree on that date provided the weather is reasonable."

The date was agreed and we discussed all the details of the climb. We were complete beginners—pioneers—and we had only enthusiasm and determination behind us. I suddenly had an idea:

"Wouldn't it make the climb a cakewalk if we could fuse all the lights? I believe I could do it."

"How?"

"You know the wires run round the walls of the buildings on insulators, and they're only about eighteen inches apart. It's just a matter of shorting them."

"And how do you think you can do that?"

I thought for a moment. "I know. One of the windows in room 44 is only about four feet above the wires and is in pretty good shadow. If we can collect about forty razorblades I'll attach these with drawing-pins to a piece of wood, forming a conductor and sharp knife at the same time. I can screw the piece of wood on to a broom-handle and there we are."

"A good idea," said Rupert, "and if June 30th is our zero date, then the sooner the fusing is done the better."

"I meant to fuse them on the 30th."

"I don't think that's wise. It might create an uproar, and they might get the lights working again just when you were hanging somewhere in mid-air. It would be better to make the fusing a try-out too. Then we can see how long it takes them to repair the fuse."

"All right," I agreed, "then I'll do the job, and while I'm fusing, you three had better take up positions around the buildings to note if any sections of the lighting do not go out with the rest."

In due course the fusing was carried out. The razor-edged 'short circuit' worked perfectly. I cut through the heavy insulation in a matter of a minute with a gentle sawing motion. There was a brilliant flash and all the floodlights I could see went out. There was some shouting and running about near the guard-house. In three minutes the lights went on again. This interval of time would not be enough for our purposes.

One of the main problems in escaping, which in course of time and through bitter experience we recognised, was that of deciding at a moment's notice whether all the conditions for an escape were right, or if not, which of them could be ignored. An opportunity once missed might not occur again for months or years, which made one keen to take it; yet if it were taken under adverse conditions, or if more important conditions were misjudged as being of less importance, then the escape was ruined. Another chance was gone and another gap in the enemy's defences closed for good.

There was a second problem. Whether a sentry would shoot or not on detection was entirely a matter for conjecture; probably he would. His orders were to shoot; this had been explicitly pointed out to us by the Camp Commandant at his memorable parade on our arrival. He had delivered a long harangue, and on the subject of escaping had said, "It is useless to try to escape. Look around you at the impregnable barriers, the formidable array of machine-guns and rifles. To escape is impossible. Anyone attempting it will be shot." He spoke English well and he spat out the word 'shot' with a malicious staccato that was no doubt intended to put escaping out of our minds for ever. "These are my strict orders to the guards, who will carry out the command to the letter." Awed silence was followed by roars of laughter as he added with Teutonic seriousness, "If you escape a second time, you will be sent to a special camp."

June 30th was a fine day. Evening approached and the stars came out—not a breath of wind, not a cloud! At 10.30 p.m. Rupert and I crept from our room and along the corridors, which were irregularly patrolled, to the room where the job was to begin. We looked carefully through the window, and listened. It was disconcertingly light outside, but the shadows were correspondingly dark and there was a new sound which we had not noticed before. The river, that pleasant gurgling stream rushing talkatively down from the mountains, made up for the silence reigning elsewhere. Yes, it was worth trying.

Rupert fetched Nealy and Lockwood, who took up positions at key windows. I estimated the trip would take about an hour and said I would not return earlier than that. Zero hour was 11.30 p.m.

The drop was in full view of a sentry about fifty yards away, who could play a searchlight at will on any desired spot. I dropped quietly and quickly to the flat roof as the sentry's footbeats indicated his back was turned. I had stockings on my feet, old stockings cut out as mittens on my hands, and a borrowed balaclava helmet concealing the greater part of my face. All was well. Once on the flat roof I was hidden from view and I continued to the higher sloping roof which ran at right angles to the flat one. I had just succeeded, making a certain amount of noise, in climbing the five feet to the gutter in full view of a second sentry but helped by shadow, when a commotion began among the guards, a running hither and thither with torches flashing and orders shouted. I lay like a dead thing, spread-eagled on the roof. The commotion increased, but it did not approach the quarter where I was. At midnight a continuous sound of murmuring voices broke out in the most distant of the four courtyards and, after listening for some time, I decided that the noise must be due to the arrival of another batch of prisoners. I continued with a lighter heart, for though the noise was far off, it would help me. As I moved, slates cracked like pistol-shots, so it seemed to me, and broken pieces slid to the eaves with a long-drawn-out rattle. I had to cross over the ridge of the roof, because on the near side I was visible as soon as I left the gable end. On the far side I was out of sight and in deep shadow. I tried to spread my weight as evenly as possible and found the best way to move was to lie on my back with arms and legs stretched out and move slowly crabwise. The roof was forty yards long and the drop to the ground was sixty feet. One piece of luck that came my way on this long stretch of the journey was a roof walkway for chimney-sweeps running about half the length, but even this made the most terrifying creaks and groans. It frightened the wits out of me, especially when a loose plank fell right off and slid, rattling loudly, down to the edge. I watched, transfixed with horror, waiting for the moment when it would topple over, and then it stopped, wedged in the gutter. I had to control my movements to such an extent that I was in continual danger of cramp. At the far end of the roof I could peer over the gable end and do my reconnaissance.

The end wall of the building descended to a narrow alley outside the prison. There was a sentry who marched to and fro along the street running parallel with the building. By studying his routine and timing his beat, we had previously established that a blind interval of some three minutes might be expected in the alley at each turn of the sentry's walk. We hoped to make use of this; provided there was sufficient deep shadow or other concealment in the alley. That was the purpose of the reconnaissance—a survey of the alley and of its precincts at the time of night when the escape was projected. There were other points to be established too; whether the climb was feasible, the speed at which we could move without making a noise loud enough to attract attention, and whether at the exposed points of the climb the darkness was sufficient.

Three and a half hours later I returned, having spent about half an hour at the prospective point of descent. I nearly failed at the twelve-foot climb back through the window. I was tired and a month's starvation diet had told on me. Rupert hauled me in. I made a most unholy row, but the sentry must have been only half-awake. It was 3 a.m.

The next day we held a second meeting, and I gave my opinion.

"The proposed point of descent isn't good. The nearest anchor for a rope will mean carting along with us about twenty-five sheets or blankets. We would also have rucksacks and boots. The alley is a cul-de-sac, but I'm afraid the shadows are not helpful. The rope would be clearly visible in any position."

"I heard you distinctly on several occasions," reported Kenneth, to which Nealy added:

"Once I thought you'd fallen off the roof. I couldn't see you because you were on the far side, but there was a long rumble and a crash against a gutter."

"I think we may as well call it off," said Rupert. "If one man without luggage makes all that din, what are four going to do? Frankly, Pat, I think you were saved by the noise of the new arrivals. And, to clinch it, if the rope has got to dangle in the limelight, we shall never get away with it. I couldn't descend sixty feet on a homemade rope and give you time to heave it up again all within three minutes."

We all agreed and decided to prospect further along the lines of Rupert's tunnel idea.

As for the new arrivals of the night, they turned out to be four hundred officers of the 51st Division who had been captured at St. Valéry on the north coast of France on about June 12th. This meant crowding in the rooms, and our No. 66 finished up with fifty-seven occupants. The room was about fifteen yards by twelve yards by twelve feet high. In this space there were nineteen wooden three-tier bunks, half a dozen tables, a heating stove, and ten small wardrobe cupboards. Fifty-seven officers ate, slept, and lived in this room, for at that time day-rooms were unheard of.

While I had been concentrating on my idea of escaping over the roofs, Rupert had been doing some quiet 'snooping' on his own. The word 'snooping' soon became recognised camp terminology. It meant touring the camp in a suspicious manner and was applied to both Germans and British. The Germans employed professional snoopers who became familiar figures in the camp. It was extraordinary how few people snooped effectively. Snoopers could usually be distinguished in a crowd a mile away, looking like habitual burglars searching for another safe to break.

Rupert was a good snooper chiefly because it was impossible for anyone to look at him without taking him for a man too honest and proud to demean himself. He noted a small locked room in the corner of the building backing against the alley (cul-de-sac) that I had examined from the roof-tops, and discovered that the room was a semi-basement. One day, while Kenneth kept watch for the German snoopers, Rupert, Nealy, and I undid the lock of the door and went in. We found some steps leading down to the floor, which was about five feet below the outside ground-level. Rupert proposed piercing the wall at floor-level, digging a tunnel across the street, and through or under the foundations of an old stone building at the other side. Nealy preferred crossing under the alley and coming up inside a small lean-to shed against a private house. The walls of the shed were made of vertical wooden slats with gaps in between. We could see piles of wooden logs inside. We adopted Nealy's suggestion because we thought we would have no heavy foundations to circumvent at the far end of our tunnel. As things turned out we were right, although even in this direction we did not know what form our exit would take.

We started to break through the wall on July 14th. I thought it was a propitious day—the anniversary of the storming of the Bastille!

We decided to work two shifts of two hours each per day, and in the afternoon, this being the quietest time from the point of view of internal camp disturbance, and at the same time the noisiest for external street sounds which would help to cover up the sound of our working. We kept the tunnel a complete secret except for one officer, Major Poole, who had been a prisoner-of-war in the 1914–18 War, and whose advice we sought. The routine was simple enough; one man worked at the wall-face, another man sat on a box inside the room with his eye glued to the keyhole of the door looking along the passage, a third man read a book, or otherwise behaved innocently, seated on the stone steps at the only entrance to the building a few yards away from the passage, a fourth man lounged, or exercised, in the farthest courtyard. After a couple of hours the two men outside and the two men inside would change places. Warning of the approach of any German was passed by noncommittal signals, such as the blowing of a nose, along the line, depending upon the direction from which he appeared. The man on the wall-face would immediately stop work on receipt of the signal.

The door of the room was opened by removing the screws holding the latch of the padlock. The latch was screwed up during each shift. The room contained lumber, including a large variety of rifle-range targets. There were painted French soldiers and English Tommies—lying, kneeling, and charging, as well as the usual bull's-eye type. If a German decided to come into the room, the only hope for the men inside was to hide amongst the lumber or in a small triangular space underneath the stone steps. The entrance to the tunnel was in the farthest corner of the room and was hidden in the darkness under an old table. For tools, we began with three stout six-inch nails. After some days we received an addition of a small hammer.

The hammer was the cause of one of the first major camp 'incidents,' and gave us a 'friend in need' in a Royal Tank Regiment lieutenant called O'Hara, who as time went on became 'Scarlet O'Hara,' one of the most notorious POWs in Germany. His face was so ruddy that the slightest excitement made it live up to the name.

On this particular day, a lorry came into one of the

courtyards to deliver goods to the canteen, and although it was guarded by a sentry, O'Hara, with a confederate, 'Crash' Keeworth, secured the hammer and a very fine road-map of Germany from the tool-kit under the driver's seat. Keeworth pretended to steal something from the back of the lorry, distracting the sentry enough to ensure that Scarlet could perform his task with the utmost ease. The loss was, of course, soon discovered. The guard was called out and a special *Appell,* or parade, sounded. Incidentally, this *Appell* gave us some anxious moments, for we had to extract our two men from the room in double-quick time: a contingency for which we always had to be prepared, as we never knew what mischief the other prisoners might be up to.

The Commandant appeared at the parade foaming at the mouth. All his subordinates duly followed suit and shouted themselves into paroxysms of rage which were encouraged by derisive laughter from the British ranks. After interminable haranguing, both in English and German, we were given to understand that all privileges would be withdrawn until the hammer and map were returned. The parade then broke up with catcalls, hoots, and jeers. Scarlet had pulled off his job superbly, and we found a muffled hammer a much better tool than a roughly shaped stone!

*   *   *

After three weeks our tunnel had progressed three feet. We had pierced the stone and brick wall and found loose earth on the other side. Great was our rejoicing. Progress would be much faster now, but it was also obvious that shoring and timbering would be necessary to keep the roof of the tunnel from caving in. We found some lengths of three-inch by two-inch timber in the target-room where we worked, and these, together with 'bed-boards,' of which there was an unlimited supply, carried us the whole length of the tunnel.

Our wooden bunks supported the human body by means

of about ten boards spanning the width of the bed. They were about three-quarters of an inch thick and two feet six inches long, and they became invaluable in innumerable ways as time went on. They were the escaper's most important raw material. Bed-boards could be used for roof timbers in a tunnel, carved into dummy pistols or German bayonets, and made into false doors and cupboards. Jumping ahead a little in time (in fact, about a year), a tunnel was built at Laufen under the direction of Captain Jim Rogers, R.E., in which no fewer than twelve hundred bedboards were used.

We learned by experience how best to carry these boards about, and eventually we were confident enough to meet and pass a German officer with a couple of them nursed tenderly under a negligently worn overcoat.

The tunnel now progressed more rapidly. So much so that it became impossible to get rid of the soil quickly enough by the method we employed at first, which was that of taking the rubble out in our pockets, especially elongated for the purpose to reach our knees, and emptying it surreptitiously as we lay on the grass in the compound. Rupert and I were one day carrying out this thankless task.

"At this rate, Pat," protested Rupert, "the tunnel will take us six months."

"The only alternative is to pile up the soil in the target-room, and I don't like that," I retorted.

"We can hide it in the corner under the steps."

"Not all of it. The space isn't big enough."

"We can cover what remains with old targets and rubbish."

"If the Jerries take more than a glance at the room, they can't fail to notice it."

"And if we plod on for six months, the Jerries will find the tunnel anyway," rejoined Rupert.

"Why?"

"It's only a matter of time before we're caught. We take risks every day, and the longer we work the shorter the odds become against us. One day a Jerry will just be in the wrong place at the wrong time. The longer we work the more chance there is of that happening."

"All right," I concluded, "then I agree. We'll make a 'blitz' of it."

In the week following our decision, we progressed three yards.

On the right of the tunnel we ran along the side of an old brick wall. Curiosity as to the purpose of this wall led to a lucky discovery and also to an unlucky incident. We made further measurements and found that we were not outside the main wall of the building as we had thought, but were running beside what was a completely sealed-up room under the lavatories on the first floor. By using a small mirror held out of the lavatory window we could see a manhole cover in the alleyway adjacent to the sealed chamber. We assumed that the chamber was an old sewage-pit, of which the manhole cover was the exit. If we could enter the sewage-pit and go out by the manhole cover, we would have a perfect exit to the tunnel which could be used over and over again. We decided to risk breaking through the wall on our right. It was lucky we made the measurements, for if we had proceeded with the tunnel, thinking we were outside the main wall, we would always have been three yards short in our calculation of the length of the tunnel.

But we nearly wrecked the whole scheme by breaking through the wall on our right! I was working away at the wall, which came away easily. As I removed a final brick, a flood of foul sewage rushed out at me, extinguishing the light. (Light was provided by German cooking-fat in a cigarette-tin with a pyjama-cord wick.) I lay prone in total darkness with a gushing torrent sweeping around me. I shouted to Rupert who was keeping guard:

"There's a flood coming in. I've got to stop it. The stench is asphyxiating. For God's sake, pull me out of the tunnel if I pass out."

I heard Rupert say:

"I can smell it from here. I'll call you every half-minute and if you don't answer I'll come for you."

I set about the hole as best I could with bricks and clay mud, in feverish anxiety. The tunnel was built downhill and the flood was mounting! Fortunately the pressure could not have been great on the other side, and after five minutes of frantic work I managed to reduce the torrent to a small trickle. I wormed my way back out of the tunnel. Rupert nearly fell off his box when he saw the appalling object which rose from the hole. Not much sewage had come into the room because of the downward slope of the tunnel made to provide ventilation at the working end. We knocked off for the day to let the flood settle. I cleaned myself up in the bathroom next door, and dry clothing was produced.

Next day I went in again with a light and made a proper dam of puddled clay, of which there was no lack, supported by boards driven into the floor of the tunnel. Needless to say, we abandoned the pit scheme and carried on in a forward direction. There always remained a small leak which necessitated our putting duck-boards along the whole length of the tunnel. As luck had it, the tunnel-level carried us just beneath the base of the main external wall. It would have been a heartbreaking job to tackle three feet of masonry in the confined space of the tunnel. Without further incident, towards the end of August we arrived under the lean-to woodshed at the other side of the alleyway.

Nealy had been given orders, in the middle of August, that he would move at short notice to a naval camp, as he belonged to the Fleet Air Arm. At the same time, with the lengthening of the tunnel we needed more workers. We sought Major Poole's advice. Finally, we asked 2nd Lieutenant 'Peter' Allan, Captain 'Dick' Howe, and Captain Barry O'Sullivan to join us, which they did with alacrity.

Our choice fell on Peter first because he could speak German fluently, and in fact was used as an interpreter with the Germans on many occasions. When the escape took place, it would be helpful to have a German speaker. The rest of us knew nothing of the language. Major Poole warned us to be careful to check up on his credentials: Where had he learnt German? The reply was—at school in Germany. Why was he at school in Germany? His father had business relations with Germany. These and other pointers as to his past were probed, mostly indirectly and unostentatiously through officers who said they knew him before the war.

All this goes to show how, from the start, in prisoner-of-war camps we were suspicious of the possibility of the planting of an 'agent provocateur' in our midst. Officers had read how these were placed in camps in the First World War to spy, and we certainly thought Nazi Germany would be capable of it in this war. Later these agents became known as 'stool pigeons.'

Peter passed the tests—we often laughed about it in later days—and he was as keen as mustard. A 2nd-Lieutenant of the Cameron Highlanders, standing only five feet six inches, he nevertheless swung his kilt as well as the tallest, and his tough legs showed he could walk long distances. He was fit in spite of the starvation. Educated at Tonbridge, he played both rugby and soccer well, and was an excellent bridge and chess player. He always managed to drive chess opponents into a frenzy by his unvarying stratagem of taking a pawn or two early in the game, and swopping like piece for like. He and Rupert were a match at bridge.

Dick Howe and Barry O'Sullivan were likewise tested. Neither proved difficult to check up on. Barry was the son of a British General and Dick had been known in England by a large number of the prisoners now at Laufen. Both belonged to the Royal Tank Regiment. Barry was of an effervescent nature and had been for some time in India. He was recommended by Poole for our acceptance on account of his keenness and determination to escape at all costs. The recommendation proved well founded.

Dick Howe was our own choice. He lived in room 66 with us and showed initiative combined with good sense, which made him the possible leader of a second group to escape via our tunnel. Already we had ideas of concealing our tunnel exit so that it could be used repeatedly.

Dick was a Londoner educated at Bedford Modern School and possessing a flair for mechanical engineering, and for wireless theory and practice. He had just been awarded the M.C. for his gallantry at Calais, where he had been landed with his group at a moment's notice to fight an action postponing the capture of that port by the Germans for several precious days.

He was good-looking and strongly built, if anything burly, and was about five feet ten inches tall. He laughed with a neigh like a horse, had a great sense of humour, and went about everything in a quiet manner with a slight grin as if he was looking for the funniest way of doing it.

Nealy left towards the end of August. I agreed to write to his parents if the escape was successful to let them know how he was faring.*

A few days later we had a bad scare. Barry O'Sullivan was digging at the face, I was hauling back the earth in improvised boxes—a tiring job crawling back and forth on one's tummy—and Peter Allan was doing 'keyhole' watch. From outside he received the signal—'danger, cease work.' No sooner had he warned us than a German non-commissioned officer came down the corridor and, without hesitating, approached our door, unlocked the padlock, and pushed. The door did not open. We had devised a safety-catch on the inside—a rough-and-ready affair. It was our last defence for just such an event as this. The German swore, pulled the door with all his strength, tearing the latch off, then pushed again and peered through the narrow chink, to discover a rough piece of iron barring his way. This delaying action gave Peter Allan just sufficient

* Nealy escaped from Stalag Luft III in the 'Great Escape' of March 1944, when fifty out of seventy-six officers were shot by the Gestapo. Nealy was a survivor.

time to jump down the steps and crawl behind the targets and into the tunnel. We all wore soft-soled shoes, otherwise Peter would have been heard.

A moment later the Jerry burst open the door. What he thought I do not know, but he must have been deceived by our safety-catch. This was made of rusty-looking material and fell downwards into position very easily so that the explanation might offer itself to a person finding an empty room barred on the inside, that it had fallen into position of its own accord on the last occasion when the door was shut. This we knew was about two or three months before. It was a long chance, but our only one, and it worked. Peter reported action at our end and later we heard the rest from our confederates. The Jerry came in, pushed the targets farther against our tunnel corner and went out again. After an interval Peter was sent to inspect, but soon scuttled back saying, "Jerries are returning!" This time several came in, carrying an assortment of targets which they piled up wherever there was room. They then nailed on the latch with some four-inch nails, turning them over on the inside, locked the padlock, and departed. Five minutes later a surreptitious knock on the door told us our own guard was outside. Peter and I went to the door and I whispered:

"We can't get out. They've driven in four-inch nails and turned them over on the inside. You'll never be able to remove the latch."

"A prison within a prison," mused Kenneth from outside. "Can't you bend the nails?"

"Not a hope! The wood will split if we try. The nails are as thick as my little finger."

"Well, what a pity! You'll just have to stay there until you've starved enough to crawl out under the door."

"Shut up that nonsense, Kenneth! I've got an idea. Can you fetch me a file?"

"Why, certainly, old man! The ironmonger's shop is just around the corner," and I heard him chuckling maddeningly on the other side of the door.

"It's not at all funny. You're on the right side of the door, but we're on the wrong side. I'm sure Scarlet O'Hara can produce a file. For heaven's sake, hurry!"

The file was produced in a very short time and passed under the door. I filed the nails through at the point where they were bent over. Kenneth on the outside levered the latch from the woodwork, drawing out the bitten-off nails. We left the room, replacing the nails quickly, and departed. The next day, in the interest of silence, we again shortened the nails and, rebending the filed-off ends, stuck them into their original positions, leaving no trace of the tampering.

The tunnel progressed. We were all interviewed and recommended to have a medical examination to see that we were fit enough for the arduous trek to the frontier. The examination included running up and down four flights of stairs at full speed, followed by a heart test. The result of the medical exam. was reported, and unfortunately Barry O'Sullivan was asked to stand down in favour of someone else. His trouble was recurring malaria, contracted in the East. He was far too honest to conceal it from the doctor. The latter considered it a serious handicap and with reason.

We were very sorry to lose Barry. Although it consoled nobody at the time, it is pleasant to recall that Barry escaped shortly afterwards from another camp, and was about the first British escaper to reach Switzerland safely.

We chose Harry Elliott, a captain in the Irish Guards, to take his place. He passed all the tests, and his inclusion was agreed, so that the first escaping party still consisted of six officers. I hoped that others would be able to follow subsequently.

I had an important reason for limiting the first batch to six persons. Our sortie would be made from the woodshed and thence up the side street, for about thirty yards, to the main road. The side street was in full view of a permanent day-and-night sentry-post on a cat-walk about forty yards away from the woodshed alley. Although we would be walking away from him, the sentry would see each one of us. Six men appearing from a little-used cul-de-sac was quite a mouthful to swallow. So much so that I planned we should leave by ones and twos at intervals and, moreover, that at least two of us should dress up as women for the occasion. We also decided that after the escape we should separate for good into two parties of three each. Rupert and Peter Allan agreed to join me as one party, and the other three formed the second. My party made plans to go to Yugoslavia, while the other three were to head for Switzerland.

I asked that Scarlet O'Hara should be placed at the top of the list for any subsequent escape from the tunnel. He was already a man marked down by the Germans as dangerous, and wherever he was seen by a 'snoop,' there suspicion followed. He was never long out of trouble and was quite irrepressible. Scarlet soon possessed a wide range of useful tools and implements, odd civilian attire, maps and other escape paraphernalia, which he concealed in various hide-outs all over the camp. He was a Canadian, small and wiry, and he loathed the Jerries so much that he was unable to pass one without muttering semi-audible curses and insults. He had a nature that craved excitement and intrigue; he was never so happy as when he was tinkering with some implement with a view to breaking out of the camp. He and 'Crash' Keeworth were the pet aversions of the Germans.

One day Scarlet was going through one of his hides. It was behind the cleaning-hatch of a chimney-flue. He had a square key to fit the hatch and used the large space within as an extra cupboard—mostly for contraband. The hatch was at the corner of a corridor, about nine feet from the ground.

The Camp Commandant had just declared that Army mess-tins were to be handed in as being illegal escape equipment. Any officer retaining a tin would be liable to heavy punishment. So Scarlet was busy hiding several mess-tins. His 'stooge,' that is the officer keeping watch, passed him up the tins one after the other. As he handed the last one, a

Goon (the senior Sergeant, or *Feldwebel* as it happened) surprised them. The stooge had only time to say, "Goons," giving Scarlet's trousers a tug at the same time, and then walk away unconcernedly as the Goon approached and stared up at Scarlet. Scarlet's head was inside the hatch and he did not hear the operative word. He shouted:

"What in hell's name do you think you're doing, trying to knock me off my stool?"

No answer.

"There's not enough room in this b—— hole. I reckon some of you guys'll have to find your own holes. I'm not a b—— storage contractor, anyway. B—— those b—— Huns. I'd like to wring their necks and knock their square heads together till their gold teeth fall out. Hey! hold this tin! I've got to make more space."

Silence.

"Take the b—— tin, I said."

The mess-tin was taken from his hand by the *Feldwebel*, who started pulling violently at the seat of his pants.

"For crying out loud! You'll have me over. What in hell's name do you want?"

At this juncture Scarlet's ruddy face appeared from the hatch and surveyed his mortal enemy beneath him holding one of his precious mess-tins.

* * * * *

It was obvious that Scarlet was not the right person to assist in building the tunnel. He was too conspicuous. So he was allotted the task of closing it up after our six had departed, with a view to his learning the job and going with the second batch.

Harry Elliott was introduced to tunnel work in a curious way. On his first shift he was given the post of keyhole stooge. Incidentally, this usually entailed suffering from a strained bloodshot eye for several days after the shift. No sooner had Harry taken up his position on this, his first day, than one of the camp's 'athletic types' approached the door. We had various 'athletic types.' Some ran round the compound for hours on end, others walked as if the devil was after them, others again did physical jerks and acrobatics, appearing to stand on their hands for more hours per day than on their feet.

The particular 'athletic type' that approached the door was a boxer. Harry told us the story afterwards:

"The man was obviously punch-drunk from his earliest childhood. His nose told his life-story. I thought he was heading for the bathroom next door. He certainly needed a shower—he was perspiring so much, as a matter of fact, that he looked as if he'd just come from one. He was shadow-boxing his way down the corridor with massive gloves on his fists. He started snorting vigorously as he passed out of my keyhole line of vision. The next thing I knew was a terrific crash against the door which sent me reeling backwards. I quickly put my eye to the keyhole again to see what was the matter. I was sent reeling again as the door shuddered under another blow. Another and another followed in quick succession. He was a formidable opponent even with a door between us. I shouted at him through the keyhole, but between his loud snorts and the drum-like blows, a ship's siren couldn't have been heard. I just gave up and disappeared into the tunnel. I thought it the best place to be when the Jerries arrived.

"After ten minutes, when the door showed signs of decomposing, the athletic type retired—I suppose finally to cool himself off in the bathroom. The silence that followed made me feel I was in a tomb rather than a tunnel."

Harry had an infectious laugh, almost a giggle, which was irresistible. When he told a story, listeners invariably started to laugh at the beginning and did not stop for a day or two. He was an Harrovian, older than most of us, and had several children. He loathed being a prisoner more than anyone else I knew in the camp, but he never showed it except when he took 'time off' to express his feelings for the German race, the *Herrenvolk*, with a picturesque invective difficult to equal. He was small and wiry, with darting blue eyes set in a sunburnt face. His voice was reminiscent of the 'Colonel Sahib' home from India after years of polo and pigsticking. He said he could always tell whether a man was an 'officer and a gentleman' by asking him to repeat one sentence, namely, "I saw thousands and thousands of Boy Scouts routing around in their brown trousers." He tested many officers, roaring with laughter at the result. No offence was ever taken or implied. It was Harry having his fun!

The tunnel drew towards completion and we were under the lean-to shed which I have mentioned before and which we now called the woodshed. We had to determine our exact position. The woodshed contained a pile of logs each about one yard long, and we dare not break cover under the passage of the shed immediately beyond the logs. I found a thin-steel rifle ramrod about three feet long in the target-room. While Rupert observed with a mirror the ground outside the shed from the lavatory window above, I made a small vertical hand-hole in the roof of the tunnel and slowly pushed the rod upwards. As soon as Rupert saw it he was to kick the lavatory wall once and make a mental note of its position. The alarm signal was two knocks in case of danger. The sound carried down the wall and was to be reported to me by a listener in the tunnel immediately beneath the wall foundations. I started at a point I estimated to be just outside the woodshed and pushed the rod upwards, digging away with the same hand until I began to think our tunnel was deeper underground than we had estimated. Suddenly the double knock was heard. I withdrew the rod like lightning and awaited a report. Some minutes later it came—whispered up the tunnel (noise carries like thunder in a tunnel). My rod had been waving about two feet above the roadway, but was so close to the shed that even Rupert had not noticed it for some time.

Now we continued with confidence, and after a few days I broke the surface under the wood-pile and first smelt wholesome fresh air. I was delighted, for whereas I had envisaged perilously removing logs to leave a natural archway, I found the logs were on a platform of wood raised some six inches above the earth. Furthermore, by inspection I found that a wainscot board had been placed along the shed passage against the platform, closing it off down to the ground.

The next thing to figure out was how to make a concealed exit. We were determined this tunnel should work for several escapes. Besides, the position of the exit and of the woodshed made it dangerous to attempt sending off a large number of officers at one time. Eventually I decided to dig away the ground just inside the wainscot and to support the earth of the passage-way with narrow wooden horizontal slats backed against two stakes driven vertically into the floor of the tunnel. Actually Dick did most of the work on his shift, and had to work very carefully and silently, hammering the stakes into the ground. The vertical wall of comparatively loose earth was thus held up by a little wooden dam. We christened it 'Shovewood.' The scheme of opening was simple. When all was ready, the slats would be removed and an opening quickly made at an angle of forty-five degrees upwards and out into the passage-way, pulling the earth into the tunnel.

The escaping party having scrambled out, one person remaining behind would close up the tunnel again by replacing the slats one by one and filling the earth back behind them. Everything that would speed up this process was seized upon. Thus to save putting back earth that needed tamping, a couple of small strong wooden boxes were made ready which, placed behind the slats, would fill up much space and save valuable seconds. The final slat immediately beneath the wainscot was only two inches wide. In this way the last layer of earth outside could be spread, then tamped with a flat board and made to merge with the passage-way, the slat would be put in, and the earth backed up behind. It could not be a perfect job, but it was the best we could do, and we estimated that the owner of the woodshed would imagine that a chicken had been there and scratched about, or maybe that a rat had been at work.

The tunnel was ready on August 31st. It had taken just under seven weeks to build, and was eight yards long.

We were pleased with our work, especially when we thought of the slow progress made in the early days when we had stood a pint of beer to the one amongst us who had extracted the largest stone from the wall in each series of working shifts. I remember the first winner was Rupert, with a stone the size of an egg, then I won a pint with a half-brick. We closed the competition with two pints for Rupert when he cleared the wall by removing a piece of masonry twice the size of a man's head, which we could hardly lift.

The next decision ahead of us was the date and time of the escape. It was essential to be able to forecast the movements of the household which occupied the building beside the woodshed. From behind the wainscot in the tunnel, a watch was kept through a tiny peephole, which revealed a doorway into the house, a window and a washing-machine, but alas! not enough of a slatted door opening on to the roadway to allow us to ascertain what kind of a lock, if any, was on this door, which was to be our gateway to freedom. I made a mental note that, when we escaped, I would take a screwdriver with me. It might be useful!

The watch was maintained at first over the whole day, quickly shortening to concentrate on the more quiet periods. A graph was made of movements against the hours. A German *Frau* spent much of her time in the shed.

We needed a definite 'all-quiet' period of at least half an hour, estimated thus: five minutes to open up, twelve minutes (two minutes per person) to sortie, and thirteen minutes to close up the tunnel again.

Two periods showed promise, but not the certainty, of half an hour's quiet. A sentry came on before dusk at the woodshed corner, and left after dawn. In fact, he spent most of the night leaning against the shed, and one fine morning had the audacity to relieve himself immediately over my head. The two periods were: one, immediately prior to the sentry's arrival, and the other immediately after his departure. He usually left at 6 a.m., and was followed by a patrol. These patrols had always to be reckoned with; some were at regular intervals, but most of them were irregular. They were always a nuisance, and much more so now in the final stage of arranging the getaway.

On the morning of September 4th, our watchers informed us that the woodshed sentry had departed at 5 a.m. This was good news and placed the early-morning escape in the most favourable light. The *Hausfrau*, according to the graph, could be relied upon not to enter the woodshed before 6.30 a.m., and usually she arrived a little later. Thus, at the best we would have an hour and a half, and at the worst half an hour. We decided to waste no further time, and to escape next morning. Our zero hour was 5 a.m. on Thursday, September 5th.

CHAPTER II

THE FIRST BID FOR FREEDOM

W E ate well on September 4th and prepared our kit, putting the final touches to our clothing. Maps— good survey maps which had been found, and others carefully traced on thin lavatory paper—were distributed. Our staple diet of raw oatmeal mixed with sugar provided at the expense of the German kitchen, was packed. My portion of staple diet went into two small sacks of strongly sewn canvas which were to be hung round my neck so as to fall over my chest and form a buxom bust, for I was to escape as a woman. I still possessed a large brown canvas pouch, which I had found in a caserne at Charleville. This I could carry by hand when dressed as a woman, and later on my back as a man. There was no room for my boots, so I made a brown-paper parcel of them.

My female attire consisted of a large red spotted hand-kerchief for my head, a white sports-shirt as blouse, and a skirt made of an old grey window-curtain, which I had also picked up during the trek into Germany. My legs were shaved and 'sunburnt' with iodine, and I wore black plimsolls.

Once clear of the camp, I would change into a man again, wearing a green-grey Tyrolean hat, cleverly made and dyed from khaki by a British sergeant (a former tailor), a heavy pullover to go over my shirt, a small mackintosh groundsheet for wet weather (also picked up during the journey to Germany), a pair of dark-blue shorts cut from a Belgian airman's breeches (obtained by barter), white Bavarian woollen stockings of the pattern common to the country, purchased at a shocking price in the German canteen, and my brown army boots dyed black.

The others had similar clothing, with minor individual differences. The tailor had devised enough Tyrolean hats to go round and had fashioned an Austrian cloak for Harry Elliott. Lockwood was also to make his exit disguised as a woman, and his costume was more or less like mine. Rupert had an old grey blanket which he converted into a cloak. We were a motley crowd and hardly fit to pass close inspection by daylight, for we had not the experience required to produce really finished garments from scratch. But the idea was that we were young Austrian hikers, and we would only be seen at dusk or dawn.

That night our room-mates made dummies in our beds, good enough to pass the cursory glance of the German night patrol through the room. We all slept in different rooms in the same building as the tunnel, doubling up with other officers, and these arrangements were made as secretly as possible to avoid any hubbub or infectious atmosphere of excitement. The Senior Officers of the rooms in question, who had to declare nightly to the German Officer on the rounds the number of officers present, were not even aware of the additions to or subtractions from their flock.

We were to rise at 4 a.m. None of us slept much, though we took precautions against oversleeping by having a couple of 'knockers up' in reserve. I remember banging my head on the pillow four times—an old childhood habit which for some unaccountable reason usually worked. It was hardly necessary on this occasion. I passed a most unpleasant night with the cold sweat of nervous anticipation upon me, and with that peculiar nausea of the stomach which accompanies tense nerves and taut muscles. My mind turned over the pros and cons a hundred times; the chances of success, immediate and later, and the risks. If they shot, would they shoot to kill? If they caught us sooner or later, what were our chances—to be liquidated or to disappear into a Concentration Camp? At that period of the war, nobody knew the answers. It was the first escape from this prison, probably the first escape of British officers from any organised prison in Germany. We were the guinea-pigs.

Lt. W. L. B. O'Hara ('Scarlet')

We undertook the experiment with our eyes open, choosing between two alternatives: to attempt escape and risk the ultimate price, or face up to the sentence of indefinite imprisonment. There were many who resigned themselves from the beginning to the second of these alternatives. They were brave, but their natures differed from those of the men who escaped and failed, and escaped again; who, having once made the choice between escape and resignation, could not give up, even if the war lasted the remainder of their lives. I am sure that the majority of the men who sought to escape did it for self-preservation. Instinctively, unconsciously, they felt that resignation meant not physical but mental death—maybe lunacy. My own case was not exceptional. One awful fit of depression sufficed to determine my future course as a prisoner. One dose of morbidity in which the vista of emptiness stretched beyond the horizon of my mind was quite enough.

$$*\qquad *\qquad *\qquad *\qquad *$$

At 4 a.m., in grisly darkness, I fastened my bosom in place, put on my blouse and skirt. We crept downstairs to our collecting-point in the washroom beside the tunnel-room. A tap was turned on quietly to fill a water-bottle. It went on dripping. The sound of the drops was loud and exasperating. A sentry stood only thirty yards away by the courtyard gate. I felt he must hear it. . . . It was nerves. Captain Gilliat, one of the assistants, wore a gas-cape. Why he chose this garment for the occasion I never knew. It crackled loudly with every movement and nearly drove us mad. A watcher was by now at the end of the tunnel, waiting to pass the signal when the sentry near the tunnel exit went off duty. Other stooges were posted at vantage-points to give the alarm in case a patrol suddenly appeared in the buildings. We waited.

At 5.15 a.m. the sentry outside the tunnel still remained at his post. It was probable now he would not leave till 6 a.m. There was nothing to do but wait quietly while our hearts pounded through our ribs with suppressed excitement.

There was a thundering crash and a reverberating clang as if fifty dinner-gongs had been struck hard with hammers all at once. There was a second crash and a third, diminishing in intensity, and, finally, some strident squeaks. This must be the end—but no one was allowed to move. We had our stooges and we had time after a warning to disappear. The men in the tunnel-room were safely locked in and could hide in the tunnel. A panic would have been dangerous.

Dick Howe and Peter Allan, tired of the long wait, had leant against one of the twelve-foot-long, solid cast-iron troughs which were used as communal washbasins, and finally they had sat on the edge of it. The next instant the whole trough collapsed on to the concrete floor. If I had tried for weeks I doubt if I could have thought of a better way of making the loudest noise possible with the least effort. The succeeding crashes and squeaks which kept our hair standing on end were caused by Dick and Peter who, having made a frantic attempt to save the crash, were extricating themselves from the wreckage and bringing the trough to rest quietly on the floor.

We waited for the signal to return. A minute passed, five minutes passed, and ten—and we began to breathe again. No Germans appeared. I never found out why they did not come. The noise woke up most of the officers in the building, which was a large one, and the sentry thirty yards away near the courtyard must have jumped out of his skin. Yet for some unaccountable reason he did not act.

Six o'clock chimed out from a distant steeple. We waited more anxiously as every minute passed. At last, at 6.15 a.m., the signal came through: 'All clear!' In a moment the door was unlocked and we hustled into the tunnel. I crawled quickly to the end, listened for a second, and then set to work like a demon. Down went the slats and I shovelled earth and cinders to my right and below me as fast as I could. It was light outside. As the hole enlarged I could see the various shed details. All the usual household cleaning equipment, piles of cardboard boxes at one end,

clothes drying on a line, and then the slatted door and its
lock—a large and formidable-looking padlock on a hasp.
Once I tried to get through, but the opening was still too
small. I enlarged it further and then squirmed upwards
and into the shed. I pulled Rupert and then Peter through
after me, telling Dick, who was next, to wait below while
we found the way out. We searched quickly. The padlock
would not open to a piece of wire which I inserted as a key.
I climbed the cardboard boxes to reach a large opening in
the slats near the roof and slipped, nearly bringing the
boxes down on top of me. Peter held them and we re-
adjusted the pile. We tried the door into the house; it was
locked. Then in a flash I thought of the screwdriver. (I had
asked Scarlet to lend me one—just in case.) I looked more
closely at the hasp on which the padlock was bolted. What
a fool I was!

The way was clear. With hands fumbling nervously, I
unscrewed three large screws securing the hasp to the
wood and the door swung open. I looked at my watch.

"Dick!" I whispered hoarsely down into the tunnel.
"You'd better come up quick, it's 6.30."

As he started to worm himself up through the hole,
there came the sound of an approaching horse and cart.

"Hold everything, Dick!" I said, "don't move," and to
the others: "Flatten yourselves against the walls!"

A moment later the cart appeared. Dick remained rigid
like a truncated man at floor-level! The driver did not
look our way and the cart passed on. We pulled Dick out
of the hole. I repeated to him what he already knew.

"We're late. Our safe half-hour is already over and the
Frau may come in any moment. Someone's got to replace this." I pointed at the hasp and padlock. "It will take
five minutes. Add to this twenty minutes to clear the six
of us."

"It will take Scarlet fifteen minutes to close and camouflage the hole," said Dick. "It's now 6.35. That means 7.15
before everything is clear."

We looked at each other and I knew he read my

THE LAUFEN TUNNEL

SITUATION AT 6.36 a.m.
ON 5th SEPTEMBER, 1940

KEY :—

1. Bathroom door.
2. Stooge No. 2.
3. Stooge No. 1.
4. Target room.
5. Scarlet O'Hara.
6. Tunnel entrance beneath table.
7. Lavatories.
8. Cess-pit.
9. Harry Elliott.
10. (Fräulein) Kenneth Lockwood.
11. Roadway. Sentry post, now vacated.
12. Exit to tunnel in woodshed.
13. Rupert Barry, Peter Allen, Dick Howe already in woodshed.
14. (Frau) Pat Reid.
15. Position of tunnel shown by dotted lines.
16. Man hole entrance to cess-pit.
17. Outside wall of cess-pit.

thoughts. We had gone over the timetable so often together.

"I'm sorry, Dick! The graph has never shown the *Hausfrau* to be later than 7 o'clock, and she may arrive any minute. You'll have to lock up and follow tomorrow," and I handed him the screwdriver.

"Make a good job of closing up our 'Shovewood,'" I added. "Your escape depends on it."

We quickly brushed each other down. I was worried about the back of my skirt, which had suffered in the exit as we had to come out on our backs. I repeated nervously:

"Is my bottom clean? Is my bottom clean?"

For the sentry, about forty yards away on the trestle walkway, would see my back view and I did not want him to see a dirty skirt.

I tied my spotted handkerchief around my head, opened the door, and walked out into sunlight. I turned the corner into the side street leading to the main road, and felt a gooseflesh sensation up my back and the sentry's stare burning through my shoulder-blades. I waited for the shot.

For thirty yards up the side street I walked with short steps; imitating what I thought to be the gait of a middle-aged peasant woman, and thereby prolonging the agony of every yard. At last I reached the main road. There was no alarm and I turned the corner.

The road was almost deserted. A few people were cleaning their shop-windows, a restaurant manager was pinning up his menu, and a girl was brushing the pavement. A cyclist or two passed. The hush of dawn and of sleep still lay over the town. I received casual glances, but did not attract any stares.

After I had gone about two hundred yards I heard the heavy footsteps of two persons following me, marching in step. I turned into a square and crossed it diagonally towards the bridge over the river. The footsteps grew louder and nearer. I was being followed: a patrol had been sent after me by the suspicious sentry. They did not run for fear of making me run. I was finished—the game was up—but, I thought, I may as well play it to the end and I ambled along with my bundles across the bridge, not daring to turn round. How those footsteps echoed, first in the street, now on the bridge! The patrol came alongside and passed me by without accosting me. I raised my head and to my relief saw two young hikers. They were Rupert and Peter, walking briskly away from me. I had never expected them so soon.

About a hundred yards past the bridge I turned right, following the other two. This route brought me alongside a local railway line and towards the outskirts of the town. We could see the line from the camp, and it had been arranged we should follow the path beside it and rendezvous in the woods about a quarter of a mile out of the town.

As I turned the corner, a little girl, playing with a toy, looked up at me and caught my eye. Astonishment was written all over her face. I might take in a casual adult observer, but I could not pass the keen observation of a child. She continued to look wide-eyed at me as I passed and when I was a few yards farther on I heard her running into a house—no doubt to tell her parents to come and look at the extraordinary man dressed up as a woman. Nobody came, so I presumed they just did not believe her. Grown-ups always know better than their children!

It was a misty morning heralding a hot day. I followed the railway into the woods, where it swept to the left in a big curve. I heard a train approaching and made for cover among the trees. It passed and I continued a short distance, expecting to see the other two waiting for me. There was no sign of them and I began to worry. I whistled, but there was no answer. I continued slowly, whistling "We're going to hang out our washing on the Siegfried Line." . . . They must be close by in the woods. Still no answer. Then I heard shots in the distance and dogs barking. I immediately dashed into the woods and decided to hide and change rapidly. I could not go on in my makeshift skirt. Maybe the child's parents had 'phoned the camp or the police. They might search for someone with a skirt on!

I found myself close to the river and was soon in among high reeds, where I started to change. It was about 7.15 a.m. Shots continued spasmodically and the barking of dogs increased. I was at my wits' end and sure the 'hunt was up,' and I had lost the other two. Rupert had the only compass—a good army one given him by a fellow-officer, who had managed to conceal it through all searches. I could not travel far without one.

I suddenly heard people approaching along a wood path close to the reeds. I crouched and waited until I saw them. Thank God, it was my two hikers once more!

"I thought I'd lost you for good," I said, quickly completing my change and hiding my skirt in the reeds. "I was already bothering about how I was going to reach Yugoslavia without a compass."

"What's all the shooting about?" said Peter.

"I haven't the foggiest idea. I don't like it. They've probably discovered something and are shooting up the camp. They'll be after us in no time. We'll have to hide up."

"It sounds to me like rifle-range shooting," said Rupert.

"Well, why have we never heard it before, then?" I questioned, "and how do you account for the dogs?"

"Probably the village dogs barking at the gunfire."

"The fact is, Rupert, we've never heard shooting like this before, and besides, it's still misty in places. I believe they're after us and we'd better hide up quickly."

"I bet you five pounds it's range-shooting. Anyway, it's no use hiding here. We're much too close. Come on, let's make tracks!"

We made for the top of a high wooded hill which lay in our general direction southwards. From it we would see all the surrounding country. We crossed the railway, then a road and some open fields before entering the friendly cover of more woods. We simply scuttled across the fields, Rupert, who was the calmest, doing all he could to make us walk normally. In the woods we disturbed some chamois which fled away noisily, giving us the fright of our lives.

We had left tracks in the dew-laden grass of the fields and we were out of breath from the steep uphill-going. We rested for a moment and smeared our boots with German mustard, which we had brought for the purpose of putting dogs off the scent, and then continued, climbing steeper and steeper. We heard woodcutters at work and kept clear of them. Eventually, at about 9 a.m., we reached the top of the hill.

The shooting and the barking of dogs had ceased. We gained confidence. Either the hunters had lost track of us or it had been a false alarm, as Rupert thought.

The camp *Appell*, that is, roll-call, was due and soon we should have an important matter decided. We had arranged that, from a window high up in the camp build-ing, a sheet should be hung, as if to air; white for 'all clear,' blue check if our absence had been discovered.

The Germans held two separate *Appells*, one for the Officers, and immediately afterwards one for the Other Ranks—-in another courtyard. This gave us an opening of which we were not slow to avail ourselves. I had arranged with six 'good men and true' that they would stand in for the officers' *Appell* and then do a rapid change in a lavatory into orderlies' attire and appear on the Other Ranks parade. Only three of them would be necessary today.

It was a glorious morning and I climbed a tree to look down into the valley, now clear of mist and bathed in luxurious sunshine. The view was beautiful, rich in September fruitfulness, with the river in the foreground rushing over its pebbly bed, a ribbon of sparkling light.

I could see our prison in the distance reflecting a warm golden colour from its walls. I had never thought that our Archbishop's Palace could be called beautiful, but from a distance it certainly was so. Then I realised why; I could not distinguish the windows in the walls. We were farther away than we had estimated, and the sunlight was at a bad angle. There was no hope of seeing a sheet of any colour. Later, when the sun had moved round, Peter climbed the tree, but he could scarcely distinguish the windows and, although his sight was keen, could see no sign of a sheet.

We hid the whole day in a copse of young fir-trees on the top of the hill. We were only disturbed once, by a woodman who passed close by but did not see us. We reconnoitred the southern slope of the hill along the route we were to take that night, but it was wooded for a long distance so we soon gave up, letting the darkness bring what it might. We were in very good hiding. I believe only dogs would ever have found us.

We lay in long grass in an open patch among the trees, dozing from time to time, scarcely ever talking. The sun shone in a cloudless sky. It was good to be alive, to breathe the air of freedom, the scent of pines and dry grass, to hear the murmur of flying insects around and the distant chopping of a woodman's axe, to listen to a lark above one's head—a fluttering speck against the infinity of the clear blue sky. We were free at last. A restful calm, a silent relish of this precious day spread over us. There was a hush on the sunbathed, pleasant countryside. We felt attuned to it. Our hearts were full of thanksgiving. Animals do not need to speak, I thought.

At meal-time we sat up and ate our meagre ration. We had worked it out to last us twelve days. We drank a mouthful of water each from a small bottle, exchanged a few remarks on the chances of Dick and the others the next day and then returned to our dreaming.

A beautiful autumnal evening set in, and with it came a chill in the air as the sun sank peacefully over the horizon. I have seldom in my life spent a happier day. The war did not seem to exist.

We clothed ourselves, put chalk in our socks and boots, and, as darkness approached, set off downhill through the woods—southwards to Yugoslavia. It was about one hundred and fifty miles away across the mountains of the Austrian Tyrol. We hoped to make it in ten days.

CHAPTER III

THE PRICE OF FAILURE

WE had a large-scale survey map which covered the first sixty miles of our journey. It showed all the contours, and even tiny villages and mountain paths. Its acquisition deserves an explanation.

Our camp was formerly the depôt of the 100th Gebirgs-jäger Regiment—mountain troops. At the top of one of our buildings was a staircase leading up to an attic. The former was entirely shut off by a wood partition and a door made of slats which was heavily chained and padlocked. We could not see far up the staircase, but its situation was intriguing and invited inspection.

One day Scarlet O'Hara solved the problem of how to by-pass the door. The stair passed diagonally across a window, the springer being about eight inches away from the glass. The sill of this window could be reached from the flight of stairs below by climbing on a man's shoulder. A thin man could worm himself up through the eight-inch gap on to the forbidden staircase, and thus the secrets of the attic were revealed. A few doors with very simple locks were no barrier to Scarlet, and an old storeroom was found in which there were many copies of survey maps of the district around Laufen. Other useful things, such as small hatchets, screws and nails, pens and coloured inks, were found, and even badges of the mountain regiment. We took away a small proportion of everything, hoping the stock had never been accurately counted.

Before we escaped, someone a little too fat had tried the window route and split the glass. The Jerries realised what was happening and barred off the window completely. There was not much left in the attic by that time. The Germans created a big fuss and searched the camp and the prisoners individually. The search lasted a day, but nothing seriously incriminating was found, and our tunnel, being behind German locks, was not troubled.

Rupert's compass had survived many such searches by employing the following simple ruse. Before being searched, the owner of the compass demanded urgently to go to the lavatory, meeting there by arrangement a friend who had been searched already. Although the owner was accompanied by a sentry while carrying out this simple duty, a moment always arrived when it was possible to slip the article to the friend unobserved. The method required good synchronisation and deft handling of an opportunity, or even the making of an opportunity by diverting the attention of the sentry.

There was no moon and it soon became pitch-dark in the woods. We were in thick undergrowth and brambles and made slow progress, so much so that we altered our compass bearing and headed south-east, trying to find easier going. After about two hours we cleared the woods and were able to trek across country at a good speed, aiming at a chosen star which we checked by the compass as being in our line. It was then only necessary to look at the compass every hour or so and change our guiding star as the constellations moved in the sky.

Walking at night straight across country is an eerie experience. Only the actual ground for a few yards around is real, be it long grass, corn stubble, potato field, or moorland. Beyond this island lies an ocean composed entirely of shadows, unreal and mysterious. Into this outer world one gropes with the eyes, peering and straining all the time, seeking to solve its mysteries. Shadows of every shape, some grotesque, some frightening, varying infinitesimally and subtly in depth from the deepest black, through blues and greens to the patchy greys and whiteness of the ground mist. One walks into the unknown; one might be walking on the moon. Shadows are deceptive things. A little copse seems like an impenetrable forest. A field of hay may turn into a discouraging reedy marsh. A stook of corn suddenly takes on a fantastic resemblance to a silent listening man.

A sheet-white ghost looms out from the mist. It moves—a stray cow shies off, as frightened as ourselves by the encounter. Stately mansions turn into derelict barns, and a distant hedge becomes a deep cutting with a railway line at the bottom. On this unreal planet one walks with every sense alert to the 'sticking-point.'

We went in single file spaced as far apart as possible, taking turns at leading with a white handkerchief draped over our backs. We would follow the leader, listening for the muttered warnings: 'ware wire, brambles, a ditch, marsh, and so on. We often stumbled. We avoided buildings, but even so, in the silence of the night, our progress would be heard by dogs and they would start barking as we hurried off into the shadows. We knew there was no big river in our path but we had to ford several streams, sometimes taking off boots and stockings and wading knee-deep to do so. We stopped to rest occasionally, and had a meal under a haystack at about 1 a.m.

As dawn approached, we searched for a hiding-place for the day and found one in a grove of trees far away from any buildings. We had done only thirteen miles, and were rather disappointed. We did not sleep much and were anxious to move on. The first part of our next night's march lay across a wide valley. Noting landmarks on our line, we set off a little before nightfall. Our feet were sore and blisters were appearing. Peter had borrowed a pair of suitable-looking boots which, however, did not fit him too well, and he developed enormous blisters on his heels. I had warned him what to expect. He stuck it well.

Later we found ourselves in mountainous country with occasional rushing torrents, waterfalls, and deep gorges, and mostly wooded. Farms, surrounded by small patches of cultivation cleared out of the woods, were few and far between.

The weather held fine. On our third day of freedom we considered making a start in daylight. By the early afternoon our impatience got the better of us and we set off.

After some steep climbing, we found a sparkling stream where in the clearer pools basked mountain trout.

"Rupert," I said "I can't resist this. My clothes are wringing wet; I'm perspiring like a pig. I'm going to have a bathe."

I started to undress. Rupert bent over a rock to feel the water.

"Ye gods!" he shouted, withdrawing his hand as if he had been scalded. "This water comes straight from the North Pole."

"Just what you need to freshen you up." I thought of my long walking tours as a student, when I learnt the benefit of bathing my feet frequently in cold water.

"Peter," I added, "it'll do your blisters no end of good. I insist we all sit with our feet dangling in a pool for at least ten minutes."

We all had a lightning dip, while our damp and sweaty clothes lay drying in the sun, and then we dangled our feet until we could not feel them any more. When we set off again, we were walking on air.

The going soon became so difficult that we took to paths and cattle tracks, and for the first time met another human being. Previously we had narrowly escaped being seen by some Hitler youths and girls whom we heard singing and laughing on our path close behind us. The new intruder was a woodman—we passed him with a casual "Heil Hitler!" He took no notice of us.

Later we came upon a small farm and Peter made so bold as to ask the farmer the way. Although our survey map could hardly have been better, our route was strewn with deep narrow valleys and we became confused as to which one we were in.

As evening drew on we found another gurgling stream and, piling up some stones on its bank, we made a fire. We had hot soup from cubes and roasted some potatoes, which we had collected earlier from a potato patch. It was a heavenly meal. After a good rest and a doze, we pushed on again as night fell.

We tried to maintain our direction on the small mountain paths, but found ourselves more and more frequently consulting our map with the aid of matches. This was an unwelcome necessity, for we did not want a light to give us away, and, even in woods, shielded the matches with our capes. Eventually we found a minor road and embarked on it. Soon it started to wind downhill and in a general direction at right angles to ours. At the same time we became hemmed in with impenetrable-looking forest which we dared not enter. We did not want to go downhill; it was out of our way and, in any case, it is always an advantage when walking across country to keep high up; then, with a map, one's position can be checked by bearings taken on the surrounding country. At the rate we were going we would be in the main Salzburg (Salzach) valley by morning. Even from our map we could not be certain which road we were on. In fact, we were lost.

We decided to wait till dawn and retrace our steps until our position could be checked up. Penetrating about fifty yards into the woods, we lay down to sleep in a leafy hollow. It was bitterly cold and we huddled together for warmth, with our scanty coverings spread over all three of us. Our muscles ached and we spent a miserable few hours dozing fitfully. Just before daylight we could stand it no longer and were about to move off when Rupert suddenly declared in a horrified tone:

"The compass is gone, I can't find it!"

There was a long silence as we regarded each other. I broke the awkward spell.

"That's a nice kettle of fish! When do you last remember having it?"

"Miles away! Before we started coming downhill—the last time we lit those matches."

We stared blankly at each other in the cold dawn, shivering miserably and depressed beyond description.

"Well! let's start searching," I said. "Be careful where we've been lying. Start from one end of the hollow and let's work on our hands and knees in line. Feel first for lumps and don't turn over more leaves than you can possibly help."

We searched, carefully patting the leaves and moss, advancing slowly yard by yard over the whole area of our bivouac.

"I've got it!" said Peter in triumph suddenly, holding it up like a trophy.

We sighed our relief. In this country, without a compass we could not keep a consistent course for five minutes.

After about two hours' walking, as the dawn came up we were able to locate ourselves and once more set off in the right direction across meadows and along the edges of woods, following a mountain ridge while it ran more or less parallel with our course.

This was our fourth day of freedom and we had had no rain. We met nobody all day. By evening we had reached the main road which heads south-east from Golling to Radstadt and across the mountain hump by way of the Radstädter Tauern pass. From now on it was apparent we should have to follow the road, because the mountains were high and the valley was a gorge. We set off along the road in the cool of the evening. Within ten minutes several people passed us on foot or on bicycles, and a Jerry soldier ambled by with a "Heil Hitler!" to which we replied with gusto. Although he had not appeared to see anything unusual in our now ragged and dirty clothing, we decided to retire into the woods and continue only after dark. This we did, and during the night we walked fast and with few stops, for the cold was becoming intense.

Our feet were at last becoming hardened. We made good going and by dawn had done about twenty-four miles. There were two incidents during the night. At about 11 p.m. a girl on a bicycle caught us up and insisted on talking to us.

"*Guten Abend! wo gehen Sie hin?*" she volunteered, dismounting and walking along beside us.

"Forward hussy, what?" murmured Rupert under his breath.

"Peter, you're a lady-killer," I whispered; "go on, do your stuff."

Peter took over.

"We're going to Abtenau. We've got army leave and are hiking. And where might you be going?"

Peter's German was correct even to the Austrian accent. The girl was pleased.

"I live at Voglau. It's only two miles from here on the main road. You come from Salzburg?"

"No, from Saalfelden," replied Peter, naming a place as far away from Salzburg as possible.

"I'll walk with you to my house. Father may offer you beer."

I understood enough to know that the conversation was taking an unhappy turn. I promptly sat down on a grass bank at the edge of the road and, pulling Rupert by his sleeve, said in an undertone, hoping my indifferent German accent would not be noticed, *"Hans! Kommen Sie hier. Ich gehe nicht weiter."* Rupert took the hint and sat beside me. Peter and the girl were already some yards ahead. I heard her say: "Your friends do not seem to like me. They will not speak. How rude they are."

"They are not rude but very tired, *Fräulein,*" put in Peter. "I am too tired to continue farther without a rest. *Auf Wiedersehen!* You must hurry home, for it is very late and your father will be worried. *Auf Wiedersehen!*"

With that Peter practically sat her on her bicycle and finally got rid of her. She left us a bit disgruntled and probably with some queer impressions. I doubt if she suspected us, though she was capable of talking to someone in a village who might. This was an added reason for our making good headway during the night and moving out of the district.

Occasionally a car passed with headlights blazing—no thought of blackout!—which gave us enough warning to take cover. We did not take cover for pedestrians who passed or for cyclists who, in any case, were liable to catch us up, unheard above the roar of a mountain river which the road now followed. We walked together, feeling that if we were accosted there was always one of us who could reply.

Approaching a small village beyond the junction town called Abtenau, we saw several lights and torches flickering. We hastily took to a field. The lights persisted for a long time—about two hours—and garrulous voices could be heard. Finally the episode wound up when a very drunken man passed down the road reeling from side to side, throwing and kicking his bicycle along in front of him. He was shouting and swearing and could be heard a mile away. Loud crashes punctuated his tirade, indicating that the bicycle was the victim of his rage and presumably the cause of it!

The lights were ominous. We continued when all was quiet and shortly afterwards encountered a small house with an army motor-cycle standing outside. Dogs barked as we passed, so we hurried on.

We were about three thousand feet above sea-level. The valley became narrower than ever and it was out of the question to travel other than on the road. In daylight we would be conspicuous walking through the small villages.

We rested during the fifth day (a Monday) on a promontory overlooking the road. Towards late afternoon a cold drizzle began to fall. We became restless and argued about going on. One by one we gave in and agreed to move. With our odd-looking capes and blankets over our shoulders, we trudged uphill along the now muddy road—passing a sawmill where a few men were working. They stared at us, and later a motor-lorry from the mill caught us up before we had time to take cover. As it passed, a youth leaned out and had a good stare at us.

This was disquieting. I insisted we should disappear again until nightfall. We found a resting-place beside the river among trees about fifteen yards from the road. The rain continued till nightfall and then ceased, leaving us cold, wet, and dispirited. I was nervous after the experience of the sawmill. We drank water copiously before starting. If a man drinks far more than he has the desire for, he can walk for eight hours without feeling unduly thirsty. We continued up the winding valley past straggling villages and small chalets. The night was pitch-dark and there were no stars. We were nearing the top of the pass and were only a few miles from Radstadt, which was the half-way point on our journey to Yugoslavia. We had walked about seventy-five miles.

We entered a small village at about 11.30 p.m. It was called Lungötz. All was quiet. Suddenly the light of an electric torch was directed down at us from a window high above. After a few seconds it went out. Very suspicious! But there was nothing we could do about it in the middle of a village. We had been seen, so we had to bluff our way out. Coming to a fork in the road, we hesitated a moment while I peered at the signpost, and then took the left branch. After a couple of hundred yards we left the village behind and the road entered deep woods. We breathed more freely.

The next moment there was a loud crashing of branches and undergrowth. Beams from powerful torches flashed on us and we saw the gleam of rifle barrels. Men shouted "Halt! Halt! Wer da?" We stopped, and Peter, a few steps ahead, answered "Gut Freund." Three men jumped down to the road from the banks on either side and approached, with their rifles aimed at us from the hip. At a few yards' distance they began shouting at Peter all together. I could see they were very nervous.

"Who are you? What are you doing in the woods at this hour? Where are you going? Produce your papers."

"One at a time! One at a time!" shouted Peter. "What is all this fuss? We are innocent people. We are soldiers on leave and we go to Radstadt."

"Where are your papers? We do not believe you. Show us your papers."

"We do not carry any papers. We are on leave."

One of the men approached Rupert and me and knocked

the sticks which we held, out of our hands with his rifle, jabbering hysterically at us. We could not have answered him if we had wanted to.

"So you have no papers. Why are your two companions silent? We think you are spies, enemies of the Reich!"

There was a moment when Rupert and I might have run for it—back down the road, zigzagging—leaving Peter. But the opportunity passed before we had time to pull our wits together. We might have got away with it if there were no patrols behind us.

Then the men were all shouting, "*Hände hoch! Hände hoch!*" and we put up our hands, Peter still protesting we were innocent and anxious to get on to Radstadt. It was no use. If Peter had been alone he might have deceived them, but we two were just so much dead weight and our dumbness or sullenness was the last straw.

We were marched back at the bayonet point to a small inn in the village. Several windows in a house opposite were lit up. I recognised it as the house from which the torchlight had first been flashed at us. The owner of the torch had probably been in touch with the ambush party by signal. In the *Gaststube* (dining-room) of the inn, we were lined against a wall and ordered by one of the three policemen, more ferocious and nervous than the rest, to keep our arms stretched upwards. We were then left with two guards until about 1.30 a.m., when the third guard returned. We were marched out and put in the back of an open lorry, which I recognised as the one which had passed us, and were driven off down the road along which we had come. It was heartbreaking to see the landmarks we had passed only a few hours before as free men. The two guards sat facing us with their rifles at the ready. Since our capture there had not been the faintest chance of a getaway. The remainder of the night was spent at the police-station at Abtenau, then two hours' drive under armed guard, and we were back in the German *Kommandantur* at Oflag VII C, a depressed and sorry-looking trio.

A German under-officer approached us and we

were 'for it.' He was the one who checked numbers at *Appells*, and he knew Peter well, since Peter had acted as camp interpreter on many occasions. He roared at us, forcing us to stand rigidly to attention while he tore off pieces of our clothing. He shook Peter wildly by the shoulders, spluttering into his face. It was a wonderful exhibition. He had obviously had a bad time since our absence was discovered.

After working off his revenge he led us to the German Camp Adjutant, who took us one by one into his office and questioned us. He began with me.

"It was useless to try to escape. You were warned. Now it is proved. You were fortunate not to have been shot. When did you leave?"

"I cannot say."

"But what difference does it make? We know everything. Six of you escaped. You left on Saturday, did you not?"

"I don't know."

"Herr Hauptmann, you are an officer and I understand your point of view, but when the whole matter is closed and finished, surely we can talk together freely?"

"Of course, Herr Oberst, I understand. I did not know you had recaptured three more officers."

"That is a leading question. Please remember 1 am questioning you—and that you are not here to question me. You had money, of course?"

"Money? No."

"Then how have you travelled so far in such a short time?"

"There are ways of travelling, Herr Oberst."

"Hah! So you stole bicycles?"

I was becoming involved. My 'No' to the question concerning money was not a good answer. I fell back upon "I cannot reply to your questions."

"Unless you tell me the day you escaped, I shall have to assume you have stolen bicycles. This is a very serious charge."

"I cannot help it."

"You have concealed your absence at one *Appell*. How did you do it?"

"I did not do it."

"You did not, but others did. You see, your absence was known at evening *Appell* on Saturday. Your escape was made at night. Therefore at the morning *Appell* your absence was concealed. You admit it was at night, do you not?"

"I admit nothing."

"Do not be so silly. It was, of course, clever of you to hide in the grass compound. We are building a guard ring of barbed wire two yards from the fences now. You will not be able to repeat your escape. Did you hide near the river or high up?"

"I just concealed myself."

"But where?"

"I cannot say."

"I know that soldiers concealed your *Appell*. Unless you tell me their names, I shall be compelled to have them all punished. That is not fair, to punish all for the offence of six. What were their names?"

"I do not know."

"You know well. If you do not give the names, it will be bad for all. You can save much hardship by a simple answer."

"I am sorry, Herr Oberst."

"Well then! You have either stolen bicycles or you have had assistance from outside the camp. For a prisoner to steal a bicycle is punishable with death. If you have received help, you can say so. I shall not ask the names and shall not charge you with theft of German private property. Come now, that is fair."

"Your offer is so fair, Herr Oberst, that I know you will understand my inability to answer you."

"You are a fool," he answered, becoming angry. "I have given you enough chances. You will suffer for your silence. Do you like concentration camps? Do you like to starve? Do you like to die? I give you one more chance. Your obstinacy is madness—it has no reason. Did you receive any help?"

I did not answer.

"So you insult me. Very well. You will be punished for silent insolence as well. About turn! March!"

I left the room and the others were paraded in turn. The questioning and tactics were the same in each case, as I found out. Rupert and Peter gave nothing away. We had a pretty good idea by now of German bluff, and in our three months' imprisonment we were beginning to learn that even a POW had rights and that a document known as the 'Geneva Convention' existed.

I learnt in time to bless this International Convention for the Treatment of Prisoners-of-War and must record here my gratitude to its authors. This product of the League of Nations stands as a testimony to our civilisation. Its use in World War II demonstrated the force of that civilisation amidst the threat of its ruin.

Our questioning ended, we were marched off to the town jail, which was close by, and each locked in a separate cell. For several days we languished in our dungeons like forgotten men. My cell was empty except for an unused heating stove, a bucket, and a jug of water. Wood floor, stone walls, and a tiny window just below a high ceiling made up my surroundings. There was no bed or bedding. At night the cold was intense, though it was only September.

During the day we walked our rooms or sat on the floor. We tried knocking to each other through the walls, which annoyed the guards, who cursed and threatened us if we continued. This depressing period was no doubt intended to demoralise us, for we were again taken individually and questioned, and when we refused to speak we were informed that we would be held for court martial.

When an officer is recaptured after an escape, the same principle holds good as when he is first taken prisoner—namely, that it is better to say nothing than tell lies. Lies may temporarily deceive the enemy in one direction, but they often lead him to unearth something which was never intended to be discovered. If I had replied to the question "How did you escape?" by saying we escaped over the roofs, it was quite liable to upset a plan being prepared by other officers in the camp unknown to us.

If to the question "When did you escape?" I gave a date several days before the actual event, I ran a good risk of being found out in a lie through a chance identification, or I might make the Germans so aghast at the length of my absence that the repercussion on future *Appell* precautions might be disastrous. If I named a date sometime after the actual event, I immediately gave the Jerries false ideas as to how far I could travel in a given time and thereby enlarged the circumference of cordons for future escapers. I found also that Jerry quickly lost respect for an enemy who talked. He expects silence. It is in accord with his own rules.

We returned, to languish in our jail. Every second day we were thrown a slab of brown bread in the morning and given a bowl of soup at midday.

On the fourth day there was a loud commotion and we heard the voices of Dick Howe, Harry Elliott, and Kenneth Lockwood! They were locked in neighbouring cells. Their arrival was further cause for depression.

We soon made complaints about the bucket sanitation and were eventually allowed to use a lavatory at the end of the corridor. Then we complained of lack of exercise and were allowed to walk for half an hour daily in single file at twenty-five paces from each other in a circle in the Oflag courtyard, the other officers being temporarily shut off from the area.

We established communications with the camp and among ourselves. With the aid of pencil butts dropped in the courtyard where we walked, notes were later written on pieces of lavatory paper, and left to be picked up by officers. The first Red Cross parcels had just arrived. We asked for food in our notes and were soon receiving it: chocolate, sugar, Ovo-sport, cheese!

We would enter the courtyard carrying our towels as sweat-rags. After a turn or two we would notice an inconspicuous pile of swept-up dust. This was the food done up in a small round parcel. A towel would be dropped carelessly in the corner over the rubbish and left until the end of the half-hour's exercise. The towel and the parcel would then be recovered in one movement and nonchalantly carried back to the cells to be divided later and left in the lavatory.

Gradually we learnt each other's stories. We found out also that no one else had escaped, and were aghast at this and extremely disappointed. Men could have been escaping every other day or so. We could not understand it.

Dick Howe, Harry Elliott, and Kenneth Lockwood had been recaught about sixty-three miles away, on the road to Switzerland, after eight days of freedom. Their escape worked to plan. Scarlet O'Hara closed up the hole. After two days' march the three of them jumped a goods train near Golling which took them to a place called Saalfelden. Although they gained about four days' march by this, they had to retrace their steps for some two days to regain their correct route. They had some bad going and bad weather, and had to lie up for a day or two in deserted mountain huts. Walking along a river bank close to a village, they were accosted by two women who appeared to suspect them. Harry's German passed. The women were looking for a man who had burgled their house. Farther on they were trapped by a policeman who conducted them to the village to question them concerning the burglary. Only when they were searched did the local bobby realise he had 'fished for a sprat and caught a mackerel.'

After ten days in the cells we were told that there would not be a court martial after all, but we were to await our sentences. In due course these were meted out, and to our surprise varied considerably. Peter got off with a fortnight, Rupert and I were the longest with a month each, without retroactive effect from our first day in cell. The differences were explained by minor offences, such as carrying a cut-up

Captain Richard Howe, M.B.E., M.C.
Escape Officer, Colditz 1942-45.
Photograph of a pastel drawn in his fifth and last year of
captivity, by John Watton.

German blanket or being in possession of a compass or a map and so on. The sentences were 'bread and water and solitary'; that is to say, bread and water only and a board bed for three days out of every four. On the fourth day the prisoner was given a mattress and two meals of thick potato soup or other gruel. As sentences finished we were allowed to live together in one cell: a large one with mattresses, blankets, and German prison ration food. Thus it came to pass, after forty days, that all six of us were together again. We wondered what would happen to us next. We knew that escaped prisoners were usually moved to new camps.

One day a camp padre was allowed to visit us and give us spiritual comfort. We had complained repeatedly that we were not allowed to read books, not even a Bible. Padre Wynne Price Rees gave us the first news as to what had happened to our tunnel.

For some inexplicable reason Scarlet O'Hara and others had postponed using the tunnel, at first for a week and then, upon our recapture, indefinitely. Finally, questions having been asked in the town as to whether any suspicious individuals had been seen between certain dates, a little girl was brought by her mother to the Camp Commandant. She reported having seen one morning, in a woodshed near the camp walls, a man in pyjamas whom she did not recognise as being anyone belonging to the household of the woodshed owner. A stranger in pyjamas in the woodshed of a house in the early morning—wonderful food for gossip in Laufen! This event occurred about three weeks after our escape. Little notice was taken of the child's story by anyone except an elderly *Feldwebel* who had been a POW in England during the First World War and who had helped German officers to build a tunnel. He went 'snooping' in the part of the camp near the woodshed, sounding the walls and floors. Eventually he arrived at the little locked room, where he came upon the hidden piles of earth and finally our tunnel entrance in the darkest corner under a table. It was camouflaged against casual observation by a large piece of painted cardboard made to fit the hole.

We could pride ourselves on the fact that the camouflage of the tunnel exit had held out. I felt a little ashamed that our entrance had not been better finished. My excuse was that I had never meant it to last three weeks and, moreover, we found from later experience that it was difficult under any circumstances to keep an escape-hole concealed for long after prisoners were known to have escaped.

The figure in pyjamas turned out to be Scarlet O'Hara, who was feverishly screwing up the woodshed door-bolt when he looked up to see the face and startled eyes of the little girl peering at him through the slats of the door. She bolted in terror, and Scarlet, equally frightened, disappeared backwards down our rabbit burrow at high speed. Scarlet's face was at no time beautiful, and I am sure the little girl had nightmares for weeks afterwards.

A few days after the padre's visit we were summoned and, to our utter astonishment, sent back to the camp. We became once more normal prisoners-of-war. It was not to be for long. A week later we were given an hour's notice to assemble for departure to an unknown destination.

The six of us had profited by our week to pass on what information and experience we had gained to the others, and we could not understand why the Germans had given us the opportunity. They had no microphones in Laufen; of that we were certain. Before we departed, our Senior British Officer (always known as the S.B.O.) insisted on being told our destination. I believe he also insisted on this information being cabled to the International Red Cross. We packed our meagre belongings and, with a large five-gallon drum filled with cooked potatoes which we took it in turn to carry, two at a time, we set off on foot for the station under heavy guard. Our destination was Oflag IV C, Colditz, Saxony.

II

Escape Officer

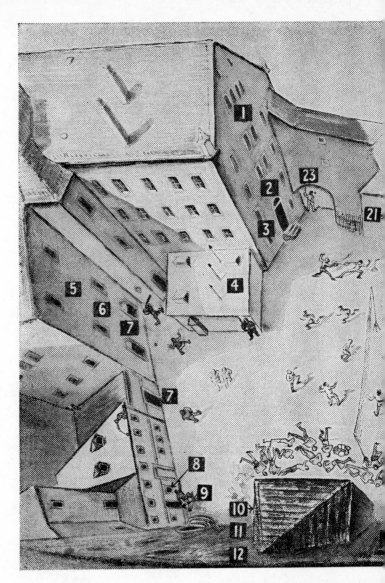

Bird's-eye view of the Prisoners' Quarte

1. Theatre.
2. Senior Officers' quarters: British, French, Polish and Dutch.
3. Shower baths.
4. Delousing shed.
5. British orderlies' quarters.

6. French and Polish orderlies quarters
7. Kitchens.
8. Camp Office.
9. Canteen entrance.
10. Barber's shop.
11. Polish quarters.

Note: The various quarters were put to different uses at d

Reproduced, from a sketch drawn by John Watton whi

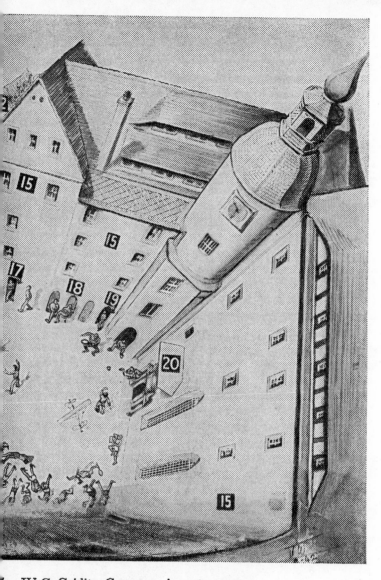

Stalag IV C, Colditz, Germany, August 1942.

12. Dutch quarters.
13. British quarters.
14. Medical inspection and Dentist rooms.
15. French quarters.
16. Belgian quarters.
17. Parcel office.
18. Cellar door.
19. Parcel office and Hospital entrance.
20. The Chapel.
21. Punishment cells.
22. The German Guard House.
23. Courtyard entrance.

times, but this was how they were employed in August 1942.

in Colditz, by courtesy of "The Illustrated London News."

CHAPTER IV

THE FORTRESS PRISON

W E left Laufen on November 7th, 1940, and arrived three days later in Colditz, Oflag IV C.

There was little or no chance of escape on the journey. Moreover, we had no escape material or reserve food (except potatoes!). The guards were watchful; we were always accompanied to the lavatory. We travelled sometimes in second class, sometimes in third, at all hours of the day and night. There were many changes and long waits, usually in the military waiting-rooms of stations. Passers-by eyed us curiously but without, I thought, great animosity. Those who made closer contact by speaking with our guards were concerned at our carrying potatoes with us. We, who had had three months of starvation diet, followed by many weeks of bread and water, were taking no risks and would have fought for those cold soggy balls of starch with desperation!

We arrived at the small town of Colditz early one afternoon. Almost upon leaving the station we saw looming above us our future prison: beautiful, serene, majestic, and yet forbidding enough to make our hearts sink into our boots. It towered above us, dominating the whole village; a magnificent Castle built on the edge of a cliff. It was the real fairy castle of childhood's story-books. What ogres there might live within! I thought of the dungeons and of all the stories I had ever heard of prisoners in chains, pining away their lives, of rats and tortures, and of unspeakable cruelties and abominations.

In such a castle, through the centuries, everything had happened and anything might happen again. To friendly peasants and tradespeople in the houses nestling beneath its shadow it may have signified protection and home, but to enemies from a distant country such a castle struck the note of doom and was a sight to make the bravest quail.

Indeed, it was built with this end in view. Being about one thousand years old, although partly ruined, built over and altered many times, its inherent strength had preserved it from destruction through the stormy centuries.

It was built on the top of a high cliff promontory that jutted out over the River Mulde at a confluence with a tributary stream. The outside walls were on an average seven feet thick, and the inner courtyard of the Castle was about two hundred and fifty feet above the river-level. The Castle rooms in which we were to live were about another sixty feet above the courtyard. The Castle was built by Augustus the Strong, King of Poland and Elector of Saxony from 1694 to 1733, who was reputed to have had three hundred and sixty-five children, one for every day of the year. He built it upon ruins left by the Hussite Wars of the fifteenth century. It had seen many battles and sieges in a long history, and the present name, Schloss Colditz, testified, not to its origin, but to a time when it was under Polish domination. The 'itz' is a Slavonic not a Teutonic or Saxon ending. The original spelling was Koldyeze.

The River Mulde, we later learned, was a tributary of the Elbe, into which it flowed forty miles to the north. Colditz was situated in the middle of the triangle formed by the three great cities of Leipzig, Dresden, and Chemnitz, in the heart of the German Reich and four hundred miles from any frontier not directly under the Nazi heel. What a hope for would-be escapers!

We marched slowly up the steep and narrow cobbled streets from the station towards the Castle, eventually approaching it from the rear, that is to say, from the mainland out of which the promontory protruded. Entering the main arched gateway, we crossed a causeway astride what had once been a deep, wide moat and passed under a second cavernous archway whose oaken doors swung open and closed ominously behind us with the clanging of heavy iron bars in true mediæval fashion. We were then in a courtyard about forty-five yards square, with some grass lawn and flower-beds and surrounded on all four sides with buildings six stories high. This was the *Kommandantur* or garrison area. We were escorted farther; through a third cavernous archway with formidable doors, up an inclined cobbled coachway for about fifty yards, then turning sharp right, through a fourth and last archway with its normal complement of heavy oak and iron work into the 'Sanctum Sanctorum,' the inner courtyard. This was a cobbled space about thirty yards by forty yards, surrounded on its four sides by buildings whose roof ridges must have been ninety feet above the cobbles. Little sun could ever penetrate here! It was an unspeakably grisly place, made none the less so by the pallid faces which we noticed peering at us through bars. There was not a sound in the courtyard. It was as if we were entering some ghostly ruin. Footsteps echoed and the German words of command seemed distorted out of reality. I had reached the stage of commending my soul to the Almighty when the faces behind the bars suddenly took on life; eyes shone, teeth flashed from behind unkempt beards and words passed backwards into the inner depths:

"*Anglicy! Anglicy!*"

Heads crowded each other out behind tiny barred windows, and in less time than it took us to walk thirty yards there was a cheering mob at every window; not only at the small ones which we had first seen and which we were to come to know so well, but from every other window that we could see there were jostling heads, laughing and cheering. Welcome was written on every face. We breathed again as we realised we were among friends. They were Polish officers.

Relief was quickly followed by amazement as we heard the men behind the bars shout insults at the Germans in their own language, at the same time making violent gestures indicating throat-cutting of the unmistakable ear-to-ear variety. The Jerries were angry. They threatened reprisals, and quickly hustled us away to a building and up many flights of stairs into a couple of attic rooms, where they left us under lock and key behind a wooden grill.

We were not the first arrivals: three R.A.F. officers were there to greet us! They were Flying Officers Howard D. Wardle, Keith Milne, and Donald Middleton.

Wardle, or 'Hank' as he was called, was a Canadian who had joined the R.A.F. shortly before the war. He was dropping propaganda leaflets over Germany in April 1940, when his bomber was shot down. He parachuted and landed in trees as his parachute opened. He was one of the earliest British POWs of the war. He had escaped from the Schloss camp of Spangenburg, about twenty miles from Kassel, by climbing a high barricade on the way to a gymnasium just outside the camp precincts. The other two, also Canadians, had escaped dressed as painters complete with buckets of whitewash and a long ladder, which they carried between them. They had waited for a suitable moment when there appeared to be a particularly dumb Jerry on guard at the gate, marched up briskly, shouted the only words they knew in German and filed out. Having passed the gate, they continued jauntily until they were halfway down the hill on which the Schloss reposed. They then jettisoned ladder and buckets and made a bolt for the woods.

These escapes were in Augst 1940, and were probably the first escapes of the war from regular camps. None of the three travelled very far before recapture and it was, alas, only a matter of hours before they were back behind the bars. They suffered badly at the hands of their captors, being severely kicked and battered with rifle-butts. The local population were bitter and revengeful.

The three R.A.F. officers had arrived a couple of days before us at night and had seen no one. They were told that sentences awaited them and that they would probably be shot. On the first morning at dawn they had been marched out to some woods in a deep valley flanking one side of the Castle and halted beside a high granite wall. . . . They had then been told to exercise themselves for half an hour! The Germans took a sadistic pleasure in putting the complete wind up the three of them. By the time they reached the high wall in the early half-light they had given up hope of ever seeing another sunrise. This joke over, the Jerries took them back to the rooms in which we found them.

Later that evening we made our first acquaintance with the Poles. There were hushed voices on the staircase, then four of them appeared beyond the grill. They unlocked the door with ease and advanced to greet us. We were the first English they had seen in the war, and the warmth of their welcome, coupled with their natural dignity of bearing, was touching. Each one of us might have been a hero, for to them we represented the friend who had come to their aid when in dire need, who had been prepared to fight in their cause. The Polish people are above all loyal, and they have long memories too—a capacity worth noting in our present times.

They brought food and some beer. Two of the four could speak English and the remainder French. They all spoke German. The meeting soon became noisy and there was much laughter, which the Poles love. Suddenly there was a warning signal from a Pole on the look-out by the stairs, and in less than no time they were all distributed under beds in the corners of our two rooms, where suppressed laughter continued up to the instant of the entry of a German officer with his *Feldwebel*.

The attic door, and others below, had, of course, been locked by the Poles, so that there was nothing to cause suspicion other than our laughter, which the Germans had overheard and had come to investigate. The officer was shocked that we, reviled prisoners, whose right to live depended on a word from him, should find occasion to laugh. It was like laughing in church, and he implied as much to us. He noticed we had shifted all the bunks to make more floor space and promptly made the *Feldwebel* move them back again into orderly rows. The Poles moved with the beds. No sooner had they departed than the Poles, like truant schoolboys, reappeared, laughing louder than ever at the joke. They called the sergeant '*La Fouine,*'

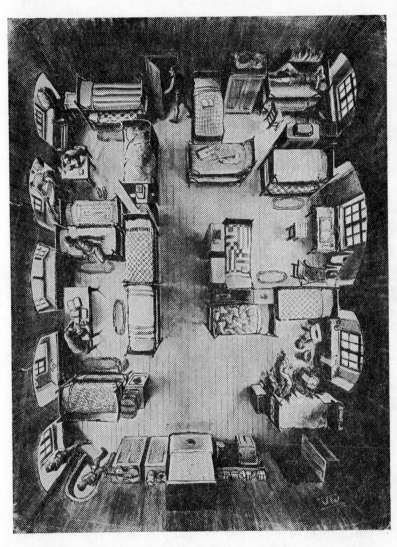

Bird's-eye view of a British bedroom at Oflag IV C. Redrawn from a water-colour painted in June 1942 at Colditz.

the French for a marten, which has also a figurative meaning, namely 'a wily person,' whose propensities have been translated into English as 'ferreting.' The merriment continued for a while, then they departed as they had come, leaving us to marvel at the facility with which they manipulated locks. In order to visit us they had unlocked no fewer than five doors with a couple of instruments that looked like a pair of button-hooks. Such was our introduction to Colditz, which was to be our prison house for several years.

There were about eighty Polish army officers in the camp when we arrived. They were among the cream of the Polish army and some had undoubtedly charged tanks at the head of their troop of horse. Although stripped of much of their military attire, they were always smartly turned out on parade. They wore black riding-boots which they kept in beautiful condition. Their Senior Officer was General Tadensz Piskor, and there was also an Admiral named Joseph Unrug.

The officers had all committed offences against the German Reich and the majority had escaped unsuccessfully at least once. They had been prisoners, of course, since the end of September 1939. So many of them had prison sentences outstanding against them that the half-dozen cells normally set apart for solitary confinement housed about six officers each. The cells were about three yards square and each had one small, heavily barred window. These were the windows we saw, crammed with grimy faces, immediately on entering the prison upon our arrival. Thus nearly half of their contingent was officially in solitary confinement!

Time passed more quickly in the new surroundings and in making new friends. The Germans, after a week or so, gave us permanent quarters: a dormitory with two-tier bunks, a washroom, a kitchen, and a day-room in a wing of the Castle separated from the Poles. The courtyard was the exercise area. At first we were given different hours to exercise, but the Jerries eventually gave up trying to keep us apart. To do so would have meant a sentry at every courtyard door, and there were half a dozen of these. Moreover, the Castle was a maze of staircases and intercommunicating doors, and the latter merely provided lock-picking practice for the Poles. We were so often found in each other's quarters that the Germans would have had to put the whole camp into 'solitary' to carry out their intentions, so they gave it up as a bad job.

A trickle of new arrivals increased the British contingent, until by Christmas we numbered sixteen officers. A few French and Belgian officers appeared. All the newcomers were offenders, mostly escapers, and it was impressed upon us that our Castle was 'the bad boys' camp,' the '*Straflager*' or '*Sonderlager*' as the Germans called it. At the same time we also began to appreciate its impregnability from the escape point of view. This was to be the German fortress from which there was no escape, and it certainly looked for a long time as if it would live up to that reputation. As I said in my Prologue, the garrison manning the camp outnumbered the prisoners at all times; the Castle was floodlit at night from every angle despite the blackout, and notwithstanding the sheer drop of a hundred feet or so on the outside from barred windows, sentries surrounded the camp within a palisade of barbed wire. The enemy seemed to have everything in his favour. Escape would be a formidable proposition indeed.

*   *   *   *   *

The Poles entertained us magnificently over the Christmas period. They had food parcels from their homes in Poland. We had nothing until, lo and behold, on Christmas Eve Red Cross parcels arrived! The excitement had to be seen to be believed. They were bulk parcels; that is to say, they were not addressed individually, nor did each parcel contain an assortment of food. There were parcels of tinned meat, of tea, of cocoa, and so on. Apart from a bulk consignment which reached Laufen the previous August, these were our first parcels of food from England and we felt a surge of gratitude for this gift, without which our Christmas would have been a pathetic affair. We were also able to return, at least to a limited extent, the hospitality of the Poles, whose generosity was unbounded. We had to ration severely, for we could not count on a regular supply, and we made this first consignment, which we could have eaten in a few days, last for about two months. Our estimate was not far wrong.

Throughout the whole war, in fact, supplies of Red Cross parcels to Colditz were never regular and a reserve had always to be stocked. Parcels were despatched from England at the rate of one per person per week. In Colditz we received normally one, on rare occasions two, parcels per person in three weeks. The parcels both from the United Kingdom and from Canada were excellent in quality and variety. The 'individual' as opposed to the 'bulk' parcels weighed ten and a half pounds each and contained a selection of the following: tinned meat, vegetables, cheese, jam and butter, powdered egg, powdered milk, tea or cocoa, chocolate, sugar, and cooking-fat. These parcels were paid for to a large extent by a prisoner's relatives, but it became almost a universal rule at all camps that 'individual' parcels were put into a pool and everybody shared equally.

The Poles prepared a marionette show for Christmas. It was 'Snow-White and the Seven Dwarfs.' They had the full text of the story, and the characters were taken by persons behind the screen. It was a picturesque show, professionally produced both as to the acting and the décor. The marionettes were beautifully dressed and the frequently changing scenery was well painted. It lasted about two hours and was a great success. During the interval, sandwiches and beer were served and afterwards a feast was offered. The Poles had saved everything for months for this occasion. The beer was a ration, also saved. It was bottled lager which was handed out by the Jerries against prison money on spasmodic occasions. To begin with, in Colditz, it was not too scarce, but by the middle of 1941 it had disappeared completely.

CHAPTER V

ROUTINE

PRISONERS were not allowed so much as to look at a real Reichsmark; instead, the special paper money known as *Lagergeld* was issued. *Lagergeld* did not go far. The canteen offered for sale the usual razor-blades, tooth-paste, shaving soap, and occasionally some turnip jam or beetroots in vinegar, and saccharine tablets. We could also buy musical instruments by order. They were very expensive—in fact, the prices were downright robbery—but they gave satisfaction to many amateur musicians.

During my sojourn in prison I bought two guitars, one for about £10 and the other for about £25, and a brass cornet for about £30. I must admit that the cornet was of good quality and the more expensive guitar was a beauty. The instruments came from a well-known firm in Leipzig. I studied the guitar for a year and a half, becoming fairly proficient. I could read music slowly and could play some classical pieces by heart. The cornet provided me with a means of letting off steam when I had nothing better to do. My colleagues limited the use of it to the washroom, with the door closed, in fine weather, at hours when they were normally out in the courtyard.

The German food was cooked in a large, well-equipped, and clean kitchen off the prison courtyard. Private cooking by the prisoners could also be done in our small kitchen provided with a cooking-stove and a hopelessly inadequate supply of coal. All loose and unessential items made of wood, together with large numbers of fixtures, partitions, floorboards, beds and the like, quickly disappeared into the greedy mouth of our grubby little pot-boiler and frying-pan heater. However, the smells which exuded from that murky room invariably outweighed any pangs of conscience, not to mention fears of reprisals, on account of the dubious origin of most of our fuel. My favourite meal was corned beef fried with dried currants or sultanas. Even today my mouth waters in grateful memory of the delectable dish which warded off many an incipient depression. Rupert Barry was the *chef par excellence* for this *specialité de la maison*. It was not an everyday meal—indeed, it was a rarity—which perhaps accounts for the poignant memories I still have of it.

The daily course of life, as may be expected, did not vary much. We awoke in the morning at 7.30 a.m. to shouts of *'Aufstehen'* or 'get up' from a couple of German non-commissioned officers who passed through the dormitories. At 8 a.m., breakfast orderlies (our own troops), helped by officers, carried up from the German kitchen a large cauldron of 'ersatz' coffee (made from acorns), a certain number of loaves of bread, a small quantity of margarine, and on certain days a little sugar. At 8.30 a.m. there was *Appell*. All ranks formed up in the courtyard, the Poles in one contingent, the British in another, with their respective senior officers in front. A German officer would appear. Everybody would salute everybody else and the German non-commissioned officers would go through a painstaking count of the bodies. When all was found correct there would be more saluting and the parade would break up. As time went on, the first of four daily *Appells* was sounded at 7 a.m. by means of a factory hooter. By 9 a.m. we were free to carry on any lawful pursuit such as reading, studying, language lessons, music lessons, or exercise. The Poles knew every language imaginable between them, and most Englishmen took up a foreign language with a Polish teacher in exchange for English lessons.

Teachers and pupils paired off and sought out quiet corners all over the Castle, where they would settle down to explain to each other the intricacies of the various European languages. Our living-room became a hive of industry and the low murmur of voices continued unabated throughout the morning hours. Those who sought more privacy chose to sit on the staircase or on blankets in the lobbies or out in the courtyard, if it was fine. Here, voices did not have to be hushed and temperament could be indulged in. I remember passing a couple once, deep in the throes of an English lesson, and I overheard the following instruction:

Teacher: "Now we shall read. Start where we left off yesterday."
Pupil (*reading*): "Thee leetle sheep——"
Teacher: "Not 'thee,' say 'the.'"
Pupil: "The leetle sheep——"
Teacher: "No! 'The little ship!'"
Pupil: "The little sheep——"
Teacher: "*Not* 'sheep,' you ass, but 'ship.'"
Pupil: "The leetle ship——"
Teacher: "Damn it! Are you deaf? I've already said 'little ship,' not 'leetle ship.' Start all over again."
Pupil: "Thee little ship——" and so on.

When books started to arrive from the U.K., study courses began. Later, a prison theatre was opened and plays, varieties, and concerts occupied much of the time of officers with any talent for amateur theatricals or musicals.

One variety concert, arranged by Lieutenant Teddy Barton, R.A.S.C., played to packed houses for several nights. It was called *Ballet Nonsense*. Costumes were made mostly out of crêpe paper, which served the purpose well. The orchestra was of surprisingly high quality and the airs and lyrics, composed by 'Jimmy' Yule (Lieutenant J. Yule, R.C.S.) and Teddy Barton, gave the show a professional touch which savoured poignantly of Drury Lane and the Hippodrome. The orchestral talent was provided by a mixture of all the nationalities under the able band leadership of John Wilkins, a naval (submarine) Leading Telegraphist who had a fantastic aptitude for playing any wind instrument he chose to pick up, in a matter of days. The underlying theme of *Ballet Nonsense* was provided by a *corps de ballet* consisting of the toughest-looking, heaviest-moustached officers available, who performed miracles of energetic grace and unsophisticated elegance upon the resounding boards of the Colditz theatre stage attired in frilly crêpe paper ballet skirts and brassières.

Ballet Nonsense very nearly never came off! A grand piano was to be installed for the occasion. When it arrived in the courtyard, the workmen engaged in hauling it up the narrow stairs took off their jackets and waistcoats for the job. These, of course, quickly disappeared. The contents of pockets were left intact, but the civilian clothing was considered by the vast majority of the camp to be fair game!

The Commandant promptly closed the theatre and demanded the return of the clothing. Monetary compensation was offered by the POWs, but the return of the clothes —no! It was all very upsetting for the Management, who had gone to endless trouble over advertisement with decorative posters spread about the Castle. They, the Management, were in the throes of preparing postponement strips beginning with 'The Management regrets . . .' and were haggling over the phrases to follow, which were quite likely to put the author in 'solitary' for a month if he was not tactful as to their content, when their worries were dispelled in an unforeseen manner. The French, true to a Riviera tradition, solved the problem in their own way. When the morning after the piano incident dawned, a second poster had been superimposed over the *Ballet Nonsense* Folly Girls. It read:

> For Sunshine Holidays
> visit
> Sunny Colditz
> Holiday Hotel
> 500 beds   one bath
> Cuisine
> by French chef
> Large staff
> always attentive and vigilant
> Once visited, never left

(The camp cook was a French chef, though he had no scope for his talent.)

After a month of futile searching for the clothes by the Jerries, the money was accepted and the theatre reopened. *Ballet Nonsense* was a far greater success, due to a month of extra rehearsals!

* * * * *

The midday meal at Colditz was sounded at 12.30 p.m. and consisted of thick barley gruel. Occasionally, pieces of hog's hide were cut up and put into the soup, which gave it a delicious odour of pork and that was about all. On such days the German menu on the blackboard outside the kitchen triumphantly announced '*Speck*'—in other words, Bacon. It deceived nobody but the far-away 'Protecting Power' who read the menus, sent by the German *Kommandatur* in answer to questionnaires. Nor did it deceive the 'Protecting Power' for long either; the latter was quickly disillusioned on its representatives' first visit to the camp. The 'Protecting Power' is a neutral government which represents the interests of one belligerent power in the territories of the other. In the case of the U.K. the government was Switzerland's, and unstinted praise is due for its good work on behalf of British prisoners throughout the war.

The rations deteriorated as the war progressed. An idea of the German ration of food provided from about 1942 onwards is given by the table on the following page, which has been taken from a 'Protecting Power' report on Colditz.

It was inevitable that the camp should possess a cat. It arrived, of course, as a kitten and in time grew up into a fine brindled specimen through the undisputed and indulgent care of a rather fat Belgian officer. The two were inseparable, for the Belgian never stinted the cat's rations and the latter grew fat while the Belgian grew thin. One day the cat disappeared. His absence was mourned by all,

(One English pound equals 454 grammes)

Day	Breakfast	Lunch	Dinner
Monday	Coffee-subst. 4 gr.	Potatoes 400 gr. Turnips 500 gr.	Jam-subst. 20 gr. Bread 300 gr.
Tuesday	Coffee-subst. 4 gr.	Potatoes 400 gr. Turnips 600 gr.	Jam-subst. 20 gr. Bread 300 gr.
Wednesday	Coffee-subst. 4 gr.	Potatoes 400 gr. Turnips 500 gr.	Jam-subst. 20 gr. Bread 300 gr.
Thursday	Coffee-subst. 4 gr.	Potatoes 400 gr. Turnips 600 gr.	Jam-subst. 20 gr. Bread 300 gr.
Friday	Coffee-subst. 4 gr.	Potatoes 400 gr. Turnips 600 gr.	Jam-subst. 20 gr. Bread 300 gr. Cheese 31·25 gr.
Saturday	Coffee-subst. 4 gr.	Potatoes 400 gr. Peas 112·5 gr. Millet 75 gr. Oats 62·5 gr. Cooking-fat 68 gr. Barley 37·5	Jam-subst. 20 gr. Sugar 175 gr. Jam 175 gr. Bread 300 gr.
Sunday	Coffee-subst. 3·5 gr.	Potatoes 350 gr. Fresh meat 250 gr. Turnips 600 gr.	Jam-subst. 30 gr. Bread 425 gr.

while his master, though visibly moved, bore the loss with a smile. As the days passed it was assumed that the cat, tiring of monastic life, had gone a-roaming to find a mate; and the affair was forgotten. Then, a British orderly, while emptying the camp dustbins, came across a brown-paper parcel. Curiosity led him to open it and, as the layers of paper were unfolded, out fell an unmistakable brindled pelt. The cat was out of the bag; the smile had been on the face of the tiger.

*   *   *   *   *

In the afternoon, sport came to the fore. Foils made their appearance at one time and many took up fencing.

The little courtyard only lent itself to games such as volley-ball; that is to say, a football pushed backwards and forwards over a high badminton net with about three players on each side. Boxing was another favourite pastime.

There was one game which deserves special mention. It was invented by the British and belonged to that category of local school game devised in almost every public school of England. The wall game at Eton is an example. The rules soon become a matter of tradition and depend on the surface and shape of the ground, the buildings round it, and various hazards such as jutting corners or stone steps. The Colditz variety, which we called 'stoolball,' was played, of course, in the granite cobbled courtyard. It is the roughest game I have ever played, putting games like rugby football in the shade. The rules were simple. Two sides, consisting of any number of players and often as many as thirty a side, fought for possession of the football by any means. A player having the ball could run with it but could not hold it indefinitely; he had to bounce it occasionally while on the move. When tackled, he could do whatever he liked with it. A 'goalie' at each end of the yard sat on a stool—hence the name—and a goal was scored by touching the opponent's stool with the ball. Goal defence was by any means, including strangulation of the ball-holder, if necessary. There was a half-time when everybody was too tired to continue. There was no referee and there were, of course, no touch-lines.

The game proceeded as a series of lightning dashes, appalling crashes, deafening shouts, formidable scrums—generally involving the whole side—rapid passing movements, as in a rugby three-quarter line, and with a cheering knot of spectators at every window. Nobody was ever seriously hurt, in spite of the fury and the pace at which the game was played. Clothing was ripped to pieces, while mass wrestling and throwing of bodies was the order of the day. To extract an opponent from a scrum it was recommendable to grab him by the scalp and one leg. I never saw any 'tripping.' This was probably due to the instinctive

reaction of players to long schooling in our various ball
games where tripping is forbidden. I realise now that this
game was a manifestation of our suppressed desire for
freedom. While the game was in action we were free. The
surrounding walls were no longer a prison, but the confines of the game we played, and there were no constrain-
ing rules to curtail our freedom of action. I always felt
much better after a game. Followed by a cold bath it put
me on top of the world.

The Poles, and later the French when they arrived, were
always interested spectators. Although we had no monopoly of the courtyard, they naturally took to their rooms
and watched the game from windows. They eventually put
up sides against the British and games were played against
them, but these were not a success. Tempers were lost and
the score became a matter of importance, which it never
did in an 'all-British' game.

As time went on, the Jerries allowed us a couple of
hours' exercise three times a week in a barbed-wire pen in
the wooded grounds below the Castle, but within the external castle walls. Here we played something resembling
soccer—the hazards were the trees amongst which the game
surged backwards and forwards. Our ball games amused
the Jerries. Officers and N.C.O.s were occasionally caught
watching them surreptitiously—not because they were
afraid of being seen as spectators, but because their
vantage-points were supposed to be secret and were used
for spying upon us.

Towards the afternoon musical instruments could be
heard tuning up on all sides. As soon as they could be
purchased, many officers started practising one type or
another. In the late afternoon, too, we could usually rely
upon a *Sondermeldung*—which was always a good diversion.

What happened was that the Germans, who had placed
loudspeakers at strategic points throughout the Castle,
would switch on the power when a German *Sondermeldung*
or Special War Progress bulletin was announced. These

Stoolball

were calculated to raise German morale throughout the Reich to incredible heights and correspondingly to demoralise Germany's enemies to the point of throwing in the sponge.

Anyway—in the camp—the power would suddenly be

switched on with unmistakable crackling noises as the loudspeakers heated up. First a fanfare of trumpets sounded. Then, the strains of Liszt's preludes would come over the air, followed after a few moments by the announcer's proclamation in solemn and sonorous tones:

Das Oberkommando der Wehrmacht gibt bekannt! In tagelangen schweren Kämpfen gegen einen stark gesicherten Geleitzug im Atlantik haben unsere Unterseeboote sechzehn Schiffe mit insgesamt hundertfünfzigtausend Bruttoregistertonnen versenkt. Ferner wurden zwei Zerstörer schwer beschädigt.

As soon as the announcer had ceased, German brass bands would strike up *Wir fahren gegen Engeland,* and to the additional accompaniment of the whine of descending bombs, the crackle of machine-guns and the bursting of shells the act would attain a crescendo of power and then end with trumpets heralding victory.

The show was intended to make the bravest quail. It regularly produced pandemonium in the camp. No sooner had the ominous crackle of the loudspeakers started than windows all over the Castle would open, heads would reach out to the bars and every musical instrument that could be mustered was automatically requisitioned for the coming spectacle. As Liszt's preludes softened to give way to the announcer, this was the signal: drums, cymbals, clarinets, cornets, trombones and accordions, all gave voice at once in a cacophony that could be heard re-echoing from distant hills. The German *Kommandantur* shook with the reverberations.

But the Germans persevered and the war went on in earnest for several months, until eventually they gave in and the loudspeakers were for ever silenced.

Of course they tried all means at first to stop our counter-attack—but that was not easy. What broke the German morale, in the end, over the battle, was not so much the opposition we put up, as the insidious counter-propaganda we produced. For we recorded regularly the numbers of *Bruttoregistertonnen* involved, until we could show the Germans in the camp that there could not be a British ship left afloat, according to their figures.

In our less energetic moments, especially in the evenings, we played bridge and chess. Chess games, in a community where the passage of time was of no importance, went on for days. Players were known to sit up all night with a homemade, foul-smelling oil-lamp (for the electricity was turned off). The light had to be shaded so as not to show through the windows and bring the Jerries in.

There was also a card game for two players which we learnt from the Poles, called 'Gapin,' which means, in Polish, 'a person who looks but does not see!' The term applied well to the game, for it was one in which many cards lay face upwards on the table. These cards could be made use of, provided a player held certain corresponding cards in his hand. The open cards were continually changing, so that concentration and quick thinking were necessary. The game was aggravating, for after finishing a turn an opponent could promptly make good use of a card overlooked. It was so exasperating a game that I have known friends not to be on speaking terms for days because of humiliation and wounded pride involved in the showing up of an opponent's obtuseness. Rupert Barry and I had a running 'Gapin Contest' with high stakes in *Lagergeld* which ended with the payment, after the war, of a fat cheque—to Rupert!

The last roll-call of the day occurred usually at 9 p.m., after which soon came 'lights out.' At this 'witching hour' many of the nefarious escape activities of the camp started up. They were lumped together under the general heading of 'night shift.'

CHAPTER VI

THE SECOND TUNNEL

WITH Christmas fare inside us, optimism returned, and we began to wonder how the walls of our unbreachable fortress could be pierced. Tunnelling seemed to be the only solution, and we (the British) were such a small number, and so united in our resolution to escape, that we worked as one team. Lieutenant-Colonel Guy German (Royal Leicestershire Regiment), our senior officer, placed me in charge of operations, and kept aloof from them himself so as to be in a strong position *vis-à-vis* the Jerries. Nevertheless, he was keen to take part in any escape into which he could be fitted.

As at Laufen, we concentrated on parts of the Castle not used by ourselves. Our début was made early in January 1941 in a room on the ground floor under German lock and key. We were learning from the Poles their art of picking locks, and in this empty room, with our usual guards on the look-out for alarms, we started work. Unloosening floorboards, we came on loose rubble and in a short time had a hole big enough for a man to work in, with the floorboards replaced over him.

I was dissatisfied with this tunnel entrance before long, because the boards were very old and one of them could be lifted easily; moreover, they sounded ominously hollow underfoot. I made a sliding trap-door out of bed boards, which fitted between the floor supporting-beams. The trap-door itself was a long, open-topped box which slid horizontally on wooden runners. The box was filled with the under-floor rubble. When the trap-door was closed, a German could lift the floorboards and see nothing suspicious; he could even stand on the trap-door. At the same time, the rubble filling damped out the hollow sound. Without any discussion, the trap-door became known as 'Shovewood II'!

The trap was soon tested in action. Hank Wardle and I were surprised one day when the Germans came to the room before we could disappear, but luckily not before we had closed the trap and replaced the floorboards.

I do not know why they came directly to this room. It was most unlikely they had then—as they had later—sound detectors around the Castle walls, which picked up noises of tunnelling. Their spies, set at various windows, may have remarked an unusual movement of British officers through certain doors in the buildings, not previously employed, or again some Polish orderlies (prisoners-of-war), whose rooms were close to where we worked, may not have been trustworthy.

In any event, it was an awkward moment when the Germans unlocked the empty room and gazed upon two British officers doing physical jerks and press-ups, counting audibly "One—two—one—two—three and four—one—two——" with seraphic innocence written all over their faces. Luckily we spoke no German and had only to gesticulate in reply to their shouts. We were allowed to leave, but given to understand that the matter was not closed. The Germans searched the room after our departure, prised up floorboards, and then left.

The tunnel would never succeed now; that, at least, was plain. We promptly gave it up. The same afternoon, Hank and I, along with four others who had committed some minor offence, were called for, escorted to the room in which 'Shovewood II' reposed, and locked in.

Curiosity could not keep Kenneth away long, and almost as soon as the 'Goonery' had departed, he was at the door asking puckish questions.

"How do you like your new quarters?"

"I don't. Go and tell Colonel German what has happened. He'll kick up hell with the *Kommandant*. This is imprisonment without trial!"

"I shouldn't worry, Pat. They'll let you out in a month or so and it's a fine room for doing physical jerks in! You'll be so fit when you come out."

"I'm fit enough now," I answered, "to knock your head off like a ninepin, if you don't do something quickly."

"But there's the tunnel to get on with! No need to bother about shifts—you can just go on and on. Maybe you'll be out in a month by the tunnel instead of by the door!"

"Kenneth," I shouted, exasperated, "I'm getting out of this today. Go and fetch my 'Universal.'"

He went, and a few moments later returned with it.

"What do you want me to do with it?" he said.

"Open the door, you idiot; what else do you think?"

"But why? It's such a lovely opportunity to go ahead with the tunnel, I think I'll leave you there."

"Open up!" I yelled.

Inside, the six of us were champing at the bit over the curtailment of our liberties. Hank, tall six-foot length of loose-limbed Canadian, with freckles and curly hair, and handsome withal, suggested:

"Let's take the ruddy door off its hinges and drop it over a cliff somewhere."

"Good idea," I said, "if you'll hack the bars away from a window first. I propose we carry the door in procession round the camp in protest and then dump it at the top of the Castle."

Kenneth opened the door.

"Kenneth," I said, "go and get someone upstairs to play the Dead March!"

We had the door off its hinges in no time. The six of us then carried it solemnly like a coffin—marching in slow time—around the courtyard. In a few minutes the Dead March started up. After three turns of the courtyard, by which time a crowd of mourners had fallen in behind the cortège, we started to mount the winding stairs slowly.

The staircases, of which there were three in the Castle, though of simple design, were beautiful, consisting of flat stone steps about two yards wide, winding upwards in a perfect spiral around a central column. Each staircase formed a round tower built into the corners of the Castle, and the doors to all rooms opened outwards from the towers at various levels. At one period of our imprisonment, the British contingent were housed eighty steps above ground-level! To the top was a matter of about a hundred steps.

By the time our procession with the door was halfway up the stairs, a German officer and two corporals, all panting hard, caught us up and joined in behind us. The officer, who was known as Hauptmann Priem, possessed a rare quality among Germans—a sense of humour. An interpreter was demanded.

"Herr Hauptmann Reid, what does this mean? A few moments ago I locked you all into close confinement."

"That is exactly why we are here now," I replied.

"Not at all, Herr Hauptmann, you are here now because you have unlocked and removed the door of your prison cell. Why have you done so?—and how have you done so?"

"We protest at being imprisoned without sentence and pending fair trial. We are prisoners-of-war, and you should treat us according to the German Army Code and the Geneva Convention."

Priem smiled broadly and said:

"Very well! If you will return the door to its hinges, you shall go free, pending trial!"

I agreed, and the whole solemn procession wended its way downstairs again. The door was replaced ceremoniously with saluting and heel-clicking.

Priem was intrigued to know how we unhinged a locked door, so I gave him a short piece of twisted wire, which I had obtained specially for the eventuality of a search. This may seem an unwise thing to have done, but by now the Germans knew well that we could pass through a simply locked door. They had given up separating the different nationalities for that reason among others, and a piece of useless wire gave nothing away. We heard no more of the incident.

We continued our search for the weak spots in the Castle's armour. I was next attracted by the drains, and a trusted Polish orderly told me that once, when a certain

The door episode

manhole cover in the yard had been raised, he had seen small brick tunnels running in various directions. This sounded promising. There were two round manhole covers in the courtyard, but alas! they were in full view of spy windows and of the spyhole in the main courtyard gate.

I decided to make a reconnaissance by night. In the darkness we could unlock our staircase door into the courtyard —we were always locked into our quarters at night—and provided the guard outside the gate was not disturbed or tempted to switch on the courtyard lights, we could proceed with our examination. The moon was not up. It was February and bitterly cold. We knew the manhole covers were frozen solid to their bases, but we had prepared boiling water in our black-out kitchen. With Kenneth acting as doorkeeper with the key, Rupert made sorties at ten-minute intervals and poured the boiling contents of a kettle around the nearest cover. Then we both sortied, I with a stout piece of iron unscrewed from a door support, and together we managed to loosen and lift up the cover. The hole was not deep and there were tunnels as the orderly had said. I jumped in and Rupert replaced the lid and disappeared. He was to return in half an hour.

My reconnaissance along the slimy tunnels, which were about three feet by two feet in section, arched and flat-bottomed, revealed one leading up to the camp building in which the canteen was housed. This was bricked up at the canteen entrance, but obviously continued inside. Another led to the kitchens, which accounted for the slime. A third was the outfall sewer and ran under the courtyard to another manhole. It looked promising and I followed it, but a couple of yards beyond the second manhole it, also, was bricked up with only a small pipe at the bottom serving to drain the system. The pipe headed out under the courtyard gateway. I had my iron tool, a cigarette-lighter, and one of our homemade lamps. I tackled the brick; the joints were very tough indeed and I made little impression. The wall had been recently built and obviously with special attention to strength.

Rupert returned on time and the two of us—myself pushing upwards from within—managed to remove the heavy cover. I was filthy and smelling badly, but there was hope in two directions!

During several nights following I took turns with Rupert and Dick Howe in attacking the brick wall in the tunnel with an assortment of steel bits and nails which we 'won' by various means.

The task proved hopeless, especially as we dared make very little noise. In the silence of the night, the sound of hammering could be plainly heard in the courtyard even from below ground. The tunnels and pipes echoed the sound and carried it a long way.

We thought of doing the job in daylight and I actually descended two days running in full view of those officers who happened to be exercising in the yard, but protected from the direction of the main gate by a small knot of Britishers while the manhole cover was being removed. Although I hammered loudly enough to awake the dead, I made little impression. The joints in the brick-work were made with 'ciment fondu'—a specially tough cement.

We tried the second direction. Inside the canteen, where we bought our razor-blades and suchlike, in front of the counter on the buyers' side was a manhole cover. I had not far to seek for assistance in opening up this manhole, for Kenneth had already provided the solution. Some weeks before he had had himself appointed assistant manager and accountant of the canteen!

Kenneth was a London Stock Exchange man and the idea of keeping even the meagre canteen accounts evidently made him feel a little nearer home. He had been educated at Whitgift School and was by nature a tidy person, meticulous in his ways and in his speech. He made a point of buckling the nib of the pen used by the German *Feldwebel* (sergeant) in charge of the canteen so that that unfortunate man invariably started his day's accounts with a large blot at the top of his page. Kenneth explained to the *Feldwebel* on the first occasion that nibs made with poor wartime steel always buckled if used with bad wartime ink owing to the 'springiness' of the nib being affected by a film of corrosion. Thereafter he consoled the *Feldwebel* whenever the latter fell into his trap. He always added a titbit of demoralising propaganda such as that the whole war was a shame and he was sure the Germans didn't want it any more than the English. Within a few

In the canteen

months he had broken down the morale of the *Feldwebel* to such an extent that the latter was preaching sedition to his colleagues and had to be removed.

The table which Kenneth and the *Feldwebel* used for writing was situated under the only window in the room, at some distance from the counter. While a few people stood at the counter, and Kenneth distracted the German's attention with some accounting matter at the table, it was comparatively simple to tackle the manhole cover.

Incidentally, Kenneth in his position as canteen accountant had also to deal with the mail. This brought him into contact with the German camp interpreter, who was responsible for censoring our letters home. His name was Pfeiffer—in English 'Whistler'—and to suit his name his voice never descended below the treble clef.

Our group were leaning over the counter preparatory to dealing with the manhole when Pfeiffer entered the canteen and demanded to see Kenneth. I should say, in parenthesis, that we had been allowed, on rare occasions, to send home with our mail photographs taken by a German civilian photographer.

Pfeiffer addressed Kenneth:

"Herr Hauptmann, once again must I not tell you that officers on the backside of photographs to write forbidden are. Will you please foresee that my instructions be carried out?"

Before Kenneth had time to make any retort, a Polish officer, Felix Jablonowski, rushed into the canteen, beaming all over, and shouted:

"Have you heard the news? Benghazi has fallen down!" (It was early February 1941.)

We forgot the manhole and started cheering. Pfeiffer's brain must have been working at top pressure conjuring up a sarcastic retort to combat this exhibition of non-defeatist morale. There was a moment's lull in the cheering and he piped up shrilly:

"All that you too to the Marines can tell."

The cheering redoubled in intensity.

When the excitement had died down, we continued our work. The manhole came away after some persuasion. Sure enough, there were tunnels leading in two directions, one connecting with the tunnel already noticed from the yard, and the other leading out under the window beside which Kenneth and the German worked. A second reconnaissance in more detail showed this latter to be about eighteen yards long and built on a curve. Under the window it was blocked up with large hewn stones and mortar. Outside the shop window and at the level of the canteen floor was a grass lawn, which also abutted the German section of the

PLAN OF

COLDITZ
CASTLE

OFLAG IVC 1939~45

NOTE: The plan of the older Northern part of the Castle is copied from an MS of the Seventeenth Century

STEEP DROP TO ROAD

Sentry
Gate in Barbed Wire PARAPET

GRASS AREA

Sentry

Sanitary Tunnel into Kommandantur

Sentry
Canteen Tunnel Exit

Sentry
Machine Gun

CELLS FOR PROMINENTE

DENTIST'S Room

CANTEEN

Sentry with Machine Gun in Roof.

PRECIPICE

WIRE

Route of Lawton and Fowler

CHAPEL

Ida Haida Clothes Store
German Office
Clothes Store

Capt aut's Office

INNER (PRISONERS') COURTYARD

PRISONERS' KITCHEN

Sentry

Delousing Shed

Sentry

Sentry

DOWN TO CELLARS

Light

SOLITARY CONFINEMENT CELLS

Shower Baths

THEATRE (2nd Floor)

SICK WARD

PARCELS OFFICE

ROUND TOWER

Sentry with Machine Gun in Roof

TERRACE

Entrance
Sentry Gate

PARAPET

Flood Light

Sentry

GUARD HOUSE

NEAVE'S ROUTE
RAMPART

Sentry

Flood Light

PARAPET

GARDEN

Sentry Machine Gun

BARBED WIRE

PRECIPICE

Sentry Machine Gun W

PRECIPICE

ESCAPE ROU

112

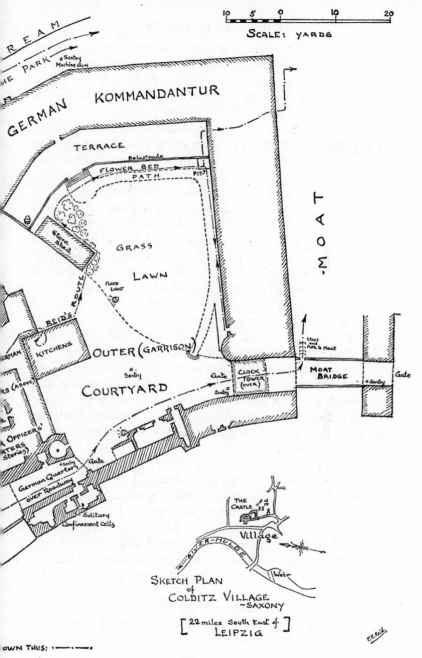

SCALE: YARDS
10 5 0   10   20

STREAM
THE PARK
o Sentry
Machine Gun

GERMAN KOMMANDANTUR

TERRACE

Balustrade
FLOWER BED
PATH
PIT?

MOAT

Stone Shed

GRASS LAWN

FLOOD LIGHT

REID'S ROUTE

GERMAN KITCHENS

OUTER (GARRISON)

o Sentry

COURTYARD

Gate
o Sentry

CLOCK TOWER (over)

Steps and Path to Moat

MOAT BRIDGE

o Sentry

Gate

OFFICERS' QUARTERS (Stories)

ABOVE)

German Quarters over Roadway
o Sentry
Gate

Solitary Confinement Cells

THE CASTLE

Village

RIVER MULDE

Weir

SKETCH PLAN
of
COLDITZ VILLAGE
~SAXONY

[22 miles South East of]
LEIPZIG

SHOWN THUS: ——·——·

P.R.Reid.

113

Castle. At the outer edge of this lawn was a stone balustrade, and then a forty-foot drop over a retaining wall to the level of the roadway which led down to the valley in which our football ground was situated. Maybe the tunnel led out to this wall. We had to find out.

A few days later we had made out of an iron bedpiece a key which opened the canteen door. Working at night as before, we would open our staircase entrance door and cross about ten yards of the courtyard to the canteen door. This opened, we would enter and lock it behind us. We then had to climb a high wooden partition in order to enter the canteen proper, as the door in this partition had a German-type Yale lock which foiled us. The partition separated the canteen from the camp office: a room in which all the haggling took place between our Commanding Officer and the German Camp Commandant on his periodic visits. The partition was surmounted with the aid of a couple of sheets used as ropes.

Entering our tunnel, we tackled the wall at the end. This time we were lucky. The mortar gave way easily and we were soon loosening huge stones which we removed to the other tunnel (the one leading back to the courtyard). Although the wall was four feet thick we were through it in a week of night shifts. Alas! the tunnel did not continue on the other side. Beyond the wall, under the grass, was sticky yellow clay.

My next idea was to make a vertical shaft which would bring the tunnel up to the grass. I would construct a trapdoor which would be covered with grass and yet would open when required, thus repeating my Laufen idea of having the escape tunnel intact for further use. Escapes involved such an immense amount of labour, sometimes only to serve in the escape of one or two men, that it was always worth while attempting to leave the escape exit ready for future use.

Once out on the grass patch we could creep along under the Castle walls in the dark; descend the retaining wall with sheets; then continue past the guards' sleeping·

quarters to the last defence—the twelve-foot wall of the Castle park surmounted for much of its length with barbed wire. This obstacle would not be difficult provided there was complete concealment, which was possible at night, and provided there was plenty of time to deal with the barbed wire. We had to pass in full view of a sentry at one point. He was only forty yards away, but as there were Germans who frequently passed the same point, this was not a serious difficulty.

I constructed out of bed boards and stolen screws a trap which looked like a small table with collapsible legs— collapsible so as to enter the tunnel. The legs were also telescopic; that is to say, they could be extended by degrees to five feet in length. The table-top was a tray with vertical sides four inches deep. It sat in a frame and had shutters so that I could excavate upwards from below, removing half the table area at a time. As soon as the edge of the tray came to within an inch of the surface of the lawn I merely had to close both shutters and cut the last inch of earth around the tray with a sharp knife. Then, pushing the tray up I could lift it clear, still full of undisturbed grass. The last man out would replace the tray in the frame and patch up carefully any tell-tale marks around the edges. The frame, supported on its extended legs, set on stones at the bottom of the tunnel, would take the weight of a man standing on the tray. The tunnel floor (in the clay) was just five feet below the lawn surface. I need hardly mention that the contraption was christened 'Shovewood III'!

Before all this happened, our plans were temporarily upset. Two Polish officers got into the canteen one night when we were not working and tried to cut the bars outside the window which I have mentioned before. Cutting bars cannot be done silently. They did not take the precaution of having their own stooges either to distract the attention of the nearby sentry or to give warning of his approach. Throughout our work on the tunnel we had a signalling system from our rooms above which gave warning of this sentry's approach. He was normally out of sight from where our tunnel exit was to be, but he only had to extend his beat a few yards in order to come into view.

The Poles were caught red-handed and within a few days a huge floodlight was installed in such a position as to light up the whole lawn and all the prison windows opening on to it.

This was a good example of what was bound to happen in a camp holding none but officers bent on escape. We had already asked the Poles for liaison on escape projects so that we would not tread on each others' toes all the time, and now Colonel German called a meeting with their Senior Officers, at which an agreement was reached. The Senior Polish Officer was in a difficult position because he frankly could not fully control his officers; he knew that they might attempt to escape without telling him or anybody else. However, after this meeting the liaison improved, and when we offered some Poles places in our tunnel escape, mutual confidence was established.

Shortly after this incident about two hundred and fifty French officers, led by General Le Bleu, arrived at Colditz. All of them were not escapers by any means, but about one hundred of them were. Among the remainder were many French Jews who were segregated from the rest by the Germans and given their own quarters on the top floor of the Castle.

We had to come to an arrangement with the French Senior Officer over escape projects similar to that agreed with the Poles, but unfortunately the French liaison system was also found wanting—at the expense of our tunnel— before a workable understanding was reached.

To return to the thread of my story: we were not allowed to store any tinned food, expressly because it was potential escape rations. Over a period of time we had all stinted ourselves to collect a reserve for distribution when our tunnel would be ready. It amounted to three heavy sack-loads. One night we were busy transporting the sacks into the tunnel from our quarters, where they were badly

hidden. Rupert carried them one by one out of our courtyard door into the canteen. On the last trip all the courtyard lights were suddenly switched on from outside, and
Rupert found himself between the doors, like Father
Christmas caught in *flagrante delicto!* He made for the
door of our quarters, which had to be unlocked again for
him to re-enter. To our astonishment nothing further happened, so we completed our work for the night and returned to bed. Whether the Germans saw Rupert or not
we shall never know, but since the Polish attempt they
seemed to be more on the qui vive.

This incident was followed by a still more unfortunate
one. Although the Germans often paid nocturnal visits to
our quarters without warning, this did not seriously bother
us. If we were in the tunnel, the doors were locked as
usual, and pillows were placed in our beds to pass the
casual inspection of a torch flashing along the rows of
sleeping bodies.

One night, however, the Germans had been carousing—
we could hear them. In fact, they kept our orderlies awake,
and that was the start of the trouble. We had five staunch,
'game' orderlies, who had places reserved on our tunnel
escape.

On this particular night, being unable to sleep for the
Germans, one of the orderlies named Goldman, a Jew from
Whitechapel, who had a sense of humour, started to
barrack the German sentry outside the nearest window.
Goldman had arrived at Colditz as Colonel German's
orderly and was so voluble at their interrogation by the
Camp Commandant that he was mistaken by him for our
new S.B.O. The barracking must have been reported to the
carousing Goons, for after some time, they arrived in the
courtyard in force and headed for our quarters. Priem and
another officer, the Regimental Sergeant-Major—Oberstabsfeldwebel Gephard, the corporal known as the 'fouine'
and half a dozen Goons entered and began shouting
'*Aufstehen!*' They woke everyone up, poked the beds, and
discovered that four officers were missing.

The Germans lost their heads. They had come upstairs drunk and disorderly, intent on having some fun at our expense and had not expected this new turn of affairs. Gephard, who looked like the fat boy of Peckham, was wearing his dress parade uniform. He carried an enormous curved sword, which every now and then caught between his legs. He was despatched to count the orderlies.

"*Aufstehen! Aufstehen!*" he shouted. "You English pig-dogs! I shall teach you——" Crash!—as he tripped up over his 'battle-axe.' Then, picking himself up he started again:

"You English pig-dogs! I shall teach you to laugh at German soldiers carrying out their duty! Tomorrow morning at dawn you shall be shot. All of you! I shall give the firing order myself."

He strode up and down the room trying to increase his stature to cope with his sword which clattered and jangled along behind him. "Goldman!" he screamed, "what are you doing with those playing-cards?"

Goldman had quietly given each orderly a card face downwards.

"We are about to draw for places in the order of shooting," he replied.

Gephard spluttered and drew his sword.

"Swine! You dare to insult me personally!"—still struggling with his sword, which was too long for him to extract comfortably from the scabbard—"Put down those cards at once. You will be the first and I shall not wait longer. I shall remove your head."

Finally unsheathing the sword by holding the blade with both hands, he advanced on Goldman, waving it wildly around his head. The latter disappeared under a bed. Gephard's dignity prevented him from following. Instead, he performed a dance of rage around the bed hacking at the wooden supports. Having let off steam, he sheathed the 'battle-axe' once more, quickly counted the orderlies, noting significantly the presence of Goldman still underneath the bed, departed with much jingling, and tripped up once more as he slammed the door behind him.

The confusion in the officers' dormitory became indescribable. The officers were paraded along the middle of the room while Goons turned every bed inside out, and emptied the contents of cupboards all over the floor.

Priem, with his face glistening and his nose distinctly showing signs of the bottle, was torn between rage at having his carousal upset for longer than he had anticipated, and high spirits which were his more natural reaction to alcohol. He compromised between the two moods by seizing a pickaxe from one of his soldiers, and started to hack up the floor.

With mighty swings, accompanied by gleeful war-cries, he smote the floorboards, wrenching off large pieces of timber. With each blow he shouted a name "Benghazi"; "Derna"; "Tobruk" (Rommel was advancing in Africa at the time). As he shouted "Tobruk," a huge length of flooring came away on the end of his axe and impaled to it under the board was a brand-new civilian felt hat! It had been very carefully hidden there by Lieutenant Alan Orr Ewing, Argyll and Sutherland Highlanders, nicknamed 'Scruffy,' who had only the day before paid a large sum in *Lagermarks* to a French orderly to smuggle it into the camp.

This gave Priem an idea. He sent out orders for the dogs to be summoned. They arrived; were led to the beds of the missing officers; encouraged to sniff; and then unleashed. They left the dormitory and made for the foodbin in the kitchen where Goldman was already pottering. Priem followed them. Spying Goldman, he seized him by the collar and demanded:

"What direction have the missing officers taken?" to which Goldman answered:

"That's right! Hauptmann Priem, pick on me! Every time an officer wants to escape, he comes up to me and says: 'Please, Goldman, may I go to Switzerland?' "

Priem saw the point, relaxed his grip, and shooed the

dogs out of the food-bin. These promptly dashed out of the quarters and headed up the stairs, followed by Priem and Goldman's parting shot:

"That's right, Fido—they jumped off the bleedin' roof."

When the dogs produced nothing, Priem sent out orders for the whole camp to be paraded. It was about 2 a.m. by then. Suddenly, 'stooge' Wardle, a submarine officer lately arrived who was our look-out, shouted, "They're heading for the canteen." He had scarcely time to jump down into the tunnel, and I to pull the manhole cover over us, before the Jerries were in. They searched the canteen and tried hard to lift the manhole cover, but were unable to do so as I was hanging on to it for dear life from underneath, my fingers wedged in a protruding lip of the cover.

As soon as we noticed that a 'General *Appell*' had been called, I told Rupert and Dick (the others in the tunnel with me) to start at once building a false wall half-way up the tunnel, behind which they put our food store and other escape paraphernalia such as rucksacks, maps, compasses, and civilian clothing which we normally kept hidden there.

The hubbub continued in the courtyard for about an hour. The count was taken about half a dozen times amidst as much confusion as the prisoners could create without having themselves shot, and aided by the chaos caused by the Germans themselves, who were rushing all over the camp searching every room and turning all movable objects upside-down.

Rupert and Dick quietly continued their work and in a few hours had constructed a magnificent false wall with stones from the original wall which we had demolished, jointed with clay from under the lawn and coated with dust wherever the joints showed.

By 5 a.m. all was quiet again. We departed as we had come and went to bed wondering how the Germans would react to our appearance at morning *Appell*. We had apparently put them to a great deal of trouble, for we heard that, while the Jerries had had the whole camp on parade, they had carried out an individual identity check. Every officer paraded in front of a table where he was identified against his photograph and duly registered as present. We were recorded as having escaped, and messages, flashed to the O.K.W. (*Oberkommando der Wehrmacht*), brought into action a network of precautions taken all over the country as a matter of routine for the recapture of prisoners.

At the morning *Appell,* when we were all found present again, confusion reigned once more. The Goons decided to hold a second identification parade which they completed after about two and a half hours. They then called out our four names, which they had managed to segregate at last, and we were paraded in front of everybody. They dismissed the parade and led us to the little interview room, in which most of our fights with the *Kommandantur* took place. We refused to explain our disappearance and were remanded for sentence for causing a disturbance and being absent from *Appell!* The O.K.W. orders had all to be countermanded and the Commandant, we heard, had a 'rap over the knuckles' for the incident.

The Goons were upset and watchful during the next few days. They again visited the canteen, and this time the manhole cover came away—too easily for our liking, of course! But they had done some scraping around the edges before trying it and were apparently satisfied it was the result of their own efforts. The dust and grit, inserted around the manhole cover, were placed there by us as a matter of routine after every working shift, so that the cover always looked as if it had not been touched for years. A Goon descended and, after an examination, declared 'nothing unusual' below. Kenneth, who was in the background of the shop, trying to appear occupied with his accounts, breathed an audible sigh of relief, which he quickly turned into a yawn for the benefit of his German colleague, busy at the same table.

The Germans were suspicious of this tunnel, either because they had seen Rupert doing Father Christmas in the courtyard or because they were warned by a spy in the camp. A third possibility would have been microphones, set to detect noises. Microphones were installed, to our knowledge, in many places later on, but it is doubtful whether the Jerries had them in Colditz at this period of the war. Microphones were installed in newly built hutted camps for the R.A.F., but their installation in an old Schloss would have left tell-tale marks which we could have traced.

The spy—that is to say, a 'stooge' or prisoner in the camp—set by the Germans to report on us was a definite possibility, and our suspicions were later proved correct. Suffice it to say that we repeatedly found the Goons very quick on the trail of our activities. We tried hard to make our actions look normal when among other prisoners, but it was not easy, especially on escapes such as tunnels, which involved preparation over a long period of time. Incidentally, we employed the term 'stooge' very loosely! Our 'stooge' Wardle was certainly no spy.

The Goons concreted four heavy clasps into the floor around the canteen manhole cover. However, we dealt with these forthwith by loosening them before the concrete was set, in such a way that they could be turned aside. This was done in daylight while Kenneth as usual occupied the Goon, and a few officers acted as cover at the counter. In their normal position the clasps still held the cover firmly.

This done, we decided to give the tunnel a rest, as things were becoming too hot for our liking.

CHAPTER VII

THE COMMUNITY OF NATIONS

IT was March 1941. The camp was slowly filling up; the British contingent had increased by a steady trickle of new arrivals, escapers all, except for a sprinkling of 'Saboteurs of the Reich'—we had three Padres who were classed in the second category. One day about sixty Dutch officers arrived. Curiously enough, their Senior Officer was Major English, ours being Colonel German! The Dutchmen were a fine company of men and a credit to their country. They were all Netherlands East Indies officers. At the outbreak of war, they had sailed home with their troops to Holland in order to help the Mother-Country. When Holland was occupied, the German High Command offered an amnesty to all those Dutch officers who would sign a certain document; this, if treated honourably, precluded an officer from acting in any way contrary to the wishes of the German Reich; it also laid down conditions relative to the maintenance of law, order, and subservience within the country. It was apparently a cleverly worded document and most Dutch officers of the home forces signed it.

The Colonials, on the other hand, refused to sign it almost to a man and were promptly marched off to prison in Germany. After many vicissitudes, including unending wordy battles with the Germans and numerous escape attempts, they finally ended up lock, stock, and barrel in Colditz. Since they all spoke German fluently, were as obstinate as mules and as brave as lions, heartily despised the Germans and showed it, they presented special difficulties as prisoners!

They were always impeccably turned out on parade and maintained a high standard of discipline among themselves. I regret to say that the French and ourselves were the black sheep in matters of parade 'turn out.' The French officer is never tidy at the best of times. His uniform does not lend itself to smartness, and the French do not care about 'turn out' anyway.

The British were more unfortunate. and had an excuse for appearing a straggly-looking crowd. The British battle-dress is not particularly smart, and most of us had lost a part of it at our time of capture—a cap, or jacket, or gaiters —and many of us had to wear wooden-soled clogs, given us by the Germans. Occasionally a much-needed parcel came from home containing replacement for our wornout kit, and the Red Cross once sent a bulk consignment of uniforms which were of great help. Still, we were a picturesque if not an unsightly company. The other nationalities had somehow succeeded in bringing much of their wardrobe with them, and, at any rate until time wore these out, they had a definite advantage over us. It was common for a Britisher to appear on parade, for instance, wearing a woollen balaclava or no cap at all, a khaki battledress blouse, blue R.A.F. or red Czech army trousers, home-knitted socks of any colour, and trailing a pair of clogs on his feet.

Speaking of the picturesque, colour was lent to our parades by two Yugoslav officers who had joined our happy throng. Their uniform, consisting of voluminous red trousers and sky-blue embroidered waistcoats, brought home to us what a Community of Nations we had become!

First, there was the Polish contingent. Then there were Englishmen, Irishmen, and Scotsmen. The Empire was represented by R.A.F. officers from Canada, Australia, and New Zealand, and by an Army Doctor, Captain Mazumdar, from India. The French included some officers from Algeria and the Jewish contingent. There were the two Yugoslavs and some Belgian officers. The Netherlands were represented by an aide-de-camp of Queen Wilhelmina, and last, but not least, the Dutch East Indies Company completed this procession of nations.

Colditz was the only camp of this kind in Germany. The

solidarity that existed among the various nationalities was always a matter of surprise to the Germans. The alliance amongst us was not fostered by any artificial means. It was natural, springing from something deep within us, and it withstood many tests. It was a sufficiently strong link to withstand any attempt by the Germans to alienate one nationality from another.

A favourite communal punishment meted out to any particular contingent was the curtailment of the hours of recreation allowed in the wooded park of the Castle. When this happened, the recreation parade was ostracised by all until the Germans withdrew the ban. If an officer of any one nationality was unfairly treated, the whole camp would go on strike without hesitation, the only condition agreed between us being the form of the strike! On one occasion, Captain Mazumdar, true to a noble tradition, went on hunger strike. I regret to say the whole camp did not follow suit! It was not easy to obtain unanimity and mutual sacrifice where such an elemental means of survival was concerned.

On another occasion the German camp doctor worked himself into a Polish 'hate' neurosis. He insisted that Poland no longer existed, and that in consequence every Polish officer, of whatever rank, should salute him smartly. He was a captain or *Stabsarzt*. When he tried to make the Polish General salute and went into a tantrum about it, this was too much for the Poles. The whole contingent went on hunger strike. The rest of the camp supported them in spirit! The S.B.O.s of all the other nationalities sent parallel complaints concerning the doctor's attitude to the German commandant. After three days the commandant hauled his junior officer over the coals and the famished Polish officers, having registered a grudging salute from the *Stabsarzt*, took to their vittles again with ravenous ardour.

*   *   *   *   *

The German sentence upon the four of us who had disappeared for a night was a fortnight's solitary confinement.

During this confinement a third unlucky incident occurred which piled up further difficulties in the way of our canteen tunnel escape. A Frenchman and a Pole managed to disappear one day, and were not missed until the evening *Appell*. The Goons suspected a getaway during the return of the prisoners from their recreation in the park, and searched all possible places of concealment in the proximity of the roadway leading down to it. The two officers were found, hiding up for nightfall, in the seldom-used basement of a house near the path (it was used as an air-raid shelter), into which they had slipped undetected. This operation was by no means easy. It had been done by split-second timing, with the assistance of officers who had successfully distracted the attention of the guards accompanying the parade on the march. The assisting officers placed themselves in the ranks so as to be near the guards who walked at intervals on either side. When the officers who were to escape reached a predetermined spot on the march, the others made gestures or remarks calculated to draw the attention of their nearby guards away from the scene of action. Three seconds after the predetermined spot was reached, the escaping officers bolted. In five more seconds they were behind a concealing wall. During these five seconds some eight guards in view had to be made to 'look the other way'! The chances of success were very slight, but the trick worked. When the count was taken after the recreation period outside the courtyard gate, the assisting officers created confusion and a German-speaking officer browbeat the sergeant in charge into thinking he had made a wrong count to start with, and bluffed out the discrepancy in numbers.

It was a pity that in this case a brilliant beginning was not carried through to a successful end, and that the concealment of the count was not maintained at the later general *Appell*. The *Appell* normally called after dark in the lighted courtyard was, on this day, called in daylight, possibly due to the German sergeant's suspicions getting the better of him. *Appell* times were often changed without warning, especially to catch prisoners out, and this should not have been overlooked.

Be that as it may, the officers, when caught, made up a story concealing their real method of escape and leading the Germans to suspect a rope-descent from an attic sky-light on to the grass lawn under which our tunnel exit lay hidden. A sentry was now placed with a beat which brought him in full view of our projected tunnel exit at intervals of one minute both day and night.

This incident led me to make a complaint through Colonel German and to request closer liaison and more co-operation among the various nationalities so that we did not continually trip over each other in our hurry to leave the camp! Common sense prevailed, and from this date I can record no further serious instances of overlapping in escape plans.

Our tunnel was, nevertheless, in 'Queer Street.' I disliked the idea of lengthening it and making a long-term job of it, as any prolonged lapse of time worked against the success of the venture. The Germans also started gradually to install new locks on certain doors at key-points throughout the camp. They began with the lock of the canteen, thereby foiling us temporarily in any attempt to spend long hours at work in the tunnel underneath.

We called the new locks 'cruciform' locks. The simplest description I can give of them is to compare them to four different Yale locks rolled into one. Kenneth Lockwood obtained an impression in candle-wax of the four arms of the cruciform key to the canteen. I worked for a long time on the manufacture of a false key. There was a dentist's room in the camp which was normally locked, as was also the dentist's cupboard of instruments, but these had presented little difficulty to budding burglars like ourselves. I wore out many of the bits of the dentist's electric drill in the process of making my key, but all my efforts were in vain. I am afraid the drills after I had finished with them were very blunt. Ever afterwards when I heard the agonising shrieks of sufferers in the dentist's chair I felt a twinge of remorse that I should have been the cause of so much fruitless pain! I often wonder what would have been my fate if all the dentist's visitors had known my secret sin. Luckily for me, only one or two of my trusted confederates knew, and they kept the secret. The dentist, who was a French officer and fellow-prisoner, must have thought little of German tool-steel! He filled one of my teeth excellently before I had ruined his drills, using I do not know what kind of rubbish as filling. I cannot explain the existence of the up-to-date dentist's chair and equipment. The Poles said it was there when they arrived. Before the war the Castle had been used, among other things, as a lunatic asylum. Maybe it was thought too risky to allow lunatics to visit a dentist in the town!

At this unhappy stage, when we were casting around to decide what to do with our tunnel, Peter Allan and Howard Gee (a newcomer), both excellent German speakers, reported the existence of a helpful Goon sentry. He was a sympathetic type, and he started smuggling for us on a small scale: a fresh egg here and there in return for English chocolate, or a pound of real coffee in exchange for a tin of cocoa, and so on. He ran a terrific risk, but seemed to do it with equanimity—perhaps too much equanimity—and we decided also to take a risk and plunge. At several clandestine meetings, in doorways and behind angles in the courtyard walls, Peter and Howard Gee primed the sentry and eventually suggested that he might earn some 'big' money if he once 'looked the other way' for ten minutes while on sentry duty.

The sentry fell for the idea. He was told that we would have to arrange matters so that he did a tour of sentry duty for a given two-hour period, on a given day, on a certain beat, and that in the ten-minute interval, between two predetermined signals, he was to stand (which was permitted) at one particular end of his beat. He was to receive an advance of one hundred Reichsmarks on his reward, which was settled at five hundred Reichsmarks (about £34), and the remainder would be dropped out of a convenient window one hour after the ten-minute interval. The sentry was told also that no traces would be left which could lead to suspicion or involve him in accusations of neglect of duty. To all this he listened and finally agreed. The escape was on!

The first escape party consisted of twelve officers, including four Poles. The French and Dutch were as yet newcomers, whereas the Poles were by now old and trusted comrades, which accounted for their inclusion. Further, the participation of officers of another nationality was decided upon for reasons of language facilities offered, and for camp morale. The Poles had been most helpful since our arrival; the majority of them spoke German fluently, some of them knew Germany well, and those of us who thought of aiming for the North Sea or Poland took Poles as travelling companions. A few decided to travel alone.

My mind was occupied with another problem—how to arrange for the entry of thirteen officers, twelve escaping and one sealing up the entry, into the canteen? During opening hours I examined the cruciform lock closely and came to the conclusion that, from the inside, I could dismount the lock almost completely, allowing the door to open.

The escape would have to be done after the evening roll-call and in darkness.

The fateful day was decided upon—May 29th. I arranged to knock down the false wall the day before and extricate all our provisions and escape material. This was comparatively simple. During the two-hour lunch interval the canteen was locked. Before it was locked, however, I hid in a triangular recess which was used as a store cupboard and to which I had the key. When the canteen was locked up I had two clear hours to prepare everything. I removed the false wall, took out all our escape paraphernalia, hiding it in the cupboard, and prepared the tunnel exit so as to give the minimum amount of work for the final opening. After 2 o'clock, with a suitable screen of officers, I came out of the cupboard and all the stores were carried to our quarters.

The arrangements for the escape were as follows: Howard Gee, who was not in the first party, was to deal with the sentry. He would pass him the first signal on receipt of a sign from us in the tunnel. This was to be given by myself in the first instance at the opening end of the tunnel, passed to our thirteenth man on watch at the canteen window in the courtyard, who would then transmit it to our quarters by means of a shaded light. Gee could then signal to the sentry from an outside window. The 'all clear' was to be given in the same way, except that our thirteenth man had to come to the tunnel exit and receive the word from me when I had properly sealed up the exit after all were out. A piece of string pulled out through the earth served the purpose. I would be over the wall at the far end of the lawn before the signal would be transferred to the sentry.

May 29th loomed overcast and it soon began to rain. It rained all day in torrents, the heaviest rainfall we had ever had, but this would mean a dark night and it did not upset our plans. The sentry was told during the course of the afternoon what post he was to occupy. He was given his advance in cash and instructed to avoid the end of his beat nearest to the canteen on receipt of an agreed signal from a certain window, and to remain away from that end until another signal was given.

As the evening approached, the excitement grew. The lucky twelve dressed themselves in kit prepared during many months of patient work. From out of astonishing hiding-places came trousers and slouch caps made of grey German blankets, multicoloured knitted pullovers, transformed and dyed army overcoats, windjackets and mackintoshes, dyed khaki shirts and home-knitted ties. These were donned and covered with army apparel. Maps and home-made compasses appeared, and subdued last-minute discussions took place concerning routes and escape instructions. As the time passed, impatience for the 'off' increased. I became alternately hot and cold, and my hands were clammy and my mouth was dry. We all felt the same, as I could tell by the forced laughs and the nervous jokes and banter which passed around.

I remained hidden in the canteen when it was locked up for the night, and dismounted the lock. When the evening *Appell* sounded, I slipped out of the door behind a well-placed crowd of officers. If a Goon pushed the door for any reason whatever we were finished. A wedge of paper alone held it. Sentries were posted for the *Appell* at all vantage-points, and one stood very close to the canteen. Immediately after the *Appell* we had to work fast, for all the prisoners then had to disperse to their rooms, the court-yard doors were locked, and every door tried by the German duty officer. All thirteen of us had to slip into the canteen behind the screen of assisting officers while German officers and N.C.O.s were in the courtyard, and the lock had then to be remounted on the canteen door in double-quick time. The twelve escapers had to appear on parade dressed ready in their escape attire suitably covered with army overcoats and trousers. Assembled rucksacks had been placed in order in the tunnel during the lunch-time closing hours in the same way as before.

The *Appell* went off without a hitch. Colonel German, who had to stand alone in front, was looking remarkably fat, for he was escaping with us. He aroused no comment. Immediately after the 'dismiss' was given, and almost in front of the eyes of the sentry nearby, the thirteen chosen ones slipped silently through the door until all were in.

"Where do we go from here?" asked one of the Polish officers who had not worked on the tunnel.

"Over the palisades!" I replied, pointing to the high wooden partition, over which sheets had already been thrown.

He grabbed them and started to climb, making a noise like a bass drum on the partition door. A loud "Sh! Sh!" as if a lavatory cistern was emptying greeted his effort.

"For God's sake!" I said, "you're not in Paderewski's orchestra now."

"No," replied the Pole dramatically from the top of the partition, "but his spirit is living within me, this night!"

Luckily the din in the courtyard covered any noise we made at this juncture.

While the lock was remounted on the door, I removed my army uniform and handed it to our thirteenth man. He was to collect all discarded clothes, conceal them in the

The Pole on the palisades

cupboard, and remove them with assistance next day. I went straight away to the end of the tunnel, closely followed by Rupert Barry, for we were going together, and started work on the last few inches of earth beneath the surface of the opening. It was dark by now outside, and the rain was still pelting down. It began pouring through the earth covering of the exit, and within five minutes I was drenched to the skin with muddy water. The lock-testing patrol tried the canteen door and passed. Soon all was quiet in the camp. Within an hour the sentry was reported by light flashes to be at his post. I gave the signal for him to keep away from the canteen window.

I worked frenziedly at the surface of grass, cutting out my square, and then slowly heaved the tray of the exit upwards. It came away, and as it did so a shaft of brilliant light shot down the tunnel. For a second I was bewildered and blinded. It was, of course, the light of the projector situated ten yards away from the opening, which lit up the whole of the wall-face on that particular side of the Castle.

The second tunnel

I lifted the tray clear. Streams of muddy water trickled into the tunnel around me. I pushed myself upwards, and, with Rupert's assistance from behind, scrambled out.

Once out, I looked around. I was like an actor upon a stage. The floodlight made a huge grotesque image of my figure against the white wall. Row upon row of unfriendly windows, those of the German *Kommandantur*, frowned down upon me. The windows had no blackout curtains and a wandering inquisitive eye from within might easily turn my way. It was an unavoidable risk. Rupert began to

climb out as I put the finishing touch to the tray for closing the hole. He was having some difficulty. He had
handed up my rucksack and was levering himself upwards
when I happened to look from my work at the wall in
front of me, there to see a second giant shadow outlined
beside my own crouching figure. The second shadow held
a revolver in his hand.

"Get back! Get back!" I yelled to Rupert, as a guttural
voice behind me shouted:

"*Hände hoch! Hände hoch!*"

I turned, to face a German officer levelling his pistol at
my body, while another leaped for the hole. He was about
to shoot down the opening.

"*Schiessen Sie nicht!*" I screamed several times.

A bullet or two down that stone- and brick-walled tunnel
might have wrought considerable damage, filled as it was
with human bodies. The officer at the hole did not
shoot.

Germans suddenly appeared from everywhere, and all
the officers were giving orders at once. I was led off to the
Kommandantur and conducted to a bathroom where I was
stripped completely and allowed to wash, and then to an
office where I was confronted by Hauptmann Priem.

He was evidently pleased with his night's work and in
high spirits.

"*Ah hah! Es ist Herr Hauptmann Reid. Das ist schön!*"
he said as I walked in, and continued:

"Nobody could recognise who the nigger was until he
was washed! And now that we have the nigger out of the
woodpile, what has he got to say for himself?"

"I think the nigger in the woodpile was a certain German sentry, was he not?" I questioned in reply.

"Yes, indeed, Herr Hauptmann, German sentries know
their duty. The whole matter has been reported to me
from the start."

"From before the start maybe?"

"Herr Hauptmann Reid, that is not the point. Where
does your tunnel come from?"

"That is obvious," I replied.

"From the canteen, then?"

"Yes."

"But you have been locked into your quarters. You have a tunnel from your rooms to the canteen?"

"No!"

"But yes! You have just been counted on *Appell*. The canteen has been locked many hours ago. You have a tunnel?"

"No!"

"We shall see. How many of you are there?"

"So many I have never been able to count them properly!"

"Come now, Herr Hauptmann, the whole camp or just a few?"

"Just a few!"

"Good, then I hope our solitary confinement accommodation will not be too overcrowded!" said Priem, grinning broadly. He added:

"I was perturbed when first I saw you. I gave orders at once not to shoot. You see I had my men posted at all windows and beneath on the road. They were to shoot if any prisoners ran or struggled. I saw this figure which was you, writhing upon the ground. I thought you had fallen from the roof and that you were in great pain!"

While this was going on, hell had broken loose inside the prison. The courtyard was filled with troops, while posses dashed around wildly trying to locate the inside end of our rat-hole. In our quarters there was the usual parade in the day-room while Goons prodded beds and unearthed the customary thirteen inert corpses made of coats and blankets. At first they were convinced the tunnel started in our quarters on the first floor and they uprooted floorboards accordingly. Slowly it dawned upon them that it might be worth while to try the canteen.

Once there, as body after body issued from the manhole amidst shouts along the tunnel of "Goonery ahoy!" mingled with shouts from above of *"Hände hoch! Hände hoch!"* the Goons began hopping with excitement and revolvers were waving in all directions. The Jerry officer-in-charge was an elderly 2nd-Lieutenant. He was white to the lips and shaking all over. It was a miracle the weapons did not go off, for the Jerries were out of control. They practically stripped all the escapers naked in their anxiety not to miss any escape booty.

The escapers, on the contrary, appeared reasonably calm. When one of them lit a cigarette, it was the signal for an outbreak. The Goons turned on him in a fury. The German 2nd-Lieutenant was near him and the two of them were penned in a corner surrounded by an angry armed mob. A further uproar occurred when Colonel German's face appeared at the tunnel entrance. Consternation was followed by action and our Colonel could hardly rise out of the tunnel on account of the number of Germans who pressed around him. This was 'big-game' hunting, they must have thought.

Eventually some semblance of order was established and each officer in turn, after a thorough inspection, was escorted back to our quarters in his underclothes.

The next day the usual inquiry took place. The Germans had overhauled the tunnel, but what puzzled them was how thirteen men could be inside the canteen, which was locked with their unbreakable cruciform lock, so soon after an *Appell,* and after having been apparently closed up in their quarters for the night.

Special attention was paid to Kenneth Lockwood, of course, as canteen assistant. He was made to sit in front of a table on which a solitary object reposed—the official key of the canteen. Two German officers faced him and repeated ominously in German the question:

"How did you get into the canteen?"

Kenneth ignored the hypnotic key and asked them in return:

"Have you ever read *Alice in Wonderland?*"

This was duly interpreted.

"No," they said. "Why?"

"Because Alice got through small doors and keyholes by eating something to make her smaller."

The interpreter had difficulty in getting this over, but suddenly they broke into roars of laughter and Kenneth was dismissed without further questioning.

For a long time they searched for a tunnel connecting with our quarters, but eventually gave it up. I imagine that, after some time, they worked out the method used— this was not difficult.

In due course we were all sentenced to a fortnight's 'solitary,' but as usual, the solitary cells were all occupied and, instead, we carried out the sentence in two small communal rooms. Funnily enough, one of the rooms was that in which we had started our first tunnel, and in which Hank and I had been caught.

'Shovewood II' was still in good working order, and as we had previously concealed some food reserves there, it at last came into its own—we were not short of extra rations during our term of 'solitary'! The 'solitary,' in this case, with thirteen officers jammed into two small rooms, was of the 'Black Hole of Calcutta' variety.

Needless to say, we never saw 'our' sentry again! He did not receive his four hundred Reichsmarks, which was a good thing. It also puzzled the Jerries how we were getting supplies of German money.

CHAPTER VIII

THE HEAVY PALLIASSE

NO sooner were we all free again after our 'solitary,' than a rare opportunity presented itself. One day, without warning, a large German lorry was driven into the courtyard under guard and stopped outside the doorway to our quarters. Some French troop prisoners descended. We knew a couple of them. They were not lodged in the camp but somewhere in the town where they worked, and they occasionally came into the camp to carry out odd jobs. We had naturally made contact to nose out particulars concerning the orientation of the village and the life of its inhabitants. Unfortunately, these Frenchmen appeared so rarely that they were useless as trafficking agents.

This time they had come to collect a large number of straw palliasses—the standard prison mattresses consisting of large canvas sacks filled with straw—which were stored on the floor above the Dutch quarters. The palliasses were needed for troops' quarters being prepared in the village to house, as it turned out afterwards, Russian prisoners-of-war. The French prisoners each collected a palliasse and, descending the winding staircase past our quarters, continued to the ground floor and then outside the main door swung the palliasses on to the lorry.

There was no time to waste. After hasty consultation, Peter Allan was selected for the attempt. He was small and light and could speak German fluently—so he was an ideal candidate for a one-man effort. We were prepared to try more, but Peter was to be the guinea-pig.

We rigged him out in what was left of our depleted stock of escape clothing, gave him money and packed him in one of our own palliasses, and then tackled the French.

On the stairway outside, I stopped our most likely

Frenchman as he descended and pulled him into our quarters with his palliasse, saying:

"I want you to carry an officer downstairs inside a palliasse and load him on to the lorry."

"*Mais c'est impossible*," said the Frenchman.

"It is simple," I assured him. "It will be over in two minutes; nobody will notice it."

"And if I am caught?"

"You will not be caught," I argued, and pressed a tin of cigarettes into his hand.

"But the others?"

"They will not give you away. Give them some of the cigarettes."

"I am not so sure," was his reply. "No! It is too dangerous. I shall be caught and flogged, or they may even shoot me."

"You know you will not be shot. Courage! Would you not risk a flogging for the Allies, for France? We are all fighting this war together."

"I would not risk much for many Frenchmen," he said, cryptically, "and France is no more!"

"Come now!" I cajoled, "that is not a Frenchman speaking; that sounds like a collaborator. You are no collaborator. I know your reputation from Frenchmen in the camp who speak well of you. You have helped them. Can you not help us now?"

"Why should I suffer because a British officer wishes to be mad?"

"He is not mad. He is just like you and me. Remember, we officers are not able to move around like you. Why should he not want to escape?"

"*Eh bien!* I'll do it!" he consented, softening at last.

I breathed a sigh of relief and patted him on the shoulder. If he was caught, he was liable to suffer rough treatment.

Peter was already packed and waiting in another palliasse, which was propped over the Frenchman's shoulder. I never saw a bundle of canvas and straw looking less like a palliasse in my life, but the corners soon seemed to settle themselves out. By the time the Frenchman made his exit to the courtyard, he was looking much more as if he was carrying ten pounds than ten stones.

Alas! he could not off-load the mattress on to the high floor of the lorry alone, so he did the sensible thing; he dropped his load on the ground and looked around, pretending to wipe his brow. An opportune moment arrived almost immediately, as a couple of our stooges on 'attention

The heavy palliasse

distracting' duty promptly started to tinker with the front of the car. The Jerries on guard moved to the front, and our Frenchman asked for help from a compatriot just relieved of his mattress. The two of them swung Peter as if he were a feather on top of the rapidly growing pile.

That was enough for the morning. We had no intention of risking another body on that lorry. In due course it departed and was ineffectually prodded by guards at the various gates before trundling off down to the town below.

Peter was duly off-loaded by his guardian, although some of the French were becoming 'windy' as to the enormity of their crime. The guardian was subjected to a good deal of barracking and some threats from his compatriots about the loss of privileges, food and suchlike, which was the usual whine of all prisoners who preferred the *status quo* to doing anything that might hurt the feelings of their captors.

Peter understood French well, and heard it all from his recumbent position as he busily imitated an inert mattress in a hurry to be put on a nice board bed in an empty room somewhere in the town of Colditz. He was eventually so deposited and the lorry team disappeared for the lunch interval. All was silent.

Peter extricated himself and found that he was on the ground floor of a deserted house in the town. He opened the window and climbed into a small garden and from there to a road. Our bird had flown!

Peter reached Stuttgart and then Vienna. His greatest thrill was when he was picked up by a senior German S.S. officer travelling in style in a large car, and accompanied him for about a hundred miles on his way. Only a man like Peter Allan, who had spent six months at school in Germany, could have got away with the conversation involved in a cheek-by-jowl car journey of such a kind.

Meanwhile, in the afternoon, work was resumed by the French on a second load of mattresses and we resumed work on the preparation of a second 'heavy' mattress. Peter had been instructed to make his getaway quickly for the reason that if we failed in the second attempt we did not want the Germans to find Peter quietly lying in his mattress awaiting nightfall!

By now, however, the Frenchmen were frightened and even our staunch French orderly wilted under the weight of the second mattress, duly prepared by us with Lieutenant J. Hyde-Thomson, M.C. (Durham Light Infantry), resting inside. Unfortunately Hyde-Thomson weighed nearly twelve and a half stone and was sufficiently tall to give the lie to the desired impression of a well-stuffed palliasse. In the courtyard he was dumped on the ground next to the lorry and the Frenchmen refused to load him. Our distraction stooges worked overtime, but the

French strike continued and eventually the Jerries became suspicious. The non-commissioned officer-in-charge called for an officer, and by the time the latter arrived the lorry was loaded and our 'heavy' mattress still lay leadenly on the ground.

The officer prodded and then ordered the non-commissioned officer to investigate, while he held his revolver cocked, expecting the worst. Hyde-Thomson duly appeared covered in straw, and was ignominiously led off for examination and a month's cooling off in the cells.

Fourteen days later we heard the sad and discouraging news that Peter Allan had been recaught. His story was depressing.

He had reached Vienna and, having spent the last of his money, was looking around for ways and means to carry on to Poland. He thought of the American consulate—for the U.S.A. was still not at war. He went there and disclosed his identity. The Americans politely but firmly refused him any kind of help. After this he became despondent. He was worn out from long trekking and the insidious loneliness of the solitary fleeing refugee in an enemy land descended on him. This curious sensation has to be lived through to be appreciated. It can lead a man to give himself up voluntarily, despite the consequences; to talk and mix with other human beings, be they even his jailers, means something to a hunted man, particularly in a city. He must have a strong inner fibre who can withstand the temptation for long. It was for this reason among others that escapers found it advisable to travel in pairs, where possible.

Peter Allan went into a park in Vienna and fell asleep on a bench. In the morning he awoke and found his legs paralysed with cramp. He crawled to the nearest habitation and was taken to hospital, where his resistance broke down. He was quite well looked after and was soon fit to be escorted back to Colditz, where the greater despondency of failure was to hold sway over him during a month's lonely imprisonment.

Two questions, at least, arise concerning this escape. First, why was a tall and heavy person selected for the second attempt? The answer is the same as that which accounts for pure strategy so frequently becoming modified by paramount policy, often, as in this case, resulting in the failure of the project. Hyde-Thomson had arrived in Colditz with a considerable amount of German money in his possession, following an abortive escape attempt. Although the money was not officially his own, he had had the wit to save it through many searches and he had a justifiable lien on it. Officers were searched on departure from one camp and again on arrival at a new one. This consisted of being stripped naked and having each piece of clothing carefully examined, while luggage was gone through with a toothcomb. Hyde-Thomson had given a large proportion of the money to me with alacrity for the canteen tunnel attempt, and some more had gone with Peter Allan. It was time he should be rewarded, and the mattress escape was offered.

Secondly, one may wonder at the attitude of the Americans in Vienna. The explanation is probably twofold. The official one is that the Americans, though neutral, were having a hard time holding on to their Vienna Consulate, and were continually in danger of being ordered out of the country at a moment's notice. They were doing important work and could not risk their position officially. The other explanation, which is quite plausible, is that Peter did not succeed in convincing the Consulate that he was not a German 'agent provocateur.' He had nothing to prove his case and he spoke German perfectly. His English might have been sufficient proof to an Englishman if tested *in extenso*. Yet I dare any Englishman to accept in a similar situation, but with the nationalities reversed, the voice and accent of an alleged American as being that of a genuine American.

CHAPTER IX

FRENCH DASH AND POLISH TEMPERAMENT

LIEUTENANT MAIRESSE LEBRUN was a French cavalry officer, tall, handsome, and debonair, and a worthy compatriot of that famed cuirassier of Napoleon whose legendary escapades were so ably recounted by Conan Doyle in his book, *The Adventures of Brigadier Gerard*.

Lebrun had slipped the German leash from Colditz once already by what seems, in the telling, a simple ruse. In fact, it required quite expert handling. A very small Belgian officer was his confederate. On one of the 'Park' outings the Belgian officer concealed himself under the voluminous folds of a tall comrade's cloak at the outgoing 'numbering off' parade and was not counted. During the recreation period in the Park, Lebrun, with the aid of suitable diversions, climbed up among the rafters of an open-sided pavilion situated in the middle of the recreation pen. He was not missed because the Belgian provided the missing number, and the dogs did not get wind of him. Later he descended and, smartly dressed in a grey flannel suit sent by a friend from France, he walked to a local railway station and proffered a hundred-mark note at the booking-office in exchange for a ticket. Unfortunately, the note was an old one, no longer in circulation. The station-master became suspicious and finally locked Lebrun up in a cloakroom and telephoned the camp. The Camp Commandant replied that nothing was amiss and that his prisoner complement was complete. While he was 'phoning, Lebrun wrenched open a window and leaped out on top of an old woman, who naturally became upset and gave tongue. A chase ensued. He was finally cornered by the station personnel and recaptured. In due course he was returned to the Castle and handed over to the protesting Commandant.

This adventure lost Mairesse his fine suit and found him doing a month's 'solitary' confinement at the same time as Peter Allan.

One fine afternoon we heard many shots fired in the playground and rushed to the windows, but could see nothing because of the foliage. Terrific excitement followed in the German quarters and we saw posses of Goons with dogs descending at the double from the Castle and disappearing among the trees. Shouts and orders and the barking of dogs continued for some time and eventually faded away in the distance.

We heard by message from Peter Allan what had happened. The 'solitaries'—at the time a mere half a dozen—were having their daily exercise in the park, during which period they could mix freely. Being only a few, they were sparsely guarded, though confined to one end of the compound, where the prisoners played football among the trees. Lebrun was in the habit of doing exercises with two other Frenchmen, which included much leapfrogging. Now Lebrun was athletic. It was high summer and he was dressed in what remained to him of his former finery—shorts, a yellow cardigan, an open-necked shirt, and gym shoes—not good escaping clothes, but that was also what he reckoned the Germans would think. While a couple of the latter were lolling rather sleepily outside the wire and looking at anything but the prisoners, Lebrun innocently leapfrogged with the other Frenchmen.

It all happened in a flash. His French colleague stood near the wire and, forming with his two hands a stirrup into which Lebrun placed his foot, he catapulted him upwards. Acrobats can heave each other tremendous distances by this method. Precision of timing of muscular effort is its secret. Lebrun and his friend managed it, and the former sailed in a headlong dive over the nine-foot wire.

This was only half the battle. Lebrun ran twenty yards along the fence to the main wall of the park. He had to reclimb the wire, using it as a ladder, in order to hoist himself on to the top of the wall which was, at this point, about thirteen feet high. Rather than present a slowly moving target during this climb, Lebrun deliberately attracted the fire of the two nearest sentries by running

The escape of Mairesse Lebrun

backwards and forwards beside the wall. Their carbines once fired (and having missed), the reloading gave him the extra seconds he needed. He was on top of the wall by the time they fired again and dropped to the ground on the other side in a hail of bullets as the more distant sentries joined in the fusillade.

He disappeared and was never recaught. He certainly deserves the greatest credit for this escape, which was in the true French cavalry tradition and demanded the very quintessence of courage, remembering the effort was made in cold blood and with every opportunity for reflection on the consequences of a false step. A British officer, in a similar attempt a few years later, was shot dead. The escape savours of a generation of Frenchmen of whom the majority disappeared on the battlefields of the First World War and who, alas, never had the chance to sire and educate a generation like themselves to follow in their footsteps.

The loss, which was so deeply felt in the 'thirties and which found physical expression during the critical days of 1940, is happily in these days of the 'fifties fading like a bad dream. The young blood of France is quickening again and there is a new courage in the air.

I met Lebrun again long afterwards, when the war was over, and here is the end of his story.

Lebrun escaped on July 1st, 1941. Although he had the sleuth-hounds and a posse of Goons on his tail within ten minutes, he managed to hide in a field of wheat. (You must walk in backwards, rearranging the stalks as you go.) There he hid the whole afternoon with a search 'plane circling continuously above him. At 10 p.m. he set off. He had twenty German marks which were smuggled into his prison cell from the camp. He walked about fifty miles and then stole a bicycle and cycled between sixty and a hundred miles a day. He posed as an Italian officer and begged or bought food at lonely farmhouses, making sure, by a stealthy watch beforehand, that there were only women in the house. His bicycle 'sprang a leak,' so he abandoned it and stole a second. On the journey to the Swiss frontier he was stopped twice by guards and ran for it each time. On the second occasion, about twenty-five miles from the frontier, he tripped the guard up with the aid of his bicycle and knocked him out with his bicycle pump. He took to the woods and crossed the frontier safely on July 8th.

Within a week he was in France. In December 1942 he crossed the Pyrenees and was taken prisoner by the Spaniards, who locked him up in a castle. He jumped from a window into the moat and broke his spine on some rocks at the bottom, was removed, laid down on a mattress, and left to die. A local French Consul, however, who had previously been endeavouring to extricate the incarcerated Lebrun, heard of the accident and insisted on an immediate operation. Lebrun's life was saved. He eventually reached Algeria to carry on the war. Today, though permanently crippled by his fall, he is a pillar in his own country.

If any German had examined Lebrun's cell at Colditz when he left for his daily exercise on July 1st, he might have nipped Lebrun's escape in the bud. Lebrun had packed up his belongings and addressed them to himself in France. Months later they arrived—forwarded by Oberstleutnant Prawitt, the Colditz Camp Commandant!

*   *   *   *   *

The most daredevil Polish officer at Colditz among a bunch of daredevils was 'Niki,' 2nd-Lieutenant (Ensign) N. Surmanowicz. He was a small weedy-looking young man with an untidy face made up of unequal-sided triangles. The fire that burnt in his soul showed only in his eyes, which glowed with fanatical ardour. He was a great friend of mine and we went on many marauding expeditions together through the forbidden parts of the camp. He taught me all I ever knew about lock-picking, at which he was an expert. It was Niki who had been one of our first visitors up in the loft on our arrival at Colditz. The manufacture of magnetic compasses was also a pastime of his. This he carried out with the aid of a homemade solenoid, employing the electric current of the main camp supply, which happened to be 'direct' current. The number of compasses fabricated by him alone, together with their pivots, compass cards, and glass-covered boxes, went into the fifties.

His schemes for escaping were, to my mind, mostly too

wild to bear serious examination. He, on the other hand, thought my ideas were prosaic and I know he inwardly deprecated my painstaking way of setting about escape problems.

Like Lebrun, he relied on 'dash,' to which he added a depth of cunning hardly to be equalled. In common with all the Poles, he despised the Germans, but, unfortunately also like many Poles, he underestimated his enemy; a form of conceit which, however, is not a monopoly of the Poles.

Niki spent as much time in solitary confinement as he spent with 'the common herd.' On one occasion, in the summer of 1941, he occupied a cell which had a small window, high up in the wall, opening on to our courtyard. Another Polish officer, Lieutenant Mietek Schmiel, a friend of Niki, occupied the cell next door. I received a message from him one day, saying that he and Schmiel were going to escape that night and would I join them!

I declined the invitation for two reasons; firstly, I thought Niki was crazy, and, secondly, I had given up the idea of escaping myself so long as I remained Escape Officer. With the British contingent on the increase rapidly, this latter course was the only one open to me if I wished to retain the confidence of our group as an impartial arbiter and helper.

I passed on Niki's invitation to a few of the most harebrained among our company, but Niki's invitation was politely refused by all!

Nobody believed he was serious. Nobody believed he could ghost his way out of his heavily barred and padlocked cell, then open his friend's cell and then unlock the main door of the 'solitary' cell corridor which opened on to the courtyard. Having accomplished this feat he was inside the prison camp, the same as everyone else! Niki loved a challenge and he would chuckle with laughter for the rest of his life if he could show the Jerries once and for all that it took more than they could contrive to keep a Pole down.

He left the invitation open, giving a rendezvous in the

courtyard outside the solitary confinement cells at 11 p.m.
that night.

I was at my window watching as 11 p.m. struck, and on
the minute I saw the door of the cells open slowly. All was
dark and I could only faintly distinguish the two figures as
they crept out. Then something dropped from a window
high up in the Polish quarters. It was a rope made of
sheets with a load strapped at the bottom—their escape kit,
clothes and rucksacks. Next I saw the figures climb the
rope one after the other to a ledge forty feet above the
ground. What they were about to do was impossible, but
they had achieved the impossible once already. I could no
longer believe my eyes. The ledge they were on jutted four
inches out from the sheer face of the wall of the building.
They both held the rope, which was still suspended
from the window above them. My heart pounded against
my ribs as I saw them high above me with their backs
against the wall moving along the ledge inch by inch a
distance of ten yards before reaching the safety of a gutter
on the eaves of the German guardhouse.

Once there, they were comparatively safe and out of
sight if the courtyard lights were turned on. I then saw
them climb up the roof to a skylight through which they
disappeared, pulling the long rope of sheets, which was let
loose by Polish confederates, after them.

Their next move, I knew, was to descend from a small
window at the outer end of the attic of the German guardhouse. The drop was about one hundred and twenty feet,
continuing down the face of the cliff upon which the
Castle was built.

I retired to my bunk, weak at the knees and shaking, as
if I had done the climb myself.

The next morning the two of them were back in their
cells! I find it hard to tell the end of the story. Niki wore
plimsolls for the climb, but his colleague, with Niki's
agreement, preferred to wear boots of the mountaineering
type. As they both descended the long drop from the guardhouse, the mountaineering boots made too much noise

against the wall and awoke the German duty officer sleep·
ing in the guardhouse. He opened his window, to see the
rope dangling beside him and a body a few yards below
him. He drew his revolver and, true to type, shouted
"Hände hoch!" several times and called out the guard.

I spent a month in Niki's cell later on without being
able to discover how he had opened the door!

After this episode the Germans placed a sentry in the
courtyard. He remained all night with the lights full on,
which was to prove a nuisance for later escape attempts.

CHAPTER X

JUST TOO EASY

THE summer months were passing—slowly enough for us—yet too fast for all our plans. Winter, relatively speaking, is the escapers' 'close season,' though the Second World War was to see many time-hallowed rules of this nature broken.

There was a long curved room over the canteen where a batch of our British contingent slept and passed much of their time. Roughly speaking, two sides of this room backed on to the German section of the Castle, and these two walls always attracted our attention as holding out possibilities. A door in the end wall, in the very early days, had been opened by Niki, who had been beyond into a deserted attic. He could describe no more than that. The doorway had promptly been walled up. Although efforts were made to break through the wall, this had been constructed with such tough cement that noise gave us away and the Germans calmly replastered our puny efforts. This is possibly where they planted one of their microphones, which they later had everywhere.

The second wall, according to the officers who slept near it, backed on to German lavatories.

Tommy Elliott (Lieutenant, Royal Northumberland Fusiliers) and Ted Barton announced to me one day that they had started a fair-sized hole which was making good progress. In a matter of a couple of days they were practically through. Listening carefully, they established by sounds from the other side that the hole was near floor-level and appeared to be close to a lavatory bowl. A pinhole was made through the plaster face from the inside, and it was confirmed that the opening would be just off centre and below the seat of a porcelain water-closet.

No time could be lost—the Germans appeared unconscionably quiet and they might start a series of searches any day. The opening was not well concealed on our side and any search would have revealed it. I had my own misgivings, too, concerning the hole, but without evidence I could not withstand the enthusiasm of my fellow-officers for the venture.

The plan was simple. Towards late evening on the coming Sunday, when the German quarters would be at their quietest, the hole would be broken through and twelve officers at five-minute intervals between pairs or individuals, would pass through in civilian attire and make their best way out. In effect, the entry into the German quarters would be only the beginning of their troubles, for they would still have to find their way to the exits of the German side of the Castle, then brave the various gates or, more probably, disappear into the wooded playground below the Castle and climb over the main wall under cover of trees.

Sunday arrived and the tension grew apace. The escapers appeared for a passing-out parade. Civilian attire was checked and in some cases altered or substituted by articles of civilian clothing supplied from the private hoards of willing helpers.

* * * * *

At this period of our captivity, escape equipment was becoming organised. Although every officer had not yet been equipped with identity papers, each had a homemade compass of one kind or another, a set of maps painfully traced over and over again from originals, and each was given some German money.

Every officer possessed his private escape kit, which he had ample time to devise during the long hours of enforced idleness—the devil indeed 'finds mischief still for idle hands to do' in a prison camp! And it was surprising what could be produced in the way of civilian clothing by dyeing and altering, by cutting up blankets, and by clever sewing and knitting. Many officers had their specialities and turned out articles in quantity.

I concentrated on the manufacture of 'gor blimey' caps and also rucksacks. My particular brand of cap, cut out of any suitably coloured blanket, having a peak stiffened with a piece of leather or other water-resisting stiffener and lined with a portion of coloured handkerchief and a soft-leather head-band, looked quite professional. My rucksacks were not always waterproof; they were made from dark-coloured or dyed, tough army material, with broad trouser braces adapted as straps, and the flaps and corners neatly edged with leather strips cut from boot tongues. They would pass in Germany as workmen's rucksacks.

Dyeing with 'ersatz' coffee or purple pencil lead became a fine art. The blue Royal Air Force uniform was readily adaptable and with skilful tailoring could become a passable civilian suit. Of course, real civilian clothing was what every officer ultimately aimed at possessing. This urgent desire accounts for the high premium set on the workmen's clothing which gave rise to the 'grand piano' incident.

A similar occasion arose once during one of the very rare visits of a German civilian dentist to supplement the work of our French army dentist. He was accompanied by two leech-like sentries, who kept so close to him that he hardly had room to wield his forceps.

The dentist's torture chamber was approached through a maze of small rooms and had two doors, one of which was supposed to be permanently locked but which we opened on our nefarious occasions with the aid of our universal keys. On the back of this door was a coat-hook, and on the hook our German dentist hung his Homburg hat and a fine fur-collared tweed overcoat.

This was indeed 'big game,' and Dick Howe, with another British officer, 'Scorgie' Price, and a French officer named Jacques Prot were soon hot on the trail.

Dick arranged to pay an officer's dentist's bill. The dentist was paid in *Lagergeld* and Dick sought out an officer with a heavy bill—it came to a hundred marks. He collected the whole sum in one-mark notes. This would

give him plenty of time. He arranged a signal with the
other two. The operative word was 'Right.' When Dick
said 'Right' loudly, Price was to open the locked door
and remove the coat and hat.

Dick went to the dentist's room and insisted on interrupting the dentist's work to pay his brother-officer's bill.
He drew him over to a table; the two sentries dutifully
followed; and Dick started to count out laboriously his
Lagergeld.

"Eins, zwei, drei, . . ." he started and carried on to *zehn,*
at which point he looked up to see if he had the full attention of the dentist and his guards. 'Not quite,' he thought,
and he carried on painfully, *"elf, zwölf . . ."* By the time
he reached *zwanzig* he had all their eyes riveted on the
slowly rising pile of notes, so he said "Right." As he continued he sensed nothing had happened. At *dreiszig* he repeated "Right" a little louder. Again nothing happened.
At *vierzig* he filled his lungs and shouted "Right" again.
Still nothing happened. Doggedly he continued, holding
the attention of all three, as his reserves of *Lagergeld*
dwindled. As *fünfzig, sechzig, siebzig* passed, his 'Rights'
crescendoed, to the amusement of his three spectators.
Nothing happened. An operatic bass would have been
proud of Dick's final rendering at *achtzig, neunzig,* and
hundert. The scheme had failed, and the only persons
laughing were the Germans at Dick's, by this time, comic·
act.

The dentist, still guffawing, collected all the notes together and before Dick's crestfallen gaze started recounting
them. As he reached *zehn* he shouted "R-r-right," and
Dick, to his own utter astonishment, felt rather than heard
the door open behind them, and sensed an arm appearing
around it. Before the dentist had reached *zwanzig* the door
had closed again. Dick continued the pantomime and
eventually, after assuring himself that the coat and hat had
really disappeared, he retired from the scene with apologies—a shaken man.

The concealment of contraband material presented great

difficulty, and many were the hours given up to devising ingenious ways of hiding our precious work. The common hiding-places and those at various times found out by the Germans were: behind false-backed cupboards and in trap-door hides, under floorboards, and sewn into mattresses and overcoat linings. Small items were often sealed in cigarette-tins, weighted and dropped into lavatory cisterns or concealed in stores of food. There were myriads of possibilities, and it is appropriate that the better ways remain undisclosed for the present. Men who may have nothing to think about for many a long, weary day in the years to come will rediscover them and sharpen their wits in the exercise.

*   *   *   *   *

To return to our twelve stalwarts perspiring with nervous anticipation, some even vomiting quietly in the seclusion of an *Abort*, waiting for the zero hour! At the appointed time, all was reported quiet on the other side of the wall. The hole was quickly broken out and the escapers started to squirm through in their correct order and at the appropriate intervals of time, while watchers at different vantage-points scanned the exits from the German quarters.

Soon reports began coming in: "No exits!" and again "No exits!" We persisted, however, for forty minutes, by which time eight officers had passed through the hole. At this point I turned to the remaining four:

"I think it's too risky to continue without having a pause. What do you think?"

"It's suspicious that not one has poked his head out of the other end of the rabbit run yet!" said the next on the list to go.

"I don't think we can spoil anything by holding off and watching for results. If we go on pumping any more through as it is, they'll soon be bulging out of the *Kommandantur* windows."

"Shall we stay on the field during half-time or go and have a drink?"

"Better stay here," I advised. "You may be wanted at a moment's notice, but have all your kit ready to hide too. Make a plan for a split-second hideaway in case the Jerries are on to the scheme and try to catch us in the rear."

After fifteen minutes of inactivity the alarm was suddenly given. "Jerries *en masse* entering courtyard, heading for our staircase!"

Well, that was the end of that! The Germans had laid a trap and we had walked into it, or eight of us had. The hole must have been marked during operations upon it, and a secret guard kept. As each of the eight escapers left the *Abort,* and proceeded down a long corridor he was quietly shepherded into a room and put under guard!

Thus ended another depressing chapter for British morale in Colditz. The Germans had gained the upper hand and were playing with us. Our efforts were beginning to appear ridiculous.

CHAPTER XI

DUTCH PORCELAIN

BRITISH escaping reputation had reached rock bottom, and whatever conceit we had left was soon to receive a further blow, this time at the hands of the Dutch. From the beginning close relations were maintained with them, and, though at the start this did not involve revealing the full details of our respective plans, it soon developed into a very close co-operation, which was headed on the Dutch side by a Captain Van den Heuvel.

The Dutch were not very long at Colditz before Van den Heuvel warned me of an impending attempt. 'Vandy,' as he was inevitably called, was a fairly tall, big-chested man with a round face, florid complexion, and an almost permanent broad grin. His mouth was large enough in repose, but when he smiled it was from ear to ear. He had hidden depths of pride and a terrific temper, revealed on very rare occasions. He spoke English well, but with a droll Dutch accent.

"How are you, Vandy?" I would ask him, to which his unvarying reply was: "Rather vell, thank you," with emphasis on the 'rather.'

"Patt," he said to me one day, "ve are about to trry our virst vlight vrom Golditz. I can only zay it is vrom the direczion ov the park and it vill take place on Zunday."

Sunday passed calmly and in the evening I went to see Vandy.

"Well, Vandy, there's been no excitement. What have you got up your sleeve?" I asked.

"Aah! Patt," he replied, with a mischievous twinkle in his eye, "I haf two more op my sleeve vor next Zunday, two haf gone today!"

He was grinning as usual and was like a dog with two tails. His pleasure was infectious and I could not help laughing.

At the morning *Appell* on Monday, however, two Dutchmen were missing. Some time later (not the next Sunday, for technical reasons), two more disappeared.

The Germans were worried enough over the first two. They were 'hopping mad' when the number rose to four. When it had risen to six, they forgot even to hop. There was a series of searches of the camp premises, and the park was given a very careful scrutiny. I noticed the Jerries placed bars across the small wooden cover to a manhole in the football ground which had, in any case, one large nut and bolt securing it.

Eventually I managed to worm out of Vandy how he, a comparative newcomer to the camp, had managed with such ease to arrange the escape of his six Dutchmen from the fortress of Colditz.

His trick was so simple that it shook me to think that the rest of us—Poles, French, and British, numbering now some two hundred and fifty—could not have thought of it. The escape was indeed from the manhole in the football ground.

"All very well," I said to Vandy. "We've all looked at that manhole cover till we were blue in the face without arriving at a satisfactory scheme."

"Ah!" he replied, "Patt, vat is that game the Poles taught you? Gapin? Vell, I tought of Gapin and looked at the manhole cover vrom another angle!"

On the first two occasions in question, a few Dutchmen, led by a venerable-looking bearded one named Van Doorninck, had held Bible-reading meetings, curiously enough, around the manhole. Previously they had measured the size of the nut and bolt. During the Bible-reading, the bolt was undone with a pair of large homemade spanners filed out of iron bed-parts. The bolt had about a 3/4-inch diameter thread. When the sentries' notice was attracted to a football game in progress, two Dutchmen disappeared into the manhole. Now this was the crux. Immediately after the recreation, and before the prisoners returned to the Castle, the football ground was carefully examined, invariably including the manhole, by two or three Jerries appointed for the purpose. They also let loose dogs to trace possible hideouts or graves among the trees.

"How," I asked, "did you conceal the opened manhole? That is what beats me."

"Ve made another bolt; a fery special kind of bolt," Vandy replied. "It vas made of glass tubing with a vooden head, and painted just like the real vone."

That in effect was the secret of this simple yet brilliantly conceived escape. The two escapers in the manhole had the real bolt with them. At nightfall they pushed up the lid, breaking the glass bolt. They cleaned away the bits as best they could before leaving, and replaced the original bolt exactly as it was before, applying mud and dirt to cover any marks left on the iron. Their exit thereafter, only impeded by a high wall and some barbed wire, presented no difficulty in the dark with the nearest guard over four hundred yards away. By this time the Germans had enforced no fewer than four roll-calls on the daily recreation parade; two in the park and two at the courtyard gate. How Vandy managed to cover these he kept a secret for a little while longer!

The first four who escaped were Captains A. L. C. Dufour and J. G. Imit (Royal Netherlands Indies Army) and Lieutenants E. H. Larive and F. Steinmetz (Royal Netherlands Navy), and the latter two reached Switzerland. The other two were caught on the frontier and eventually returned to Colditz. The third couple disappeared about a month after the others during a Polish-Dutch International Soccer match. They were Major C. Giebel and 2nd-Lieutenant O. L. Drijber, both of the Royal Netherlands Indies Army. They reached Switzerland safely.

The Germans still believed they could make Oflag IV C impregnable (from within), so that escapers, when recaught, were not sent elsewhere according to normal custom but invariably returned to Colditz. For this reason, it was always growing in population; a centre of gravity, towards which escapers moved from all over Germany, when not moving in the opposite direction under their own steam! It was likewise a fortress, which required an ever-increasing garrison. The Germans greatly outnumbered the prisoners. Admittedly our jailors were not class A 1 soldiers. The swollen number of the garrison was probably a source of irritation to the German High Command, because they held a series of inspections at one period, including a visit by two German officers who had escaped from Allied hands. One was Hauptmann v. Werra, the German airman who gave our POW authorities much trouble and eventually escaped from Canada to the U.S.A. The story has it that he jumped from a train near the St. Lawrence River, stole a motor-boat in which he crossed and eventually reached the German Consulate in New York. He visited our camp during his leave to give the Commandant advice. Shortly afterwards he was reported to have been shot down and killed somewhere on the Russian front.

The return of escaped officers to their original camp provided certain advantages for the inmates, by which we were not slow to profit. It was inevitable, however, that, if the war lasted long enough, in the end the Germans would win the battle of Colditz and the camp would become practically unbreakable, but none of us thought that stage had arrived in the autumn of 1941. In fact, although every escape discovered meant that one more foxhole had been bunged up, the prisoners really never gave up trying until the Allied advance into Germany.

The 'Prominten,' as they were called by the Germans, also drifted gradually towards Colditz. Winston Churchill's nephew, Giles Romilly, arrived. He was given the honour and the inconvenience of a small cell to himself, which had a sentry outside it all night. He was free to mix with the other prisoners during the day, but he had to suffer the annoyance of being called for by his guardian angel—a heavy-booted Hun—every night at 9 p.m., and escorted to his bedroom and locked in!

Like everybody else, he wanted to escape, but it was

naturally more difficult to arrange. I once succeeded in substituting him for one of several French orderlies who were off-loading coal from a lorry in the courtyard. The coal-dust was a helpful disguise—smeared over his face—but he did not even pass the first gateway. It was obvious that he was either watched from within the camp by other than his ostensible jailors, or, which is equally likely in this case, a French orderly—perhaps the one substituted—reported to the Germans what was happening, to save his own skin. We never found out, but it was Hauptmann Priem himself who entered the courtyard when the lorry was ready to leave and calmly asked Romilly to step down from it. I think he was awarded only a week's solitary confinement and then returned to his normal routine.

It was also in the late summer of 1941, when I was doing one of my customary periods of 'solitary'—three weeks in this case—that the cells became overcrowded and Flight-Lieutenant Norman Forbes joined me for a spell. The cells were tiny, about four yards by three yards. We were given a two-tier bed, however, which helped, but to compensate for this, our cell was built immediately over a semi-basement cellar in which the camp garbage-cans were housed.

Norman and I managed very well and did not get on each other's nerves. One day, shortly before his 'time' was finished, he remarked to me casually that he needed a haircut.

"Ah ha!" thought I, "anything to relieve the monotony!"

"What a curious coincidence," I said, "that you should be doing 'solitary' with an expert amateur barber. I learnt the art from my school barber, who said I had a natural talent for it."

"Well, have a shot at mine, then," was the reply.

Soon I was busy with a pair of nail-scissors and a comb, which I periodically banged together in a professional manner. I tried for a few minutes to cut his hair properly, then realised that a barber's skill is by no means easy to acquire. I carried on, extracting large chunks of hair here and there, until the back of his head looked more like a gaping skull than anything else. At the front of his head I cut a neat fringe. The rest of his head was a jumble. As the front was all that Norman could see in the tiny mirror we had, he was unaware of his predicament until a day or two later, when he rejoined the camp and became a standing joke for several days.

After Norman left, boredom settled on me once again. I was studying economics, but found it heavy reading when continued for weeks on end. One day I thought of my cornet. As a concession I had been allowed to take into 'solitary,' along with books and other paraphernalia, my guitar and my brass cornet.

Norman had only just managed to withstand my guitar crooning, and categorically refused to let me practise my cornet. Now I was alone, I thought, and I could practise in peace. But so many objections were raised from nearby cells and also from the courtyard—which my cell faced— in the form of showers of pebbles, shouts, and insults, that I was driven to practising my cornet at the only time (apart from the dead of night) when nobody could stop me, which was during the half-hour of evening *Appell*.

This seemed to satisfy everybody; for the German officers and N.C.O.s taking the parade could hardly hear themselves speak, and the numbers invariably tallied up wrong, necessitating several recounts. By the third evening the hilarity grew to such an extent that the parade almost became a shambles. Apparently many of the German troops thought the cornet practice funny too—which made it all the worse for the German officer-in-charge, who was beside himself. By the fourth day I was feeling so sorry for the Jerries having to put up with the ear-splitting noises which coincided with their commands, that I decided to show a gentlemanly spirit and refrain from practising that evening.

Evidently I was not the only one who had been reflecting, for when the evening *Appell* was assembled, and the German officer-in-charge entered the yard (Hauptmann

Püpcke was his name), he made straight for my cell with two soldiers and swung open my door with violence.

"*Geben Sie mir sofort ihre Trompete,*" he shouted.

I was so taken aback by his abruptness after my good intentions and sympathy for the German position that I thought it was my turn to feel insulted.

"*Nein,*" I said. "*Ich will nicht; es ist meine Trompete, Sie haben kein Recht darauf,*" and with that I hid the trum-

The cornet incident

pet (cornet) behind my back. He seized it and we began a violent tug-of-war. He ordered his two cohorts to intervene, which they did by clubbing my wrists and arms with their rifle butts, and I gave up the unlucky instrument.

"You will have a court martial for this," the officer screamed as he slammed the door behind him.

The court martial never came off, which was a pity, for it meant a journey, probably to Leipzig, and a chance of escape. Instead, I was awarded another month's 'solitary' which I began shortly afterwards in a different cell.

It was late September and the leaves were falling in the park, but all I could see from my tiny window by climbing on to my washstand was the wall of a section of our prison known as the theatre block. It was during one of my long periods of blank staring at this wall-face that a light suddenly dawned upon me. If I had not been an engineer, familiar with plans and elevations and in the habit of mentally reconstructing the skeletons of buildings, the idea would probably never have occurred to me. I suddenly realised that the wooden stage of the theatre was situated so that it protruded over a part of the Castle, sealed off from the prisoners, which led by a corridor to the top of the German guardhouse immediately outside our courtyard.

This discovery was a little goldmine. I tucked it away and resolved to explore further as soon as I was free.

CHAPTER XII

THE RIOT SQUAD

AS I have said, 'Never a dull moment' might well have been the motto on the armorial bearings of Oflag IV C. I had hardly finished ruminating on my discovery from the cell window when a fusillade of shots sounded from the direction of the park. I was tantalised to know what was happening. Soon the 'riot squad' dashed into the courtyard and headed for the British doorway. Any posse of Goons heading anywhere at the double in an excited manner with fixed bayonets was familiarly known as the 'riot squad.'

They did not leave for hours and there was an incredible amount of shouting and barracking, mostly in French. Eventually I heard the story from Harry Elliott, who passed in a note to me describing what had happened.

He was in the Dutch quarters when the shooting, and much shouting, began from the direction of the park. Everyone rushed to the windows to see what was happening, and they saw two Belgian prisoners (Lieutenant Marcel Leroy and Lieutenant Le Jeune) running up the steep hill towards the wall which surrounded the park. They had climbed the wire (or crawled under it) and were being fired at by the sentries. As the sentries stood in a circle, some of them on the uphill side of the park came close to being hit by the ones below them. The sentries surrounding the Castle walls joined in and a regular fusillade started. The shooting was, as usual, bad, and the Germans were rapidly losing their heads. It was a wonderful opportunity for the prisoners, who wasted no time in trying to distract the sentries by shouting all sorts of abuse at them. The Dutch, who were very correct on all occasions, did not join in with as much enthusiasm as the English. So Harry ran downstairs to the British quarters to assist in the fun from there. By the time he arrived, much of the shooting was directed against the windows of the Castle and bullets were thudding against it. The Belgians had reached the high wall, but found it impossible to climb at that point and eventually stood with their hands up, still being fired at by the Germans. Luckily they were not hit.*

Next, the sentries around the Castle walls came under fire from the sentries in the park, who began firing at the jeering mob at the Castle windows. The bullets were going over their heads, but must have seemed close and they were becoming jittery. The British found this the greatest fun, and continued laughing and teasing the sentries beneath them. Eventually Peter Storie Pugh (Lieutenant, Royal West Kents) produced a Union Jack which had been used in Christmas festivities long ago, and hung it out of the window. This produced an immediate response. The hoarse shouting of the Goons increased to a thunder and the shooting redoubled its intensity until the hills echoed. It was all directed at the Union Jack.

As the walls were of stone, from time to time bullets coming in at the window ricocheted round the room. The prisoners decided it was time to lie down. At this moment the riot squad, composed of the second in command (a major) and about a dozen Goons, with bayonets fixed, clattered into the courtyard. They dashed up the staircase, and burst into the British quarters, the major leading with his revolver in his hand, white to the lips and shaking all over. The riot squad were also terrified.

"Take that flag down," said the major in German.

None of the prisoners moved—they were lying on the

* One Belgian, Captain Louis Remy, escaped successfully from the castle in April 1942 with Sqdn. Ldr. Paddon (British) and I.t. Just (Polish). The latter two were recaught. Remy reached Belgium, crossed France and Spain and swam to a British ship anchored off Algesiras. He was imprisoned for a month in England, on arrival, only being released through the intervention of Paddon who had again escaped—this time successfully—via Sweden! Remy joined the R.A.F., serving with Bomber Command (103 Squadron) until the end of the war

floor, chatting to each other—no one even looked up. There were a few loud remarks such as—

"They seem pretty windy today," and "What the hell do they want?"

"The Herr Major says you are to take the flag down," came from the German interpreter as another round of shots thudded against the walls.

Not a move. The trembling major then went up to an Australian Squadron Leader named MacColm and, pointing a pistol at him, said:

"Take the flag down."

"Why don't you take it down yourself?" replied Mac-Colm.

The major continued to threaten until MacColm finally crawled over to the window and pulled the flag inside.

All the prisoners in the room were then made to go downstairs and parade in the courtyard. They were encircled by the Goons who kept their rifles in the rabbiting position. Heads started to pop out of windows and the Senior British Officer demanded to know what was happening to his boys. The Goons said, "They fired first," which caused great amusement.

The POWs waited patiently, making pointed remarks while nothing happened. The French, however, from their windows took up their favourite refrain:

"Où sont les Allemands?"

"Les Allemands sont dans la merde," came the reply from about forty windows. And then the first chorus again,

"Qu'on les y enfonce," the reply to that being,

"Jusqu'aux oreilles."

This always provoked the Germans, who understood what it meant, and after the Litany had been chanted from the French and English quarters two or three times, the usual happened. The major started shouting at them; loud laughter from the prisoners and a few rude remarks in German; then the usual cry:

"Anyone looking out of the windows will be shot."

The sentries were in a dilemma; they did not know

whether to point their rifles at the British in the courtyard, or at the windows above. Eventually they all pointed
at the windows and a few shots were fired. This was the
signal for the British to sit down on the cobbles—a pack
of cards was produced and four prisoners started playing
bridge; the others chatted. When the Goons turned their
attention away from the windows again and saw this they
were 'hopping mad' and forced everybody to stand up
once more at the point of the bayonet, but it was not long
before small groups were again sprawling on the cobbles.
The German major, having all this time received no orders
from his higher command, departed. He was soon followed
by the riot squad, who trailed despondently out of the gate,
and the anticlimax was complete.

     ＊   ＊   ＊   ＊   ＊

Beer had long since disappeared from the camp, and
with the thought of a dreary winter ahead, a few of us put
our heads together. With the help of Niki, who had already
managed to procure some yeast from a German, we started
a brewing society. Someone unearthed a curious medal
struck to commemorate a brewing exhibition. I was elected
Chief Brewer and dispensed the yeast, and wore the medal
attached to the end of a large red ribbon. When asked by
curious Goons what the medal represented, I proudly told
them it was a war decoration for distinguished service in
the boosting of morale.

Brewing soon became a popular pastime and, with a
little instruction by the Chief Brewer and his stewards, was
highly successful. Soon, at nearly every bedside could be
seen large jars or bottles, filled with water and containing
at the bottom a mash of sultanas, currants, or dried figs—
produced from our Red Cross parcels—together with the
magic thimbleful of yeast. Curiously enough, it was
eventually found that the yeast was unnecessary, for there
was enough natural yeast already on the skins of the fruit
to start the fermentation process without assistance. The
one difficulty was the provision of gentle heat, because fer-

mentation requires a fairly consistent temperature of about 27 degrees Centigrade. This problem was overcome by the simple use of body heat, or 'hatching' as it was called. It was a normal sight to see rows of officers propped up in their beds for hours on end in the hatching position, with their jars and bottles nestling snugly under the blankets beside them. Fermentation was complete after a fortnight! Some of our amateur brewers were luckier than the ordinary run of broody officers in that their bunks were situated near an electric light. Large incubating boxes were manufactured out of cardboard and lined with German blanket. Jars were arranged in tiers in the boxes, and the heat was turned on by placing the electric-light bulbs in the boxes attached to lengths of 'won' electric cable. A flourishing commerce in brewery shares arose and combines were started.

Soon we were having gay evening parties and started entertaining our fellow-prisoners of other nationalities.

One day our Brewing Association invited a 'brilliant lecturer' to expound the secrets of distillation! Human nature being what it is, we were soon distilling briskly. I tore down a long section of lead piping from one of our non-working lavatories and made a coil, which was sealed into a large German jam-tin about twenty inches high This 'still' became the property of the Brewing and (now) Distilling Society. Almost every night distilling began after 'lights out,' and continued into the early hours. We worked shifts and charged a small percentage (of the resultant liquor) for the distilling of officers' brews. I should explain that distillation is merely a method of concentrating any brew or wine. Brandy is distilled grape-wine. We named our liquor simply 'firewater,' for that undoubtedly it was.

Over a period of time we used up nearly all the bed boards in the British quarters as fuel for our witches' cauldron. Our rows of broody officers looked more odd than ever reposing on mattresses supported only by a minimum of bed boards with pendulous bulges in between, the upper bunks in imminent danger of collapsing on the lower ones. In vain did the Germans make periodical surveys of the bed boards, even to the extent of numbering them with chalk and indelible pencil. Alas! the numbers were consumed in the flames and did not survive the boards.

The distilling process was an eerie ceremony carried out in semi-darkness around the kitchen stove with the distillers listening over the cauldron for the tell-tale hiss of

Distilling

gentle distillation—their flickering giant-like shadows dancing on the walls—as the flames were carefully fed with fuel. Distilling required most concentrated attention because the work of a fortnight could be ruined in a minute if a brew, passing through the lead coils, became overheated and the alcohol boiled away. Distillation takes place between roughly 80 degrees and 90 degrees Centigrade.

Having no thermometers, we learned to judge the temperature by sound alone—hence our experts and our right to charge a premium for the process!

The liquor, as it appeared, drop by drop, from the bottom of the still, was pure white in colour. It was bottled and in a very short time the liquor became crystal clear, leaving a white sediment at the bottom. The clear liquid was run off and rebottled. This was 'firewater.' The white sediment was probably lead oxide—pure poison—but I was not able to check this, and nobody ever died to prove it.

With experience and Polish assistance we produced various flavoured varieties, which the Poles insisted on calling 'vodka.' We did not argue over the name, but I feel sure that our liquor would never have been a suitable accompaniment to caviar. It took the roof off one's mouth, anyway.

It was not long before the British had a good cellar and 'vintages' accumulating. Christmas 1941 looked rosily ahead of us.

CHAPTER XIII

A STAGED FOURSOME

I MADE a reconnaissance of the stage in the theatre, which was on the third floor of the 'theatre block.' By removing some wooden steps leading up to the stage from one of the dressing-rooms, I was able to crawl underneath and examine that part of the floor over the sealed room leading to the German guardhouse. It was as I had hoped. There were no floorboards, only straw and rubble about four inches deep reposing on the lath-and-plaster ceiling of the room in question.

I next looked around for prospective candidates for the escape I was planning. I selected about half a dozen possibilities. To these I mentioned casually that I would get them out of Colditz if they, on the other hand, would produce first-class imitations of German officers' uniforms. It was a challenge and by no means an easy one.

We had made a start, however, on certain parts of German army accoutrements and this was reason for encouragement. What had been left over from the lead piping I removed to make the still had already been melted down and recast into perfect imitations of German uniform buttons and one or two of their insignia. The lead, unfortunately, did not go very far when melted down.

My offer was a test of ingenuity and enterprise, and it produced Lieutenant Airey Neave, R.A., an Etonian and a comparative newcomer to the Castle, and Hyde-Thomson of the 'recumbent palliasse' episode. They had teamed up and Airey promised to make the uniforms. He said he could not make them, however, without Dutch assistance, so eventually, with Van den Heuvel's agreement, two Dutch officers were selected to make the team up to four. The Dutch spoke German fluently, which was a great asset.

Neave and Scarlet O'Hara came to me in distress one day soon afterwards, while I was preparing our next evening's distilling operations. Airey said:

"We're running short of lead."

Scarlet who—it is scarcely necessary to mention—had gravitated to Colditz, was our foundry foreman. He added:

"The lead piping you gave me is finished. It didn't go very far. It's too darn thin—cheap German stuff—no weight in it." He looked towards the still.

"What are you looking at?" I asked. "I hope you're not hinting."

"Wouldn't dream of it," said Scarlet. "I just don't know where I'm going to get any lead from. We've only got three lavatories working as it is. That's not many for forty officers. If I break one up, there will be a revolution."

"Hm! This is serious." I went into a huddle with Dick Howe, who was a keen distiller, and was at that moment repairing a water-leak at the bottom of our still.

"Dick, things look bad for the still. They've run out of lead. How much liquor have we? Would you say our cellar was reasonably stocked?"

"Our cellar is not at all well stocked," Dick joined in, "for the simple reason that it's a bottomless pit. But if there's a greater need, I don't see that we can avoid the issue. We'll probably be able to recuperate our loss in due course—from, say, a Dutch or a French lavatory."

"Very good," I said to Airey, "your need is greater than ours. You'd better take the coil," and then to Dick:

"It's probably just as well to lay up for the time being, as there's a search due one of these days and we've got some stock to carry on with. The still would cause a packet of trouble if found and it's useless trying to hide it."

Dick stopped tinkering and the lead coil was handed over. It was melted down and poured into little white clay moulds which were prepared from beautifully carved patterns, sculptured by a Dutchman. Replicas, conforming perfectly as to colour (silver-grey) and size, were made of the various metal parts of German uniforms. Swastikas and German eagles, tunic buttons by the score and troops' belt-clasps with the 'Gott mit uns' monogram. The Brewing and Distilling Society resumed the title of its earlier days and became 'The Brewing Society Only,' a sad reminder of a glory that had passed.

The most important item of the German uniform was the long greatcoat of field-grey, and it was here that the Dutch came in; their greatcoats, with minor alterations, could pass in electric light as German greatcoats. The officers' service caps were cleverly manufactured by our specialists. Leather parts, such as belts and revolver holsters, were made from linoleum, and leggings from cardboard.

At a passing-out test we had to compliment Neave and the various Dutch and Britishers who had done the work. The uniforms would pass—though not in broad daylight at close range, yet under almost any other conditions.

In the meantime I had not been idle, having my share of the bargain to accomplish. From thin plywood I cut out an irregular oblong shape, large enough to fill a hole through which a man could pass. The edge was chamfered to assist in making a snug fit, and I gave one side a preliminary coat of white paint. To the reverse side I fixed a frame with swivelling wooden clamps, and I prepared wooden wedges. The result was christened 'Shovewood IV'!

I asked Hank Wardle to help me in the preparation of the escape. This tall, robust Canadian, with his imperturbable manner and laconic remarks, could be relied upon to do the right thing in an awkward moment. His brain was not slow, though his casual and somewhat lazy manner belied it.

Under the stage in the theatre we quietly sawed through the laths of the ceiling and then through the plaster. Small pieces of it fell to the floor with ominous crashes, but we were able to prevent most of it from capsizing. Then I had to descend with a sheet-rope to the room below, which was empty. The door connecting it to a corridor which passed

over the main courtyard gate and thence to the attic of the
guardroom was locked. I tested it with my 'universal key.'
It opened easily, so I relocked and began work. I had prepared two collapsible stools which fitted one on top of the
other. Standing on these, I could reach the ceiling. Hank
held 'Shovewood IV' in position while I carved out the
plaster of the ceiling to fit it. Eventually, when pressed
home and wedged from above, it fitted well enough to give
the impression of an irregular oblong crack in the real
ceiling. With a pencil I drew lines which looked like more
cracks in various directions, to camouflage the shape of the

Hank Wardle

oblong, and remove any impression that an observer might
have of a concealed hole.

The colour of the ceiling was exasperatingly difficult to
match and it took a long time to achieve a similarity of
tint between it and 'Shovewood IV.' This latter work necessitated many visits, as each coat had to dry and then be
examined in place.

Airey Neave was ready to go and was becoming impatient.
"Look here, Pat," he protested, "I've got pieces of German
clothing and gear lying about all over our quarters. It's
damn tricky stuff to hide, and if the search comes I'm
finished. When is your hole going to be ready?"

"Keep your hair on, Airey!" I retorted. "You'll go in due course, but not before it's a finished job. Remember, I want others to use this exit too."

"I wish you'd get a move on, all the same. The weather is fairly mild now, but remember, we've had snow already and we're going to have a lot more soon. I don't want to freeze to death on a German hillside."

"Don't worry, Airey! I see your point of view," I said sympathetically. "I need two more days. You can reckon on leaving on Monday evening. The 'take-off' will be immediately after evening *Appell.*"

Even when I finally launched Neave, I was not completely satisfied with my 'Shovewood.' It was so nearly perfect that I wanted to make it absolutely foolproof. Its position in the sealed-off room was unique, and I felt we could unleash officers at intervals 'until the cows came home.'

I made a reconnaissance along the German corridor and, unlocking a further door, found myself in the attic over the German guardhouse. Probably nobody had been near the attic since Niki climbed in through the skylight and left by the window at the end. The window had not been touched, but that route was no longer possible since a sentry had been positioned to cover the whole of that wall-face beneath the window. A staircase in the attic led down to the guards' quarters below. Layers of dust on everything, including the floor, were my greatest bugbear, and as I returned I had to waft dust painstakingly over fingerprints and footprints by waving a handkerchief carefully in the air over the marks.

The plan was simple enough. I would send the escapers out in two pairs on successive evenings immediately after a change of the guard stationed at the front entrance to the guardhouse. Thus the new sentry would not know what German officers, if any, might have entered the guardhouse in the previous two hours. The two officers escaping would descend the guardhouse staircase and walk out through the hall. This was the most risky part of the attempt. The stairs and hall would be well lit, and a stray

guardhouse Goon might wonder where two strange German officers had suddenly descended from. The moment of
descent from the attic had therefore to be chosen when a
period of comparative calm in guardhouse activity was
anticipated. I insisted that the two officers, on reaching the
guardhouse entrance, were to stop in full view of the
sentry, put on their gloves and exchange casual remarks in
well-prepared German, before marching boldly down the
ramp to the first gateway. This 'act' was calculated to
absorb any shock of surprise that the sentry might have if,
for instance, two strange officers were to suddenly issue
from the entrance and quickly march away.

The evening for the attempt arrived. After the last
Appell all concerned with the escape disappeared into the
theatre block instead of to our own quarters. Various senior
officers and generals lived in the theatre block and movement in this direction did not arouse suspicion.

The two escapers, Airey Neave and Lieutenant Tony
Luteyn (Royal Netherlands Indies Army) were wearing no
fewer than three sets of apparel—apart from some delicate
pieces of accoutrement, which were carried in a bag. Over
everything, they wore British army greatcoats and trousers;
underneath came their German uniforms and underneath
again they carried their civilian attire.

Although we thought highly of the German uniforms,
they were not good enough for a permanent disguise—the
cardboard leggings, for instance, would not have looked
very well after heavy rain!—and we decided they should be
discarded and hidden in the woods outside the Castle.

Our stooges were posted and we climbed—the two
escapers with some difficulty owing to their bulk—under
the stage. I opened up 'Shovewood IV,' and one after the
other we dropped quietly into the room below. I led the
way, opening the doors, along the corridor and into the
German attic. British army attire had already been discarded. The German uniforms were brushed down and
everything was checked. I said to Airey:

"It takes me eleven minutes to return, clean up and

close 'Shovewood.' Don't move before eleven minutes are over."

"Right!" replied Airey, "but I'm not going to hang around long after that. I shall take the first opportunity of a quiet period on the staircase and landings underneath us."

"Don't forget to take it easy at the guardhouse door-way," I reminded him; "remember, you own the place.

"Good-bye and good luck!" I added, "and don't come back here. Much as we like you, we don't want to see you again!"

We shook hands and I left them. I relocked doors, re-dusted traces, mounted the rope of sheets and, with Hank's assistance, wedged 'Shovewood IV' firmly in place. Before Hank and I had issued from under the stage, our watchers reported a perfect exit from the guardhouse. The 'act' went off, the German sentry saluted smartly, and our two passed on. We did not expect much difficulty from the first gate. The guard on duty would see the officers coming and the gate itself was under a covered archway very dimly lit. After this, the two were to pass through the German courtyard under another archway, of which the gates at this hour were open. They would then reach the bridge over the moat, before having to pass the last sentry at the outermost gate. There was a possibility, however, of by-passing this last gate, which might require a password.

I knew of the existence of a small garden gate in the parapet at the beginning of the moat bridge. I had re-marked on it on my first entry into the Castle just a year before. This gate gave on to a small path which led down-wards into the moat. From what I knew of the geography of the camp, I always suspected this path might lead around to the roadway, down which we passed when going for exercise in the park. If our two officers could regain this roadway, they had merely to pass some occupied Ger-man barracks and proceed a hundred yards to a locked gate in the outer wall around the Castle grounds. This gate was not guarded as far as we knew, the area would be in pitch darkness, and the wall with its barbed wire could therefore be climbed.

Our first two disappeared towards the moat bridge, and we heard no more of them.

The next day we covered the two *Appells*. Van den Heuvel arranged this with perfect equanimity. It was another professional secret of his which he promised to reveal if I told him how I launched the escapers!

In the evening I repeated the performance of the night before and Hyde-Thompson and his Dutch colleague departed from the camp.

We could not conceal four absences, so that, at the next morning *Appell*, four officers were found missing. The Jerries became excited and everyone was promptly confined to barracks.

As the day wore on and the German searches proved fruitless, their impatience grew. So did that of the prisoners. Every German who entered the courtyard was barracked until, finally, the riot squad appeared.

With rifles pointed at the windows, orders were issued that nobody was to look out. Needless to say, this made matters worse. The French started shouting their usual colloquy *"Où sont les Allemands?"* and so on. The British began singing, *"Deutschland, Deutschland UNTER alles!"* —our revised version of the German National Anthem— to the accompaniment of musical instruments, imitating a German brass band. Mock heads began bobbing up and down at windows and the inevitable shooting started, followed by the sounds of splintering glass.

From a protected vantage-point, I suddenly saw Van den Heuvel sally forth into the courtyard, having presumably opened the courtyard door with his own 'universal key.' His face was black with anger. He headed straight for the German officer in charge of operations, and with indignation showing in his every movement, he told the Jerry in his own language what he thought of him and his race and their manner of treating defenceless prisoners. His anger was justified, for hardly had he finished speaking when the

French announced in no uncertain terms from their windows that an officer had been hit.

This calmed the Jerries at once. The German officer removed his riot squad and went to investigate. Lieutenant
Maurice Fahy had received a ricochet bullet under one of
his shoulder-blades. He was removed to hospital and peace
settled on the camp once more. Fahy lost the use of one
arm through this episode. In spite of this he was never repatriated to France because he was listed as '*Deutschfeindlich,*' i.e. 'an enemy of Germany.' The personal particulars
of every allied officer POW were annotated with either a
little green or red flag. The latter meant '*Deutschfeindlich.*'

*   *   *   *   *

By the winter of 1941-42, when Neave's escape took
place, the forging of escapers' credentials had improved
considerably. A number of expert forgers were at work,
with the result that every British officer was eventually
equipped with a set of papers, as well as maps, a small
amount of German money and a compass.

Identity papers were reproduced by various means. The
imitation by hand of a typewritten document is very difficult. There were only two officers in Colditz capable of
doing it, and they worked overtime. The German Gothic
script, commonly used on identity cards, while appearing
to be even more difficult is, in fact, easier to copy, and our
staff employed on this form of printing was correspondingly
larger. The day arrived when a Polish officer, Lieutenant
Niedenthal (nicknamed 'Sheriff'), made a typewriter. This
proved a great boon and speeded up the work of our printing department considerably. The typewriter was of the
one-finger variety and its speed of reproduction could not
be compared with any normal machine, but it had the
great advantage of being dismountable into half a dozen
innocent-looking pieces of wood which did not require to
be concealed from the Germans. Only the letters attached
to their delicate arms had to be hidden.

Each officer was responsible for the concealment of his

own papers and aids; the idea being that, under such conditions, it was easier to make use of escape opportunities if
they arose without warning. One or two such occasions did
arise and were made good use of, thanks to this system. As
for concealment of the contraband, many carried their
papers about with them, relying on native wit to hide them
in the event of a 'blitz' search by the Jerries.

Searches occurred from time to time at unpredictable
intervals. Sometimes we had warning; at other times none.

On one of the latter occasions I was busily doing some
work with a large hammer when the Goons entered our
quarters.

I seized a towel lying on a nearby table and put the
hammer in its folds. The method of search was systematic.
All officers were herded into a room at one end of our
quarters and locked in. The Germans then turned all the
other rooms inside out. They tore up floorboards, knocked
away chunks of plaster from the walls, jabbed the ceilings,
examined electric lights and every piece of furniture,
turned bedclothes and mattresses inside out, removed all
the contents of every cupboard, turned over the cupboards,
emptied the solid contents of all tins on to the floor, poured
our precious homemade brews down the sinks, broke up
games, cut open pieces of soap, emptied water-closets,
opened chimney flues, and spread the kitchen fire and any
other stove ashes all over the floor.

Then, coming to the last room, each prisoner was
stripped in turn, and even the seams of his clothing
searched before he was released into the main section of
the quarters, there to be faced with the indescribable chaos
of the Germans' handiwork. The latter usually found some
contraband, though rarely anything of major importance.

On this particular occasion when I had the hammer
wrapped up in the towel, as soon as my turn came to be
searched I put the towel casually on the table beside which
the Jerry officer stood, and began stripping. When my
clothing had been scrutinised, I dressed, picked up my
'loaded' towel and walked out of the room!

Then there was the time when the Gestapo decided to search the camp and show the German *Wehrmacht* how this should be conducted. They employed electric torches to search remote crevices and borrowed the keys of the camp to make the rounds. Before they had finished, both the keys and the torches had disappeared, and they left with their tails between their legs. The German garrison were as pleased as Punch. We returned the keys, after making suitable impressions, to their rightful guardians.

*   *   *   *   *

To return to the thread of my story. The four escapers were well equipped for their journey to the Swiss frontier, towards which they headed. They travelled most of the way by train. Neave and Luteyn crossed the frontier safely. Neave was the first Britisher to make a home run from Colditz.

Hyde-Thomson and his companion were caught by station controls at Ulm. They brought back the news that Neave and Luteyn had also been caught at the same station. There had been some R.A.F. bombing, which was followed by heavy controls for the purpose of rounding up plane crews that had parachuted. Neave and Luteyn had, however, managed to escape again from the police-station during a moment's laxness on the part of their guards. By the time Hyde-Thomson reached Ulm, the Jerries were on their toes. Maybe they had received warning; in any case, once he was suspected, he had no real hope of success.

Hyde-Thomson's bad luck taught us another lesson. We paid for our experience dearly! From now on, no more than two escapers at a time would travel the same route.

[Airey Neave—at the time of publishing Conservative Member of Parliament for Abingdon—has written his adventures in a book entitled *They Have Their Exits*, published by Hodder & Stoughton in March 1953.]

CHAPTER XIV

THE INFORMER

AS I have mentioned, I was not completely satisfied with 'Shovewood IV.' When, after a week, the Germans had calmed down, Hank and I paid a surreptitious visit to the theatre and I applied a new coat of paint to the 'Shovewood,' for I knew that when more officers escaped the German efforts to discover the exit would be redoubled.

When the paint was dry we paid another visit to check the colour, and during this visit I had a suspicion we had been followed—a vague impression and no more. I was more careful than ever about our movements and disappearance under the stage. It was curious, though, that the *fouine,* our German 'ferret,' paid a visit to the theatre and I even heard him speaking (presumably to a prisoner) close to the stage.

The next two officers were preparing for their exit, due for the following Sunday, when, on Saturday, we learnt that the Jerries had been under the stage and discovered my 'Shovewood.' This was more suspicious than ever, as no traces were left to indicate the position of the 'Shovewood,' buried as it was under a four-inch layer of dirt and rubble, which extended uniformly beneath the whole of the stage; an area of one hundred square yards.

My suspicions increased further when the German Regimental Sergeant-Major, Gephard, who on rare occasions became human, remarked in a conversation with Peter Allan:

"The camouflage was *prachtvoll*! I examined the ceiling myself, and would not have suspected a hole."

"Well, how did you discover it then?" asked Peter.

"*Ach!* That cannot be revealed, but we would never have found it without help."

"Whose help? A spy?"

"I cannot say," replied Gephard with a meaning look, then, changing the subject:

"The photographer has been called to take photographs of the camouflage for the escape museum."

"So you make records of our escapes?"

"*Jawohl!* We have a room kept as a museum. It is very interesting! After the war, perhaps you shall see it."

The remark concerning 'help' was reported to the various senior officers and escape officers. It meant we had to act in future under the assumption that there was a 'stooge' or 'planted man' in the camp and, sure enough, it transpired that there was.

Gephard was a strange character. He gave the impression of being sour and ruthless with his harsh, deep voice and unsmiling face. But he was probably the most intelligent of the Jerries at Colditz. I am sure he was one of the first to realise who would win the war! Apart from this, under his gruffness, there was honesty, and it is possible he disliked the idea of sending blackmailed spies into a camp, enough to warrant his dropping hints about it.

The stooge was not unearthed for some time. There was no evidence from the theatre escape to commit anyone. However, certain Poles had been keeping their eye on one of their own officers over an extended period and had slowly accumulated evidence.

Not very long after the theatre escape, we heard a rumour that the Poles were about to hang one of their own officers. The same day a Pole was hurriedly removed from the camp.

What I gleaned from Niki and others—the Poles were reticent about the whole incident—was that they had held a court martial and found the man guilty of aiding the enemy, though under duress. The officer had been blackmailed by the Germans, having been tempted in a weak moment while he was ill in a hospital somewhere in Germany. He was allowed to return home and see his family, and thereafter was threatened with their disappearance if he did not act as an informer.

I would go so far as to say that the German army officers
in the camp did not use him willingly. They were probably
presented with an informer by the Gestapo and given
orders to employ him. This would also account for
Gephard's reaction in giving us the hint.

In any case, the upshot was that the Polish Senior Officer,
rather than have a dead body on his hands, called on the
German Commandant, told him the facts—which the Commandant did not deny—and gave the latter twenty-four
hours to remove the man.

*   *   *   *   *

Towards the end of 1941 the Goons also tried to per-
suade the French and Belgian officer prisoners to 'collab-
orate' and work with them. Their efforts in Colditz had
little success; only two or three Frenchmen disappeared.
The Germans were keen to employ engineers and chemical
experts. On a couple of days, a Goon officer addressed the
French and Belgian officers at the midday *Appell*—by this
time we were having three *Appells* daily—asking if there
were any more volunteers for work, saying that officers
should give in their names and state their professions in
order to see if they could be fitted into the 'Economy of the
Reich.' There was no response on the first day, except much
laughter and derisive cheers. On the second day a French
aspirant, Paul Durand, stepped smartly forward and said:

"I would like to work for the Germans."

There was a gasp of surprise from the assembled parade
and a beam from the Goon officer.

"You really want to work for the Reich?"

"Yes, I would prefer to work for twenty Germans than
for one Frenchman."

More gasps and looks of astonishment from the
prisoners!

"All right! What is your name?"

"My name is Durand, and I wish to make it clearly
understood that I would prefer to work for twenty Germans than for one Frenchman."

"Good! What is your profession?"

"Undertaker!"

Jacques Prot, a *sous-Lieutenant d'Artillerie*, was another Frenchman whose puckishness was irrepressible and whose quick-wittedness won him freedom and later glory. I have mentioned his name along with that of 'Scorgie' Price in connection with the requisitioning of the German dentist's hat and overcoat. Prot contrived to escape during a visit to the German dentist in the village of Colditz. The visit was an unheard-of relaxation, but he worked it. He set off under heavy guard with another Frenchman also suffering from some galloping disease of the teeth. 'Scorgie' Price's teeth did not warrant the visit and he was left behind. The other Frenchman was *Sous-Lieutenant d'Artillerie* Guy de Frondeville. They escaped from the guards when leaving the dentist's house, and that was that.

The two friends separated for safety at Leipzig. Prot, tall, dark, and well-built, aged about twenty-six, went through Cologne to Aix-la-Chapelle. As he neared the frontier he saw to his horror that his false papers were not at all like those in current use. The frontier station was heavily patrolled and guarded. He closely followed the crowd, mostly Belgian passengers, towards the barrier. He was at his wits' end. Then the light dawned! He grabbed a suitcase out of the hand of an astonished fellow-passenger and took to his heels, through the barrier and away. The psychology behind this move was inspired. For the passenger created a tremendous uproar, attracting everybody's attention for a few minutes—then, as soon as the Germans were fully aware of what had happened, they couldn't care less. An escaping French officer might have been something, but a thief running away with a Belgian's suitcase did not raise the slightest interest!

Nine days out from Colditz, Prot arrived in Paris, to the surprise and joy of his family, on Christmas Eve 1941.

He reached Tunis via the French Free Zone in 1942, and joined the 67th Artillery Regiment (Algerian). From Paris he returned the suitcase to the owner, whose address

The Snake Dance, New Year's Eve (1941-42)

he found inside, and from Tunis he sent to the German dentist a large consignment of real coffee with apologies for the removal of his hat and coat. He fought through the Tunisian Campaign to Casino, where during the First Offensive (Mount Belvedere) on January 29th, 1944, he gave his life for France. May his honoured memory remain long with his countrymen as it is cherished by every Escaper of Colditz!

*   *   *   *   *

Christmas 1941 and New Year's Eve were gay affairs. There was deep snow everywhere and there was a spirit of hope, for the Germans were halted in Russia and having a bad time.

Our cellar of wines and firewater added to the fun! Teddy Barton produced another good variety show which played to overflowing houses for three nights. On New Year's Eve, towards midnight, the British started a 'snake chain': men in single file each with an arm on the shoulder of the man in front. Laughing and singing, the snake passed through the various quarters of the Castle, growing in length all the time, until there must have been nearly two hundred officers of all nationalities on it. As midnight struck, the snake uncoiled itself into a great circle in the courtyard and struck up 'Auld Lang Syne.' The whole camp joined in, as the courtyard refrain was taken up from the windows in the Castle. The snow was still falling. It had a peaceful and calming influence on everyone. If we prisoners could ever have felt happy and unrepressed, we were happy that evening.

CHAPTER XV

WINTER MEDLEY

THERE were many heavy snowfalls during the winter of 1941–42. I used to pass hours in a sleepy trance looking out of my window, hypnotised by the slowly gyrating flakes. I think it was a Chinese philosopher who once said that everything in Nature can be turned to man's advantage, if only man can find the way! I pondered long over the possibilities of using snow in an escape. I thought of snowmen and then of snow tunnels, but the stuff melted so quickly. A short snow tunnel maybe—and as I stared out of my window, once more I saw an opportunity before my eyes.

There below, at the other end of the courtyard, was the canteen, and at a high level above the canteen were the dormer windows of that room into which only Niki had once been, over a year ago, and which was sealed off from the end room (the curved room) of our quarters. There was a small flat roof over the canteen doorway which abutted both a window of the curved room and also a vertical slate-covered gable of the sealed room. The window-sill was at the level of the roof. The snow on the flat roof was nearly three feet thick.

Here was an opportunity not to be missed. I had no idea where we could go from the sealed room, but Niki had reported a further door opening on to the German quarters.

'Scruffy' Orr Ewing and another British officer, Lieutenant Colin McKenzie, M.C., Seaforth Highlanders, had always wanted to tackle this room, and as they were high on the escape roster I gave them the plan and offered to help. Our curved-room window was, as usual, barred, and the filing of bars would be visible to anyone in the courtyard under normal circumstances. Certainly any persons climbing out of the window would have been seen. Now the snow hid everything.

The bars were cut in no time and Scarlet O'Hara manufactured thin metal sleeves so that the cut bars could be replaced and the sleeves slid over the ends. The metal was worked to a superlative fit and when in place each broken bar could be shaken without its falling out. Quick-drying black paint completed the camouflage after every workshift.

A short snow tunnel of four yards' length was burrowed. It was shaped like an arch, one foot nine inches high, resting on the flat roof. The snow roof caved in a little at one point but some cardboard helped to prop it. The tunnel did not melt with my body heat but, on the contrary, formed a compact, interior ice-wall. On reaching the vertical gable I removed some slates and found only laths and plaster beyond. This presented no difficulty. After a day's work the hole was big enough and the three of us crawled through to inspect the sealed room—it was the middle of the afternoon. We were examining the door into the German quarters when we received an alarm signal. Hauptmann Priem and a couple of his stooges on one of their lightning 'catch you out' visits had entered the courtyard. He headed straight for the British door and immediately started a close scrutiny of the British quarters—starting, unfortunately, in the curved room. We were trapped and the bars which had been cut were not in place! It was also standard routine for the Jerries to tap all window bars. For one moment the officers in the room thought the Jerries might overlook our window as it opened into the courtyard and was not therefore as suspect as windows facing the outside of the Castle. But alas! They opened the window, saw the gaping hole in the bars, and then the fun began.

Priem sent an N.C.O. along the snow tunnel. We could see him coming. In a matter of seconds I gathered up the tools we had brought—a hammer, screwdriver, a small saw, a file and some keys, and forcing open one of the dormer windows I have already mentioned, I shouted to a couple of Britishers walking around the courtyard.

"Tools coming out; save them, for heaven's sake!"

Lockwood was one of the two Britishers; he immediately

A man from Mars

saw the position. The particular window I was at had never been opened since Colditz had become a prison! The tools descended and, before an astonished sentry's gaze, Kenneth collected them and headed for the Polish doorway. He had disappeared before the sentry, who was

standing close to the canteen, had recovered from his surprise.

This was not the end, in another five seconds I followed,
leaving the window just as the Jerry N.C.O. began waving
his revolver, with his head and arm protruding through
the hole in the gable. I was fed up with repeated 'solitary'
confinements; this would mean another month and I was
just not going to do it. Although the snow in the cobbled
courtyard had been cleared, there was a thin film about
half an inch thick on the ground. This might soften the
drop, which was about twenty feet after a three-yard slide
down to the gutter from the dormer window. I leaped out
of the window, slithered, fell, and landed squarely, then
doubled up forward, hitting my forehead hard on the
ground. I wore a balaclava helmet with only eyes and nose
showing, many layers of outer clothing, and thick leather
gloves. To the sentry, just recovering from the rain of
tools, the descending body must have looked like a man
from Mars. As I picked myself up and ran for it, he stood
transfixed and I was able to make a clean getaway. Orr
Ewing and McKenzie did not follow. By that time the
Jerry in the hole had advanced sufficiently to be able to
make respectable use of his revolver.

After this setback we had another in which the Dutch
came off badly. They lived on the floor just above us,
and had discovered the existence of a hollow vertical shaft
in the outer wall of the Castle. It was a mediæval lavatory.
The Castle had many curious buttresses and towers, and
once before, during explorations, the Dutch had come
across a secret staircase, bricked up in the thickness of one
of the walls. Unfortunately, it only led to another floor-
level and was of little use for escape purposes. It may have
seen curious uses in bygone days!

The vertical shaft, on the contrary, held definite
promise. Vandy constructed a superbly camouflaged entrance to it in the urinal wall of the Dutch lavatory. As the
urinal was kept wholesome by applications of a creosote-
and-tar mixture, Vandy had little difficulty in obtaining a

supply of it from the Jerries, which served to hide the shaft entrance from even the most experienced snoop or 'ferret.' The entrance was about three feet from the ground and was closed with a thick concrete slab. Beyond the urinal was a small turret room. Through the outer wall of this turret, Vandy pierced a second hole which he camouflaged equally well by means of a door, made of the original stones of the wall cemented together. The door swung open on pivots and gave directly on to the vertical shaft, which was about one yard by four yards in size. The drop to the bottom was seventy feet. Vandy had a neat rope-ladder made for the descent.

At this stage he came to me with a proposal for a joint escape effort if I would provide him with some experienced tunnellers. This was not difficult. I proposed Jim Rogers, engineer of the long Laufen tunnel in which twelve hundred bed boards were used, and Rupert Barry, the best tunneller of our team, who had constructed the shorter Laufen woodshed tunnel. When Jim Rogers's huge bulk was not tunnelling, it was sitting on a stool playing the guitar. Jim took up the instrument on his arrival at Colditz, saying he would give his wife a surprise when he returned home after the war. He never mentioned it in his letters. By the time he left prison camp years later, he was a highly proficient player. Without considering the difficult classical music he played, it was sufficiently amazing to watch his massive fists manipulating the delicate strings. His index finger alone could easily 'stop' about three strings at once.

He and Rupert, with Dutch assistants, set to work at the bottom of the shaft, but the going was hard and rocky in parts. Tunnelling continued for a week and then the Jerries suddenly pounced. It was becoming painfully obvious by now that they had sound detectors around the Castle walls. Our tunnellers were experienced, knew exactly what they were up against and could be trusted not to do anything stupid. Yet again they were taken by surprise. This time Priem and his team of ferrets entered the Castle and made straight for the place where the shaft was located at ground-level. This implied that the Germans knew the invisible geography of the camp, presumably from plans of the Castle in their possession. Without a moment's hesitation, Priem set his men to attack a certain false wall with pickaxes, and in less than ten minutes they had pierced it and a man put his head and arm through and shone a torch up and down the shaft.

The two tunnellers on shift had succeeded in climbing the seventy feet, one at a time—for the rope-ladder was not reckoned strong enough to carry two—and Vandy was busy pulling up the ladder when the torch flashed around the shaft. A few seconds later and the ladder would have been out of sight. The Jerries would have had no clue as to the entrance and the betting was that they would not search for an underground tunnel entrance on the third floor of the Castle. It was such a close shave that Vandy was not even sure they had seen the dangling ladder, but, unluckily for Vandy and his team, they had.

Nevertheless, the tunnellers had time to clear out and Vandy was able to complete the sealing of the two entrances, with the result that when the Jerries arrived in the upper stories they were at a complete loss. Eventually they pierced new openings on the same lines as the 'blitz' hole made down below. They first reached the small turret room, where, unluckily for all, they found important booty. Vandy had hidden much contraband in this room; no fewer than four complete German uniforms—our joint work—were found; and also Vandy's secret *Appell* 'stooges.' After this débâcle he told me the following story of his 'stooges.'

During one of the periodic visits of the Castle masons, doing repairs, he had managed to bribe one of them into giving him a large quantity of ceiling plaster. The Dutch amateur sculptor had carved a couple of life-size, officer-type busts which were cleverly painted (I saw one later) and as realistic as any of Madame Tussaud's waxworks. They were christened Max and Moritz by Vandy. Each bust had two iron hoops fixed underneath the pedestal, which was shaped to rest on a man's arm, either upright, or upside-down hanging from the hoops. A shirt collar and tie were fitted to the bust and, finally, a long Dutch overcoat was draped over the bust's shoulders.

When not in action the dummy hung suspended under the forearm of the bearer, concealed by the folds of the overcoat. In fact, to outward appearances the bearer was carrying an overcoat over his arm. When the *Appell* was called, officers would muster and fall into three lines. With a screen of two assistants and standing in the middle line of the three, the bearer unfurled the overcoat, an army cap was placed on the dummy's head by one assistant and a pair of top boots placed neatly under the coat in the position of 'attention' by the other assistant. The dummy was held shoulder high and the helpers formed up close to one another to camouflage the proximity of the 'carrier' officer to his Siamese twin!

The ruse had worked perfectly for the *Appells* in connection with the Dutch park escape and the theatre escape. Although Max and Moritz were discovered by the Jerries in Vandy's hide, they were found as unclothed plaster busts and Vandy hoped that he might be able to play the trick again.

CHAPTER XVI

THE RHINE MAIDEN

SINCE Niki's last escape attempt over the guardhouse roof, and two successive attempts from hospitals by a Lieutenant Joseph Just, which took him to the Swiss border but alas! not over it, the Poles seemed to retire from the escape front. Of course they were pestered for a long time by the 'informer,' whom they must have suspected and who must have hampered their efforts greatly. They were also liable to be blackmailed for the slightest offence, as their families were at the mercy of the Germans. In January 1942, without any warning, they were told to pack. With many regrets we said good-bye, and as we shook hands we expressed the mutual wish:

"*Auf Wiedersehen—nach dem Krieg!*"

We saw very few of them again. They went to semi-underground fortress camps in the Posnan area. A very few managed to trek westward towards the end of the war. Niki died of tuberculosis.

For a long time the Polish rooms were vacant. Then, one spring morning, the 'ghetto' arrived. French Jewish officers sifted out from many camps were gathered together and sent to Colditz. Why were they being incarcerated here? The question made one reflect a little as to what was to be the ultimate fate of all the Colditz inmates. We were 'bad boys,' and a public danger and nuisance. I, personally, did not think that we had much hope of surviving the war. If the Allies won, which we considered almost a certainty, Hitler and his maniacs would see that all possible revenge was wreaked before they descended the abyss and their Führer fulfilled the prophecy of his favourite opera, 'Götterdämmerung.' The gathering of the French Jews was a bad omen. If the Germans won the war, they, at least, would not survive. Would we?

The French contingent had also been quiet for some time. They seemed to be resting on the laurels of Lebrun's escape for too long.

It was with pleasure therefore, although with considerable misgivings for its ultimate success, that I received the news of the commencement of a French tunnel. Its entrance was at the top of the clock-tower, a hundred feet from ground-level; that, at any rate, I thought, was a good beginning.

So many tunnels, and exits generally, begin at ground-level, that at Colditz, at least, it was almost a waste of time to start work in the conventional manner. If someone thought of a tunnel, we examined the attics; if someone thought of escaping by glider (do not laugh! for one was made in Colditz and is to this day, as far as I know, concealed there), we started, if possible, underground! The short Laufen tunnel and the Colditz canteen tunnel began at ground-level, although the entrances to both were under German lock and key. Clandestine entrances rose to the second-floor level in the theatre escape; hovered on the first floor with the snow tunnel; then rose to the third floor in the Dutch vertical-shaft tunnel, and now, the French capped all by starting their tunnel at the top of the clock-tower!

The most serious danger, of course, for all tunnel attempts nowadays in Colditz was that of sound detectors placed around the Castle. The lightning descents of Priem on our snow tunnel and on the Dutch tunnel were too speedy compared with what we could expect of normal Jerry vigilance. At the same time, as far as tunnel entrances were concerned, German scrutiny of floors and walls decreased in inverse ratio as one increased one's height from the ground!

The French tunnel was a gigantic undertaking. I shall leave it for the present at its entrance.

Further French originality displayed itself shortly after their tunnel had begun. One spring afternoon a mixed batch of French, Dutch, and British were marching through the third gateway leading down to the exercise ground, or park as it was called. The majority had just 'wheeled right,' down the ramp roadway, when a gorgeous-looking German Lady passed by. She haughtily disdained to look at the prisoners, and walked primly past, going up the ramp towards the German courtyard of the Castle. There were low whistles of admiration from the more bawdy-minded prisoners—for she was a veritable Rhine maiden with golden blonde hair. She wore a broad-brimmed hat, smart blouse and skirt, and high-heeled shoes; she was large as well as handsome—a fitting consort for a German Demi-God!

As she swept past us, her fashionable-looking wrist-watch fell from her arm at the feet of Squadron-Leader Paddon, who was marching in front of me. Paddon was familiarly known as 'Never-a-dull-moment' Paddon, because he was always getting into trouble! The Rhine maiden had not noticed her loss, but Paddon, being a gentleman, picked up the watch and shouted:

"Hey, Miss! You've dropped your watch."

The Rhine maiden, like a barque under full sail, had already tacked to port, and was out of sight. Paddon thereupon made frantic signs to the nearest guard, explaining:

"*Das Fräulein hat ihre Uhr verloren. Ja!—Uhr— verloren,*" and he held up the dainty article.

"*Ach so! Danke,*" replied the guard, grasping what had happened. He seized the watch from Paddon's hand and shouted to a sentry in the courtyard to stop the Lady.

The Lady was, by now, primly stepping towards the other (main) gateway which led out of the camp. The sentry stopped her, and immediately became affable, looking, no doubt, deeply into her eyes from which, unfortunately, no tender light responded! "Hm!" the sentry reflected, as she did not reply to his cajoling. "She is dumb or very haughty or just plain rude."

He looked at her again and noticed something—maybe the blonde hair had gone awry. The second scrutiny, at a yard's distance, was enough for him. By the time our guard arrived panting with the watch, the Rhine maiden stood divested of her *Tarnhelmet*, a sorrowful sight, minus her wig and spring bonnet, revealing the head of Lieutenant Bouley (Chasseur Alpin), who unhappily did not speak or understand a word of German.

This escape had been the result of many months of

Paddon picks up the fateful watch

patient effort and was prepared with the assistance of the officer's wife in France. The French were allowed to receive parcels direct from their next-of-kin, which made this possible. He had a complete lady's outfit including silk stockings. The golden hair was a triumph of the wigmaker's art, of real hair, collected, bleached, curled, and sewn together. The wig was put together in Colditz. The large straw bonnet was the product of French patterns and Colditz straw weaving.

The transformation had been practised for weeks and was a conjuring trick which, I regret, I never saw enacted. The 'conjurer' had three accomplices and the usual 'stooges' to distract momentarily the attention of the guards as he turned the corner out of the gateway leading to the park. At this point, the 'conjurer' could count on a few seconds of 'blind-spot,' which might be drawn out to, say, ten or twelve seconds by a good 'stooge' attending to the guard immediately behind him. The guards were ranged along the ranks on both sides at intervals of ten yards.

Part of the transformation was done on the march, prior to arrival at the corner—for instance, strapping on the watch, pulling up the silk stockings, the rouging of lips and the powdering of the face. Once in the gateway, the high-heeled shoes were put on. The blouse and bosoms were in place, under a loose cloak around his shoulders. The skirt was tucked up around his waist. His accomplices held the wig, the hat, and the lady's bag.

There is a moral to this story which is worth recording. I had not been informed of the forthcoming attempt and certainly I sympathised with the French in their desire for complete surprise. It was much better, for instance, that the parade going to the park should be unconscious of what was taking place. The participants behaved naturally in consequence, whereas the least whispering or craning of necks or rising on tiptoe—any conscious movement—might have upset the effort. Yet the fact of having informed me would not have made much difference to all this. Neither would I have been able to warn all the British on the parade; it would have been dangerous. Nevertheless, the moral emerges: the fateful coincidence that I happened to be behind Paddon on the walk; that, if I had been warned, I might have nipped the watch incident in the bud, and the escape would probably have succeeded.

This escape, as usual, closed the park to the prisoners

for a period. Hardly had walks recommenced, however, when Vandy announced another attempt to be made by his contingent. I asked from what direction, and he answered, "Vrom the park, ov course!"

The 'privilege' of going to the park for a two-hour walk around a barbed-wire enclosure at the bottom of the valley was continually being withdrawn by the Goons, because of insubordination of the prisoners, in consequence of escapes or just to annoy us. During those periods in the late spring of 1942, when the privilege was not withheld, the Dutch used to sit together on the grass in the middle of the wire enclosure while one of them would read to the others. Personally, I did not go very often to the park—it used to depress me. The Goon sentries stood close up to the wire, so that when officers walked round the path of the perimeter, they came within a few yards of them. I am sure the Germans put English-speaking sentries on this job who listened to one's every word. They could not have been edified, because many prisoners made a point of saying exactly what they thought of the Goons, the German race, and the Third Reich in general, for their benefit.

On the day appointed by Vandy, I went there for a change, and noticed the Dutch in their usual group, with a huge, black-bearded man in his army cloak sitting in the centre, reading to them. I happened to notice also that he was fidgeting all the time, as if he had the itch. He held a book and continued reading for an hour and a half. The walk lasted officially two hours, but a quarter of an hour was allowed at the beginning and at the end to line us up and count the numbers present.

The whistle blew and the prisoners slowly collected near the gate where they lined up to be counted before marching back to the Castle. All went off as usual and we started to march back. It was the custom that, as soon as the prisoners left the park, the Goons unleashed their dogs. Suddenly hoarse shouts were heard behind us. We were halted and again counted. This time the Goons found one prisoner missing.

What had happened was that the huge Dutchman with
the black beard had been sitting on a small Dutchman
who had been entirely hidden by his black cloak (an alternative to the Dutch colonial army overcoat) and who had
dug a 'grave' for himself. The others had all helped to hide
the earth and stones and cover the small Dutchman with
grass. When the whistle blew they moved towards the gate,
leaving the little man in his grave, ready to escape when
the coast was clear. They managed to cover up the first
count so that the Goons did not notice that a man was
missing. By bad luck, one of the Alsatian police dogs took
it into his head to chase another. The leading animal ran
straight over the 'grave' and the other followed. When he
reached the grave the second dog was attracted, possibly by
the newly dug earth, and started digging; in a few seconds
he unearthed the Dutchman.

Vandy had once more employed a dummy Dutchman—
the third he had made. When the alarm was raised, however, he had not used it again. He knew the parade would
be carefully scrutinised and he hoped to save the dummy.
He was out of luck. The Germans searched all the officers
carefully before they re-entered the Castle and the dummy
was found in its full regalia.

It was always questionable whether a dog was much use
immediately after a parade, unless he found himself almost
on top of a body, because the ground must have reeked
with the scent of many human beings who had just vacated
the area. It cannot be denied, however, that in this case
the dogs found the man; whether it was by coincidence or
by astuteness, I do not know. The Germans were again
having the better of the battle of Colditz. We would have
to improve our technique. . . .

III

Escaper

CHAPTER XVII

THE 1942 FEELING

IN April 1942, I asked to be released from the post of escape officer. It was high time someone else took on the job. I had visions of a month or two of rest, followed by an attempt in which I could take part myself. As escape officer it had become morally impossible for me to take part in any escape.

Colonel Stainer replaced Colonel German in the New Year as Senior British Officer, after the latter's departure to another camp. I think Colonel German was the only

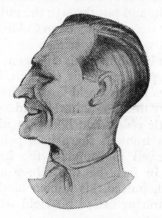

Ronnie Littledale

British Officer who was removed from Colditz, once having been incarcerated there. Needless to say he returned about a year later on account of further 'offences' against the German Reich.

I suggested Dick Howe as successor to the post of escape officer. I deputised once again for him in July, while he did a month's 'solitary.' After that he carried on for a long time.

Throughout 1941 the British contingent had slowly risen from a mere handful of seventeen officers to about forty-five. During 1942 the number rose further, until by the summer there were about sixty. Late arrivals included Major Ronnie Littledale and Lieutenant Michael Sinclair, both of Winchester and of the 60th Rifles, and ten Naval officers and two Petty Officers from Marlag Nord. Group-Captain Douglas Bader also arrived.

Ronnie Littledale and Michael Sinclair had escaped together from a camp in the north of Poland and had travelled South. They were given assistance by Poles and lived in a large town somewhere in Poland for a while. When properly organised they headed for Switzerland, but were trapped in Prague during a mass check-up of all its inhabitants on account of the assassination of Heydrich. They were caught and put through the mill, including torture, before they were despatched to Colditz.

Ronnie was a very rare specimen on this earth. There was not a flaw to be found in his character. Quiet and even shy in his ways yet firm in his opinions, he suffered 'the slings and arrows' of this world to strike harmlessly against him. He was very thin, too thin. He had 'been through it.' He looked a little older than his age, with hair thinning unmistakably in front. A sharp nose pointing towards a hatchet chin served to complete the impression of an ascetic, which, in fact, he was. He would never have admitted it, and, indeed, his human kindly side and his alert sense of humour belied his rigid self-discipline and dogged determination.

Fate was to draw us close together.

Before long Michael Sinclair, his colleague, had a court-martial charge read against him for an offence he had committed in his earlier camp. We waved him good-bye as he left for his trial under guard. He was completely equipped for a getaway with transformable clothing, chiefly of R.A.F. origin. His court martial was at Leipzig, but he managed to elude his guards in a lavatory at a Leipzig barracks before it took place, and a few days later turned up in

Cologne. There had been heavy Allied bombing and the colour of most of his clothing was unfortunate because a witch-hunt of R.A.F. parachute survivors was in progress. He was caught in the meshes and duly returned to Colditz under a three-man guard.

Returning escapers were bad for morale. Each successful getaway was like a tonic for the rest of the prisoners even though it usually meant one less bolt-hole for those who remained. Michael Sinclair felt this very much, though he had no reason to. His record clearly showed that he was the type of man who would not miss 'a hundred to one against' chance of an escape.

It was, nevertheless, becoming obvious to everybody that, once out of the Castle, it was an escaper's duty to take very heavy risks rather than return to the fold within the oppressive walls of Colditz. It was in the summer of 1942 I resolved I would not come back if I ever escaped again, and I know it was the decision which many others made as the months of 1942 dragged on. We already had one temporarily insane officer on our hands (he recovered after the war). He remained with us for months before the Germans were convinced he was not shamming, and we had to maintain a permanent guard from among our own number to see that he did not attempt suicide. The guard, which was worked on a roster, soon had to do double duty to cope with a second officer who tried to slash his wrist with a razor, but, luckily, made a poor job of it and was discovered in a washroom before he had completed his work. This type of guard duty had a decidedly bad effect on the guards.

Then there was a third British officer who was not so mad as he looked. He confided to me one day, early in 1941, when he was perfectly normal:

"Pat, I think the only way I shall ever escape from Colditz is by going insane."

"It's not a bad idea," I replied, "in so far as the Swiss have at last got things moving over the repatriation of wounded, sick, and insane POWs."

"I know."

"Do you realise what it means?" I said. "Have you thought out all the ramifications?"

"Well, it'll be a long job, I know."

"Much more than a long job! I read a book before the war called 'The Road to Endor.' It is the best escape book I have ever read. In it a British officer feigned madness for months—and what he went through was nobody's business. He nearly hanged himself. Yet it was child's play compared with what you would have to do in this war by way of convincing experts."

"I realise that," said the officer, "and I'm prepared for it. I'm ready to behave as insane before the whole camp and convince my friends also that I'm cuckoo."

"More than that," I said, "you'll have to write insane letters to your people at home! Have you considered that?"

"No," he admitted, "it might be better not to write at all."

"You're going to cause a lot of suffering, but if you're determined, go ahead. First, you'll have to have medical advice as to symptoms so that you can develop slowly and correctly. Your insanity will have to become your second nature. Do you realise there is a possibility of its becoming your real nature?"

"I've heard it," he agreed, "but I'm prepared to risk it."

"I shall have to obtain all the medical symptoms for you from the French camp doctor," I continued. "You must not approach him yourself because he is one of the first you will have to convince of your authenticity. The job will take six months at least before you get on to a repatriation train."

"Good, I'm ready to start as soon as you've got all the dope."

"All right," I concluded. "I'll let you know when I have it. I shall not tell anyone. If you mean to succeed, everyone around you must be convinced. It is the only way. If a rumour once starts that you're feigning, it will spread and eventually get to the Germans. Then you're finished for good."

Two months after this conversation I handed over my job to Dick Howe and told him of the case of our pseudo-lunatic. Dick would not believe me at first. He thought that our pet lunatic (for he was of the harmless type) had pulled the wool over my eyes. It was a tribute to the officer's acting!

The arrival of the Navy in force gave rise to an incident which echoed through the halls of Colditz for many a day. The 'new boys' arrived one evening at about 9 p.m. Howard Gee, who had helped in the affair of the canteen tunnel, was a civilian. He had volunteered for the expedition to help the Finns against Russia, had been captured by the Germans in Norway, and inevitably gravitated to Colditz. He was a clever man, aged about thirty, dark and handsome; he loved adventure and sought it out; journalism was one of his hobbies and practical joking was another. He spoke German fluently—so, upon the arrival of the Navy, he dressed up as the German camp doctor in one of our German uniforms (between the Dutch and ourselves there were still several wardrobes available). Our 'medium-sized' R.A.F. officer, as he called himself—he was 5 ft. high—acted as his British medical orderly, wearing a white jacket and apron. Entering the room where the Navy had just bedded down and bellowing with rage, Gee ordered them all out of bed to parade in front of him in their pyjamas. He shouted for a 'Dolmetscher'— that is, an interpreter—from among them. A fair-haired officer advanced and stood smartly at attention in front of him. In Colditz it was an unwritten law that nobody stood at attention before a German officer (except on *Appell*) unless ordered under threat to do so. The officer's action in this case, being unprecedented, inflamed our 'camp doctor' so much that he promptly ordered the 'Dolmetscher' two months' 'strenger Arrest,' otherwise 'solitary.' He then delivered a harangue, which the interpreter did his best to translate, saying the Navy were all lousy, that they should never have been allowed into the camp without first passing through the 'delouser' and consequently they would all be court martialled. Then, with vociferous references to *les papillons d'amour*—he used the French term —he commanded his British orderly to produce the bucket of 'blue.' This is a strong bright blue-coloured disinfectant which is applied to the body to kill lice, fleas, and so on. It is also a paint which takes weeks to remove. He made the parade strip naked and told the British orderly to apply a lavish coating of 'blue' to the bodies assembled. This done, he inspected the result, calling for more 'blue' where he thought it necessary, and then retired, still muttering threats and Prussian curses. The parade was left standing at attention, a row of bright blue nudists, while the laughter of the twenty or so 'old lags' who occupied the same room could be heard throughout the Castle.

The Navy saw the joke and Gee was known as the 'Herr Doktor' ever after.

Douglas Bader's arrival also heralded an increase in practical joking of the particular form which was known as 'Goon-baiting.' Bader, a character already famous for his exploits, was irrepressible, undaunted by catastrophe, a magnetic leader and a dangerous enemy. He had hardly been in Colditz a few weeks, when he—a man with no legs from the knees downwards—volunteered for partnership in an escape attempt over the roofs of the Castle!

Goon-baiting was a pastime indulged in when one had nothing better to do—a frequent occurrence in a POW camp. It varied from the most innocuous forms, such as dropping small pebbles from a hundred feet or so on to the head of a sentry, through less innocent types as the release of propaganda written on lavatory paper and dropped out of windows when the wind was favourable, up to the more staged variety like the case of the 'corpse.'

A life-size 'lay figure' was made out of palliasses and straw by Peter Storie Pugh and clothed in a worn-out battle-dress. We were having frequent air-raid alarms by the summer of 1942, during which the normally floodlit Castle was blacked out. On one of these raids the 'lay figure' was eased through the bars of a window and left suspended with a long length of twine attached, some of which was held in reserve.

As soon as the floodlights went on again, the figure was jerked into movement and in less than no time the firing started.

After a good 'value for money' volley, the figure was

The lay figure

allowed to drop to the ground. Goon sentries immediately rushed to recover the corpse, which thereupon came to life, and rose high into the air again. A Goon approached nearer and the lay figure was promptly dropped on his head!

It was difficult for the Jerries to find the culprits. It was even difficult for them to locate the window from which the figure had sallied, as thin twine was used. The result was the withdrawal of the 'park' privilege for the whole camp during a month.

At first sight it might appear to be unfair that other nationalities should suffer for our sins, but we were not the only sinners and we suffered reciprocally! It was the expression of our unity against the common enemy.

Harry Elliott also indulged in a cold war against the Goons, but of a type which they never actually discovered. In the intervals between escape attempts he was always inventing new ways of waging war inside the prison walls. Thus while languishing in 'solitary' after an 'attempt' from the air-raid shelter on the road to the park along with a Pole, Captain Janek Lados, in which he was caught by the German sleuthhounds, he conceived the 'Razor-blades in the Pig Swill' campaign. With the aid of volunteers and large numbers of broken razor-blades, the camp garbage was heavily and regularly impregnated. All razor-blade pieces were carefully inserted and hidden completely inside rotten potatoes and vegetable remains. The results of the campaign were never known except by inference. The Germans made it a court-martial offence, punishable by most severe sentences including the possibility of the death penalty, to endanger the lives of German animals by tampering with the camp swill. Incidentally, while Harry was hatching this scheme in one prison cell, Janek Lados succeeded in escaping from another—it· was conveniently situated in the outer walls of the Castle. Janek cracked his shin-bone in the fall from the cell window. He reached the Swiss frontier, nevertheless, but was recaptured within sight of freedom.

Another campaign which Harry initiated was 'the Battle of the Dry Rot.' In conversation with a fellow-prisoner, Lieutenant Geoffrey Ransome, who was an architect by profession in peacetime, he learnt that dry rot could be propagated by making 'cultures' of it. He argued, quite logically, that whereas an R.A.F. bomb could remove the roof of a building in a second or so, dry rot could do the same thing though in a somewhat longer space of time— say twenty years or so. The war, according to him, might easily last that long, so that in the end his work might equate to the work of a fair-sized bomb, and there was nothing that could please Harry more than the thought that he was dropping a bomb on Colditz—however long the time-fuse.

In less than no time rows of innocent-looking, almost empty jam-jars made their appearance in dark corners under the beds of Harry and his disciples. In each jar was a sliver of wood, but wedged to it somehow was 'the culture.' The jars had to be kept damp and in the dark. On their periodic searches the Jerries were always puzzled by these jars, but they looked so harmless that they never removed them, ignorant of the dangerous 'explosive' they contained. In due course, when ripe, the slivers of wood were distributed throughout the roof timbers of the camp, where no doubt they still repose.

Harry had another habit. At night, after 'Lights Out,' he would often hold the stage as we all reclined on our beds in the darkness. A flow of funny stories would issue from the corner where he lay, and then he would start recounting some rather involved incident of his career—I think he did it on purpose. About halfway through it he would stop, and after a pause, during which heavy breathing would become audible, he would say:

"Don't you think so, Peter (or Dick, or Rupert)?"

A long pause was followed by:

"Hm! No answer. Time I turned in."

And, to the sound of grunts and rustling straw, Harry would turn in. The silence of 'a prisoner's vigil' would descend upon the rows of wooden bunks, faintly reflecting the glow of the searchlights outside.

CHAPTER XVIII

ESCAPE STRATEGY

MIKE SINCLAIR'S fear that he had closed another bunk-hole for his fellow-prisoners proved groundless. Soon after his attempt, Squadron-Leader 'Never-a-dull-moment' Paddon was called to face a court-martial charge at a former prison camp in the north-east of Germany. He was duly equipped for an escape and left for his destination under heavy guard. It was a long journey and he would be away several days. As the days turned into weeks, Colonel Stainer naturally became concerned, and demanded an explanation from the Camp Commandant. The latter replied with a resigned shrug of the shoulders:

"Es war unmöglich, trotzdem ist er geflüchtet"—"It was impossible, none the less he escaped!" Paddon eventually reached Sweden and then England safely. He was the second Englishman to do the home run from Colditz.

* * * * *

I was lying on my bunk one hot day in August 1942. 'Lulu' Lawton (Captain W. T. Lawton, Duke of Wellington's Regiment), was lying in another nearby. Lulu had one short break from Colditz and had been recaught after a few hours' journey outward bound. He was a Yorkshireman and he naturally preferred the smell of the fresh air outside the precincts of the camp. He lay ruminating for a long time and then in a sad tone of voice, turning towards me, he said:

"As far as I can see, Pat, it's no good trying any more escapes from Colditz—the place is bunged up—a half-starved rat wouldn't find a hole big enough for him to squeeze through." Then he added soulfully: "I wouldn't mind havin' another go, all the same, if I could only think of a way."

"You've got to consider the problem coldly," I replied. "The first principle for success in any battle is to attack the enemy in his weakest quarter, but what is always confused in the question of escape is our understanding concerning the enemy's weakest quarter. It isn't, for instance, the apparent weak point in the wire or the wall, for these are his rear-line defences. We have to go a long way before we reach them. It's his front-line defences that count, and they are inside the camp. Jerry's strongest weapon is his ability to nip escapes in the bud before they are ready. This he does right inside the camp and he succeeds ninety-eight per cent. of the time. His weakest quarter inside the camp has therefore to be found; after that, the rest is a cakewalk."

I added: "For instance, if you were to ask me where the German weak spot in this camp is, I should say it's Gephard's own office. Nobody will ever look for an escape attempt being hatched in the German R.S.M.'s office."

"That's all very well," said Lulu, "but Gephard's office has a cruciform lock and an ugly-looking padlock as well."

"All the better," I answered. "You won't be disturbed then."

"But how do I get in?"

"That's your problem," I concluded.

I never dreamt he would take the matter seriously, but a Yorkshireman's thoroughness is not to be denied.

There was a Dutchman in the camp, the red-bearded Captain Van Doorninck. He used to repair watches in his spare time, and he even repaired them for the German personnel occasionally, in return for equipment with which to carry on his hobby. Thus, he possessed a repair outfit consisting of miniature tools and various oddments in the way of materials, which were rigorously denied to other prisoners. He never gave his parole as to the employment of the tools.

Van Doorninck was 'brainy.' He had a wide knowledge of higher mathematics, and at one period he gave me, along with one or two others, a university course in

Geodesy—a subject I had never thoroughly grasped as a student.

Besides tinkering with watches Van Doorninck was not averse to tinkering with locks, as Lulu Lawton found out, with the result that the former devised a method of lock-picking that any Raffles might have been proud of.

I have described the outward appearance of the cruciform lock before as resembling a four-armed Yale lock. Its essential internal elements consisted of between six and nine tiny pistons of not quite one-eighth of an inch diameter each. In order to open the lock these pistons had to be moved in their cylinders by the insertion of the key. Each piston moved a different distance, the accuracy of which was gauged to a thousandth of an inch.

The principle involved was the same as that employed in the Yale lock. The keyhole, however, was like a cross, each limb being about one-sixteenth of an inch wide, whereas the Yale has a zigzag-shaped keyway. The latter keyway might have presented more difficulty to Van Doorninck, though I am sure he would have overcome it. However, he solved the cruciform problem by manufacturing a special micrometer gauge, which marked off the amount of movement that each piston required. He then made a key to conform, using his gauge to check the lifting faces of the key as he filed them. The key looked rather like a four-armed Yale key.

Van Doorninck succeeded brilliantly where I had failed miserably. I blushed with shame every time I recollected the tortures I had inflicted on so many wincing sufferers in the dentist's chair! The new key was a triumph. Moreover, Van Doorninck was in a position to 'break' all the cruciform locks, though each one was different. Thereafter, like ghosts we passed through doors which the Germans thought were sealed.

Returning to the door of Gephard's office: once the cruciform lock was 'broken' the other lock, the padlock, presented no difficulty.

The plan evolved. Lulu Lawton had teamed up with

Flight-Lieutenant 'Bill' Fowler, R.A.F., and then made a foursome with Van Doorninck and another Dutchman. Dick Howe, as escape officer, was in charge of operations. He came to me one day.

"Pat, I've got a job for you," he said. "Lulu and three others want to break out of Gephard's office window. Will you have a look at it? I'd also like you to do the job for them."

"Thanks for the compliment," I replied. "When do we start?"

"Any time you like."

"I'm not so sure of the window idea, Dick," I said, "but I'll check up carefully. It's pretty close to a sentry and it may even be in his line of sight."

"Kenneth Lockwood will go sick whenever you're ready," Dick continued, "and he'll live in the sick-ward opposite Gephard's office and manipulate all the necessary keys."

"Good! There's no German medical orderly at night, so I can hide under Kenneth's bed after the evening *Appell* until lights out. Then I can start work. I'll take someone with me."

"Yes, do," said Dick, "but don't take Hank this time. He's an old hand. We've got to train more men in our escape technique. Choose someone else."

I had a look at the office. It was small and oblong in shape, with a barred window in an alcove at the far end from the door. Gephard's desk and chair were in the alcove. The remainder of the office was lined with shelves on which reposed an assortment of articles. Many of them, such as hurricane lamps, electric torches, dry batteries, and nails and screws, would have been useful to us, but we touched nothing. The window exit was thoroughly dangerous. I saw by careful inspection and a few measurements that with only a little more patience we could rip up Gephard's floor, pierce a wall eighteen inches thick, and have entry into a storeroom outside and below us. From there, by simply unlocking a door, the escapers would walk out on to the sentry path surrounding the Castle. There was one snag. Did the storeroom have a cruciform or an ordinary lever lock?

This was checked by keeping a watch from a window for many days upon the area of the storeroom. The store-room door was not visible, but a Jerry approaching it would be visible and, in due course, a Jerry was seen going to the door holding in his hand an ordinary lever key! Van Doorninck would take a selection of keys and there should be no difficulty. The alternative, which would have taken much longer, would have been for me to construct a camouflage wall and examine the storeroom at leisure. This escape was to be a blitz job. The hole would be ready in a matter of three days. Experience was proving that long-term jobs involved much risk due to the time element alone. I often mused on the chances of the French tunnel which was advancing slowly day by day. . . .

The work would have to be done at night; Gephard's office was in use all day. The office was situated near the end of a ground-floor corridor, on the opposite side of which was the camp sick-ward. This ward was across the courtyard from our quarters, so that the undertaking in-volved entering the sick-quarters before the main doors were locked up for the night and hiding there, under the beds, until all was quiet—there was a sentry in the court-yard all day and night nowadays. The hospital beds were not high off the ground and were rather crammed together, giving ample concealment for superficial purposes.

I chose Lieutenant Derek Gill (Royal Norfolks) to come along and help me; he was the right type—imperturbable. We started operations as soon as Kenneth was snugly ensconced in his sick-bed, with serious stomach trouble. When the doors were locked and the patrols departed, Kenneth manipulated the keys, opened the sick-ward door and then Gephard's door, locked us in for the night and returned to bed.

I removed the necessary floorboards underneath the window and also, incidentally, under the desk at which Gephard sat every day! I started work on the wall. The joints between the stones were old, as I suspected, and by the morning the two of us had reached the far side. I noticed there was plaster on the other side. This was what I expected; it was the wall-face of the storeroom. That was enough for the first night. Most of the large stones were removed in a sack, and in the under-floor rubble a passage was cleared at a forty-five-degree angle so that a person could ease himself down into the hole. Blankets were laid down so as to deaden the hollow sound, and the floor under Gephard's desk was then very carefully replaced. Nails were reinserted and covered with our patent dust-paste. All cracks were refilled with dirt. In the early hours, Kenneth, by arrangement, let us out and locked up. We retired to the sick-ward, the door of which also had to be locked, and rested comfortably until the German medical orderly arrived on his morning rounds, when we retired under the beds.

The next night Derek and I went to work again. This time the job was more difficult; the hole in the wall had to be enlarged enough to allow a large-sized man's body (Van Doorninck) to pass through. At the same time, the plaster on the further face was to be left intact. I knew the hole was high up in the storeroom wall, probably eight to ten feet from the floor-level. We finished the task successfully and in the morning retired as before.

The escape exit was now ready. Dick, Lulu, Bill, and myself worked out the plan together. It was based on the fact that German N.C.O.s occasionally came to the storeroom with Polish POWs who were working in the town of Colditz. They brought and removed stores, baskets of old uniforms, underclothing in large wooden boxes, wooden clogs and a miscellaneous assortment of harmless soldier's equipment, as far as we could see. They came at irregular hours, mostly in the mornings, sometimes as early as 7 a.m. and seldom more often than twice a week. These habits had been observed and noted over a period of a month. It was agreed that the escape party should be increased to a total of six. Two more officers were therefore selected.

They were 'Stooge' Wardle, our submarine type, and Lieutenant Donkers, a Dutchman. It was arranged that Lulu
should travel with the second Dutchman, and Bill Fowler
with Van Doorninck.

Sentries were changed at 7 a.m., so the plan was
made accordingly. Van Doorninck, who spoke German
fluently, would become a senior German N.C.O. and
Donkers would be a German private. The other four
would be Polish orderlies. They would issue from the
storeroom shortly after 7 a.m. Van Doorninck would lock
up after him. The four orderlies would carry two large
wooden boxes between them, the German private would
take up the rear. They would walk along the sentry path
past two sentries, to a gate in the barbed wire, where Van
Doorninck would order a third sentry to unlock and let
them pass. The sentries—with luck—would assume that
the 'fatigue' party had gone to the storeroom shortly before
7 a.m. Once through the barbed wire the party would proceed downhill along the roadway which went towards the
park. They would, however, turn off after fifty yards and
continue past a German barracks, and farther on they
would reach the large gate in the wall surrounding the
Castle grounds; the same over which Neave and Thompson
had climbed in their escape. At this gate, Van Doorninck
would have to use more keys. If he could not make them
work, he had to use his wits. Indeed, if he managed to lead
his company that far, he could probably ring up the Commandant and ask him to come and open the gate!

The plan necessitated the making of two large boxes in
sections so that they could be passed through the hole into
the storeroom, and yet of such construction that they could
be very quickly assembled.

The day for the escape was fixed shortly after a normal
visit to the storeroom, in order to lessen the chances of
clashing with a real 'fatigue' party. We prayed that a clash
might not occur, but the visits were not accurately predictable and we had to take this chance.

The evening before the 'off,' after the last *Appell*, nine

officers ambled at irregular intervals into the sick-ward corridor. There was other traffic also, and no suspicion was aroused. The sections of the wooden boxes had been transferred to the sick-ward at intervals during the day under coats. Eight officers hid under the beds, while Kenneth retired to his official one and saw to it that the hospital inmates remained quiet and behaved themselves. They were mostly French and were rather excited at the curious visitation. Kenneth had a way of his own of dealing with his brother officers of whatever nationality. He stood on his bed and addressed the whole sick-ward:

"I'll knock the block off any man here who makes a nuisance of himself or tries to create trouble. *Comprenez? Je casse la tête à n'importe qui fait du bruit ou qui commence à faire des bêtises.*"

Of course, Kenneth knew everybody there intimately and could take liberties with their susceptibilities. He continued:

"What is going on here is none of your business, so I don't want to see any curiosity; poking of heads under beds, for instance; no whispering. When the patrol comes round, everybody is to behave quite normally. I'll be sitting up looking around. If I see the slightest unnecessary movement, I'll report the matter to General Le Bleu as attempted sabotage."

Kenneth's mock seriousness had an edge to it. Among those in the sick-ward were a few more or less permanent inhabitants—the neurotic ones. They were capable of almost any absurdity and a firm line was the only one to take in their case.

The sick-ward was duly locked and night descended upon the Castle. Quietly the nine arose, and as Kenneth unlocked one door after another with ease, we 'ghosted' through. Eight of us squeezed into the small office and Kenneth departed as he had come.

"Derek," I whispered, "we've got a long time in front of us before we start work. There's no point in beginning too early in case of misfires and alarms."

"How long do you think it will take to break out the hole?" he questioned.

"About an hour, I should say, but we'll allow double that amount."

"That means," said Derek, "we can start at, say, four a.m."

"Better make it three a.m. We must allow much longer than we anticipate for pushing this crowd through, along with all the junk. There's also the hole to be made good. Have you brought the water and the plaster?"

"Yes. I've got six pint bottles and enough plaster to do a square yard."

"Good. What time do you make it now?"

"Nine-forty-five," Derek replied. We sat around on the floor to pass the vigil.

At midnight there was an alarm. We heard Germans unlocking doors and the voice of Priem in the corridor. He went into the sick-ward for five minutes, then came out and approached Gephard's office door. We heard every word he said as he talked with the night-duty N.C.O. The latter asked:

"Shall I open this door, Herr Hauptmann?"

"Yes, indeed, I wish to control all," answered Priem.

"It is the office of *Oberstabsfeldwebel* Gephard, Herr Hauptmann."

"Never mind. Open!" came the reply.

There was a loud noise of keys and then Priem's voice:

"Ah! of course Herr Gephard has many locks on his door. I had forgotten. Do not open, it is safe."

The steps retreated and then died away as the outer door was relocked. We took several minutes to recover from this intrusion. Eventually Lulu Lawton, who was beside me, whispered into my ear, "My God! You were right, and how!"

It was uncanny the way Priem scented us out and nearly caught us in spite of all our precautions.

In the dog-watch, I started work quietly by making a small hole through the plaster and then cutting and pulling inwards towards myself. Minute pieces fell outside and made noises which sounded like thunder to me, but which were not, in reality, loud. In due course the hole was enlarged for a hand to pass through, then the rest was removed with ease. I had a sheet with me to help the escapers down into the storeroom beyond. Van Doorninck went first. He landed on some shelves and, using them as a ladder, descended safely to the floor. A few minutes later he reported that the outside door of the storeroom had a simple lock and that he had tried it successfully. This was good news. The other five officers followed: then the sections of the two boxes; the various bundles of escape clothing; the Polish troops' uniforms; the German soldiers' uniforms, and lastly, the plaster and the water. We could have made good use of a conveyer belt!

Derek and I wished them all good luck and, wasting no time, we started to refill the hole in the wall as neatly as possible, while Van Doorninck on the other side applied a good thick coat of plaster. The wooden boxes would come in very handy for carrying away the empty water-bottles and surplus plaster as well as all the civilian outfits! Finally, as the last stone was ready to go into place, Van Doorninck and I checked watches and I whispered 'Goodbye' and 'Good luck' and sealed the hole.

Derek and I then replaced blankets and floorboards carefully. By 6 a.m. the operation was finished, just as we heard Kenneth whispering through the door: "Is all well, are you ready?"

"Yes, open up."

Kenneth manipulated the locks and we retired to the sick-ward.

From there we would not see the rest of the act. The escapers would leave at 7.10 a.m., while the sick-ward would not open up until 7.30 a.m. Morning *Appell* was at 8.30 a.m. This was where the fun would start!

At about 7.30 a.m. we sallied forth unobtrusively. Dick was waiting for us and reported a perfect take-off!

Van Doorninck's uniform was that of a sergeant. The

sentries had each in turn saluted smartly as the sergeant's
'fatigue' party wended its way along the path towards the
barbed-wire gate. Arrived here, the sentry in charge
quickly unlocked it, and the party passed through and was
soon out of sight of our hidden watchers in the upper
stories of the Castle.

As minutes passed and there were no alarms, we began
to breathe more freely. By 8 a.m. we could almost safely
assume they were away.

The *Appell* was going to cause trouble. We had for the

Van Doorninck walks out

time being exhausted all our tricks for the covering of
absentees from *Appell*. We had tried blank files, with our
medium-sized R.A.F. officer running along, bent double,
between the ranks and appearing in another place to be
counted twice. We had tried having a whole row of officers
counted twice by appropriate distraction of the N.C.O.s
checking off the numbers. We had tried bamboozling the
Germans by increasing the returns of officers sick. The
Dutch dummies were no more.

If the escape had been in the park, we had a greater

variety of methods from which to choose. Park parades, in the first place, did not cover the whole prisoner contingent. We could add bodies to begin with; as we had done, for instance, by suspending our medium-sized officer, on occasion, around the waist of a burly Dutch officer, whose enormous cloak covered them both with ease! On another attempt, we had staged a fake escape to cover the real one, by having two officers cut the park wire and run for it—without a hope of escape, of course. The deception, in this case, was that the two officers acted as if a third was ahead of them among the trees. They shouted encouragement and warning to this imaginary one, whom the Jerries chased round in circles for the remainder of the day!

By now we had temporarily run out of inspiration. We might manage to conceal one absence, but six was an impossibility. So we did the obvious thing. We decided to lay in a reserve of spare officers for future escapes. We concealed four officers in various parts of the Castle. There would be ten missing from the *Appell*! With luck the four hidden in the Castle would become 'ghosts.' They would appear no more at *Appells* and would fill in blanks on future escapes. The idea was, by now, not unknown to the Germans, but we would try it.

The morning *Appell* mustered and, in due course, ten bodies were reported missing. There were hurried consultations, and messengers ran to and fro from the *Kommandantur*. We were counted again and again. The Germans thought we were playing a joke on them. Guardhouse reports showed there had been a quiet night, after Priem's visit, with no alarms.

The Germans kept us on parade, and sent a search-party through all the quarters. After an hour, they discovered two of our ghosts. This convinced them we were joking. They became threatening, and finally held an identification parade while the Castle search-party continued its work. Eventually the latter found two more ghosts. By 11 a.m., not having found any further bodies, they concluded that perhaps six had escaped after all. The identification parade continued until they had established which officers were missing, in the midst of tremendous excitement as posses of Goons were despatched in all directions around the countryside.

We were satisfied at having increased the start of our six escapers by a further three hours. Later in the day we heard that the Jerries, after questioning all sentries, had suspected our fatigue party, and working backwards to the storeroom, had discovered my hole. There was much laughter, even among the Jerries, at the expense of Gephard, under whose desk the escape had been made! I leave it to the reader to imagine the disappointment and fury of Priem at our having eluded his grasp so narrowly during the night!

Before the evening was over, we had our disappointment too; Lulu Lawton and his companion were recaught. I was sorry for Lulu. He had put so much effort into the escape. It was largely his own idea and he had displayed cleverness and great pertinacity. These qualities, I thought, deserved better recognition than a month of 'solitary' in the cells.

Lulu told us how Van Doorninck led the fatigue party past the German barracks and onwards to the last gateway. As he approached it, a Goon from the barracks ran after the party and asked Van Doorninck if he wanted the gate opened. "Naturally," replied the latter!

The Goon hurried off and returned shortly with the key. He opened the gate and locked it again after them!

A day later, Stooge Wardle and Donkers were recaptured.

Bill Fowler and Van Doorninck carried on happily. They slipped through the net and reached Switzerland safely in six days. That was September 1942. Two more over the border! We had no reason to be ashamed of our efforts!

CHAPTER XIX

FORLORN HOPE

IT was high time Bruce, our medium-sized officer, was given a chance of escape. He had done such good work unobtrusively! The opportunity arrived when the Germans decided we had too much personal property in our rooms. It was September, and they issued orders that all private kit not immediately required, as, for instance, summer clothing, was to be packed. The Jerries provided large boxes for the purpose. We were informed on the word of honour of the Camp Commandant that the cases would be stored in the German *Kommandantur* (the outer part of the Castle) and would be made available again in the spring.

The cases were duly packed, closed, and removed on a lorry. Several of them were Tate and Lyle sugar-boxes, about three feet square by three feet high, which had contained bulk consignments of Red Cross food, and in one of these travelled our medium-sized officer!

He had his civilian clothes and escape equipment with him, as well as a knife to cut the cords holding down the lid of his case, and about a forty-foot length of rope in the form of sheets. We knew the cases were to be stored in an attic at the top of a building which we could see from our windows.

Bruce reached Danzig, bicycling much of the way. Unfortunately, he was recaught on the docks, trying to stow away on a neutral ship, and returned in due course to Colditz where he was placed in solitary confinement.

I would like to have heard his full story but I never saw him again. I was doing two successive bouts of 'solitary' in the 'cooler' when he returned, and I did not even meet him during the daily exercise hour.

My 'solitary' was due to two abortive escape attempts.

The first was a short tunnel, mostly vertical, built to con-
nect up with the drains in the courtyard, which I have
mentioned before. Rupert Barry and Colin McKenzie were
my confederates. I had long ago noticed, on a photograph
of the prisoners' courtyard taken before the war, a manhole cover near the entrance gateway. This manhole cover
no longer existed and I was sure it had been covered over
for a good reason. We were trying to find out why, by
means of the tunnel, when the unannounced arrival of a
batch of Russian prisoners proved our undoing. Our vertical shaft began in what was known as the 'delousing shed,'
a temporary structure in the courtyard built to house the
portable ovens, which looked like boilers and into which
clothing was put and baked in order to kill lice and other
pests.

The sudden arrival of the Russians necessitated the use
of these portable ovens, and Rupert and I were caught red-
handed. McKenzie was lucky. He was doing earth-disposal
duty and was not in the shed! The boilers were hardly
used once in six months, and it was unfortunate the
Russians arrived just during our working hours!

The incident, however, enabled us to meet the Russian
soldiers, who were to be housed in the town where normally we should never see them. They were a sight of
which the Germans might well have been ashamed. Living
skeletons, they dragged their fleshless feet along the ground
in a decrepit slouch. These scarecrows were the survivors of
a batch ten times their number which had started from
the front. They were treated like animals, given no food,
and put out into the fields to find fodder amidst the grass
and roots. Their trek into Germany took weeks.

"Luckily," said one of them, "it was summer-time. In
the winter," he added, "nobody bothered even to move us
to the hinterland from the front. We died where we were
captured."

How many times, in my life as a prisoner, did I murmur
a prayer of thanksgiving for that blessed document, 'the
Geneva Convention,' and for its authors! But for its

humane principles, I saw myself standing in the place of these wretched creatures. Needless to say, as between Germany and Russia, there were no recognised principles for the treatment of prisoners-of-war. Neither of them had signed the Convention.

My second bout of 'solitary' was due to the fact that I tried to escape from my prison cell. It happened to be in the town jail because, as usual, all the camp cells were full, and the overflow nowadays went to the jail.

By placing my cell table on the bed, I could reach the ceiling of the cell. I had a small saw, which was normally hidden in my guitar. Breaking through the plaster one evening, I started work on the wood. I had to work noiselessly, for the guards lived next door. In spite of every effort, I was not finished by morning and, of course, the jailer saw my handiwork when he came with my bread and ersatz coffee.

I was evidently doomed to spend another winter in Colditz.

*   *   *   *   *

September was nearly over. Dick Howe came up to me one day.

"I have another job for you, Pat," he said. "Ronnie Littledale and Billie Stephens have teamed up and are clamouring to leave. Their idea isn't in the least original, but that doesn't stop their clamouring," he added.

He then described to me roughly what they intended to do.

"That old chestnut," I commented, "has grown a long beard by now. It has about as much chance of success as the famous camel that tried to go through the eye of a needle! What's the idea, Dick?" I asked. "I thought we were going to keep that type of lunacy till the very end, and that we wouldn't even consider it until every hole in the camp was completely bunged and we were desperate?"

"We're not desperate, Pat. I hope we never shall be. Still, I don't mind letting them have a shot. I want you to go with them," he added as an aside, "just to see they don't get into any trouble!"

"Well! I seem to be doomed. I'll do it for the fun of the thing, but it's a mad idea and it will mean another month in the 'cooler' for me without a shadow of a doubt," I concluded.

I knew the scheme well. A child could have thought of it. It involved making a sortie from one of the windows of the kitchen over the low roofs of various store buildings in the adjoining German *Kommandantur* courtyard. Then, descending to the ground, one had to cross over the path of a sentry's beat when his back was turned, and then crawl across the dimly lit area in front of the *Kommandantur* to a small open pit, in the far corner of the courtyard, which was visible from our windows. That was as far as the plan went! We were still in the midst of the enemy and how we were supposed to extricate ourselves was a mystery to me.

Dick, Ronnie, Billie Stephens, and myself discussed the plan.

I suggested an addition to the team:

"We may as well be hung for a sheep as a lamb, so why not add a fourth to our group of three? Then, when we get out, *if* we get out, we can travel in independent groups of two each."

"All right," said Dick, "who do you suggest?"

"Well, if Ronnie and Billie are going to travel together, it's rather up to me, I suppose, to choose someone. I think Hank Wardle is the man. It's time he had a turn."

"Good. I don't think there will be any objections, but I'll just confirm this," rejoined Dick. "He's the right man as far as I'm concerned. He has all the qualifications; he's high on the roster and has helped other escapes; and he's R.A.F."

Ronnie put in: "This attempt will be an 'All Services' venture then, Billie being a naval type. A good idea, I think!"

"You'll have to travel by different routes, of course," said Dick. "What do you suggest?"

"Well, if it's all the same to Ronnie and Billie," I answered, "I've studied the route from Penig via Zwickau to Plauen, Regensburg and Munich, and thence to Ulm and Tuttlingen. I'd like to stick to it. How about it, Ronnie? You could go from Leisnig to Dobeln, then via Chemnitz to Nürnberg and Stuttgart."

"That suits us," said Ronnie. "We prefer Leisnig, as it's

Billie Stephens

only a few kilometres away and we reckon to catch a train before the morning *Appell*."

"All right," said Dick, "you're agreed then. We'll go into questions of detail, dress, food, and so on, nearer to the date for the 'off.' Let me know if you are stuck for anything."

Lieutenant-Commander William Stephens, R.N.V.R. (Billie), had been captured during the St. Nazaire raid, when the dock gates were blown up in an effort to imprison a large number of German U-boats. He had tried to escape twice, and was a new arrival at Colditz. In fact, when he arrived he was promptly put into 'solitary' for several weeks to complete his sentences before he was let loose into the camp. His school was Shrewsbury and he came from Northern Ireland. He was handsome, fair-haired, with piercing blue eyes and Nelsonian nose. He walked as if he was permanently on the deck of a ship. He was a daredevil, and his main idea appeared to be to force his way into the German area of the camp and then hack his way out with a metaphorical cutlass.

The one hope I could see was of forcing an entry into the tall block of buildings, at the top of which our medium-sized officer had been deposited in his Tate and Lyle sugar-box. As he had been able to make an exit from there, maybe we could also. It was important to have Bruce's comments, and I managed to pass a message to him in some food and, eventually, had an answer. Once inside his building, it was possible to descend from unbarred windows on the far side into the moat of the Castle. The top floors were unoccupied, but care was necessary to avoid noise as Germans occupied floors below. There was a large heavy door into the building which was visible from our quarters and which gave on to an unused stair-case leading to the top.

There were two principal snags: the door mentioned above was visible from almost everywhere and in full view of the sentry in the German courtyard; secondly, the door was locked. We could assume the lock was not cruciform in type, but beyond this we knew nothing. At night, when the floodlights were blazing, this door was in shadow. I might be able to work at the lock, but the risk was tremendous because the door was beside the main path, leading from the outer Castle gateway to the entrance of the *Kommandantur*—all pedestrians passed within a yard of it. Besides, would the shadow be sufficient to hide a man from the eyes of the sentry? Lastly, the door was twenty yards from the pit of which I have spoken—and the nearest place of concealment—so that a person going to and from the door had to flit twenty yards each way in a penumbra where movement would be visible.

When Hank's nomination had been agreed, I broached the subject to him:

"Ronnie and Billie want you and me to join them on

about the most absurd escape attempt I know," I opened by way of invitation.

"One thing seems to be as good or as bad as another in this camp nowadays," was Hank's reply.

"That means you're not fussy, I take it?"

Hank's answer was a typical shrug of the shoulders and "I couldn't care less, I've got nothing to do till the end of the war, so it's all the same to me!"

I described the plan to him in fair detail, and when I had finished he said:

"I'll try it with you. I agree there's no hope of success, but we've got to carry on trying just the same."

The whole scheme assumed that we could reach the pit safely and hide inside it. For all we knew it might have been deep. Our hope that it was shallow was based on the fact that the pit was not balustraded and a man might easily have fallen into it. To reach the pit would be a prolonged nightmare.

The camp kitchen was in use all day. Towards evening it was locked up. It was in full view of the sentry in the prisoners' courtyard. A pane of glass in one of the metal-framed windows was half-broken. I had preparatory work to do in the kitchen and this window was my only means of entry. I employed a stooge to help me. After the evening *Appell* on the first day of operations, he sat on a doorstep near the kitchen, watching the sentry, while I remained out of sight behind the protruding wall of the delousing shed, about five yards from the window. The sentry's beat varied between eight and twelve seconds. I had to be inside before he turned round.

My stooge gave me the O.K. signal. I ran and hopped on to the sill. Reaching through the broken pane of glass on tiptoe, I could just grasp the lever which opened the window. I pulled it upwards gently, withdrew my arm carefully so as not to break what was left of the glass pane, opened the window and crept through. If the sentry stopped short or turned in the middle of his beat, I was caught. I jumped down on to the kitchen floor and silently closed the window. I was safely inside, with a second to spare.

Leaving the kitchen was a little easier, as one faced the sentry and could see him through cracks in the white paint of the lower glass panes of the window.

I repeated this performance five evenings running along with one assistant. We usually entered after the evening *Appell*, at about 6 p.m., and returned again before locking-up time, at 9 p.m.

During these periods of three hours, we worked hard. The windows on the opposite side of the kitchen opened on to the flat roofs of a jumble of outhouses in the German courtyard; all the roofs were about twelve feet above the ground. The kitchen windows on this side, as well as the whole wall of the building, were in bright floodlight from dusk onwards.

I opened one of the windows by removing a number of wire clips which were supposed to seal it, and examined the bars beyond. I saw that, by removing one rivet, I could bend a bar inwards, providing enough room for a body to pass. The hole through the bars opened on to the flat roof.

The rivet was the next problem. I could saw off the head, but it was old and rusty and would obviously require great force to withdraw it. Yet the method would involve much less sawing: 'Silence was golden.' A sentry plied his beat just beyond the outbuildings, about fifteen yards away. Luckily the window was not in his line of vision, unless he extended his beat to nearly double its normal length. This he did from time to time. Of course, the window and the flat roof were in full view of all the windows of the *Kommandantur* above the ground floor!

The less sawing I did, the better. Sawing the head off the rivet was the solution, if only I could withdraw it after-wards.

My assistant was E.R.A. 'Wally' Hammond, R.N. He was one of the naval types who had been painted blue! He and his friend E.R.A. 'Tubby' Lister arrived by mis-take at Colditz, this being an officers' camp, while they were chief Petty Officers. They made good use of their sojourn.

Soon afterwards, when they were removed to their rightful prison, they escaped, and with the advantage of their Colditz 'education' behind them, they reached Switzerland with comparative ease!

These two submarine men deserve to be placed on pedestals in a conspicuous place somewhere in England. They were the quintessence of everything for which our island stands. If a hundred Englishmen of every rank and county were put together in a pot and boiled down, the remaining crust would be Wally Hammond and Tubby Lister. Their sense of humour was unbeatable. It rose to meet dangers, knocking them on the head with a facetiousness capable of dispersing the most formidable army of adversities.

During their escape, for instance, for lack of a better language they spoke pidgin-English with the Germans throughout, posing as Flemish collaborators. They stayed at middle-class German hotels, and before leaving in the mornings, usually filled any army top-boots which happened to be outside the doors of neighbouring rooms with water, as a mark of their respect for the *Oberkommando der Wehrmacht*—the German High Command! ... Their full story belongs to another book; their journey through Germany was a pantomime.*

*   *   *   *   *

To return to the story of the rivet which required attention; the head was sawn through during the fourth evening shift. Next, we needed a high-powered silently-working punch which would force the rivet out of its socket.

Wally Hammond made one in the space of a few hours out of a bar used for closing the grate door of a German heating stove. The bar was about a foot long. At each end

* See *The Latter Days* (page 464).

he made clamps which could be fixed to the iron bar out-side the kitchen window. In the centre there was, already, a half-inch-diameter screw. The end of this was filed to fit into the quarter-inch-diameter rivet-hole. The head of the screw was a knurled wheel of two inches diameter. To the latter, Hammond arranged to clamp a lever one foot long.

On the fifth evening of work I applied Hammond's punch, turned the lever, and the rivet, which had been corroded in its position for probably twenty years, slid smoothly and silently out of its hole and the job was done!

I camouflaged the joint with a clay rivet, sealed the win-dow as usual, and, redusting everything carefully, we left the kitchen as we had come.

The escape was on and we wasted no time. Our two groups would travel by different routes to the frontier crossing-point on the Swiss border—a Colditz secret! Although I had never been there, I knew the area in my mind's eye like the back of my hand. Every Colditz escaper's first and last duty was to learn this crossing by heart; for I had forbidden frontier-crossing maps to be carried many months ago. We had the master map in the camp and it was studied by all.

We each had our identity papers, our general maps, money, and compass. We kept them usually in small tubes. I had once received a present from friends in Eng-land which actually arrived—two boxes of twenty-five Upman Havana cigars. The cigars were in light metal con-tainers about five inches long. These cases were much in demand. All the above documents, money, and a compass fitted into the metal tube, which was easily carried and could be easily concealed, even by sleight of hand if neces-sary.

I had printed my own identity papers. German Gothic script is not easy to copy, but it was possible with practice. We had a primitive, yet highly successful, system of duplicating, and reproduced typewritten orders and letters as desired. A multitude of lino-cut stamps provided all the officialdom necessary, and photographs were managed in

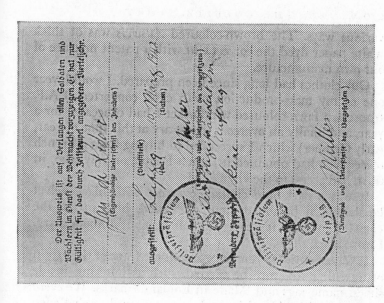

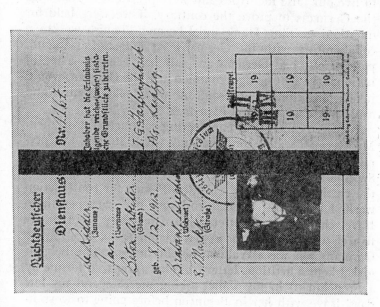

The author's passport (*Ausweis*)

various ways. The brown-coloured *Ausweis* was of thick white paper dyed the correct tint with a patent mixture of our own manufacture.

Our clothes had long since been prepared. I would wear one of my mass-production cloth caps, converted R.A.F. trousers, a fawn-coloured windjacket I had concealed for a year, and finally an overcoat (necessary at this time of year, early October) which I succeeded in buying from a French officer who had obtained it from a French orderly who, in turn, had access to the village.

It was a dark-blue civilian overcoat with black velvet lapels and it buttoned, double-breasted, high up on the chest! I imagine it was a German fashion of about 1912. I wore black shoes.

It was essential to remove every single trace of the origin of anything we wore or carried, such as lettering inside shoes, name tags and 'Made in England' marks. We were to live our false identities and were prepared to challenge the Germans to prove the contrary, if we were held for questioning. Thus Hank and I became Flemish workmen collaborating with the Germans. As *Flamands* we could pass off our bad German and our bad French—a useful nationality! Not being a common one, the Germans would take a long time to find someone who spoke Flemish and could prove we were not *Flamands*.

We were concrete or engineering contractors' workmen. My German wallet contained my whole story. I was permitted to travel to Rottweil (some thirty miles from the Swiss border), in reply to newspaper advertisements—I had the cuttings—requiring contractors' men for construction work. I also had a special and very necessary permit to travel close to the frontier. Part of my story was that my fiancée worked at Besançon as a telephone operator for the Germans. She was a Walloon—or French-speaking Belgian girl. I kept a fictitious letter from her (prepared for me by a Frenchman) in my wallet asking me to spend my few days' leave with her in Besançon before going to work in Rottweil. By a curious coincidence the railway line going

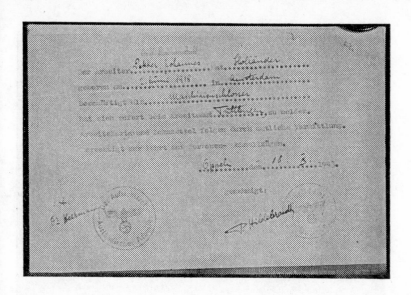

A typical travelling permit and identity card as
manufactured at Colditz

Nur gegen Vorzeigung des Urlaubscheines und des Sichtvermerks ist die Grenzübertritt bei der Hin- und Rückreise möglich. Der Urlaubschein ist daher bis zur Beendigung der Urlaubsreise sorgfältig aufzubewahren

Urlaubsſchein

Der belgische Arbeiter, de Ridder, Jan.
(Vor- und Zuname)

aus Dieghem, Brabant.
(Heimatland, Heimatort)

geb. am 8. 12. 12. beſchäftigt als Betonarbeiter.

iſt vom 15/10/42 bis 31/10/42 nach Belfort, E
Frankreichs. beurlaubt.
(Urlaubsort)

Grund des Urlaubs: Heimaturlaub.
(Familienheimfahrt, Krankheitsurlaub, Heimaturlaub, besondere Anläſſe uſw.)

Der Urlauber hat Arbeiterrückfahrkarte bis Keine erhalten

Der Urlauber iſt über die für die Mitnahme von Geldmitteln in deutſcher bzw. der betreffenden ausländiſchen Währung geltenden Beſtimmungen unterrichtet worden.

Der Urlauber iſt verpflichtet nach Beendigung des Urlaubs die Arbeit in unſerm Betrieb wieder aufzunehmen.

Leipzig den 10/10/42 1942   Habecher
(Firmenſtempel und Unterſchrift)

Beſcheinigung des Arbeitsamts

Der Erteilung des Sichtvermerks zur einmaligen Aus- und Wiedereinreise wird zugeſtimmt.

Leipzig   den 12 - 10 - 1942

J. A. Schein
(Unterſchrift)

Arbeitsamt
(Stempel)
Leipzig

100005 4. 43. C.8500

The author's leave permit
The obverse carried a special pass and stamp permitting travel in the frontier zones

to Besançon from my direction passed within fifteen miles of the Swiss frontier!

My trump card was a real photo, which I had, of a girl I met in France. One day, while looking through a German weekly newspaper, I had come across a German propaganda photograph showing German and foreign girls working together for the Germans in a post office and telephone exchange. One of the girls in the picture was the double of the girl whose photo I carried. I immediately cut out the press photo and kept it as a treasured possession. It would prove to any German where my imaginary fiancée's loyalties lay. My private snapshot was conclusive evidence and I was prepared to battle with any German who dared to doubt my identity.

The other three of our team had different case-histories, more or less as conclusive as mine.

Towards the end of our final preparations I held a last consultation and, among many items, we discussed food.

"You all realise that we can't take anything with us by way of food except normal German rations," I pointed out.

"Yes, I agree," said Billie, "but all the same I'm taking enough corned beef and tinned cheese to make sure of one good meal before we board the train."

"Our sugar is all right too," added Ronnie. "We can carry that with us indefinitely. It looks the same as the German and would pass."

"Now I've got a sticky proposition to make," I began, changing the subject. "There are a few of those small ersatz leather suitcases lying about—you know, the ones that came with that last batch of parcels. They had army clothing in them. I propose we each carry one."

"H'm! That's a tall order!" retorted Billie. "It's going to be hard enough to get out of the camp, climbing over roofs and walls and down ropes, without being pestered with suitcases into the bargain."

"I agree, but remember, Billie, when we *do* get out of the camp we are a long way from Switzerland and freedom," I argued; "it's no use planning only for the begin-

The wallet photograph of my pseudo
fiancée

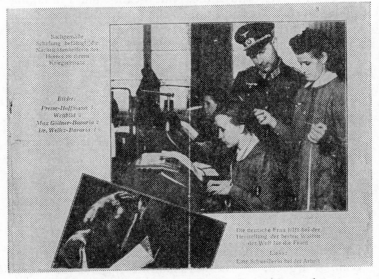

My alleged fiancée at work with the Wehrmacht

My 'fiancée's' letter asking me to come to Belfort on leave

ning and leaving the rest to look after itself. The rest in this case is just as important, and a little extra risk to begin with—in conditions over which we have some control— may be amply repaid later on, in circumstances over which we have no control at all."

"What does all that imply?" queried Billie.

"It means," I said, "that I don't think it's such a tall order. Once outside the camp, a suitcase becomes the hall- mark of respectability and honesty. How many people travel long journeys on main-line expresses in wartime with nothing at all in their hands? Only fugitives and rail- way officials. And the Germans know this well. They know that to look out for an escaped prisoner means to look out for a man travelling light, with no luggage—without a suitcase."

"I see your point, Pat," agreed Billie.

"At railway-station controls or in a round-up, a suitcase will be invaluable," I continued. "You can wave it about and make it prominent and the betting is it'll help a lot. Moreover, it will be useful for carrying articles of respect- ability: pyjamas—without tags and hall-marks—razors, bootbrushes, and German boot polish, German soap, and, of course, your German food. Otherwise your pockets are going to be bulgy, untidy, and suspicious-looking. I know it's going to be hell lugging them with us out of the camp, but I think it will be worth the effort in the end."

They all agreed and so it was fixed. We procured four of the small fibreboard suitcases and packed away our escape-travelling kit.

I could hardly believe we were going to do the whole four-hundred-mile journey by train. I thought of our naïve escape from Laufen and realised how much experience counted in escaping.

CHAPTER XX

THE WALLS ARE BREACHED

IT was October 14th, 1942. As evening approached, the four of us made final preparations. I said "Au revoir till tomorrow" to Van den Heuvel, and to Rupert, Harry, Peter Allan, and Kenneth and Dick. Rupert was to be our kitchen-window stooge. We donned our civilian clothing, and covered this with army trousers and greatcoats. Civilian overcoats were made into neat bundles.

In parenthesis, I should explain why we had to wear the military clothes over everything. At any time a wandering Goon might appear as we waited our moment to enter the kitchen, and there might even be delays. Further, we had to think of 'informers'—among the foreign orderlies, for example, who were always wandering about. If orderlies saw one of us leap through the kitchen window, it was just too bad—we might be after food—but it would be far worse if they saw a number of civilian-clothed officers in a staircase lobby—the orderlies' staircase as it happened—waiting, apparently, for their taxi to arrive!

Our suitcases were surrounded with blankets to muffle sound, and we carried enough sheets and blankets to make a fifty-foot descent, if necessary. Later we would wear balaclava helmets and gloves; no white skin was to be visible. Darkness and the shadows were to be our friends, we could not afford to offend them. Only our eyes and noses would be exposed. All light-coloured garments were excluded. We carried thick socks to put over our shoes. This is the most silent method of movement I know, barring removal of one's shoes—which we were to do for the crossing of the sentry's path.

Squadron-Leader MacColm was to accompany us into the kitchen in order to bend the window bar back into place and seal up the window after we had gone. He would have to conceal the military clothing we left behind in the kitchen and make his exit the next morning after the kitchen was unlocked. He could hide in one of the enormous cauldrons so long as he did not oversleep and have himself served up with the soup next day.

Immediately after the evening *Appell* we were ready and started on the first leg of our long journey. It was 6.30 p.m.

I was used to the drill of the entry window by now. At the nodded signal from Rupert, I acted automatically; a run, a leap to the sill, one arm through the cracked pane of glass, up with the window lever, withdraw arm carefully, open window—without noise—jump through, and close again softly. I was through. Only two had done it before at any one session. The question was, Would five succeed? One after another they came. At least, they had not the window-lever latch to bother about.

The sentry was behaving himself. At regular intervals, as he turned his back, the signal was given. I could not see Rupert—but he was timing perfectly. I could see the sentry from behind the window throughout his beat.

Each time, as the sentry turned away, I heard a gentle scurry. I automatically opened the window, in jumped a body, and I closed the window again, breathing a heavy sigh. The drill was becoming automatic. It was taking as little as five seconds. Then, suddenly, just as the last of the five was due, I sensed—I do not know how—an uncertainty, a hesitation in the manner of the sentry as he turned away. I knew that he would behave oddly during this beat. My heart was in my mouth, for I expected to hear the scurry and anticipated a clash. But there was no scurry, and in the next instant the sentry stopped dead and turned around! It was nothing less than intuition on Rupert's part that saved us.

On the next turn of the sentry's beat, I heard the scurry, opened and closed again. At last all five of us were safe.

We removed our military clothing and handed it to MacColm.

I set about the window overlooking the German courtyard, and as darkness fell and the floodlights went on, I
heaved on the bar until it was bent horizontal, and immediately attached to the unbent portion a long strip of
black-painted cardboard resembling the bar. This hung
downwards in the correct position and camouflaged the
opening.

"All set!" I whispered to the others. "I'm going out now.
Hank! Wait until I'm hidden by the shadow of the large
ventilator out there. Then join me as quickly as you can.
Billie and Ronnie, remember not to follow until we have
crossed the sentry's path safely."

I squirmed through the hole in the bars on to the flat
roof beyond. The roof joined the kitchen wall just below
our window-sill. I crept quietly forward in a blaze of light.
The eyes of a hundred windows glared down upon me.

The impression was appalling. "Does anybody ever look
out of a window at night?" I kept asking myself.

Happily there was shelter from the glare about halfway
across the roof. The high square ventilator provided a deep
shadow behind which I crawled. Hank soon followed. The
sentry plied his beat not fifteen yards away.

For several days we had arranged music practices in the
evenings in the senior officers' quarters (the theatre block).
The music was to be used for signalling, and we had to
accustom the sentry in front of us to a certain amount
of noise. While Major Anderson (Andy) played the
oboe, Colonel George Young played the concertina, and
Douglas Bader, keeping watch from a window, acted as
conductor. Their room was on the third floor, overlooking
the German courtyard. Bader could see our sentry for the
whole length of his beat. He was to start the practice at
7.30 p.m., when the traffic in the courtyard had died down.
From 8 p.m. onwards he was to keep a rigid control on the
players so that they only stopped their music when the
sentry was in a suitable position for us to cross his path. It
was not imperative that they stopped playing every time
the sentry turned his back, but when they stopped playing

that meant we could move. We arranged this signalling system because, once on the ground, we would have little concealment, and what little there was, provided by an angle in the wall of the outbuildings, prevented us from seeing the sentry.

At 8 p.m. Hank and I crawled once more into the lime-light and over the remainder of the roof, dropping to the ground over a loose, noisy gutter which gave me the jitters. In the dark angle of the wall, with our shoes around our necks and our suitcases under our arms, we waited for the music to stop. The players had been playing light jaunty airs—and then ran the gauntlet of our popular-song books. At 8 p.m. they changed to classical music; it gave them more excuse for stopping. Bader had seen us drop from the roof and would see us cross the sentry's path. The players were in the middle of Haydn's oboe concerto when they stopped.

"I shall make this a trial run," I thought.

I advanced quickly five yards to the end of the wall concealing us, and regarded the sentry. He was fidgety and looked up at Bader's window twice during the five seconds' view I had of his back. Before me was the roadway, a cobbled surface seven yards wide. Beyond was the end of a shed and some friendly concealing shrubbery. As the sentry turned, the music started again. Our players had chosen a piece the Germans love. I only hoped the sentry would not be exasperated by their repeated interruptions. The next time they stopped we would go.

The music ceased abruptly and I ran—but it started again just as I reached the corner. I stopped dead and retired hurriedly. This happened twice. Then I heard German voices through the music. It was the duty officer on his rounds. He was questioning the sentry. He was suspicious. I heard gruff orders given.

Five minutes later I was caught napping—the music stopped while I was ruminating on the cause of the duty officer's interrogation and I was not on my toes. A late dash was worse than none. I stood still and waited. I waited a long time and the music did not begin again. A quarter of an hour passed and there was still no music. Obviously something had gone wrong upstairs. I decided therefore to wait an hour in order to let suspicions die down. We had the whole night before us, and I was not going to spoil the ship for a ha'p'orth o' tar.

All this time Hank was beside me—not a word passed his lips—not a murmur or comment to distract us from the job on hand.

In the angle of the wall where we hid, there was a door. We tried the handle and found it was open, so we entered in pitch-darkness and, passing through a second door, we took temporary refuge in a room which had a small window and contained, as far as we could see, only rubbish— wastepaper, empty bottles, and empty food-tins. Outside, in the angle of the wall, any Goon with extra-sharp eyesight, passing along the roadway, would spot us. The sentry himself was also liable to extend his beat without warning and take a look around the corner of the wall where we had been hiding. In the rubbish room we were much safer.

We had been in there five minutes when, suddenly, there was a rustling of paper, a crash of falling tins, and a jangling of overturned bottles—a noise fit to waken the dead. We froze with horror. A cat leaped out from among the refuse and tore out of the room as if the devil was after it.

"That's finished everything," I exclaimed. "The Jerries will be here in a moment to investigate."

"The darn thing was after a mouse, I think," said Hank. "Let's make the best of things, anyway. They may only flash a torch round casually and we may get away with it if we try to look like a couple of sacks in the corner."

"Quick, then," I rejoined. "Grab those piles of newspapers and let's spread them out a little over our heads. It's our only hope."

We did so and waited, with our hearts thumping. Five minutes passed, and then ten, and still nobody came. We began to breathe again.

Soon our hour's vigil was over. It was 9.45 p.m. and I resolved to carry on. All was silent in the courtyard. I could now hear the sentry's footsteps clearly—approaching—and then receding. Choosing our moment, we advanced to the end of the wall as he turned on his beat. I peeped around the corner. He was ten yards off and marching away from us. The courtyard was empty. I tiptoed quickly across the roadway with Hank at my heels. Reaching the wall of the shed on the other side, we had just time to crouch behind the shrubbery before he turned. He had heard nothing. On his next receding beat we crept behind the shed, and hid in a small shrubbery, which bordered the main steps and veranda in front of the entrance to the *Kommandantur*.

The first leg of our escape was behind us. I dropped my suitcase and reconnoitred the next stage of our journey, which was to the 'pit.' Watching the sentry, I crept quickly along the narrow grass verge at the edge of the path leading away from the main steps. On one side was the path and on the other side was a long flower-bed; beyond that the balustrade of the *Kommandantur* veranda. I was in light shadow and had to crouch as I moved. Reaching the pit, about twenty-five yards away, before the sentry turned, I looked over the edge. There was a wooden trestle with steps. The pit was not deep. I dropped into it. A brick tunnel from the pit ran underneath the veranda and gave perfect concealment. That was enough. As I emerged again, I distinctly heard noises from the direction of the roofs over which we had climbed. Ronnie and Billie, who had witnessed our crossing of the roadway, were following. The sentry apparently heard nothing.

I began to creep back to the shrubbery where Hank was waiting. I was nearly halfway when, without warning, heavy footsteps sounded: a Goon was approaching quickly from the direction of the main Castle gateway and around the corner of the Castle building into sight. In a flash I was flat on my face on the grass verge, and lay rigid, just as he turned the corner and headed up the path straight towards me. He could not fail to see me. I waited for the end. He approached nearer and nearer with noisy footsteps crunching on the gravel. He was level with me. It was all over. I waited for his ejaculation at my discovery—for his warning shout to the sentry—for the familiar *"Hände hoch!"*—and the feel of his pistol in my back between the shoulder-blades.

The crunching footsteps continued past me and re-treated. He mounted the steps and entered the *Kommandantur*.

After a moment's pause to recover, I crept the remainder of the distance to the shrubbery and, as I did so, Ronnie and Billie appeared from the other direction.

Before long we were all safe in the pit without further alarms, the second lap completed! We had time to relax for a moment.

I asked Billie: "How did you get on crossing the sentry's beat?"

"We saw you two cross over and it looked as easy as pie. That gave us confidence. We made one trial, and then crossed the second time. Something went wrong with the music, didn't it?"

"Yes, that's why we held up proceedings so long," I answered. "We had a lucky break when they stopped for the last time. I thought it was the signal to move, but I was too late off the mark, thank God! I'd probably have run into the sentry's arms!"

"What do you think happened?" asked Ronnie.

"I heard the duty officer asking questions," I explained. "I think they suspected the music practice was phoney. They probably went upstairs and stopped it."

Changing the subject, I said: "I heard you coming over the roofs. I was sure the sentry could have heard."

"We made a noise at one point, I remember," said Ronnie, "but it wasn't anything to speak of. It's amazing what you can hear if your ears are expecting certain sounds. The sentry was probably thinking of his girl friend at that moment."

"If it wasn't for girl friends," I chimed in, "we probably wouldn't be on this mad jaunt anyway, so it cuts both ways," and I nudged Hank.

"It's time I got to work," I added grimly.

My next job was to try to open the door of the building which I have described as the one from which our medium-sized officer escaped. The door was fifteen yards away; it was in deep shadow, though the area between the door and the pit was only in semi-darkness. Again watching the sentry, I crept carefully to the door, and then started work with a set of *passe-partout* keys I had brought with me. I had one unnerving interruption, when I heard Priem's voice in the distance returning from the town. I had just sufficient time to creep back to the pit and hide, before he came around the corner.

We laughed inwardly as he passed by us along the path, talking loudly to another officer. I could not help thinking of the occasion when he stood outside Gephard's office and did not have the door unlocked!

Poor old Priem! He was not a bad type on the whole. He had a sense of humour which made him almost human.

It was 11 p.m. when Priem passed by. I worked for an hour on the door without success and finally gave up. We were checked, and would have to find another exit.

We felt our way along the tunnel leading from the pit under the veranda, and after eight yards came to a large cellar with a low arched ceiling supported on pillars. It had something to do with sewage, for Hank, at one point, stepped off solid ground and nearly fell into what might have been deep water! He must have disturbed a scum on top of the liquid because a dreadful stench arose. When I was well away from the entrance, I struck a match. There was a solitary wheelbarrow for furniture, and at the far end of the cavern-like cellar, a chimney flue. I had previously noticed a faint glimmer of light from this direction. Examining the flue, I found it was an air-vent which led vertically upwards from the ceiling of the cavern for about four feet, and then curved outwards towards the fresh air.

Hank pushed me up the flue. In plan it was about nine inches by three feet. I managed to wriggle myself high enough to see around the curve. The flue ended at the vertical face of a wall two feet away from me as a barred opening shaped like a letter-box slot. The opening was at the level of the ground outside, and was situated on the far side of the building—the moat side for which we were heading, but it was a practical impossibility to negotiate this flue. There were bars, and in any case only a pigmy could have wriggled round the curve.

We held a conference.

"We seem to have struck a dead end," I started; "this place is a cul-de-sac and I can't manage the door either. I'm terribly sorry, but there we are!"

"Can anyone think of another way out?" asked Ronnie.

"The main gateway, I think, is out of the question," I went on. "Since Neave's escape nearly a year ago, they lock the inner gate this side of the bridge over the moat. That means we can't reach the side gate leading down into the moat."

"Our only hope is through the *Kommandantur*," suggested Billie. "We can try it either now, and hope to get through unseen—or else try it early in the morning when there's a little traffic about and some doors may be unlocked."

"Do you really think we'll ever pass scrutiny at that hour?" questioned Ronnie. "If we must take that route, I think it's better to try it at about 3 a.m. when the whole camp is dead asleep."

I was thinking how impossibly foolhardy was the idea of going through the *Kommandantur*. I remembered that other attempt—years ago now it seemed—when we had pumped men through the hole in the lavatory into the *Kommandantur*. I had considered then that the idea was mad. I thought aloud:

"There are only three known entrances to the *Kommandantur*: the main front door, the French windows behind, which open on to the grass patch right in front of a sentry, and the little door under the archway leading to the park. The archway gate is locked and the door is the wrong side of it."

In desperation, I said: "I'm going to have another look at the flue."

This time I removed some of my top clothing and found I could slide more easily up the shaft. I examined the bars closely and found one was loose in its mortar socket. As I did so, I heard footsteps outside the opening and a Goon patrol approached. The Goon had an Alsatian with him. A heavy pair of boots tramped past me. I could have touched them with my hand. The dog pattered behind and did not see me. I imagine the smell issuing from the flue obliterated my scent.

I succeeded in loosening one end of the bar and bent it nearly double. Slipping down into the cellar again, I whispered to the others: "There's a vague chance we may be able to squeeze through the flue. Anyway, it's worth trying. We shall have to strip completely naked."

"Hank and Billie will never make it," said Ronnie. "It's impossible; they're too big. You and I might manage it with help at both ends—with someone pushing below and someone else pulling from above."

"I think I can make it," I rejoined, "If someone stands on the wheelbarrow and helps to push me through. Once I'm out, I can do the pulling. Hank had better come next. If he can make it, we all can."

Hank was over six feet tall and Billie nearly six feet. Ronnie and I were smaller, and Ronnie was very thin.

"Neither Hank nor I," intervened Billie, "will ever squeeze around the curve on our tummies. Our knees are not double-jointed and our legs will stick. We'll have to come out on our backs."

'Agreed," I said. "Then I go first, Hank next, then Billie and Ronnie last. Ronnie, you'll have no one to push you, but if two of us grab your arms and pull, we should manage it. Be careful undressing. Don't leave anything behind—we want to leave no traces. Hand your clothes to me in neat bundles, and your suitcases. I'll dispose of them temporarily outside."

After a tremendous struggle, I succeeded in squeezing through the chimney and sallied forth naked on to the path outside. Bending down into the flue again, I could just reach Hank's hand as he passed me up my clothes and my suitcase, and then his own. I hid the kit in some bushes near the path and put on enough dark clothing to make me inconspicuous. Hank was stripped and struggling in the hole with his back towards me. I managed to grab one arm and heaved, while he was pushed from below. Inch by inch he advanced and at the end of twenty minutes, with a last wrench, I pulled him clear. He was bruised all over and streaming with perspiration. During all that time we were at the mercy of any passer-by. What a spectacle it must have been—a naked man being squeezed through a hole in the wall like toothpaste out of a tube! To the imaginative-minded in the eerie darkness, it must have looked as if the massive walls of the Castle were slowly descending upon the man's body while his comrade was engaged in a desperate tug-of-war to save his life!

Hank retired to the bushes to recover and dress himself.

Next came Billie's clothes and suitcase, and then Billie himself. I extracted him in about fifteen minutes. Then Ronnie's kit arrived. I gave him a sheet on which to pull in order to begin his climb. After that, two of us set about him, and he was out in about ten minutes. We all collapsed in the bushes for a breather. It was about 3.30 a.m. and we had completed the third leg of our marathon.

"What do you think of our chances now?" I asked Billie.

"I'm beyond thinking of chances," was the reply, "but I know I shall never forget this night as long as I live."

"I hope you've got all your kit," I said, smiling at him in the darkness. "I should hate to have to push you back down the shaft to fetch it!"

"I'd give anything for a smoke," sighed Billie.

"I see no reason why you shouldn't smoke as we walk

past the Barracks if you feel like it. What cigarettes have you got?"

"Gold Flake, I think."

"Exactly! You'd better start chain-smoking, because you'll have to throw the rest away before you reach Leisnig. Had you thought of that?"

"But I've got fifty!"

"Too bad," I replied. "With luck you've got about three hours; that's seventeen cigarettes an hour. Can you do it?"

"I'll try," said Billie ruefully.

A German was snoring loudly in a room with the window open, a few yards away. The flue through which we had just climbed gave on to a narrow path running along the top of the moat immediately under the main Castle walls. The bushes we hid in were on the very edge of the moat. The moat wall was luckily stepped into three successive descents. The drops were about eighteen feet and the steps were about two yards wide, with odd shrubs and grass growing on them. A couple of sheets were made ready. After half an hour's rest, and fully clothed once more, we dropped down one by one. I went last and fell into the arms of those below me.

On the way down, Billie suddenly developed a tickle in his throat and started a cough which disturbed the dogs. They began barking in their kennels, which we saw for the first time, uncomfortably near the route we were to take. Billie in desperation ate a quantity of grass and earth, which seemed to stop the irritation in his throat. By the time we reached the bottom of the moat it was 4.30 a.m. The fourth leg was completed.

We tidied our clothes and adjusted the socks over our shoes. In a few moments we would have to pass underneath a lamp at the corner of the road leading to the German barracks. This was the road leading to the double gates in the outer wall around the Castle grounds. It was the road taken by Neave and by Van Doorninck.

The lamp was situated in full view of a sentry—luckily,

some forty-five yards away—who would be able to contemplate our back silhouettes as we turned the corner and faded into the darkness beyond.

The dogs had ceased barking. Hank and I moved off

The descent into the moat

first—over a small railing, on to a path, past the kennels, down some steps, round the corner under the light, and away into the darkness. We walked leisurely, side by side, as if we were inmates of the barracks returning after a night's carousal in the town.

Before passing the barracks I had one last duty to perform—to give those in the camp an idea as to what we had done, to indicate whether other escapers would be able to follow our route or not. I had half a dozen pieces of white cardboard cut into various shapes—a square, an oblong, a triangle, a circle, and so on. Dick Howe and I had arranged a code whereby each shape gave him some information. I threw certain of the cards down on to a small grass patch below the road, past which our exercise parade marched on their way to the park. With luck, if the parade was not cancelled for a week, Dick would see the cards. My message ran:

"Exit from pit. Moat easy; no traces left."

Although I had pulled the bar of the flue exit back into place, we had, in truth, probably left minor traces. But as the alternative message was: "Exit obvious to Goons"—which would have been the case, for instance, if we left fifty feet of sheet-rope dangling from a window—I preferred to encourage other escapers to have a shot at following us.

We continued another hundred yards past the barracks, where the garrison was peacefully sleeping, and arrived at our last obstacle—the outer wall. It was only ten feet high here, with coils of barbed wire stretched along the top. I was on the wall heaving Hank up, when, with a sudden pounding of my heart, I noticed the glow of a cigarette in the distance. It was approaching. Then I realised it was Billie. They had caught us up. We had arranged a discreet gap between us so that we did not look like a regiment passing under the corner lamp.

The barbed wire did not present a serious obstacle when tackled without hurry and with minute care. We were all eventually over the wall, but none too soon, because we had a long way to go in order to be safe before dawn. It was 5.15 in the morning, and the fifth leg of the marathon was over. The sixth and last stage—the long journey to Switzerland—lay ahead of us!

We shook hands all round and with "Au revoir—see you in Switzerland in a few days," Hank and I set off along the road. Two hundred yards behind us, the other two followed. Soon they branched off on their route and we took to the fields.

As we trudged along, Hank fumbled for a long time in his pockets, and then uttered practically the first words he had spoken during the whole night. He said:

"I reckon, Pat, I must have left my pipe at the top of the moat."

CHAPTER XXI

LIBERTY EXPRESS

HANK and I walked fast. We intended to lie up for a day. Therefore, in order to be at all safe we had to put the longest distance possible between ourselves and the camp. We judged the German search would be concentrated in the direction of a village about five miles away, for which Ronnie and Billie headed and in which there was a railway station. The first train was shortly before morning *Appell*. Provided there was no alarm in the camp before then, and if the two of them could reach the station in time for the train (which now seemed probable), they would be in Leipzig before the real search started. This was the course Lulu Lawton had taken, but he had missed the train and had to hide up in a closely hunted area.

Hank and I chose a difficult route, calculated to put the hunters off the scent. We headed first south and then westwards in a big sweep in the direction of the River Mulde which ran due northwards towards the Elbe. In order to reach a railway station we had to trek about twenty miles and cross the river into the bargain. It was not a 'cushy' escape-route and we relied on the Germans thinking likewise.

We walked for about an hour and a half, and when it was almost daylight entered a wood and hid up in a thicket for the day. We must have been five miles away from the camp. Although we tried to sleep, our nerves were as taut as piano wires. I was on the alert the whole day.

"A wild animal must have magnificent nerves," I said to Hank at one point.

"Wild animals have nerves just like you and I. That's why they are not captured easily," was his comment.

Hank was not going to be easy to catch. His fiancée had been waiting for him since the night when he took off in his bomber in April 1940. It would plainly require more than a few tough Germans to recapture him. It gave me confidence to know he was beside me.

I mused for a long time over the queer twists that Fate gives to our lives. I had always assumed that Rupert and I would escape finally together. Yet it happened to be Hank's turn, and here we were. I had left old and tried friends behind me. Two years of constant companionship had cemented some of us together very closely. 'Rupert, Harry, Dick, Kenneth and Peter. Would I ever see them again?' Inside the camp the probability of early failure in the escape was so great that we brushed aside all serious thought of a long parting.

Here in the woods it was different. If I did my job properly from now on, it was probable that I would never see them again. We were not going back to Colditz; Hank was sure of that too. I was rather shaken by the thought, realising fully for the first time what these men meant to me. We had been through much together. I prayed that we might all survive the war and meet again.

As dusk fell we set off across the fields. Sometimes when roads led in our direction we used them, but we had to be very careful. On one occasion we only just left the road in time as we saw a light ahead (unusual in the blackout) and heard voices. A car approaching was stopped. As we by-passed the light by way of the fields, we saw an army motor-cyclist talking to a sentry. It was a control and they were after us. We passed within fifty yards of them!

It seemed a long way to the river. As the night wore on, I could hardly keep my eyes open. I stumbled and dozed as I walked, and finally gave up.

"Hank, I'll have to lie down for an hour and sleep. I've been sleep-walking as it is. I don't know where we're going."

"O.K. I'll stay on guard while you pass out on that bank over there under the tree," said Hank, indicating a mound of grass looming ahead of us.

He woke me in an hour and we continued, eventually

reaching the river. It was in a deep cutting, down which we
climbed, and there was a road which ran along its bank.
Towards our left, crossing the river and the cutting, was a
high-level railway bridge. I decided to cross it. We had to
reclimb the cutting. Sleep was overcoming me once more.
The climb was steep and over huge rocks cut into steps
like those of the pyramids. It was a nightmare climb in the
pitch-darkness, as I repeatedly stumbled, fell down, and
slept where I lay. Hank would tug at me, pull me over the
next huge stone and set me on my feet without a word,
only to have to repeat the performance again in a few
moments. Halfway up the embankment we stopped to rest.
I slept, but Hank was on the qui vive and, peering through
the darkness, noticed a movement on the railway bridge.
It needed a cat's eye to notice anything at all. He shook
me and said:

"Pat, we're not going over that bridge; it's guarded."

"How the hell do you know for certain?" I asked, "and
how are we going to cross the river, then?"

"I don't mind if we have to swim it, but I'm not crossing
that bridge."

I gave way, though it meant making a big half-circle,
crossing the railway line and descending to the river again
somewhere near a road bridge which we knew existed
farther upstream.

Reaching the top of the railway-bridge embankment we
crossed the lines, and as we did so we saw in the distance
from the direction of the bridge the flash of a lighted
match.

"Did you see that?" I whispered.

"Yes."

"There's a sentry on the bridge, sure enough. You were
right, Hank. Thank God you insisted."

Gradually we edged down the hill again where the river
cutting was less steep, and found that our bearings had not
been too bad; for we saw the road bridge in the foreground. We inspected it carefully before crossing, listening
for a long time for any sound of movement. It was un-

guarded. We crossed rapidly and took to the bushes on the far side, not a moment too soon; a motor-cycle came roaring round a bend, its headlight blazing, and crossed the bridge in the direction from which we had come.

We tramped wearily across country on a compass bearing until dawn. Near the village of Penig, where our railway station was situated, we spruced ourselves up, attempted a shave and polished our shoes. We entered the village—it was almost a small industrial town—and wended our way in the direction of the station. I was loth to ask our way at this time of the morning when few people were about. Instead, we wandered onwards past some coal-yards where a tram-line started. The tracks ran alongside a large factory and then switched over to the other side of the road, passing under trees and beside a small river. We followed the lines, which eventually crossed a bridge and entered the town proper. I was sure the tram-lines would lead us to the station. The town was dingy, not at all like Colditz, which was of pleasing appearance. Upkeep had evidently gone to the dogs. Broken window-panes were filled with newspaper, ironwork was rusty, and the front doors of the houses, which opened directly on the street, badly needed a coat of paint.

We arrived at the railway station. It was on the far edge of the town and looked older and out of keeping with the buildings around it. It had a staid respectable atmosphere and belonged to a period before industry had come to Penig. We entered and looked up the trains. Our route was Munich via Zwickau. I saw we had a three-hour wait and then another long wait at Zwickau before the night express for Munich. Leaving the station, we walked out into the country again and settled down for a meal and a rest behind a barn near the road. It is dangerous to wait in railway stations or public parks and advisable to keep moving under any circumstances when in a town.

We returned to the station towards midday. I bought two third-class tickets to Munich and we caught the train comfortably. Our suitcases were a definite asset. My German accent was anything but perfect, but the brandishing of my suitcase on all occasions to emphasise whatever I happened to be saying worked like a soporific on the Germans.

In Zwickau, having another long wait, we boarded a tram. I tripped on the mounting-step and nearly knocked the conductress over. I apologised loudly.

"Entschuldigen Sie mir! Bitte! entschuldigen, entschuldigen. Ich bin ein Auslander."

We sat down, and when the conductress came round I beamed at her and asked in broken German:

"Gnädige Fräulein! If you please, where is the nearest cinema? We have a long time to wait for our train and would like to see a film and the news pictures. We are foreigners and do not know this town."

"The best cinema in Zwickau is five minutes from here. I shall tell you where to alight."

"How much is the fare, please, *Fräulein?"*

"Twenty pfennigs each, if you please."

"Danke schön," I said, proffering the money.

After five minutes the tram stopped at a main thoroughfare junction and the conductress beckoned to us. As we alighted, one of the passengers pointed out to us with a voluble and, to me, incoherent stream of German exactly where the cinema was. I could gather that he was proud to meet foreigners who were working for the victory of 'Unser Reich!' He took off his moth-eaten hat as we parted and waved a courteous farewell.

Zwickau was just a greatly enlarged Penig as far as I could see. Dilapidation was visible everywhere. The inhabitants gave me an impression of impoverishment, and only the uniforms of officials, including the tram conductress, and those of the armed forces bore a semblance of smartness.

Hank and I spent a comfortable two hours in the cinema, which was no different from any other I have seen. German officers and troops were dotted about in seats all around us

and made up ninety per cent. of the audience. I dozed for
a long time and I noticed Hank's head drooping too. After
two hours I whispered to him:

"It's time to go. What did you think of the film?"

"What I saw of it was a washout," Hank replied. "I
must have slept though, because I missed parts of it. It was
incoherent."

"This cinema seems to be nothing more than impromptu sleeping-quarters. Look around you," and I
nudged Hank. The German Heer and Luftwaffe were
dozing in all sorts of postures around us!

"Let's go," I said and, yawning repeatedly, we rose and
left the auditorium.

Returning to the station in good time, we boarded the
express to Munich. It was crowded out, for which I was
glad, and Hank and I spent the whole night standing in
the corridor. Nobody paid any attention to us. We might
as well have been in an express bound from London to the
North. The lighting, however, was so bad that few passengers attempted to read. It was intensely stuffy owing to the
overcrowding, the cold outside, and the blackout curtains
on all windows. The hypnotic drumming and the swaying
of the train pervaded all.

Our fellow-travellers were a mixed bag; a few army and
air force other ranks, some workmen, and a majority of
down-at-heel-looking business men or Government officials.
There was not a personality among them; all were sheep
ready to be slaughtered at the altar of Hitler. There was a
police control in the early hours. I produced my much-
soiled German leather wallet, which exposed my identity
card or *Ausweis* behind a grimy scratched piece of cellu-
loid. The police officer was curt:

"*Sie sind Ausländer?*"

"*Jawohl.*"

"*Wo fahren Sie hin?*"

"*Nach München und Rottweil.*"

"*Warum?*"

"*Betonarbeit*" (that is, concrete work).

Hank was slow in producing his papers. I said:

"*Wir sind zusammen. Er ist mein Kamerad.*"

Hank proffered his papers as I added, taking the officer into my confidence:

"*Er ist etwas dumm, aber ein guter Kerl.*"

The control passed on and we relaxed into a fitful doze as we roared through the night towards Munich—and Switzerland.

We arrived in Munich in the cold grey of the morning— several hours late. There had been bombing and train diversions.

I queued up at the booking-office, telling Hank to stand by. When my turn came I asked for, "*Zweimal dritte Klasse, nach Rottweil.*" The woman behind the grill said:

"*Fünfundsechzig Mark bitte.*"

I produced fifty-six marks, which almost drained me right out. The woman repeated:

"*Fünfundsechzig Mark bitte, noch neun Mark.*"

I was confusing the German for fifty-six with sixty-five.

"*Karl,*" I shouted in Hank's direction, "*geben Sie mir noch Zehn Mark.*"

Hank took the cue, and produced a ten-mark note which I handed to the woman.

"*Ausweis bitte,*" she said.

I produced it.

"*Gut,*" and she handed my wallet back to me.

I was so relieved that as I left the queue, forgetting my part completely, I said in a loud voice:

"All right, Hank, I've got the tickets!"

I nearly froze in my tracks. As we hurried away I felt the baleful glare of a hundred eyes burning through my back. We were soon lost in the crowd, and what a crowd! Everybody seemed to be travelling. The station appeared to be untouched by bombing and traffic was obviously running at high pressure. We had another long wait for the train which would take us to Rottweil via Ulm and Tutt-lingen. I noted with relief that the wait in Ulm was only ten minutes. Hyde-Thomson and his Dutch colleague, the

second two officers of my theatre escape, had been trapped
in Ulm station. The name carried foreboding and I prayed
we would negotiate this junction safely. I also noticed with
appreciation that there was a substantial wait at Tuttlingen for the train to Rottweil. It would give us an excuse
for leaving the station.

In Munich I felt safe. The waiting-rooms were full to
overflowing and along with other passengers we were even
shepherded by station police to an underground bomb-
proof waiting-room—signposted for the use of all persons
having longer than half an hour to wait for a train.

Before descending to this waiting-room, however, I asked
for the *Bahnhofswirtschaft* and roving along the counter
I saw a large notice '*markenfreies Essen,*' which meant
'coupon-free meals'! I promptly asked for two and also *Zwei
Liter Pilsner.* They were duly served and Hank and I sat
down at a table by ourselves to the best meal provided us
by the Germans in two and a half years. The *Markenfreies
Essen* consisted of a very generous helping of thick stew—
mostly vegetable and potatoes, but some good-tasting
sausage-meat was floating around as well. The beer seemed
excellent to our parched gullets. We had not drunk anything since our repast on the outskirts of Penig when we
had finished the water we carried with us.

We went to the underground waiting-room. We were
controlled once in a cursory manner. I was blasé by now
and smiled benignly at the burly representative of the
Sicherheitspolizei—security police, that is—as he passed by,
hardly glancing at the wallets we pushed under his nose.

In good time we boarded the train for Ulm. Arriving
there at midday, we changed platforms without incident
and quickly boarded our next train. This did not go direct
to Rottweil, but necessitated changing at Tuttlingen. Rottweil was thirty miles, but Tuttlingen only fifteen miles
from the frontier! My intention was to walk out of the
station at Tuttlingen with the excuse of waiting for the
Rottweil train and never return.

This Hank and I duly did. As I walked off the station

platform at Tuttlingen, through the barrier, we handed
in our tickets. We had walked ten yards when I heard
shouts behind us:

"*Kommen Sie her! Hier, kommen Sie zurück!*"

I turned round, fearing the worst, and saw the ticket-
collector waving at us.

I returned to him and he said:

"*Sie haben Ihre Fahrkarten abgegeben, aber Sie fahren
nach Rottweil. Die müssen Sie noch behalten.*"

With almost visible relief I accepted the tickets once
more. In my anxiety I had forgotten that we were osten-
sibly due to return to catch the Rottweil train and, of
course, still needed our tickets.

From the station we promptly took the wrong road;
there were no signposts. It was late afternoon and a Saturday (October 17th). The weather was fine. We walked for
a long time along a road which refused to turn in the
direction in which we thought it ought to turn! It was
maddening. We passed a superbly camouflaged factory and
sidings. There must have been an area of ten acres completely covered with a false flat roof of what appeared to be
rush matting. Even at the low elevation at which we found
ourselves looking down upon it, the whole site looked like
farmland. If the camouflage was actually rush matting, I
do not know how they provided against fire risks.

We were gradually being driven into a valley heading
due south, whereas we wished to travel westwards. Leaving
the road as soon as possible without creating suspicion, we
tried to make a short-cut across country to another highway which we knew headed west. As a short-cut it
misfired, taking us over hilly country which prolonged
our journey considerably. Evening was drawing in by the
time we reached the correct road. We walked along this for
several miles, and when it was dark, took to the woods to
lie up for the night.

We passed a freezing, uncomfortable night on beds of
leaves in the forest and were glad to warm ourselves with
a sharp walk early the next morning, which was Sunday.

I was thankful it was a Sunday because it gave us a good excuse to be out walking in the country.

We now headed along roads leading south-west, until at 8 a.m. we retired again to the friendly shelter of the woods to eat our breakfast, consuming most of what was left of our German bread, sugar, and margarine.

We had almost finished our repast when we were disturbed by a farmer who approached and eyed us curiously for a long time. He wore close-fitting breeches and gaiters like a typical English gamekeeper. I did not like his attitude at all. He came close to us and demanded what we were doing. I said:

"Wir essen. Können Sie das nicht sehen?"

"Warum sind Sie hier?" he asked, to which I answered:

"Wir gehen spazieren; es ist Sonntag, nicht wahr!"

At this he retired. I watched him carefully. As soon as he was out of the wood and about fifty yards away, I saw him turn along a hedge and change his gait into a trot.

This was enough for me. In less than a minute we were packed and trotting fast in the opposite direction, which happened to be southward! We did not touch the road again for some time, but kept to the woods and lanes. Gradually, however, the countryside became open and cultivated and we were forced once more to the road. We passed a German soldier, who was smartly turned out in his Sunday best, with a friendly 'Heil Hitler!' Church bells were ringing out from steeples which rose head and shoulders above the roofs of several villages dotted here and there in the rolling country around us.

We walked through one of the villages as the people were coming out of church. I was terrified of the children, who ran out of the church shouting and laughing. They gambolled around us and eyed us curiously, although their elders took no notice of us at all. I was relieved, none the less, when we left the village behind us. Soon afterwards, the country again became wooded and hilly, and we disappeared amongst the trees, heading now due south.

As the afternoon wore on I picked up our bearings more

accurately, and we aimed at the exact location of the frontier crossing. A little too soon—I thought—we reached the frontier road, running east and west. I could not be sure, so we continued eastwards along it to where it entered some woods. We passed a fork where a forest track, which I recognised, joined it. I knew then that we were indeed on the frontier road and that we had gone too far eastwards. At that moment there were people following us, and we could not break off into the woods without looking suspicious. We walked onward casually and at the end of the wooded portion of the road we heard suddenly:

"*Halt! Wer da!*" and then, more deliberately, "*Wo gehen Sie hin?*"

A sentry-box stood back from the road in a clump of trees and from it stepped forth a frontier guard.

"*Wir gehen nach Singen,*" I said. "*Wir sind Ausländer.*"

"*Ihren Ausweis, bitte!*"

We produced our papers, including the special permit allowing us to travel near the frontier. We were close to him. His rifle was slung over his shoulder. The people who had been following us had turned down a lane towards a cottage. We were alone with the sentry.

I chatted on, gesticulating with my suitcase brazenly conspicuous.

"We are Flemish workmen. This evening we take the train to Rottweil, where there is much construction work. We must be there in the morning. Today we can rest and we like your woods and countryside."

He eyed us for a moment; handed us back our papers and let us go. As we walked on I dreaded to hear another 'Halt!' I imagined that if the sentry were not satisfied with us he would, for his own safety, move us off a few yards so that he could unsling his rifle. But no command was given and we continued our 'Sunday afternoon stroll.' As we moved out of earshot Hank said to me:

"If he'd reached for his gun when he was close to us just then, I would have knocked him to Kingdom come."

I would not have relished being knocked to Kingdom

come by Hank and I often wonder if the sentry did not notice a look in Hank's eye and think that discretion was perhaps the better part of valour! A lonely sentry is not all-powerful against two enemies, even with his gun levelled. Our story may have had a vague ring of truth, but none the less, we were foreigners within half a mile of the Swiss frontier!

Soon we were able to leave the road and we started to double back across country to our frontier crossing-point. Just as we came to a railway line and climbed a small embankment, we nearly jumped out of our skins with fright as a figure darted from a bush in front of us and ran for his life into a thicket and disappeared. I could have assured him, if only he had stopped, that he gave us just as big a fright as we gave him!

By dusk we had found our exact location and waited in deep pine woods for darkness to descend. The frontier was scarcely a mile away. We ate a last meal nervously and without appetite. Our suitcases would not be required any more, so they were buried. When it was pitch-dark, we pulled on socks over our shoes, and set off. We had to negotiate the frontier-crossing in inky blackness, entirely from memory of the maps studied in Colditz. We crossed over more railway lines and then continued, skirting the edge of a wood. We encountered a minor road, which foxed me for a while because it should not have been there according to my memory, but we carried on. Hearing a motor-cycle pass along a road in front of us, a road running close to and parallel with the frontier, warned us of the proximity of our 'take-off' point. We entered the woods to our left and proceeded parallel with the road eastwards for about a hundred yards and then approached it cautiously. Almost as we stumbled into it, I suddenly recognised the outline of a sentry-box hidden among the trees straight in front of us!

We were within five yards of it when I recognised its angular roof. My hair stood on end. It was impossible to move without breaking twigs under our feet. They made noises like pistol shots and we could be heard easily. We retreated with as much care as we could, but even the crackle of a dried leaf caused me to perspire freely.

To compensate for this unnerving encounter, however, I now knew exactly where we were, for the sentry-box was marked on our Colditz map and provided me with a check bearing. We moved off seventy yards and approached the road again. Peering across it, we could discern fields and low hedges. In the distance was our goal: a wooded hill looming blacker than the darkness around it, with the woods ending abruptly halfway down its eastern slopes, towards our left. This end of the woods was our 'pointer.' There was no 'blackout' in Switzerland, and beyond the hill was the faintest haze of light, indicating the existence of a Swiss village.

At 7.30 p.m. we moved off. Crouching low, and at the double, we crossed the road and headed for our 'pointer.' Without stopping for breath we ran—through hedges—across ditches—wading through mud—and then on again. Dreading barbed wire which we could never have seen, we ran, panting with excitement as much as with breathlessness, across fields newly ploughed, meadows and marshland, till at last we rounded the corner of the woods. Here, for a moment, we halted for breath.

I felt that if I could not have a drink of water soon I would die. My throat was parched and swollen and my tongue was choking me. My heart was pounding like a sledge-hammer. I was gasping for breath. I had lived for two and a half years, both awake and in sleep, with the vision of this race before me and every nerve in my body was taut to breaking-pitch.

We were not yet 'home.' We had done about half a mile and could see the lights of the Swiss village ahead. Great care was now necessary, for we could easily recross the frontier into Germany without knowing it, and stumble on a guard-post. From the corner of the wood we had to continue in a sweeping curve, first towards our right, and then left again towards the village. Where we stood we were actually in Switzerland, but in a direct line between us and the Swiss village lay Germany.

Why had we run instead of creeping forward warily? The answer is that instinct dictated it and, I think in this case, instinct was right. Escapers' experience has borne out that the psychological reaction of a fleeing man to a shouted command, such as "Halt," varies. If a man is walking or creeping the reaction is to stop. If he is running the reaction is to run faster. It is in the split seconds of such instinctive decisions that success or failure may be determined.

We continued on our way at a rapid walk, over grass and boggy land, crouching low at every sound. It was important to avoid even Swiss frontier-posts. We had heard curious rumours of escapers being returned to the Germans by unfriendly Swiss guards. However untrue, we were taking no risks.

We saw occasional shadowy forms and circled widely around them and at last, at 8.30 p.m., approached the village along a sandy path.

We were about a thousand yards inside the Swiss frontier. We had completed the four-hundred-mile journey from Colditz in less than four days.

Under the first lamp-post of the village street, Hank and I shook hands in silence. . . .

* * * * *

We beat Ronnie and Billie by twenty-six hours. At 10.30 p.m. the following evening they crossed the frontier safely!

EPILOGUE

A MONTH after I reached Switzerland, the invasion of North Africa occurred and the Germans took over the south of France. Switzerland became a neutral island in a belligerent's home waters. The British Legation in Berne had only the Swiss Postal wireless telegraphic facilities of communication with London.

I had made a short report on Escape from Colditz in general, which never reached home. In that report, I made a statement which I would like to repeat here. It was:

> Although in one case or another the name of practically every officer could be included in a list of those who worked for the common good at the expense of their own, I mention especially the following—not in order of priority:
>
> Lieut.-Col. Guy German, Leicester Regiment; Lieut.-Col. G. Young. R.E.; Major W. F. Anderson, R.E.; Sqd.-Ldr. H. M. MacColm, R.A.F.; Capt. R. Barry, 52nd Light Inf.; Capt. R. Howe, R.T.R.; Capt. K. Lockwood, Q.R.R.; Flight Lieut. N. Forbes, R.A.F.; Flight Lieut. H. Wardle, R.A.F.; Lieut. W. L. B. O'Hara, R.T.R.; Lieut. D. Gill, Royal Norfolks; Lieut. "Rex" Harrison, Green Howards; Lieut. J. K. V. Lee, R.C.S.; E.R.A. W. Hammond, R.N.
>
> In general these officers all placed at the disposal of the camp some flair or technical qualification without regard to personal consequences.

This story brings the war history of Colditz up to November 1942. The camp was relieved by the Americans on April 15th, 1945. The prisoners had therefore nearly another two and a half years in front of them when I left. I pay tribute to their endurance, for I could not picture myself lasting that length of time at Colditz without becoming a neurasthenic.

Two other British officers made successful escapes from the camp: Harry Elliott and 'Skipper' Barnet (Lieutenant R. Barnet, R.N.). Elliott foxed German Medical Boards for years on end, suffering from terrible stomach ulcers produced on substitute X-ray plates. He lost weight regularly and to an astonishing degree by having himself weighed to begin with, loaded with bags of sand concealed under his pyjamas. Thereafter, weight-losing was a simple procedure, and like an observation balloon he jettisoned ballast at will. Skipper Barnet practised 'Yoga' for a long time until, by muscular control, he could raise his blood pressure to incredible heights. The Germans finally repatriated him, convinced he would never survive the excitement of a homecoming. Skipper, incidentally, was the boxer at Laufen who nearly knocked Harry Elliott out with a stout door between them.

One or two French officers, also removed to hospital at death's door, managed to rise from their beds and escape successfully to France.

A time came when it was no longer worth while trying to escape. This period probably started around 'D' Day, June 1944. Then it became a question of waiting patiently for the sound of the guns and the arrival of the Allies at the gates of the Castle.

Many events of interest took place, however, before that time. There were several brilliant, though unsuccessful, escape attempts, made under the guidance of Dick Howe. Rupert Barry made another game bid for freedom but was recaught while innocently trundling a wheelbarrow out of the last gateway of Colditz. Michael Sinclair, whose name is rapidly becoming legendary among escape fans, made three more attempts. On the first occasion he did not go far; he was shot through the chest at the Castle gateway. He recovered. On his next attempt he reached Reine, twenty-five miles from the Dutch frontier, along with his companion Flight Lieutenant J. W. Best, R.A.F., before recapture. On his third attempt he was shot dead some yards from the wire of the Colditz park recreation ground.

His memory is especially honoured by every man who knew him.

Best was chiefly known for his 'mole' escape from an Air Force camp (Sagan, I think), which brought him to Colditz. In this attempt he and another officer, Bill Gold-finch, made a sufficiently long tunnel to house themselves with some space to spare for what is known as 'bulking.' They laid in a stock of provisions and had an air-tube. They then carried on digging at their leisure, and eventually surfaced at a reasonable distance from the camp and walked off!

The French tunnel was still under construction when I left. It is worth a chapter to itself. The Dutch departed from Colditz and, unhitching their railway coach in motion on the way to their next camp, the whole contingent escaped in various directions when it came to a standstill! The escape of E.R.A.s Hammond and Lister, which I have mentioned in this book, is among the cream of escape stories. Dick Howe, from somewhere high up in the Castle, eventually made contact with the concealed manhole (which I had tried to reach from the delousing shed) in the prison courtyard. From there he carried on through a maze of drains until he reached the main Castle outfall sewer. The Germans, unfortunately, discovered this attempt before it reached fruition. Dick also took over magnificently concealed wireless sets left by the French and gave the prisoners daily News Bulletins. More 'Prominenten' arrived, of various nationalities—General Bòr Komorowsky, Captain the Earl of Hopetoun, Lieutenant Alexander, Lieutenant Lascelles, First Lieutenant John Winant (U.S.A.F.), and others. American POWs joined the serried ranks of the hardbitten Colditz convicts! Finally the 'Relief of Colditz' was dramatically exciting, and carried with it a touch of pathos which it would be difficult to describe. All this and much more has been incorporated in *The Latter Days*, which concludes the saga of the Fortress Prison.

THE LATTER DAYS

Colditz Castle

TO
MICHAEL, DIANA,
CHRISTOPHER AND CHRISTINA
AND NOW HENRY

ACKNOWLEDGMENTS

My principal collaborators in the work of collecting the material for this book have been Captain 'Dick' Howe, M.B.E., M.C., formerly of the Royal Tank Regiment and Captain 'Lulu' Lawton of the Duke of Wellington's. Major Harry Elliott of the Irish Guards has been a close third. Without them this book would not have been written. It is a happy coincidence that Dick and Harry should have been my colleagues on one of the first escapes from a German Prison Camp in the last war—early in September, 1940!

John Watton, who went through the war at Colditz, has contributed the cover and the illustrations. He can bring the written word to life. His sense of atmosphere, his detail and his memory have always astonished me.

From Holland I have had unstinted, generous help from Captain G. W. T. Dames of the Royal Netherlands Indies Army. I could not have written of the Dutch without him. From France I have had the help of General Le Brigant through his well-known work, 'Les Indomptables,' the French classic on the Fortress Prison, and of Père Yves Congar, who has written a memorable epitaph to the Frenchmen who never returned, in his book, 'Leur Résistance'.

Mr. John K. Lichtblau, the well-known American critic and newspaper correspondent, has helped me to follow up trails in the U.S.A. and Major V. Dluznievski, now living in England, has traced for me many obscure details concerning the remnants of the Polish Contingent of Colditz.

Herr Hans Pfeiffer has been my link with Germany, and in a frank, friendly manner has given me the German point of view.

Returning to Britain, I acknowledge with gratitude—and pleasure, because they are still very much alive—the help of many ex-Colditz men: Alan Campbell who has contributed poetry * and notes of his legal battles with the German High Command, Rupert Barry and Peter Storie Pugh for their scrap books of the war and their notes, Geoffrey Wardle and his wife

---

* He has recently published his Colditz poems in *Colditz Cameo*, from the Ditchling Press, Ditchling, Sussex. I think *Cameo* is a highly talented and moving anthology.—P. R. R.

and children for an enjoyable evening in which the glider was rebuilt in fantasy, Peter Tunstall, Kenneth Lee, Padre Ellison Platt for the use of his sermon and his song, Edmund Hannay and Mike Harvey.

I wish to acknowledge my indebtedness to *The Times* and to the *Sunday Express* for the reproduction of extracts from editions of May, 1945, and to the publishers of 'Detour', a book from the Falcon Press, which contains an interesting series of war reminiscences and much about Colditz. This book has often helped me over questions of history, in particular with regard to the names of officers and to dates of occurrences.

Jack Best sent me the original glider plans and most useful technical notes all the way from Kenya. Lorne Welch and his wife have, together, rechecked those plans in order to confirm, once more, that the machine could take the air.

Commander and Mrs. Fowler and Wally Hammond lent me their private writings, which I found most helpful and from which I have quoted.

Lastly, to those who criticised the roughs of this book, in particular my wife and Mr. H. R. Chapman, C.B.E., I owe a great deal, and to my wife especially, who slaved through the late and early hours typing the manuscript, I am irrevocably indebted.

I have not exhausted the list of those who have helped to make this story a reality in print. I cannot forget the succulent meals with which Nanny—Miss Freda Back—kept body and soul together during the long sessions. More names spring to mind as I write: General Giebel, Colonel Guy German, Kenneth Lockwood, Roger Madin . . . I ask them all to accept my thanks and only hope that the story will do justice to their efforts.

Possingworth,   P. R. REID
    Sussex.
September, 1953.

PROLOGUE

I HAVE often been asked the question: "Why did the Germans put up with so much from the Allied P.O.W.s in Colditz? From the stories told, one is almost sorry for the Germans—the prisoners gave them such a h—— of a time"! In order to answer this question, I wrote—some years after the late war—to the only contact that I could trace among the German personalities of those days. Herr Hans Pfeiffer, the German interpreter at Oflag IV.C, Colditz, was, happily, still in the land of the living, safe in the western zone of Germany. Colditz, by the way, is in the Eastern Zone, behind the Iron Curtain. Pfeiffer's reply to my letter was written in good English and this is what he said:

'You ask for my impressions of Colditz. I think our treatment of you was correct. Of course it was your "verdammte Pflicht und Schuldigkeit" as officers to escape, if you could, and it was likewise our "damned duty" to prevent your doing so. That some of you did actually manage to get away under such difficult circumstances could only arouse the admiration of "your friends the enemy", but I think your own book shows that such a collection of "enfants terribles" as yourselves could not be handled with kid gloves. "Nichts für ungut!"—no offence meant.'

The Germans looked upon the prisoners as 'their friends, the enemy'. It was a curious friendship, but I can see what Herr Pfeiffer means. It was of the kind that springs from respect, that might easily have sprung up, for instance, between the Desert Rats and Rommel's hardened campaigners, if circumstances had ever presented the opportunity.

Colditz was the prison to which Allied officers were sent

after trying to escape from Germany. (Towards the end of the war there was not room in the camp for them all and some, who should have been there, never had the dubious honour of residence within its walls!) The initial spark of defiance thus shown in captivity, and registered by transfer to Colditz produced the reaction mentioned by Herr Pfeiffer.

In Colditz itself, however, the spirit of defiance blossomed. In the tropical atmosphere of the prison, where 'the heat' was turned on by the prisoners, this spirit thrived. The germ of admiration planted in the minds of the warders grew to a personal respect as they came into daily contact with men who would stand no bullying and who showed by their actions that the weapons in the warders' hands were not conclusive arguments as to the conduct of affairs in the prison.

The result was a *modus vivendi*, 'comparatively' neutral as opposed to hostile. The Colditz prisoners received, on the whole, what might be termed manly treatment.

Pfeiffer apologetically explains that the prisoners could not be handled with kid gloves. What he is referring to are, largely, the conditions over which he and his fellow junior officers had little control; the cramped and stifling life in the camp. The German High Command was so intent on keeping the P.O.W.s inside—with a force of guards outnumbering the prisoners—that excesses in the laying down of prison orders were inevitable. Within these limits, the Germans were almost compelled to use the kid glove.

The prisoners were hostages—that became apparent after a couple of years. If the war was to take a wrong turning for Hitler and his entourage, the prisoners of Colditz would be held up to ransom. Perhaps the emergence of this fact caused the Germans to treat the prisoners warily. A dead hostage is no use at all. Of course, he could be replaced—but there would be undesirable repercussions. So, it was worth their while to be tolerant within reason, on the principle that it is better not to tempt fate by baiting a spirited, if not dangerous animal, even though it may be, apparently, securely caged.

Where the Germans failed, was in their excess of zeal to keep the P.O.W.s in prison. Their efficiency reached regrettable heights when they refused, during the lengthening years, to remove sick prisoners and, more particularly, the unfortunate ones who went 'round the bend'. It was inevitable that in the confined atmosphere of Colditz there would be mental suffering among men whose very presence in the camp testified to their deep-seated yearning for freedom. There were several who became mentally unbalanced, even suicidal. They should have been removed. They were a menace to themselves and to the mental balance of their fellow prisoners. They had to be looked after tirelessly. They had to be guarded by men who could sense the danger to themselves, as if they were nursing patients suffering from an infectious disease.

One officer who had delusions and who, thank God, has completely recovered, described his feeling to me recently in this way:

'After this failure to escape, I was so disgusted that I took to studying and research. Shortly after "D" Day, I got some peculiar delusions—a long story in themselves. I got the impression that we were all drugged and under semi-hypnosis which was the reason the Germans caught every attempt to escape. One day I saw the Castle burning and could see the flames and the smoke and the beams crashing down. Of course, my fellow prisoners got so thoroughly scared that they got Dickie (the doctor) to give me an injection of morphia and put me in a cell.'

The desire to escape was paramount among the men of Colditz. They were of all nationalities fighting on the Allied side; Englishmen, Scotsmen and Irishmen from Britain and every corner of the Commonwealth—Canada, Australia, New Zealand and Africa. There were Poles and Yugoslavs, Dutchmen from the Netherland East Indies as well as from Holland, Frenchmen from the African colonies as well as the mother country and, long before the end, there were Americans too.

Naturally, under conditions in which everybody was trying to escape there was a serious danger that plans would overlap, if not conflict. An Englishman building a tunnel was in danger of meeting a Frenchman digging from another direction!

Each nationality had its Escape Officer; a man placed in charge of escape affairs, who was made aware of the plans of the other nationalities, who prevented congestion along the lines and initiated an orderly roster with his colleagues. The result often went like this:

'Sorry, old chap, a Frenchman (or a Dutchman or an Englishman, etc.) has already registered that plan. You'll have to wait three months when it's due to come off. If it's not blown sky high after that, I'll see you're entered on the list for the next go, by the same route.'

The reader can well understand that the position of Escape Officer was a most important and ticklish one. The holder, of necessity, had to have the implicit trust of his fellow officers. It was axiomatic that he was excluded from escaping himself; no little sacrifice for a man, who, by his nature and experience—even before his promotion to the post—possessed all the qualifications for making a successful getaway.

While on this point, I am reminded of another which I must place before the reader. Some who have read 'The Colditz Story' have said to me: "Surely the remark you made about so much having to be left unsaid was merely intended to intrigue the reader by introducing an air of mystery?"

May I be forgiven for repeating again that much interesting and exciting material has, necessarily, in the conditions of the world to-day to be omitted. If the reader feels, on occasion, that he would like to know more than he is told, I hope he will remember this point.

Apart from this, there is, nevertheless, enough material

to fill another book. I have had to pick and choose. I must, therefore, ask for the indulgence of the reader if, occasionally, I pass lightly over certain events and mention casually characters that have 'gone before'. I cannot hope to achieve the finesse of Sherlock Holmes who was wont to say, cryptically: ". . . You will notice, my dear Watson, a distinct resemblance here, to the case of the Daskerville Diamonds. . . ." I feel sure the reader will understand that, although this story should be sufficient unto itself, it is, at the same time, the second in a series.

It is with deep regret that I have had to sacrifice a heroine on the altar of truth. Neither would it be honest to the fair sex to withhold from them—or the men—the fact that there are no female characters in the story. On page 429 I have done my best. It was the nearest a woman ever approached to the forbidding portals of the Castle. Even so, she wasted no time. I can only lean on a good precedent in order to bolster up my failure to make good the omissions of history. Surely I cannot go far wrong in emulating a drama without a heroine that once held the stages of the world for record breaking runs—none other than 'Journey's End'.

With this introduction, may I usher the reader into the auditorium, where the overture is about to begin. . . .

I

1942

CHAPTER I

OVERTURE

THIS book is the story of a castle in Saxony during those years of the second World War between November, 1942, and April, 1945. It covers only a fleeting moment in the history of the Castle as measured by the life span of hewn stone and oak timbers. There must have been many periods, as the scrolls of the centuries unrolled, when the *tempo* of man's activity within its walls rose to dramatic heights; but, probably, none was more dramatic than the short interval in which this story of human endeavour unfolds itself.

Not that the interval was short for the actors who then walked upon the Colditz stage. It is short in retrospect. The passage of time is registered physically and mechanically in minutes and hours by the clock. A year may sear itself upon the soul of a man so deeply that it becomes a lifetime or it may pass so refreshingly over him that it is gone like a gay summer's day. Man measures time by happiness or sorrow, by tranquillity or torture. The one is past and gone so quickly that it is seldom seized and savoured. The other turns the hours into days, and the weeks into years, and can turn man's nature into unrecognizable shapes.

During the period of which I write, Colditz Castle was the *Sonderlager* or *Straflager* of Germany. It was the stronghold where Allied prisoners of war who had dared to break their chains were incarcerated. It was the cage in which were shut the birds that longed to be free, that beat their wings unceasingly against the bars. In such conditions birds do not usually survive long. It says something for the resilient spirit of man that those Allied prisoners, the inveterate escapers, who were sent to Colditz mostly survived the ordeal.

For such men, much more than for others, the hours

were days and the weeks were years. They were men of action by nature and they lived a long time the torture of forced inactivity. They were prisoners expiating no other crime than the unselfish service of their country.

Taking stock of the situation at Colditz in the bleak winter of 1942, entails, first and foremost, taking stock of the escaping situation.

The escape-proof castle of the 1914–18 war had been made to look like a riddled target. Holes had been made everywhere—metaphorically and literally—in its impregnable walls.

By the end of 1942, the British prisoners' contingent had risen to eighty strong. Officers from the three services and from every country of the Commonwealth, they had all committed offences against Hitler's Reich. About ninety per cent. of them had escaped at least once from other camps. There were three Padres: the Reverends Ellison Platt, Heard and Hobling, who had made themselves such nuisances elsewhere, clamouring for Christian treatment for their flocks, that the German High Command considered Colditz the only appropriate place for them. Here, at least, their clamours would not penetrate the thick walls of the fortress.

Seventy-three 'officer-attempts' to escape had been registered so far. The term 'officer-attempt' was used in the statistics so as to be able to register each attempt of each officer. Thus, seventy-three officer-attempts does not mean that seventy-three officers out of the eighty tried to escape. That figure was probably nearer forty than eighty, but as several of the forty attempted two or three times they were given their individual totals on the escape record and the total of the whole column—so to speak—added up to seventy-three. It was not often that a Senior British Officer had an opportunity to escape but Colonel Guy German was not omitted from an early attempt which would have left the camp devoid of the entire British contingent!

Out of the total recorded, twenty-two officers had succeeded in getting clear of the camp. They were 'gone away', as it was termed. The number included five Dutch officers taking part in British escape attempts. The statistic, however, that the camp was most proud of, and which has never been equalled by any P.O.W. camp in Germany, was the number of successful escapes. Officers' home-runs into neutral or friendly territory totalled no less than eleven out of the twenty-two—fifty per cent.!

The fortunate eleven were: Airey Neave and Tony Luteyn; Bill Fowler and Van Doorninck; the two E.R.A.'s, Wally Hammond and Tubby Lister; Brian Paddon; Ronnie Littledale, Billie Stephens, Hank Wardle and the author.

Coming next to the Dutch contingent, which numbered sixty at the end of 1942, the equivalent records were approximately as follows (excluding the Dutchmen above mentioned: officer-attempts about thirty, gone-aways ten, and home-runs six.

The French contingent numbered one hundred and fifty, including a batch of fifty Jewish French officers who, with rare exceptions, did not interest themselves in escaping. Frankly, the latter realised that recapture, for them, meant extermination; in prison jargon a 'Klimtin', and their lives were probably safer in Colditz than in France.

French officer-attempts numbered somewhere in the region of twenty to thirty—I cannot recollect them more exactly. Gone-aways numbered about ten and home-runs amounted to at least four.

The Polish contingent had left during the year. They had numbered eighty strong and had been at Colditz from the beginning of the war. They were already there when I arrived in November, 1940. They had come from *Sonderlager* of the First World War, Spitsberg and Hohenstein, from where they had registered twelve 'gone-aways' and three 'home runs' to the Polish Underground. Tragic, indeed, it is to recollect that they had no homeland that they could make for. When they succeeded in breaking out of the Castle they headed for Switzerland, Sweden or France, leaving their homes and loved ones further than ever behind them. Half a dozen had 'gone-aways' to their credit, but, though some of them reached the Swiss frontier they were caught and the record showed no 'home-runs' to neutral territory from Colditz for this company. Nevertheless, after leaving Colditz, two at least escaped from a camp further east in Germany and made their way to France and England. They were: Felix Jablonowski and Tony Karpf. The former, an International lawyer and University lecturer, has recently gone to America to seek his fortune and a new life; while Karpf, happily married, has settled in Glasgow.

Airey Neave was the first Englishman to reach England from Colditz via Switzerland, France and Spain.* That was in May, 1942. Paddon followed closely at his heels—in time, though by another route—Sweden.

So much for the record up to the Autumn of 1942, but what were the prospects for the future? Conditions were undoubtedly becoming more difficult. Within the Castle the roll-calls for prisoners settled down to a regular four *Appells* every day. The times at which the *Appells* occurred were, however, by no means regular. The factory siren which had recently been installed would shriek its warning at odd hours of the day, in the grey light of dawn or in the night hours. The parade started five minutes after the siren's moans had subsided. Our men, wherever they were working at their nefarious activities, had only one compensation. In the deepest shaft or the longest tunnel, the siren could be heard and tools downed at once. Nevertheless, the five minutes tolerance gave little time for sealing entrances and cleaning up. It was always a close thing and wearing on the nerves. The fact that there were four *Appells* every twenty-four hours also broke up the working shifts, impaired efficiency and slowed progress.

It was inevitable, too, that, as time went on, escape routes out of the Castle would become fewer and fewer. The Castle, as already mentioned, presented to the escaper by 1943 the picture of a target riddled with holes, but

* Neave has written the story in his book, *They Have Their Exits*.

unfortunately, at this stage, behind every hole stood a sentry. The garrison outnumbered the prisoners. Catwalks had been erected providing an unhindered view into all the nooks and crannies in the battlements. They hung suspended like window-cleaners' cradles; they stood on long poles clinging, sometimes perilously, to walls, like builders' scaffolds supported from narrow ledges in the cliff sides. Wherever a prisoner had escaped, there new and forbidding rolls of concertina wire were stretched. Jerries hung out of skylights with machine-guns beside them surveying roof ridges, slopes and gutters.

Sound detectors were being installed everywhere. The exits through the thinner walls being nearly exhausted, men were digging deeper into the formidably heavy foundations of the older structure of the Castle.

Colditz, like many other ancient buildings, was not one castle but many castles; built and ruined, rebuilt and ruined again by wars and weather, by time and usage. Thus, although some of the senior prisoners' quarters and probably the interior decoration of the Castle chapel was attributable to architects and builders working to the orders of Augustus the Strong, king of Poland and elector of Saxony from 1694 to 1733, the garrison quarters around the outer courtyard were of eighteenth and early nineteenth century design. Returning within the Keep, however, most of the architecture and the building construction bore witness of a *Schloss* built in earlier days during the sixteenth century. In these medieval halls and casemates the junior officers lived. When the tunnellers among them began delving downwards they came upon yet earlier foundations of a castle destroyed, apparently, in the Hussite Wars of the fifteenth century. In fact, it can be vouched with assurance that almost as long as man existed in those parts, and wished to defend himself against his enemies, he must have built himself an eyrie on the easily defendable, towering rock promontory of Colditz.

The searchlights increased in number dispelling the last shadow which might shelter a lurking form on its

desperate route to freedom. Then there were the Alsatian
dogs. They had not increased in number, as far as was
known, but they were worked harder. Patrols, with or
without the Alsatians, had become frequent and were the
more dangerous as they became more irregular, touring
the Castle at unpredictable intervals of time.

It was also natural that the prisoners and the guards
should learn more and more of each others' habits and
methods. As the scales were from the first weighted in
favour of the guards they held an advantage which told
more heavily as the years passed. The training of sentries
for the work at Colditz became more scientific. They were
instructed in all the known tricks and wiles of the prisoners;
warned again and again of what they might expect; their
duty stations changed often to prevent staleness dulling
the edge of their preparedness. They toured, regularly, the
escapers' museum in the garrison Headquarters, carrying
away mental pictues of the escaper's art, his tools, his keys,
his maps, papers, clothing and his false uniforms, his trap
doors and his camouflage. The prisoners' ingenuity was
stretched to limits which only the story in its unfolding
can adequately describe.

The prisoners were becoming physically weak. Even the
most robust men could not stand up indefinitely to the
meagre diet. Albeit that Red Cross food was available there
was never enough. Men were always hungry and could
only bloat themselves with unappetising mealy potatoes
and stomach-revolting turnips and swedes. Alternatively
they took to their beds for long periods of the day, pre-
serving thereby what little energy their nutrition gave
them.

The spirit was unconquered but the flesh was weak. The
change in physical condition came imperceptibly and, as
each suffered alike, a prisoner did not appreciate the altera-
tion taking place within himself, or his companions around
him. A form of evolution was going on within the Castle
walls and a different kind of human being was coming into
existence: a scrawny individual with a skin and bone

physique seriously lacking in vitamins. Mentally, the prisoner who kept himself occupied was none the worse for his captivity. On the contrary, in many cases, the enforced life of the ascetic sharpened the wits and enlarged the horizon of the mind. The age-old secret of the hermit was manifestly revealed; men's minds and souls were purified by the mortification of the body.

Unfortunately, a man cannot escape from a fortress by mind alone. He has to drag his body with him. Although the escaper's wits were sharpened and his mind as clear as a bell, his body, in 1942, could not perform the feats it did in 1940 unless scourged by the driving force of a powerful will.

So much for conditions within the fortress, but what of the great outside? The huge face of Germany lay for hundreds of miles in all directions around the Castle embedded in the very heart of the *Reich*. To the men incarcerated in the camp the changing circumstances outside were mostly a closed book. Every tit-bit of information gleaned was treasured and recorded for possible exploitation but so much was unknown. Although the Colditz techniques for the production of false papers were highly skilled, though false identities could be faithfully reproduced which would pass muster under known conditions outside the camp at a given date, these very conditions were altering rapidly for the worse and changes were unpredictable.

The change that was coming over Germany is well illustrated by the two largest breakouts of the war from camps other than Colditz. Jumping ahead in time for a moment, on the night of August 3rd–4th, 1943, sixty-five British officers escaped by tunnel from Oflag VII.B. at Eichstätt, in Bavaria. It was a beautifully engineered escape, but not one of the officers made the home run. Apart from the fact that the majority of them were ill equipped both as to civilian clothing and as to identity papers, according to the best standards, they under-estimated the reaction of the Germans to their escape. The latter, during the winter of

1942–43, were beginning to feel the flail of Allied heavy bombing; of our great aircraft sweeps over their territory. They were organising their Home Guard feverishly. It was known as the Landwacht. The *Hitler Jugend* was also mobilised, and children of tender age were not excluded from routine duties and from lessons upon how to recognise and how to capture enemy airmen. Thus, it was not a far cry to transfer their activities, at short notice, to the recapture of escaped prisoners. When large numbers escaped together, the organisation required would be no different to that which came into play after a heavy aerial bombardment.

Reports have it that after the Eichstätt escape no less than sixty thousand of the *Landwacht* were in action within twenty-four hours, searching for the escapers. It was not an escape that paid dividends. Undoubtedly, of course, it gave the Germans 'a packet' of trouble—that was a good thing. It harassed them and because of that alone it was probably worth while. But it is also argued that it gave the *Landwacht* a good field day—impromptu manoeuvres—which made them more efficient later on against our airmen parachuting in Germany and trying hard to evade capture. The escape failed on points of strategy rather than in the tactics of its execution.

Practically the same results were achieved, only with far worse consequences, by another, and the last, large British breakout recorded during World War II. This was the disastrous escape of seventy-six officers from Stalag Luft III. The escape occurred on the 24th of March, 1944.* Three made home-runs. Fifty, out of the seventy-six who escaped, were murdered by the Gestapo. Such a breakout may have been thought good for morale, but no visible uplift in escaping morale was noticeable according to subsequent accounts.

The mass escape was the ideal form that escaping could take from 1940 up to the end of 1942.

* See *The Great Escape*, by Paul Brickhill.

A superb escape and—though it is always a matter of opinion—probably the finest British escape of the whole war is another illustration of the point. It was known as the 'Warburg wire job' and it occurred on the 29th of August, 1942—within the early period of the war. Forty-three officers escaped, in one minute, over the wire barricades of Warburg prison camp with home-made storming ladders. It would be of interest to establish who provided the inspiration and leadership of this escape. He deserves a decoration.* David Walker and Pat Campbell-Preston, both of the 1st Battalion the Black Watch, had something to do with it. J. E. Hamilton-Baillie, Royal Engineers, designed the ladders. Again the accoutrement and clothing for the outside part of the attempt was incomplete. Nevertheless, three officers in battle dress made their way to France and subsequently to England. It is doubtful if they would have succeeded (in battle dress) a year later.

By 1943, a regime had come to an end and even if a great tunnel was built and completed with a good outfall beyond the camp confines, experience—bitter experience—encourages the thought that such a tunnel might have been better employed otherwise than as means for a mass break out. If a transport plane had been laid on from England at a rendezvous to take the men off—that would have been another matter.

It is only too easy to criticise after the event—and nobody could wish to detract from such magnificent escapes as those above mentioned. This said, there can be no harm in going over an exercise performed, to draw out the lessons for the future, provide food for thought and encourage the fertile imagination. The mind can exercise itself in fields of interest, not to say of entertainment, by posing a few questions. 'What might have happened if . . .?'

What would have happened if ten officers had escaped instead of seventy-six. They would have been very well equipped—for they would have had the equipment of the

* According to recent reliable information, Tom Stallard, then Major D. L. I., now Lt.-Col., D.S.O., O.B.E., was responsible.

sixty remaining behind to draw upon to fill any gaps in
their own make up. The most eligible team would be
chosen for the attempt, and every advantage would be concentrated in the team to go. Once outside the wire—and
once the alarm was given—what might the German reactions be? Ten British officers have escaped. Turn out the
local *Landwacht,* say two hundred strong; search the
locality; send out descriptions and photos; alert all railway
security police and report the escape to Corps Headquarters.
Now, consider the escape of seventy-six officers. This is
serious. It cannot be kept from the General Staff, nor from
Himmler, nor even from Hitler, and what is the result?
Landwacht alerted in their thousands—nearly a hundred
against each one, and the consequent chances of escape reduced to about the same ratio; the Gestapo sleuths placed
hot on the scent, and the revengeful spirits of the maniac
leaders of the country roused to anger: fifty of our finest
officers murdered!

If only ten men had moved out, how many might have
made home-runs? Judging by Colditz statistics the number
might have been as high as five. It would be reasonable to
say two or three.

The discussion does not end there. What is the effect on
the morale of those who stay behind; firstly, upon the whole
prison contingent amounting to hundreds of officers;
secondly upon the sixty-six standing down, who have had a
more personal stake in the escape attempt?

Are the hundreds jealous they were not included in the
escape? No! They could not be. Are the sixty-six? A few
maybe, but the majority are more pleased at the result,
feeling they have contributed to the achievement. Their enthusiasm is whetted. Encouragement at the sight of success
ensues and morale is lifted. 'Nothing succeeds like success'
applies forcibly to escaping. What is the reaction of the
hundreds to the success of the few? Morale is naturally improved. Quite the contrary is the result when many men go
out and they all come back or when a large proportion of
them are shot.

One question has been begged throughout. What is the re-action when only ten men go out where seventy-six might have gone and when ten men return? This is when the fur begins to fly and recrimination, in the confined atmosphere of a crowded camp, quickly takes on the aspects of a revolt. Among the sixty-six feeling, naturally, runs high. Why were they not all allowed to 'have a bang at it'? Herein lies the difficulty of decision, and he has a strong character who makes the unpopular decision and sticks to it. The mass break-out is the easier course to adopt. Is it the right one?

By way of a corollary, and a sop to Cerberus, the man who makes the difficult decision can partially insure himself by seeing that the tunnel is properly sealed at entrance and exit after the 'ten' have gone, with a view to a second ten departing after the first hue and cry has died down. The chance of this ever being possible is a minimum, but it pro-vides a safety valve and parries the worst fomentations aroused by disappointment.

Lastly, the value of a home-run is not to be underesti-mated. Airey Neave and Brian Paddon, returning to Eng-land in 1942, were among the pioneers, lecturing our forces training at home upon escape techniques as being developed in Colditz at the time. Their advice on the theory and prac-tice of 'evasion' and their encouragement of our thousands, flying regularly over enemy territory, was an inspiration. They, and those who followed closely after them, helped materially in the success of the 'evasion' campaign which resulted in so many Allied airmen, parachuted from crip-pled aircraft, returning home safely by devious routes, each with a story of adventure and courage in adversity .

Even the unlucky ones who were captured and thrown into prison camps had some consolation. Their numbers swelled to large proportions from 1942 onwards as our planes, in increasing avenging swarms, traversed the dis-integrating enemy cities, while more and more hatred belched upwards in screaming steel and rending explosive. Unlike the early prisoners they were not lost souls, unbe-friended and unaided. They arrived in camp knowing what to expect and what was expected of them. After the first terrible depression they had hope to buoy them up. They knew they had friends, both in England and in the prison camps who would help them to escape if possible. Moreover, the camps were well provided with the practical means to assist them.

The scene was darkening over Colditz. Men gradually realised that the difficulties were multiplying and the hazards of escape more problematical and dangerous as the days dragged on their infinitely slow and tedious procession. Around the cobbled courtyard of the inner *Schloss* the clack-clack-clack of wooden clogs wearing themselves out on the stones was interminable in the daylight hours; it bore into the head like the drops of water in a Chinese torture. It was a motif ever recurring in the symphony being played within the fortress.

There was only one silver lining for the escaper. German Army morale was on the decline and it was becoming noticeable among the camp guards.

It was possible, by slow degrees, to set up a black market, in fact many black markets. Racketeering in the produce of this illicit trade gradually became rife until it was eventually scandalous and the German profiteers were seen to be gaining.

The matter was taken in hand so that an orderly influx of escape paraphernalia took precedence over private cupidity and escapers, harassed by the infinite difficulties of escaping from the Castle, had the comfort, at least, of knowing that, once out, they could hardly be better equipped for the journey across enemy territory.

The overture continues. The cymbals and the kettle drums have had their turn. What of the undertones, the huge background in front of which the violins will play? What say the trombones, the bass drums and the deep throated cellos?

November, 1942, opened with the final phases of the Battle of Alamein which Winston Churchill describes as 'the turning of the hinge of Fate,' adding, 'It may almost be said, "Before Alamein we never had a victory. After Alamein we never had a defeat".'

Guns boomed from the Atlantic on the North African shore. The American amphibious invasion began at Casablanca on November 8th, and in the Mediterranean, around Oran and Algiers on the same day. Stalingrad was relieved at the end of January, 1943, with the capture of Field Marshal Paulus and the survivors of twenty-one German Divisions. Churchill was anxious to open the second front in Europe in 1943, and Stalin was likewise pressing for it. The British were losing an enormous tonnage of shipping every week in the Atlantic. The drain of this life blood still had to be stopped. It was one of Hitler's few remaining trump cards. The war leaders argued the pros and cons; Churchill met the Turks at Adana. The latter would not be hurried into the war on the Allied side. Hitler put all his efforts into a Tunisian campaign. The requirements for the successful completion of the Allied North African operation 'Torch' sealed the doom of another operation called 'Round up'.

The prayers and hopes of thousands of Allied prisoners all over Europe were centred on an Allied landing on the Continent—the opening of the Second Front—in 1943.

Although they did not know it by that name, 'Round up' was what they prayed for.

The Colditz inmates were by this stage of the war well equipped for the wireless reception of news from the Western Allies. They had, at the same time, by the continuous application of carefully aimed shafts of ridicule, silenced the German loudspeakers in the camp. The Germans no longer tried to switch on their news bulletins. Instead they set about dismantling the loudspeakers in the various quarters. Alas! they were too late. When the electricians took down the instruments all they retrieved were hollow shells. The works had been removed in good time and were already in the service of the Crown instead of the Corporal.

The great march of events in the latter half of the war was not lost to the prisoners. Indeed, the majority lived for the news. It was a soul assuaging consolation to the many who knew, in their hearts, that they would never make home-runs. Let the violins speak.

A seeding of players in the escape tournament began to take place. It was a voluntary affair, and brave men stepped out of the queue of their own accord. They did not speak of it.

There was no dramatic renunciation of rights; there were no recriminations. They dropped from the life-line around the over-crowded escaping life-boat and, with resignation, allowed the great ocean of world events to swallow them. They drowned their personal ambitions and drifted, each one alone with his own soul awaiting the end. The end lay over the horizon and the sky was lowering.

To these men, suspended in the boundless sea of time the broadcast news bulletins were essential for mental well-being and sanity. News was like oil poured on the waves; a protecting calm amidst the storm that threatened the balance of their minds, that was never far away, that could descend with the elemental force of a whirlwind. Sometimes, indeed, the news appeared as a mirage, deceiving them horribly, but, at least, the omissions and the veils drawn over adverse situations coming from the Western transmitters were as nothing compared with the great hoax that was played upon the German people by their wireless broadcasters. If the Allies did not tell all the truth, at least they avoided lying. So, for our men, there was always hope as opposed to the revengeful bitterness that grows from deliberate deception.

CHAPTER II

ESCAPE FEVER

NEWS of the success of the escape of Ronnie Littledale, Billie Stephens, Hank Wardle and the author, and of their safe arrival in Switzerland soon filtered through the censor's net. Four gone-aways and four home-runs! it was great news, putting the British contingent well ahead of the other nationalities in the friendly rivalry for the lead in home-runs. Many men, whose hopes of an ultimate successful escape had almost vanished, imbibed new strength and determination. A wave of enthusiasm like a gust of fresh air swept through the Castle.

Dick Howe, of the Royal Tank Regiment, and officer in charge of Escape, was overwhelmed with new schemes and the resurrections of old ones. Activity became feverish and it was clear that the Jerries were in for a difficult time. The latter soon scented trouble ahead and the German security team hardly slept at night. Hauptmann Priem and Ober-leutnant Püpcke, Hauptmann Eggers and the deadbeat Hauptmann Lange, Oberstabsfeldwebel (Sergeant-major) Gephard and his Gefreiter (Corporal), known as the *fouine* or ferret or Dickson Hawk, took turns at making the rounds. P.O.W. 'stooging' systems had to be double shifted to cope with the new circumstances. Hardly an officer was free from some duty or other.

For some unaccountable reason the word stooge, in prison jargon, had two totally different meanings, depending entirely on the context in which the term was used. 'Stooging' in the above case implied the P.O.W. 'look-out' organisation instituted to warn prisoners of Germans approaching on the prowl, 'snooping' as it was called. On the other hand, a stooge could be a person planted by the Germans in the camp to report on the prisoners' nefarious activities.

As the German security net became more closely drawn and the sentry layout more dense, it was brought home to the prisoners that escapes of almost any kind would have to rely on split-second timing. The old leisurely days were disappearing. This change implied long hours of stooging by an escape team and the plotting of enemy movements for weeks on end in order to discover the loop-holes in their defence system.

Dick, thirty-two years old, had won his M.C. at Calais in 1940. He was standing the strain of the difficult job of Escape Officer remarkably well. To any outsider, he looked sallow, hollow cheeked and terribly thin, but that was nor-mality in Colditz and passed without comment. His good humour remained his greatest friend. Demands on his time were heavy. What kept him always on top of a situation was an obstinate refusal to be flustered either by contrary events or by contrary people.

Rupert Barry and Mike Sinclair teamed up. They were a formidable pair and would take a lot of stopping. They were given what was known as the theatre shaft job.

Rupert, of the Ox and Bucks Light Infantry, tall, dark and handsome with his big brown moustache and smoulder-ing eyes, had been one of the first escapers in Germany. He, Peter Allan and the author, out of a tunnel at Oflag VII.C, near Salzburg, were half way to Yugoslavia when recaught in September, 1940. At Colditz, Rupert's luck had not been good. Two tunnels on which he worked did not succeed in putting him outside the wire, although the first was com-pleted without discovery.

Mike, of the 60th Rifles, had been free in Poland for a long time, and then in a Gestapo prison for a while before he reached Colditz. He had escaped once from the Castle only to be recaptured in Cologne. He was, by now, a fluent German speaker. He was a few years younger than Rupert —about twenty-six. His red hair and his audacity had earned him the title among the Germans of 'Der Rote Fuchs'—the Red Fox. Of medium build, tough, with a resolute freckled countenance, his life was devoted to escaping, and his determination was as valuable as a hundred ton battering ram matched against the walls of Colditz.

Mike and Rupert reorganised an old twenty-four hour watching roster, which had been started many months before, on what was known as the air shaft or light well situated in the middle of the theatre block, where, also, the senior officers were housed.

The theatre itself was on the third or top floor of this block, and the square light well was surrounded by a corridor on three sides which separated it from the theatre. A locked door gave onto the corridor, which was lighted from barred windows overlooking the well. The door was the only normal means of entry. There was no staircase. The twenty-four-hour watch was maintained in this corridor.

At the bottom of the well, fifty feet below, were doors leading into various German kitchen and canteen quarters. Thick walls, on the other hand, separated it from the prisoners' quarters at ground level. Needless to say, a sentry stood at the bottom of the well throughout the twenty-four hours.

After a fortnight's watching it was possible to confine stooging activity to some twelve hours, not consecutive, during the day; the other twelve hours being ruled out as impossible for escape purposes.

One early winter evening, as the light was beginning to fade, rehearsals of a forthcoming show were in full swing bringing many officers of all nationalities into the theatre. It was a time of activity. An orchestra was practising; the scene painters were at work; stage managers, producers, actors and staff milled around, all providing admirable camouflage for the movement of shifts of stooges through the locked door into the corridor beside the well.

The old piano clanged out its tinny tunes. Sounds of hammering and scene shifting mingled with the hubbub of voices rising and falling. Dick Howe busied himself around the stage followed by his Dutch stage lighting assistant, Lieutenant Beetes. The dreadful piano worried Dick. He mused over that dream piano—the new Bechstein Concert Grand—that had arrived one day, months ago now, in the courtyard. Workmen had toiled for hours hoisting it up the narrow staircase and had demolished a wall in the theatre in order to install it. Then the workmen's civilian coats, thrown off in the heat of the moment, had vanished. The contents of pockets reappeared mysteriously, but the coats were never found. An ultimatum from the Commandant; stubborn silence from the prisoners; and the Bechstein Grand retraced its journey down the stairs and disappeared again outside the prison gateway.

There were no less than four orchestras now; all of them suffering from the curious version of the chromatic scale reproduced by this rickety, upright cupboard-full of tangled wires.

There was the Symphony Orchestra conducted by a Dutchman, First Lieutenant Bajetto; the Theatre Orchestra with Jimmy Yule as composer, orchestrator and pianist; the Dance Band with John Wilkins as band leader; and finally the Hawaian Orchestra composed principally of Dutch colonial officers.

"What a difference it would make!" Dick sighed to himself. Then a flicker of a smile appeared at the corners of his mouth, and, as he stood in the middle of the stage by the footlights, surveying a scene, just completed, his thoughts were not on the set he was supposed to be examining. He was wondering if he could not, after all, spirit the Bechstein Concert Grand back into the theatre.

His mind was far away when a tug at his sleeve from the auditorium pulled him back to earth. He turned to see Vandy, the irrepressible Dutchman, plotter of a hundred escapes, smiling broadly as usual, looking up at him.

"I haf made a fine hole," said Vandy in a suppressed voice, "come qvick and see, my two escapers are preparing now to go."

"Fast work, Vandy," said Dick jumping down over the footlights, "I know this theatre pretty intimately and haven't noticed any rat-holes recently."

Dick Howe

"Ach no! Dick—you vould not see. I haf been vorking for a veek and you know my plaster camouflage!"

Vandy led him to the dressing-room at the right of the stage. There in the corner was a gaping hole with all the paraphernalia of camouflage strewn around.

"Why!" exclaimed Dick, "you're using Neave's old route."

"Qvite right, it is the same. This hole—qvick! bend down and look along it—you see—it is the roof of the causevay over the main gate. My men can now reach the guardhouse. They are putting on the German uniforms at this moment in my quarters. They vill be here very soon. It is a blitz."

"But," said Dick incredulously, "the Jerries blocked up that route some time ago."

"Yes," replied Vandy unshaken, "but my men haf seen Germans recently through the windows of the causevay. Where there is an entrance there must be an outrance."

"Hm!" said Dick, "I'd better get our stooges out from the corridor pretty quick. Thanks for telling me, Vandy, but give me a little more notice next time."

Vandy was full of glee. There was nothing he liked more than surprising people. He was revelling in the joke he was about to play on the Jerries and missed the note of anxiety in Dick's voice. They retraced their steps into the theatre as Vandy studied his watch and signalled to a Dutch stooge at the door leading to the stairs.

At the same moment, Rupert Barry appeared from the direction of the light well. Dick beckoned him over.

"You're in the nick of time, Rupert. Vandy has a blitz on."

They were near the orchestra which had started running over the opening bars of Chopin's Polonaise and the piano was making a noise like a broken down zither in Dick's ear.

"What did you say?" shouted Rupert. "The band has a blitz on?"

Dick took Rupert's arm and they moved away among the

chairs of the auditorium. "I said Vandy has a blitz on. He's got two Dutchmen coming up here any moment." Dick pointed to Vandy and his theatre stooge in close conversation some yards from the theatre door.

"They're going over into the guardhouse. They're dressing as Jerries. There may be trouble. You'd better get our stooge out from the corridor. Who's in there now?"

"Peter Storie Pugh," said Rupert.

They were both looking towards the door as he spoke. Hardly were the words out of his mouth when the balloon went up.

The unmistakable figure of Priem appeared framed in the doorway; a dark outline in the gathering dusk. Vandy's stooge had been caught off his guard.

Priem took a few steps into the room. From behind him stepped Gephard who made for the electric switches, and the next moment the theatre was flooded in light. A posse of Goons followed closely at Gephard's heels. The music of the orchestra tailed off to nothing as Priem grated out his orders. Hammering continued in the wings of the stage. The scene builders went on with their work—oblivious of the unrehearsed drama taking place in front. Goons were suddenly everywhere. Vandy made for the door of the staircase, but a sentry barred the way with his rifle across the jambs.

Dick noticed that Rupert had glided away in the direction of the door to the corridor. The situation was tricky. He vaulted on to the stage and collided with Scarlet O'Hara who had just emerged from the wings. Scarlet had heard the familiar guttural shouts as he was in the midst of mixing up some scenery paint for his own use. Dick whispered to him.

"Quick! Scarlet, go and help Rupert. He needs some diversion. He's got his stooge in the corridor and must get him out."

Scarlet, the Canadian Tank Lieutenant, whose complexion had earned him his name, saw the situation immediately and muttering to himself, 'These B——— Huns

again, never let you alone for a minute, the blasted Kartof-
fels.' He faded into the milling crowd of actors, scene
shifters, instrumentalists and German soldiery.

The Jerries knew what they were going for. Vandy's
hole must have been discovered from the German side.
They made for the dressing-room and herded everybody off
the stage into the auditorium as Priem and Gephard held a
conference. They were discussing what action to take.
Vandy's blitz had shaken them.

"Will they hold everyone in the theatre and search them
all?" Dick wondered to himself. It was a normal procedure.
The room would be cleared, one by one the officers would
be searched, and finally the Jerries would search the
premises and the corridor. He stood leaning against the
rickety piano and could see Rupert and Scarlet in deep
conversation in the far corner. Lulu Lawton, the black-
haired Yorkshireman from the Duke of Wellington's Regiment, Dick's second in command, was weaving his way
through the crowd towards him. In the distance Dick also
spied Harry Elliott, a captain of the Irish Guards, who
waged a private war against the Germans.

As Lulu approached Dick said casually, "I wonder what
brought Harry into the theatre. He never comes up here if
he can help it. And to choose to-day! It'll be worth listening
to what he has to say about the Jerries upsetting his routine. Look, he's arguing with the Jerry on the door now,
swearing at him like a trooper."

"He came up to get some more yellow paint for his jaundice set-up," explained Lulu ."He's going before the medical board any day now."

Priem had apparently made up his mind what to do. He
mounted the stage and addressed the assembled mixed bag
of officers of all nationalities:

"*Mein Herren*," and he continued in German with sarcasm, "I am confident that not all the officers here present
intended to escape through the hole I have just found. I
shall not inflict unnecessary punishment on you by insisting
that you remove all your clothes for searching. You will

leave the theatre one by one. My under-officers will feel through your uniforms and in your pockets. I must find the instruments with which the hole has been made, and the culprit. The theatre will probably be closed, but I shall report first to the Commandant. Will you begin to leave the theatre at once and one at a time."

Dick looked anxiously towards the corridor. He could not see Rupert or Scarlet; only a huddle of French and English officers around the locked door. Obviously a scrum was being organised—but the top of the door was clear of their heads and if it was opened it would be plainly visible. Dick thought hard. A long queue had already formed by the theatre exit where several soldiers now stood while Gephard and two Gefreite—the *fouine* and another—quickly ran their hands over officers' clothing, occasionally feeling inside a pocket. The search was cursory. One by one the queue was diminishing. He noted through the open door of the dressing-room that a sentry had been posted in front of the hole. The soldiery was all occupied. Priem was the danger.

Dick deliberately avoided the queue and approached Priem who was standing at the top of the stage steps surveying the scene before him. Dick suddenly had the inspiration he was waiting for. Looking up at Priem from the bottom of the steps he said in German:

"Herr Hauptmann, I wish to ask you a question about the theatre's requirements."

"*Na*, what is it, Herr Hauptmann Ho-ve?" said Priem, descending to his level and losing his commanding view of the corridor entrance. He always pronounced Howe as two syllables, 'Ho-ve'.

Dick drew him over to the piano and winking at Lulu who was leaning on it, he began:

"The British, Herr Hauptmann, have collected a big reserve of *Lagermarken* (prison money) which, together with subscriptions promised from other nationalities, we have calculated is large enough to buy a cinema organ for the theatre. You see, our theatre committee does not want a piano any more. This one here . . ." and Dick struck a few discordant notes on the keyboard of the upright . . . "is *Kaputt*, as you know well."

"You cannot afford an organ, Herr Hauptmann!" said Priem, raising his eyebrows and smirking incredulously.

"Oh yes we can! If you will come with me to our Senior Officer's room downstairs I can ask him to show you the figures."

"But Herr Hauptmann Ho-ve, you do not require an organ—you need a piano." There was horror in his voice. The shaft had struck home.

"*Nien, nien,* Herr Hauptmann Priem," interrupted Dick, "we are not interested in pianos any more, everybody wants to have a fine Wurlitzer organ. The protecting power will support our demand for one because this piano here is finished. We can say you refused to give us a new piano, months ago, when we asked for it."

Looking past Priem, Dick caught a glimpse of Rupert and Scarlet, and then to his relief, as the screening crowd dispersed to take up their positions in the fast dwindling queue at the exit, he noticed the figure of Peter Storie Pugh.

Priem began to walk towards the exit as well, and Dick and Lulu followed. Dick said:

"Herr Hauptmann Priem, would you like to see the accounts showing our reserve of *Lagermarken*?"

"*Nein,*" replied Priem, "I believe you." He turned away to speak to his Oberstabsfeldwebel, Gephard, and Dick turned to Lulu.

"If that doesn't bring the Bechstein Concert Grand back I reckon we'd better start saving for a Wurlitzer! I have a hunch though, that the old Commandant won't want to have a grand piano left on his hands."

The theatre emptied. Vandy had long since disappeared. Dick, Lulu and Rupert were the last to be 'frisked'. As they departed the spare Goons were already dispersing through-out the theatre rummaging in the corners and Gephard approached the corridor door with the key in his hand. . . .

In the courtyard below, Vandy was waiting for Dick.

"All is not finished, Dick, I haf a plan. You must distract the sentry who stands at the hole please."

Dick looked at him and burst out laughing, then beside Vandy he saw two bulky-looking Dutch officers. He knew them well and knew too that their bulk was not natural. There was no stopping Vandy. Weakly he said:

"Hold your horses, Vandy, Priem's still up there with his posse of Goons. Do you want me to distract them all?"

"No, Dick, vait till they haf gone. Here they come—look! ve must count them," and facing the theatre block doorway he counted, "vone, two tree, vor, vive . . ." and then finally, "Fouine, Gephard, Priem. That is all except vone," and, as the procession of Jerries filed out of the gate, Vandy sent one of his men to check if they had locked the theatre door. They had not.

"Ve are in luck, Dick! You see, you are not suspect in the theatre; you haf much vork there, you can distract the stupid German. Then I vill send my two men through the hole."

Almost wearily, Dick turned back, asking Lulu to help him do the distraction. It was dark by now outside. They climbed the stairs again and entered the lighted theatre. They pretended to go about their work, talking and laughing. Vandy quietly hid his two escapers in the wings beside the stage door leading down to the dressing-room and then joined Dick and Lulu.

"Ve vill go to the dressing-room by the other door and attract the sentry to us," he whispered.

After playing a few bars on the piano and banging some chairs about, the three of them filed into the dressing-room from the auditorium, apparently discussing heatedly the seating accommodation, the price of tickets, the timing of the various sets and finally in surprise. . . .

"Why the hell is the sentry here?"

Dick asked him what he was supposed to be doing and offered him a cigarette. The sentry took it with a 'Danke' and hid it in his tunic pocket, pointing out the large hole behind him which they all pretended to see for the first time.

Vandy chipped in with his good German and soon a political discussion was under way. The two of them eased around the sentry and Lulu started to look fixedly out of a window near the door by which they had entered. The floodlights came on with a searing flash. Suddenly he pointed and said, "Look! look!" excitedly. Dick rushed to the window and Vandy almost lifted the sentry forward. Nothing doing! The sentry stood rock-like.

The political conversation continued, with Vandy on one side of him, Dick on the other and both edging gradually towards the door in close animated discussion. Lulu, still by the window, interposed some comments at long range in halting German. Vandy and Dick feigned misunderstanding; they shuffled towards him; they enveigled the German to ask him questions, Lulu's German became more halting and less audible. Vandy became the interpreter and courier between them; standing halfway, he tried to draw them together. The sentry would not budge. Vandy was impatient at the best of times. He was working himself up and was on the point of giving the sentry a direct order to stand aside. He left the dressing-room with a growl and a wink, scowling at the sentry behind his back.

Dick and Lulu continued valiantly. More cigarettes passed hands and were lit. The sentry would not smoke. Lulu, who was nearest the door, sniffed.

"What've you got in your lighter, Dick?" he said suddenly and sniffed again.

"German lighter fuel," said Dick, "why? Does it smell like eau-de-Cologne?" Then he, in turn, sniffed. There was no mistaking that smell for German lighter fuel and it was getting stronger. "Why!" Dick exclaimed, "it's brown paper—no, it's scenery paint—no it's both."

Then he smelt wood burning and rushed from the room followed closely by Lulu. As they turned the corner they saw Vandy circling round a blaze in the middle of the floor of the auditorium, which he was fanning violently with a large sheet of cardboard. He turned to shout *"Feuer"* and, at the same time, piled more wood shavings, brown paper and bits of canvas, which he had collected, on to the flames. A thick blue cloud billowed upwards as Dick and Lulu took up the cry, *"Feuer! Feuer!"*.

Vandy rushed back to the dressing-room shouting to the sentry: *"Achtung! Feuer! Feuer! Schnell! 'raus schnell! Sie werden verbrennen wenn Sie heir bleiben.* You will be burnt alive!"

The theatre filled with smoke as more paper was applied. Again Vandy dashed to the dressing-room door, gesticulating violently, and shouted to the sentry to follow him.

The sentry would not budge.

Defeated at last, Vandy threw up his hands, "It is no use, the stupid fellow vould rather burn to death."

With that the three of them set about putting the fire out. Then, joined by the two Dutchmen from the wings, they all fled from the theatre leaving a smouldering heap on the floor. As they descended the stairs, smoke was billowing from the high windows, showing up ominously in the searchlight beams, and Germans could be heard shouting *"Feuer! Feuer!"* from the guardhouse outside.

Extraordinary to relate, the theatre was not closed and, the next day, the prison gates opened wide to allow the passage of a heavy lorry carrying the Bechstein Concert Grand piano. Amid a greater ovation than any pianist who ever pressed its keys could hope to hear, the piano was manhandled off the lorry and began its second panting, puffing journey up the narrow staircase to the theatre.

CHAPTER III

THE LIGHT WELL

THE stooging in the theatre light well was progressing
satisfactorily and without too much disturbance. But
the results coming from the graphs plotted did not give
cause for optimism. After a month of watching over the
most favourable sections of the twenty-four hours, a two-
minute blind spot stood out as a regular feature of the
graph shortly after 2 p.m. every day. It coincided with a
change of guard. The bottom of the light well remained
void of German humanity for these two minutes. They did
not necessarily occur at exactly the same time every day.
One day the two-minute gap might be at 2.10 p.m., another
day at 2.12 p.m., and even sometimes as late as 2.15 p.m.
On an average, 2.10 p.m. was the psychological moment.

The escape was decided upon, and the German uniforms
were put in hand for Rupert and Mike. These consisted of
fatigue overalls which were the standard dress of Germans
working in the kitchens and, when off duty, eating or drinking in their canteens. At the bottom of the well, doors led
off in various directions into a maze of German kitchens,
sculleries, store rooms, bakeries and canteens. A corridor
eventually led to a staircase, down one flight of stairs and
out into the German Kommandantur courtyard.

Our two escapers were to descend by rope from one of
the theatre corridor windows, a distance of fifty feet to the
bottom of the well, and find their way out to the German
courtyard. Once there, they had a choice of two routes, depending on the positions of the various gateway guards
which were not accurately predictable. The better route,
probably, would be that usually taken by the prisoners when
marched under guard for their daily recreation of one hour
in the park. Once in the park, the escapers could make for
a secluded spot near the football enclosure, climb the

barbed wire fence abutting the twelve-foot wall surrounding the park, using it as a ladder to help them to the top.

There would be little activity in the German barracks about fifty yards away at this time of day, and they could hope to scale the wall unseen. In addition, although the trees in the park were leafless, the branches provided a good screen at fifty yards, especially as the football enclosure was at a level lower than the barracks.

Preparations for the escape were nearing completion. The German overalls were ready; the civilian clothing to be worn underneath had been fitted and checked. Identity papers were in order; maps, compasses and money provided. Bos'n Crisp, R.N., who with a few assistants, manufactured all the ropes required for escapes, had made a stout sixty-foot length, fully tested for strength.

The time had come for Dick to start work on the bars of the light well window. The escape would be carried out within a few days.

With Lulu Lawton to assist him and a team of stooges in action led by Grismond Davies-Scourfield, a Lieutenant of the King's Royal Rifles, Dick repaired to the theatre. They entered the forbidden corridor by a small lattice window in the theatre wall instead of by the usual door. This window was conveniently placed for the escape, being situated in an angle of wall not directly facing the theatre exit. Although officially sealed, opening and closing it presented little difficulty, and it faced the barred corridor window from which the descent was to be made.

Crawling through the lattice window, Dick and Lulu surprised two young Frenchmen who were peering downwards into the light well from one of the corridor windows.

"Hello! Hello!" Dick greeted them with mock gaiety, "can I help you?"

"*Non merci,*" replied the Frenchmen.

Dick continued sarcastically, "You're in a forbidden zone here. I shall report this to the Germans," and then taking them to task, "What if I'd been a German—where are your stooges?"

"We have no stooges," was the answer.

"How often have you been here?"

"A few times. We intend to escape from here to-morrow. We have been observing. We think we can descend easily into the well with a rope after cutting the bars."

At this news both Dick and Lulu nearly exploded. The Frenchmen's approach, however, was so naïve that Dick recovered himself in time to burst out laughing instead.

"You b—— fools," he said, "how long have you been in Colditz?"

"Oh! a long time now."

"In that case you ought to know better than to carry on the damn silly way you're doing. Does Colonel Le Brigant know what you're up to?"

"No!"

"Then why the hell not!" said Dick, "it's about damn well time some of you gay young dogs realised that there is a Senior French officer in the camp, and that when he orders you to keep him informed of your escaping activities he means it. Get out of here quick." Turning to Lulu he added, "We'd better all get out quick and seal up. What a b—— awful mess!"

Outside in the theatre, Dick and Lulu explained to the Frenchmen that they had very nearly ruined an escape which had been in preparation for months. The Frenchmen, unfortunately, did not take kindly to the explanation. The more they realised how inept they had been, the more their pride was wounded. They insisted on their right to escape by the light well if and when they wanted to. The matter ended with both sides saying that they would refer it to their respective Commanding Officers.

"For crying out loud!" said Lulu, as they wended their way back to the British quarters, joined by Grismond on the stairs. "Months of hard work and a first-class scheme, and those two nitwits come along to break it up. I've always liked the French, but, my godfathers! the crass stupid ways they sometimes behave makes me wonder if they've any brains in their heads at all. Discipline! Great Caesar's ghost

—and they all did two years military service before the war!
They're crazy!"

Lulu, the staid Yorkshireman, could not contain himself.
Grismond could make no sense of it at all, and Dick walked
back to the quarters in glum silence. At the bottom of the
stairs he said to Grismond:

"Go and fetch Rupert and Mike—tell 'em there's a hitch
and will they come along straight away to the C.O.'s room.
You come along too. Lulu! let's go, we've got to have a
showdown and the sooner the better."

There was a showdown, and when the sheafs of graph
paper were produced showing the months of patient stooging that had been done in order to establish a two minutes
safe period in the light well, the Frenchmen at last climbed
down.

The curious attitude of the French towards their C.O.—
towards any C.O.—was always a matter of mystery to the
British. Their Commanding Officer in Colditz was one of
the finest Frenchmen imaginable. Yet a large number of
French officers felt no compunction in carrying on their
own escape schemes without telling a soul, although it was
a recognised rule of the camp, that the respective Senior
Officers should be informed so that they could compare
notes, avoid messing up each other's plans and prevent
chaos.

Frankly, some of the French were insubordinate. Presumably they thought that, so long as they told nobody, at
least their security was good. On the other hand, the Senior
Officers of the army of a defeated nation did not feel in a
position to enforce strict military discipline under prison
conditions.

This state of affairs, fortunately, seldom displayed itself
openly and, apart from one or two high spots such as the
light well debacle, the French chain of Command in the
camp was respected.

The French had to give way, but their stupidity in the
execution of the project was made up for by their astuteness in seizing an opportunity.

"If two can escape by the well, surely four can, without much more difficulty?" they queried, adding, "and if four can get out, there is more hope of at least one or two making home."

Dick and the C.O., and Rupert and Mike chewed over this proposition for a while. Finally, it was agreed:

"Yes, all right. Four will go. An Englishman with a Frenchman—in two pairs." With that the pact was concluded and the escape was on. The British were not satisfied, but, at least, they were magnanimous. Extra risk was involved inside the camp; once outside, four heads were always better than two and, after all, the 'Entente Cordiale' was being toasted daily in the camp!

German overalls were provided for the Frenchmen. Civilian clothes, paper and other paraphernalia they supplied from their own sources.

Dick and Lulu found themselves once more, some days later, mounting the stairs to the theatre on their way to cut and prepare the window bars ready for the descent.

Grismond's stooging was excellent. Nowadays, in the Castle it could not afford to be anything less. The Germans were jittery and their movements had to be watched with extreme caution.

The bar cutting was not so difficult, but it took time. The window being high above ground and overlooking a well about thirty feet square, Jerries at the bottom could not see anything going on inside the window sill. Kitchen noises and the continual hubbub of movement served to drown the tell-tale sound of sawing. Dick and Lulu cut the bars successfully, replacing the loose pieces with patent sleeves manufactured by Scarlet O'Hara. These provided a perfect camouflage against observation. The bars could even stand gentle shaking, but would not survive the violent tug of a brawny Goon. If the bars were tapped, of course, they would not ring true.

Zero hour for the descent was ten minutes past two in the afternoon on November the 20th, 1942. This is where the next snag arose. An *Appell* was, more usually than not, held at two o'clock!

Appells, when properly organised, and provided there were no unforeseen hitches, could be called to attention as the German officers appeared, and dismissed again within eight minutes. Such an *Appell* was indeed a rare occurrence. The German officer had to appear dead on time, and each contingent had to be warned to behave in exemplary manner. The French were the largest group, but as two of their own number were escaping, order and co-operation could be expected from them.

There was always the haunting fear of an unknown spy inside the camp. Sometimes, as in this case, the best that could be done to combat the possibility of such treachery was not to give the traitor enough time to 'put his spanner in the works'. Only at the last minute were officers, gathering for the *Appell,* warned to behave amenably and cut the *Appell* time to a minimum.

The afternoon arrived. Everything was prepared. The rope was concealed under the bed of Duggie Bader, the Air Force ace. His room was one of the nearest to the theatre. A vaulting horse, normally housed in the theatre, was close to the lattice window and would take the strain on the rope. Rupert, Mike and the two Frenchmen were dressed for the occasion: first, civilian clothes, then over them the German fatigue overalls, and on top of everything, army overcoats and trousers.

Rupert and Mike were both seasoned escapers. For that reason, their feelings as the crucial moment arrived, were more like those of an experienced bomb disposal officer about to begin an operation than anything else. Panic at the thought of the approaching danger, at the prospect of possibly being 'written off,' was gone. With it went the worst symptom of physical nausea which, in earlier days, brought on vomiting. There was an outward coolness, which was deceptive. The fear, which came from knowledge of the odds, lay less heavily upon the stomach. The anguish was in the conscious mind instead of in the subconscious—

the entrails. There was little nervous reaction, no visible shaking.

The suffering of the conscious mind is a stage ahead. It is fearful of overconfidence. It must remember the lessons of experience. It must not forget. The beginner has no experience to forget. His fear is of the unknown. Curiously enough, escaping is one of those adventures in which experience counts a great deal. Only the seasoned escaper knows it.

Compare a tame animal with a wild animal. They are as chalk and cheese. An experienced escaper is a tame animal that has learnt something of the wiles of a wild one.

The experienced escaper feels a heavy responsibility lying at his own door. He knows how to succeed and, if he fails, it is probably his fault. The odds are his own making. He knows he cannot blame 'bad luck' any more. The beginner does not know the odds, they are not of his own making. He is lucky or unlucky and until he has passed the stage of blaming failure on bad luck he is not a seasoned escaper. The experienced bomb disposal officer knows this too. If he is blown sky high it is because he made a blunder, though in conditions fraught with terrifying danger for the uninitiated.

The *Appell* sounded at 1.55 p.m. and the prisoners gathered in the courtyard. Obedient to whispered commands, ranks were formed in an orderly manner and in record time. As two p.m. struck Oberleutnant Püpcke, tall, in his well-fitting grey artillery uniform and highly polished jack boots, walked quickly through the gate.

"True to form," thought Dick, and he winked at Mike and Rupert forming up not far away.

The *Appell* went off without a hitch except for the ominous arrival of the Abwehr (security) officer, Hauptmann Eggers, in the middle of the proceedings. As the prisoners had nowadays come to expect, the Jerries were not far behind them. Eggers knew that something was in the wind, but evidently had few clues.

The parade was dismissed. Dick and Lulu made for the

entrance to the theatre block as nonchalantly yet as quickly as possible.

Eggers deliberately headed for them and buttonholed Dick.

With a slow calculated pronunciation he rasped out in English:

"Well, Captain Howe, and where are you going?" There was suspicion in his manner and sarcasm in his voice.

"I'm going with Captain Lawton to do some boxing in the theatre. Why do you ask?"

Eggers ignored Dick's question and said slowly, looking Dick straight in the eye, "I thought Captain Lawton was a great friend of yours. Why do you want to box him?"

"This is terrible," thought Dick, holding his gaze. The precious seconds were ticking away. He replied:

"We can have a good fight and still remain friends."

"Very remarkable! very remarkable!" commented Eggers dryly, nodding his head. He moved out of earshot, and Lulu said, as they both marched into the theatre block:

"Let's call it off for to-day. He's up to something."

"No, we go on," said Dick. "He'll have to be damn quick now to catch us and I'd much rather see him in our court-yard than waiting on the German side for our chaps to come out."

They hurried up the stairs and into the theatre to find the four escapers ready and the stooging in action. Davies-Scourfield was in charge, already giving the running commentary of Goon movements reported by signals from his staff.

"Eggers in courtyard—Dixon Hawk in sick-bay—two snoops at entrance to French quarters . . ." he reported slowly translating the signs given to him, like a bookie's mate taking his cues from the semaphore men on a race course.

Lulu secured the rope to the leg of the vaulting horse and passed it through the lattice window. Dick and Lulu then scrambled through into the corridor. The four escapers were already waiting.

"We're running late," said Dick looking at his watch, "it's ten past."

He opened the air-shaft window and listened. The next moment he was removing the sleeves and the bars. One look down the well was enough. Out went the rope, and Mike Sinclair started to descend. He seemed to be ages going down. Grismond's voice came from the theatre.

"Eggers has entered theatre block . . . he's coming up the stairs to the first floor. . . ."

Without further ado Dick and Lulu picked up the first Frenchman and threw him out of the window shouting, "*Allez, vite!*"

There was a violent jerk on the rope as the Frenchman's slack was taken up. Grismond's voice could be heard:

"Eggers on way up to second floor."

"Get the rope away, Lulu," Dick shouted, and to Rupert and the waiting Frenchman, "run for it, vamoose *vite!*" He was already sealing up the window bars and applying the camouflage.

"Eggers coming up the last flight to theatre," came through steady as a rock from Grismond.

"You must come out," said Lulu hoarsely, as Dick applied the finishing touches to the bars. Dick made a running dive through the lattice window and as Lulu locked it quietly, Dick picked himself up and gave him an almighty clout in the solar plexus.

Eggers walked into the theatre.

What he saw was a first class rough house. On the floor of the theatre auditorium with chairs flying in all directions, an irate Yorkshireman made it plain to the world that the Christian beatitude of turning the other cheek did not apply where he came from.

This might have been enough for Eggers, but, to his perplexity was added bewilderment, as the French chapel choir, which had foregathered for a practice at the other end of the theatre, entoned the opening lines of a dignified 'Kyrie Eleison.'

Eggers pulled himself together. He was accompanied by

two snoops before whom he had to keep up appearances. His sly eyes roved the theatre quickly, then, with a sudden movement, he unlocked the door into the forbidden corridor.

Dick and Lulu stopped fighting and innocently pressed forward towards the door to see what Eggers was up to. One of the snoops tried some of the window bars but missed the ones that had been out. The procession retraced its steps. Eggers relocked the door and turned to continue his tour of inspection. Spying the two Englishmen, he grinned at them, then, shaking his head as he departed, he quoted, "Mad dogs and Englishmen . . ."

The stooges reported that Mike and the Frenchman had walked casually out of the German courtyard by the deep archway leading to the park. Turning to the right, they had walked downhill, then through a wooden gateway on the left hand side, down the steep winding path to the bridge over a stream which bounded one side of the park and they were lost to view.

Half an hour passed without any alarms. It could be safely concluded that the two had succeeded in leaving the camp.

Dick had little time to congratulate himself on this achievement. The next problem loomed up like a black cloud. Rupert and the second Frenchman had not been able to go. Dick was determined that Rupert should not be disappointed. He felt his reputation was involved. If he could 'fix' three *Appells,* and provided neither of the first two escapers were re-caught, it should be possible to repeat the escape. It would have to be done the next day at the same time or never.

He decided to try a method of fixing the *Appell* which had not, to his knowledge, been used at Colditz before. It was known as the 'Rabbit' method. He had heard of its use elsewhere, but in Colditz it was thought generally that there were too many sentries present to allow of its success. He conferred with the French adjutant and called Lieutenant Gigue of the French Foreign Legion to his rescue. It was agreed that both contingents would adopt the same system and conceal one absence each at the next three *Appells*.

Bruce, 'the medium-sized man,' the indefatigable and ever willing young R.A.F. officer, who stood about five feet one inch in his socks, would be Dick's rabbit. The operation required the co-operation of a large number of officers.

With the help of Rupert and Lulu, Dick rounded up thirty of the tallest British available and in a secluded corner of a dormitory, his audience lolling on the beds and seated on the floor, Dick called for attention and began:

"We managed to get Mike away this afternoon with a Frenchman, but it was a near thing. Eggers was hot on the trail—so hot in fact, that Rupert who was the next to go couldn't make it. If we can fox the next three *Appells*, one to-night, and two to-morrow, we should be able to send Rupert out immediately after the 2 p.m. roll call. This is why I want you fellows to help. I'll have to grade you for height first. So will you please all stand up in line facing me as if on *Appell*."

With some jostling and banter a line was formed, then reshuffled, so that the tallest was at one end and the smallest at the other.

"Now," said Dick, "I think the quickest way to get what I want is for you to number off. Squad," he shouted with mock seriousness, "from the left, number!" This was followed by "even numbers, two paces backward, march!"

Having obtained two similar rows of fifteen men each, he explained:

"We've now got to re-shuffle each line so that it looks fairly natural, but I'd like the tallest in the middle of each line."

This was done and Dick continued:

"Will each of you please note your positions carefully, that is, the man on each side of you. Got it? Good, now let's break up and try a rehearsal."

The team broke up and when Dick said, "Form up!" the two lines reformed without a hitch.

The Rabbit

"That's fine. Now, for heaven's sake, remember your positions carefully. A lot depends on it. The next step is this: your two lines are to form the middle portion of the second and third ranks of the parade turn out. There will be half a dozen officers on your right flank in each row; there will be a complete rank of chaps in front of you. Those left over will tag themselves on to the left flank. Now this is where Bruce comes in." He shepherded Bruce to the right of the front rank.

"As soon as the Jerries have counted Bruce's file of three, and have passed on towards your left, Bruce will duck and run between your two ranks to the left hand end of your front rank. Let's try it, Bruce."

Bruce ducked down between the two rows and reappeared in a few seconds at the far end.

"O.K.," said Dick.

Rupert, who was watching carefully, butted in, "Dick, both ranks had better form up pretty close. I could see Bruce easily between their legs."

Dick agreed. "You'd better all wear overcoats on the *Appell*, it's cold enough, and form up close," he said; and to Bruce, "carry an R.A.F. cap with you on *Appell*. Don't wear it to begin with, but when you reappear, have it on your head with the peak well down. Last man on the left of the fronk rank: remember, on the actual *Appell*, to keep a gap on your left just sufficient for Bruce to fill in."

The parade reformed from scratch with Bruce in position, hat in hand.

"Now I'm the Jerry officer and there's a complete rank in front of you. Rupert, see how it goes as I do the counting."

Dick started to count the files in the German fashion and as he passed three files from Bruce, the latter glided out of sight and was in his new position, with his hat pulled well down over his eyes, long before Dick reached him.

"That'll do," said Rupert.

Dick then gave some final cautions and the party broke up.

The rabbit method was more foolproof the bigger the number on parade. The French were a hundred and eighty strong by now compared with the British eighty, and little difficulty was expected with their contingent. This was the kind of game which appealed strongly to the French mentality.

The evening *Appell* and the next morning *Appell* went off serenely. The French, noticing what was happening, thought it a great joke. For Dick, there was the satisfying feeling of an operation going according to schedule, but behind it was always a haunting misgiving—-the stool-pigeon; the unknown traitor who might be in their midst, who had his own secret method of transmitting information to the Germans within the prison, and who could ruin the best of schemes.

The midday *Appell* assembled as usual. Dick, Rupert and Lulu formed up at the end of the rear rank. From here they could witness the rabbit performing. To their right they could see the French forming up. Nothing looked unusual. The parade came to attention and Oberleutnant Püpcke entered the courtyard on time. He was always punctual. The counting began. As it passed Bruce, he could be seen stiffening for the 'off.' He bent his head down, looking at his feet, and as the counting reached the fourth file beyond him he seemed to slip to the earth and in a second was diving along the closely formed corridor between the two rear ranks. He reappeared, if anything rather suddenly, in his new position.

As Püpcke reached the end of the counting, a sentry near the canteen door came smartly to attention and left his post at the double. He halted in front of the German Sergeant Major, and spoke hurriedly to him. The Sergeant Major saluted Püpcke, and spoke to him. Together they accosted the sentry and a consultation took place. This was the signal for the prisoners to start barracking and shuffling their feet to register impatience. The sentry had obviously seen something. He was the one nearest to the point where Bruce reappeared. Püpcke, however, did not appear convinced. Turning away from him, he ordered the parade to dismiss.

Dick and Rupert had little time to congratulate themselves on their good fortune. In less than a minute they were in the theatre where the drill was laid on as before. Rupert, calm and collected, not showing a trace of the excitement seething within him, took up his position in the corridor and his French colleague soon stood beside him. He, too, was behaving himself well. He could hardly be excited with the coolness all around him. The operation worked like clockwork. Dick gave no orders. The men who were on this job were old hands.

The rope went over the sill; the bars came away and Rupert was outside. As he dropped down Dick whispered hoarsely after him, "Good luck, Rupert! Remember they can't shoot a British officer."

Grismond Davies-Scourfield's voice could be heard as yesterday, but to-day there was a ring of optimism in his reports:

"Püpcke walking out of courtyard through main gate . . . Gephard talking to Dixon Hawk in centre . . . two snoops at sick bay entrance . . . all clear in theatre block. . . ."

The Frenchman followed Rupert and as the rope slackened it was whipped up and removed immediately to its permanent hiding place. The camouflage replaced and the windows closed, the whole team quickly dispersed. Dick and Lulu transferred their activities to genuine theatrical preparations on the stage and awaited the reports of the stooges watching the progress of the escapers.

Ten minutes later, small, ginger-headed Peter Storie Pugh bounced into the theatre.

"They've been caught, Dick," he said, "at the gateway down to the park."

"What the hell!" exclaimed Dick. "How were they caught there? There's no sentry."

"Quite, but there was when Rupert and his Frog got there. He appeared from nowhere and stopped them."

"What happened?"

"I couldn't see much for the trees, but there was quite a lot of talking before he made them put their hands up. Then they were marched back to the Kommandantur."

"Somebody's been quick off the mark this time if you ask me. That's Egger's work all right—but what gets me is that he should know when our men were going and the direction they'd take."

"I'm afraid it's the old story, Dick—a traitor in the camp," said Peter. "This always happens when too many people get to know an escape's coming off. The whole camp knew about the escape to-day."

"You're probably right, Peter, but we'll never know for certain. A stool-pigeon would certainly account for Eggers' behaviour yesterday. But we were one step ahead luckily. Eggers wouldn't have known any more than his informer, who could only tell him an escape was likely in the afternoon and that we should be watched closely."

"But to-day," Peter interrupted, "he'd know a lot more. You can't stop people talking. He'd know about everything —except probably the actual light well."

"A damn shame!" said Dick. He was boiling with suppressed anger. He was sure in his own mind that an informer was at work, and he was impotent to trace him. The whole camp would have to be treated as suspect.

A Polish informer had been found—it was old history now—but he had been found by the Poles themselves. Dick might be able to set some sleuths at work among the British, but nothing could ever be done about the French —that was the trouble—it was his Achilles heel.

Scarlet O'Hara walked into the theatre. He had been watching the German courtyard.

"They're caught," he said grinning broadly.

"Thanks for the news," said Dick. "I can't see anything funny in it. What's the joke?"

"They were marched into the Kommandantur about ten minutes ago, from the park. I stayed put to see what happened. They've just been marched out again and they're off down to the town jail, dressed in their underpants, with their hands up and four Goons trailing 'em."

"I bet Rupert's cold, his pants always remind me of a piece of wire netting," said Dick. He was thinking, "Thank God two are out anyway—not as depressing as it could be."

Lulu had joined the group. Peter and Scarlet were re-counting their stories again. Dick changed the subject.

"I don't think the 'Rabbit' will work again in a hurry. We'd better lay up a couple of ghosts while we have the chance. That means three absent from the British ranks next *Appell*. The Jerries may call one any time now."

Lulu said, "I think Monty Bissell's our man for that. He's got the best hide-out in the camp."

"Let's get cracking," said Dick with sudden energy in his voice. He disappeared through the theatre door, and down the stairs two at a time, followed by the others.

They found Monty in the prisoners' mess room and a hurried consultation took place. Monty had recently em-barked on a tunnel scheme in the Chapel, under the pulpit. The entrance was cleverly concealed by a slab of marble forming one of the steps up to it. There was already ample space in the tunnel for the concealment of a couple of bodies which, it was now agreed, should be permanently housed there. Volunteers were quickly called for from among Monty tunnelling team, and two were elected for the job. They went straight to the Chapel and were walled in.

The *Appell* siren began to moan.

On a previous escape attempt Dick had put away no less than six ghosts. It had been too much for the Jerries to swallow. Besides, the ghosts were not superlatively well hidden, and were all, eventually, discovered. On this occas-sion Dick decided to compromise with two ghosts.

What was the purpose of a ghost? It was this: after a 'gone-away' escape the chances of success of the escaper increased tremendously the further he was from the Camp. The area of search to be covered by the Germans increased, mathematically, by the square of the increased distance away.

Thus it was of the utmost importance to give an escaper the longest start possible by concealing his absence on *Appells* as long as possible; for this purpose ghosts were created.

In this particular instance, as the two 'gone-aways'— Mike Sinclair and his French colleague—had a good twenty-four hours' start, Dick considered it unnecessary to conceal their absence any longer. On the contrary, it was now more important to think of the future. The two ghosts in the Chapel would 'fill in' on *Appells* after the next escape, whenever that might be.

German sentries entered the courtyard and took up their positions for the roll call. Their officers appeared. The parade came to attention. The count was taken. Four officers were missing. Messengers were dispatched to the Kommandantur. After a long delay they returned. The parade was dismissed.

Dick now had two cards up his sleeve.

*   *   *   *   *

Optimism ran high after Mike's escape. He was known to be heading for Switzerland, towards the hitherto almost foolproof secret Colditz frontier-crossing route.

Then after five days came the news of his recapture. The Germans were never slow to announce the recapture of an escaper: in fact, it was by the absence of such announcements that the successes were counted. An almost audible groan went up from the whole camp. He carried the hopes of so many and bore personal messages with him to so many loved ones waiting patiently at home in England for their husbands and their sons.

Within ten days Mike was back in the Castle, in a solitary confinement cell. His story came through.

When he and his French companion had walked through the German kitchens from the theatre light well, they found their way down the stairs and into the German courtyard without mishap. One quick glance had been enough for Mike to assure him of the direction to take. The gateway to the park lay open. There did not appear to be anyone on duty there. Without a word the two men, in their German overalls, passed the courtyard sentry, heading for the gate. Through this they walked and on down the hill, turning through the next gate to the left of the road-way and then down further along the steep, wide path into the park, over the bridge.

Within ten minutes they had climbed the park wall and were free. Mike parted company from his companion *en route* and in two days he was in Singen. The Frenchman made for the city of Leipzig where there were many French workmen and where, also, a convoy of lorries started for France, at regular intervals, with supplies for the occupa-tion troops. Mike was re-caught near Singen. His was the story becoming menacingly common these days; an air raid had started a round-up for parachuted airmen. Thousands of civilians were out on the manhunt. He was picked up by a patrol within half a mile of freedom and three days out from Colditz. The Frenchman was already in the cells on his return; his contacts in Leipzig had failed him.

Mike was not allowed to communicate with anyone during his stay in the 'cooler', which lasted six weeks. He was left alone with his thoughts, disconsolate and dejected, to brood upon his failure, 'so near and yet so far . . .' Mike would take himself to task seriously. He had a strongly developed conscience and an unswerving devotion to duty. A feeling that he had let down his fellow prisoners would not leave him at peace. At twenty-six he could stand a fair amount of loneliness and introspection without ill effect, but—six weeks was a long spell and, besides, Mike had taken more than his share of punishment with the Gestapo in Poland.

Resolution was the healing salve that would conquer the putrifying poison of morbidity. He would try again. He would not give up; that was certain.

II

1943

CHAPTER IV

RADIO NEWS

DURING the autumn of 1942, Dick Howe had entered into private negotiations with a French clique which possessed one of the two wireless sets in Colditz. A second group of French headed by Lieutenant Gigue owned the other. The first set had been smuggled into the prison with the arrival of a batch of Frenchmen from a camp where they had had considerable contact with the outer world, mainly through orderlies and French workmen in the town and countryside. Gigue's set had been smuggled into the camp in parts hidden in thirty-five parcels, received over a period of months, from France.

The British had no set of their own and a purchase was arranged. Dick had been Escape Officer for some months by then. From the many contacts he had and the many rather morbid impressions he picked up, he saw, only too clearly, the value of possessing such a link with the outside world. He was preparing the hide for it when a hitch occurred. The proposed purchase became widely known among the French contingent; their senior officers were told of the transaction and were prevailed upon to stop it. Feeling, among the French, ran on the lines that as they were likely to be moved at any time—which was true—they would probably be separated into groups for different destinations and would need both sets. After all, they argued, Frenchmen had gone to much trouble to obtain them, so, why should they dispose of one? They even argued that as British morale was higher than theirs they had more need of the boost given by allied news broadcasts. Of course, as long as they remained in Colditz, the British would continue to use translations of their bulletins. Dick retired from the scene.

Lieutenant Gigue came from the south of France and

had spent most of his life in Marseilles. He had the typical French accent of the region which differs from normal French, enunciated between the lips and teeth. The tongue plays a great part in producing the Marseilles accent by giving the impression of always sticking to the palate a split second too long.

Gigue carried a huge scar across his cheek and neck. His hair and eyebrows were jet black and his skin a deep suntanned brown. A pair of mischievously flashing dark eyes and a ready grin completed an appearance of good-humoured energy. His movements were unbelievably quick and he had the knack of changing his position without being thought to have moved at all. It was a most curious and even eerie propensity. If it had not struck so many different officers at different times, the likelihood is that each one would have thought he had had an hallucination or was just suffering from prison slow-wittedness. But after about a year or so, when men repeatedly found themselves talking to thin air where they had thought they saw Gigue a moment before, the matter became one of public interest. It was even advanced that possibly Gigue was endowed with occult powers. Certainly it was most disconcerting for Englishmen to be found talking out loud to themselves in French in the middle of the courtyard; Gigue understood no English. He moved without a sound wherever he went.

Marseilles is not so far from Corsica. It is said that Napoleon had the cat-like propensity of walking, not on his toes and heels, but somewhere in between. Nor was Gigue unlike a Corsican bandit in that he had a faithful company of followers who, in all escaping ventures, appeared to understand his every mood and interpreted his unspoken wishes with unfailing accuracy. Gigue's heart was made of gold and the English had no better friend among the French contingent. Long before the French left Colditz, Dick Howe and Gigue had become close collaborators and the friendship between them paid dividends.

One spring-like day in February, 1943, Dick careered down the spiral staircase from the French quarters out into the courtyard and nearly bumped into Colonel Guy German who was taking his morning constitutional.

The sun just climbed high enough at midday to peep over the steep roofs of Colditz and send a few shimmering sunbeams to scatter the shadows that ruled unchallenged in the yard during the long and dreary winter months.

There was a glow in Dick's heart and triumph in his voice as he spoke to his senior officer.

"Good morning, Colonel."

"Good morning, Dick."

"I've got good news for you, sir."

"What is it? You sound excited. Coming from you that means it must be very good."

"The French are going as you know."

"Yes, they're going very soon, I think. Colonel Le Brigant has told me. He has it on good authority from his own stooges. Incidentally, he's told me the move is to make room for British. You remember the rumours we heard of the big breakout from Warburg? Well, the British are reported to be coming from Warburg—at least some of them. So the rumour may have been true."

"Well, sir, my bit of news concerns a wireless set."

"Ah, ha! are the French coming round then? We don't want a repetition of the last effort. There was some bad feeling over that—you remember?"

"Yes, I remember well. But this time they want to present it to us."

"In that case it must be given through the Senior French Officer so that we know where we stand. I'm afraid I'll have to insist on that point."

"I think that's all laid on. Gigue tells me that he has the agreement of Colonel Le Brigant to leave one of his sets behind. You see Gigue has two now. He's damn decent about the whole business. He can claim that the sets have been obtained entirely through his efforts and he is pressing his claim and the right to dispose of the set as he likes. He says there'll be practically no opposition from the French quarters. They've two other sets now which will travel with them."

"Of course, Dick, there's our own set on the way. . . ."

"Yes, but . . . it's not here yet and may never reach us. Gigue knows about it too, and says his C.O. knows it."

"Very well! It looks as if we can accept with a clear conscience."

"Colonel Le Brigant will be speaking to you about it soon."

Dick was about to turn away when his senior recalled him.

"One moment, Dick, that's not the end of the matter. What about the use of the set? Have you thought about that? First of all there's the maintenance, then there's the stooging and the recording, and we'll have to decide on reception times and the best wave lengths and produce the best news bulletins possible."

"Yes, I've thought about it," said Dick, and the slightest trace of weariness crept into his voice. He knew what was coming. The Colonel was thinking. He had, when in thought, the unusual habit of raising his eyebrows and wrinkling his forehead. They walked together round the yard—now in shadow, now in sunlight. The Colonel always walked briskly. He had a robust physique and was still tough in spite of the years of weakening. His was a forceful character that stood no nonsense from Germans or anybody else. He could be frighteningly abrupt. To those in whom he placed his confidence he was a towering pillar of strength. He could scent out weakness like a bloodhound after his quarry, and he wasted no time. He was the ideal Commanding Officer in a difficult situation.

It was his regular exercise hour and the circle he walked never varied, though the direction in which he walked it changed unpredictably. Dick walked beside him as they speeded round in clockwise direction. The Colonel, as if to jolt his thoughts, stopped suddenly and reversed direction. Dick was well trained in his habits, and had caught him up again in a yard.

The Colonel had been ruminating and now he spoke as if unwillingly:

"I see no way out of it. You are our best wireless engineer. I daren't put the machine in anyone else's hands. It's much too valuable—our only link with reality in fact. If it broke down it would be like cutting an artery. Yes, Dick, I'm afraid it means more work for you."

"I know that."

"What you must do, at least, is to try and relieve yourself of all the news routine, and arrange the security so that you're free of that responsibility. Pass it over to someone else."

"Lulu Lawton?" queried Dick who had already given thought to the problem of stooging.

"Yes, by all means."

"Gigue has shown me the works," Dick continued, "and they're first class. We have absolutely nothing to teach that crew. I must hand it to Gigue. I can understand why the Jerries have never found it."

"Well, it's up to you, Dick, or rather to the man you appoint for stooging and camouflage to see that the Jerries continue not to find it. If they do—it'll look bad and we'll have only ourselves to blame."

Early in 1943 Gigue had received a second brand-new receiving set in another round of thirty-five parcels from France. They were smuggled, as usual, out of the German parcel office before the Germans ever set about examining the day's parcel delivery. The French were consequently happy to leave the British one of their three sets before they departed from Colditz.

There was no need even for the British to construct their own wireless hide. They took over the French set in its stronghold, lock, stock and barrel. It says much for the ingenuity of Gigue and his French colleagues that, although towards the end of the war the Germans knew the British had a set in action they never found it. They searched until they were blue in the face without success. Eventually our prisoners made no concealment of the news bulletins which were read publicly at the evening meal. The war situation was discussed openly with the Germans; their arguments contraverted and their alleged facts and figures contradicted.

As to the situation of the receiver, it was concealed in the eave of the steep sloping roof above the French quarters —which became British on the departure of the French. When a roof is forty feet high from gutter to ridge, it can be appreciated that at least two floors may be built inside it having dormer windows and comparatively high ceilings. The floor area of rooms within the roof becomes reduced at each level upwards, not only because the two sides of the roof are approaching each other, but usually because a vertical wall is built around the sides of the rooms so that the inmates do not have the impression they are living in a tent. This vertical wall, in the case of rooms at Colditz, was about five feet high and concealed behind it a small triangular space bounded by the three sides; slanting roof, vertical wall and horizontal ceiling of the room below. Actually the architectural features were slightly more complicated than this description implies. The triangular space had to be enlarged out of the seven-foot-thick walls. Within it the wireless installation was set up, complete with electric light, switch gear for the receiver, earphones, a table and two chairs for the operator and the shorthand writer acting as news-recording telegraphist. Beside it, a second cavity was enlarged to provide a hide for contraband.

Entry to these secret apartments was made from the attic which formed the apex of the roof itself.

*   *   *   *   *

Jim Rogers, the mining engineer from South Africa, could not have lived long without the news. The progress of the war could be foretold by the tilt of his broad moustache. This had grown from nothing at the time of his capture. Jim had once been a burly, tough six footer but the lengthening war was telling on him. He seemed to grow smaller. As his stature shrank and his body grew thin, his moustache alone waxed in splendour. His strength, like that of Samson, was going into his hair. Where Samson had wielded the jawbone of an ass, Jim wielded his guitar.

Before ever the B.B.C. news bulletins became an organised part of the daily schedule, Jim had developed his own system of news summaries, which he recited daily, with infinite relish, to the whole British contingent assembled for their meagre evening repast. What Jim really needed was a huge beef-steak in front of him, but alas! as that dream dish never materialised, the best that he could do was to whet his appetite with words. He revelled in his phrases and smacked his lips over his metaphors. His war appreciations were full of meat, peppered with doubtful facts, heavily salted with assumptions and blanketed with the opaque rosy coloured sauce of optimism. His prognostications were sweet fruit to the easily gullible, enriched as they were with the cream of the latest rumours. The 'Old Horse' as he was affectionately called, really had very little information to go on. His principal source was the meagre French bulletins which were often garbled with news coming from Vichy. In addition, he had the German press and the hearsay of the latest prisoner arrival from another camp.

As a writer may use a true story for the basis of his novel, so Jim used the news. He would come rushing into the common room just before the midday meal, eyes glistening, a lock of straight hair falling over his forehead, and his moustache quivering with excitement.

"Great news to-day, boys! Great news! I've just got it all straight from the horse's mouth—a chap just in from Marlag Nord—he's in the delousing shed. He was on that Dieppe raid some time ago—won't say any more now— keep it all for to-night—managed to get the whole story at last—it's terrific. It'll shake you."

"Aw, you don't say!" would come from Don Donaldson,

the Canadian, often called 'the Weasel,' who had once climbed into the cockpit of a German Messerschmitt, but could not find the starter.

"Come on, Horse! don't hold back."

Jim would then become as close as an oyster, "Awfully sorry, old chap, but simply mustn't jump the gun—besides I might give the wrong impression—got to draw the right conclusions, you know—that means some thinking—there's big strategy behind this."

It was a cat and mouse game. Don and Jim's other messmates would feign indifference. At lunch time, over the table, surrounded by eight glum officers, silence would reign. After ten minutes, with the meal practically finished and not a word spoken, Jim would realise an opportunity was slipping from him. Bursting to tell his story and thoroughly put out at the lethargy of his companions, he could not hold out any longer. In an offended tone he would blurt out:

"My God! I think you fellows are a lot of bums! Nothing to talk about—no interest in the war—I can't understand chaps not taking an interest in world events . . . terrific things going on."

There would be a pause as Don would drag out the comedy. It was like teasing a big Newfoundland dog which was your greatest friend. Jim knew he was being teased. But his nature could not be suppressed. When Don judged he had wrung the last ounce of patience out of him, he would say again:

"Aw, now Jim you're playing with us! We just can't wait to hear about Dieppe straight from the Old Horse's mouth. Just give us a hint."

So Jim would unbend, and gathering the 'chaps' around him, with their heads all bent close together over the table, he would tell them in a hoarse whisper:

"The Allies have the whole invasion buttoned up. It's coming any day now. Dieppe was terrific strategy—I've worked it out. It was all a hoax to make the Jerries think that we'd think that invasion was hopeless and so ease up on coastal defence. No more now chaps, but I'll give you the whole works to-night. Keep it dark—I want to shake everyone. Damn good for morale."

And indeed it was. Jim was our camp Goebbels—but he did a much better job than that despicable propagandist, probably because he just could not have told a lie if he had tried. He was, by nature, a good story teller. He was a spider who could weave a tantalising web to inveigle even the most suspicious fly. Once in his net, he wrapped his listeners up in a pleasantly soft cotton wool of optimism and hope which, curiously through all the years of despair, became a wonderful protection against the lengthening shadows; the misery of the polar extremes of the unknown and of reality. He was a magician who, by pretending not to be able to deceive his audience, by even encouraging their laughter and their ridicule at his naïvety in the lesser tricks of his trade, cast over them the greater spell at which he aimed; succeeding with genius, so that they were completely unaware of what he had done to them. There is no doubt he kept hope high and courage strong even in the darkest days. He was the Knight of the Silver Lining.

As with Dieppe, so it had been with the loss of the two great battleships, with Singapore and the retreats in the Libyan desert.

When Singapore fell, the French were terribly upset. The Poles were full of sympathy, and the Dutch were calm but silent. The British treated it as if one of their favourite football teams had been beaten, and as if the coming defeat had been known beforehand because the star forward line had been changed.

The fact was that the British contingent had been cushioned for the coming fall for some time by the Old Horse and a confederate, Colonel Kimber. The French came to our quarters with long glum faces wringing their hands as soon as the news was confirmed. The war in the east was over for them. They could see the Japanese hordes in the Mediterranean. They did not come to condole, but rather to join the British in a common act of despair.

Singapore appeared to them, to be for the British what Dunkerque had been for themselves. They found their allies in good spirits and were dumbfounded.

Colonel Kimber had worked on the defences of Singapore before the war. He had, even in those days, fumed at the pigheadedness of men who installed enormous guns with a traverse that covered attack from the sea, but gave no protection whatever in the direction of the Causeway.

Jim Rogers

By the time Singapore fell it was old news to the British, and Jim passed over it lightly:

"Singapore has gone, but I told you all about that three weeks ago, so there's no need to bother about it now. It merely serves to bear out the accuracy of my forecasts."

Loud cheers interrupted him and French guests, who were present, sat with mouths agape at the spectacle of British officers cheering the news of the fall of Singapore. It is not without reason that Europeans speak seriously of 'mad Englishmen'.

When the cheering, catcalls and whistling died down Jim continued his summary of the news of the day.

When he had finished, and the clatter of plates and hum of voices had resumed its normal cacophony, as if to emphasise the complete indifference of the British to a huge catastrophe, Don Donaldson's Canadian drawl would intervene:

"Come on, Old Horse! tell us a good story."

Jim had quite a fund of them and they grew longer and more elaborate with every telling.

"Well, chaps! when I was mining in Yugoslavia some queer things happened to me—you just wouldn't believe them. D'you know there was a princess out there and guess what she did?"

"No! What?"

"Well, you just wouldn't believe it."

"Aw, you don't say! Come on, Old Horse, tell us all about it."

And Jim would tell the story how, once, when prospecting in the mountains of Yugoslavia, his camp had been visited by a Royal party. They were entertained lavishly by Jim's mining team and the 'Slebovitza' flowed freely. A beautiful princess became quite incapable of retracing her steps, after the party, down the rocky gorges to the mountain road, where the cars and retinue attended. Jim and a mate formed a comfortable chair for her with their four hands interlaced, and seated upon them she slept peacefully as they carried her down the stony path.

"What happened then, Jim?"

"Her little head was against my shoulder." He paused.

"Go on, Horse!"

"I slipped on a rock. It gave the princess an awful jolt and she promptly pee'd into my hand."

CHAPTER V

THE FRENCH TUNNEL

T HE French had been digging a tunnel for eight months.
    It looked as if there might be a race between the tun-
nellers and the Germans; the former to finish the tunnel
and escape before the latter moved them all from the camp.
A small party of French had already left for Oflag IV.D.

The French architects of the tunnel consisted originally
of a team of nine officers who constituted themselves the
'Société Anonyme du Tunnel de Colditz'. To make sure
that it was 'anonyme' the tunnellers had no chief.
'Liberté, Egalité, Fraternité' was the motto they lived up
to. They were: Jean Brejoux, a professor of German;
Edgar Barras, the strong man and the champion French
'stool-ball'* player; Bernard Cazaumayou, the weight lifter;
Roger Madin, an engineer who was the tunnel electrician;
Paillé, French Sappers and Miners; Jean Chaudrut, the
chief stooge; Georges Diedler, from the Vosges; Jean Gam-
bero, the astute Parisian; and Léonce Godfrin, from the
Ardennes.

The conception of the tunnel was curious, yet typical.
The French are a logical race. They had read in the German
press that the Leipzig Fair was to be held in spite of the
war. Leipzig was only twenty-two miles away. It would
provide wonderful cover for the escape of a large body of
prisoners. Leipzig would be full to overflowing with visitors,
coming from all parts and speaking many languages. The
only way, it seemed, to dispatch a large body of prisoners to
Leipzig was by tunnel—but not the whole way by tunnel;
that opened the discussion of the next problem. Again, the
French decided where they would like their tunnel to de-
bouch so as to provide a safe get-away. From there they
worked backwards into the Castle to see where the entrance

* Described in *The Colditz Story.*

should be. Alas! none of the French quarters touched
ground level; underneath them on the ground floor were
rooms occupied by Germans during the daylight hours;
the sick-ward, the parcels office and Gephard's office. Once
more, logic saved the day. "If we can't start at the bottom,"
they said, "let's start at the top." And that was what they did.

The clock tower provided them with a means of access
to the cellar. The clock had not worked for years and the
weights, with their long chains, had also been removed,
leaving empty cylindrical sleeves which extended from the
clock down to the ground floor. There were small cubby
holes, presumably inspection chambers, giving access to
the sleeves at each floor level. The cubby holes had long
ago been bricked up by the Jerries.

A heavily barred steel door on the top landing of the
French quarters, at fourth floor level, was the first object
of attack. It led to the clock room. With men like Gigue
and Roger Madin in the camp, the padlocks, mortice locks
and cruciform locks securing the door were soon provided
with keys. Once in the clock room, a camouflaged opening
was constructed in the floor and in the ceiling below, which
let the Frenchmen down into the cubby hole on the third
floor. They could have descended through the sleeves, but
these were a tight squeeze for any adult, being only sixteen
inches in diameter, and coming up again would have been
difficult. They constructed ladders instead, piercing holes
in each cubby hole floor down to ground level. Here the
first serious tunnelling began. It consisted of a vertical
shaft through the stones and mortar of the arched roof of
the Castle cellar.

Once in the cellar, which, of course, was subject to
examination by German patrols, the Frenchmen had the
choice of digging in any direction they wished. Having
already chosen their direction—they started breaking out
a hole, four feet from the ground, in the wall facing the
chapel.

The cellar contained a stock of old Hungarian wine
reposing in bottles under a layer of dust—a serious tempta-

tion to the French. They only weakened once, according to their own admission. That was the night when they examined the cellar from end to end in search of a secret passage or other ready made exit from the camp. They were unsuccessful. Momentarily depressed at the prospect of months of tunnelling, they 'won' four bottles of wine.

Having made an entrance door on pivots like a safe door, out of the original stones from the wall, they continued, digging a horizontal tunnel behind it, through the heavy foundation which supported the dividing wall between the chapel and the spiral staircase to the French quarters. This continued for a distance of fifteen feet.

Once under the chapel, they dug a vertical shaft upwards for a distance of nine feet until they met the beams of the chapel floor. Progressing under the floor they searched for the entrance to a crypt, but found none.

The team realised, at last, that there was no short cut and that they would have to continue the tunnel until they were outside the wire. They decided to increase the number of shareholders in the Tunnelling Company. They had been working by day and night for two months and were ready to welcome new blood.

The S.A.T.C. obtained its recruits without difficulty. Many eyes had watched with envy the guarded movements and mysterious disappearances of the founder members and had noted the surreptitious washing of the dirty sweat-stained underclothing of the Société Anonyme. The Company increased from nine in number to thirty. Tunnelling continued in three shifts throughout the twenty-four hours. The spirits of the French rose as yard after yard of tunnel opened in front of them.

When the tunnel was nearing completion in the early days of 1943 Gigue, who was, by then, a long standing member of the Company and Madin, who had been one of the original members, offered to take Dick on a conducted tour of the premises. It was January, and they were hoping to break soon. When that took place the British would never have an opportunity of seeing the work they had carried out and they were genuinely proud of their tunnel.

"You know," said Dick, gladly accepting their invitation, "we've heard you digging away for months, and of course, your own people have too. Haven't you been running a tremendous risk all this time? The Germans must know well enough that a tunnel's in progress."

It was a fact that at all hours of the day, but more especially at night when the Castle was wrapped in the silence of sleep, tunnelling could be heard. The sound was definable as high up as the third floor of the Castle above the chapel where some of the British lived, and it even kept light sleepers awake. It could be compared to the regular, consecutive landing of high explosive shells over the hills some miles away. There was a gentle concussion which appeared to come from various directions, carried by the air, the walls, the floor and even the ceiling. The dull, heavy thuds struck the ear from all sides. Eventually, it was possible, by continued careful listening, to eliminate echoes and secondary sound waves, and to establish with some certainty where the sounds emanated from. Indeed, the Germans must have done this by now.

"The Jerries may know it well enough," said Gigue, "but as long as they can find no entrance we are safe."

"But the Germans will persevere...."

"Come with us this evening and you shall see why they will not find the entrance," replied Gigue. "We are on the night shift and you will spend it with us."

They met again after the last *Appell* of the day. Dick had finished his supper and was prepared for a night's vigil. Lulu would make up a dummy in his bed. He had been warned to put on plenty of warm clothing.

The Castle was in darkness, except where the reflection from the searchlights glowed. Dick mounted the French staircase with his two friends. They reached the attics at the fourth floor. From the landing, to the left was the Ghetto where the French Jewish officers lived; to the right were attics, locked and uninhabited.

Gigue looked at his watch. It was 9.30 p.m. If all went well there would be no further *Appells* until 7 a.m. the next morning.

They waited for the remainder of the shift workers to appear. It was to be a 'removal' shift. Tons of debris from a week of tunnelling had to be cleared away that night. While they were waiting Gigue explained to Dick:

"We have been lucky to find a good place for the debris of the tunnel. When we go through the steel door over there," he said pointing, "you will see a ladder leading to a skylight in the roof. Outside on the roof within a distance of two metres there is a window in the gable of the attic above your English bedroom, the one over the chapel. It has bars which we can remove and replace. In this attic we have found plenty of space for hundreds of tons of rubble between the slanting roof and the partition walls." Gigue flashed a sly grin at Dick as he caught his puzzled expression. Dick asked:

"But how do you pass the rubble from the skylight into the attic?"

"*Eh bien!* A man sits on the roof outside the skylight. He passes the sacks from one man on the ladder to another inside the attic."

"So that is why you do this at night?"

"Yes, indeed. If it was done in the day our man could be seen from the town and the countryside. At night he is in a dark shadow cast beyond the searchlight beams."

"He must get damned cold up there," said Dick. "Why, it's freezing hard."

"He freezes to begin with. But when he has lifted sacks weighing twenty-five kilos for half an hour, he is not cold any more."

The *équipe*, as the French always called their team, had, by now, all arrived. There were twenty energetic Frenchmen milling around them on the small landing. Dick was aghast at the crowd. Gigue and Madin, receiving the 'all clear' signal from their stooges, began work on the locks. Within a matter of minutes the steel door opened and the whole *équipe* was soon safely inside the clock tower. The door was locked behind them. Everybody seemed to know what to do. At signals from Gigue, who stood near the door keeping contact with a stooge outside, the team set to work. The secret trap door in the floor was disclosed, and bodies disappeared downwards through the hole. A ladder was hoisted from below and propped against a skylight window which Dick saw for the first time. Around it gathered half a dozen Frenchmen ready to go out on the roof. If there was an alarm this section of the team would have to leave the clock tower. Jerries might enter and search the room. Those who descended would have the trap door sealed above them and would remain hidden unless they had to come out because of an *Appell*.

Gigue handed over his post to a colleague and invited Dick to descend the ladder. Madin had already disappeared below. Gigue followed and the trap door was closed above them. In the small chambers at successive levels, men were changing into their tunnelling kit. Dick noted a gaudy variety of designs and colours in woollen vests, pants and stockings which the Frenchmen donned, layer upon layer. It was evidently going to be cold. Some of them wore tin helmets, and, as if answering his unspoken question, Gigue said to Dick: "Put on this English Tommy's helmet. It's the only English one we have and it's right that you should wear it. When my friends start shifting the rocks you may need it."

They were soon ready to descend to the lower regions. They stood for a moment surveying each other laughingly.

"You look like an old Roman warrior," said Dick, "with that helmet on."

Gigue indeed looked like something out of a nightmare classic. He wore gaily coloured stockings and knee-pads, a pair of dirty dark blue shorts over several pairs of pants and a bright red thick woollen sweater drawn in at the waist by a broad leather belt with a brass buckle.

Dick looked no less peculiar. From the plimsolls on his feet two pairs of long woollen pants stretched up to his waist, while, over them, a pair of white rugger shorts covered his buttocks. Three short sleeved vests clothed his chest and the tin hat crowned his head. He looked like Tommy Atkins after a bomb had blown off his uniform. Gigue said:

"You need not laugh at me. Laugh at yourself. You remind me of an English General going to have his bath in the trenches."

They climbed down the next ladder, one after the other, and carried on downwards, passing, at each floor level, through a small room packed to the ceiling with loose stones and rubble until there was scarcely sufficient room to manœuvre.

"You are now at ground level," said Gigue. "The team is about to start work—we shall watch it from here for a moment." As he spoke a blue and white check sack the size of a laundry bag, rose through a hole in the floor. Dick recognised the pattern of the standard German palliasse cover used throughout the camp.

The sack was seized by a Frenchman, standing over the hole, who checked and tightened the cord which closed it at the top, and then lifted it into a cradle made of rope with a heavy steel hook attached. Dick lifted the sack himself, out of interest, and estimated that it weighed half a hundredweight. The cradle, with the sack in it, was hooked to a loop on an endless rope that disappeared upwards through the two round sleeves which had housed the clock chains and weights. The Frenchman pressed an electric button beside him. The cradle started to move upwards and was greedily swallowed by the mouth of the sleeve above Dick's head.

"An endless rope lift?" queried Dick.

"Yes," said Gigue, "we use the original pulleys and a reduction gear from the clock at the top. It makes the work much easier for our men."

Another sack rose through the hole in the floor, was hooked to the lift and began its ascent to the attic.

"How much debris do you move in a night?" asked Dick.

"We can move nearly one ton per hour," replied Gigue.
"We shall work to-night for seven hours. If you stop for
long you catch cold. So we carry on continuously."

Dick said he could well understand it. He was already
feeling the chill of a strong draught coming up through the
hole in the floor. The clock tower was acting like a chimney.

"Let us go down further while the way is clear," said
Gigue.

They dropped through the hole feeling for the ladder
beneath them. Dick went carefully downwards in a narrow
shaft for a few feet, then found himself again in the open.
Descending further he landed on the floor of the Castle
cellar. A closely shaded electric light was focused on the
ladder to direct the worker mounting it with a heavy sack
on his shoulder. Beyond the light was impenetrable darkness. Dick looked around him wonderingly.

"Where do we go from here?" he asked Gigue quietly.

"Wait, a sack is coming," Gigue whispered as if that explained everything.

Dick heard a rumble that seemed to come towards him
out of nowhere. Gradually his eyes became more accustomed to the dark and he could see a rectangular glow of
light, bright at the edges, which appeared to shine out of a
wall at eye level some yards away. Then the rumbling
stopped, shadows moved across the glow and suddenly a
bright square patch of light showed in the wall. A Frenchman passed him and began to climb the ladder with a sack
on his shoulders.

"This is the entrance to the tunnel," said Gigue in an
undertone. "The noise you heard was a sack moving along
on the sled. We can now go forward." He beckoned Dick to
follow.

They approached the hole in the wall. Dick looked along
the tunnel. It was a little higher than it was broad; about
two feet four inches by two feet in section. It had been
hacked through stones and mortar and he began to understand the sounds he had heard for so many months. "There's

certainly no need for any shoring or timbering here," he mused.

An electric bulb burned brightly at the far end which was five yards away. The walls of the tunnel gleamed white with light reflected from stone surfaces polished by the frequent rubbing of passing bodies.

Dick stepped on to a large block of wood placed on the floor under the entrance. Then he noticed the heavy door which shut the tunnel. It was a complete section of wall, a foot thick, which had been built inside a wooden casing. A long piece of steel, three quarters of an inch in diameter, acting as a pivot, ran vertically through one end of it. The lower end of the pivot rested on a steel plate hollowed out to receive it. The plate was concreted into the floor of the tunnel. The upper end of the pivot passed through a hole in another steel plate concreted into the roof of the tunnel.

Dick recognised something familiar about the design and asked Gigue:

"Who made the door?"

"I did," was the reply. "I saw Van den Heuvel's door after the Jerries had found his secret room—you remember?—and I copied it."

Dick remembered. It had been impossible to find Van den Heuvel's door, sealed. The irregular edges of the present door were obviously carefully set to fit into crevices in the wall as a pattern fits into a mould. Putty, cobwebs and dust completed the camouflage which would defy minute investigation.

Dick was lost in admiration at the work when he heard Gigue calling from the far end of the tunnel.

"*Dépêche-toi,* Dick. Another sack is coming."

Dick hoisted himself into the hole and crawled to the far end. A rope, made of bed sheets resembling those produced by Bos'n Crisp, ran the length of the tunnel between well polished tracks of wood at each side. These, Dick realised, carried the sled with the sacks of rubble.

"Here," said Gigue, "we have buried the largest stone of all. We have had them of many sizes, but the one upon which you are kneeling weighs about one hundred and fifty kilos."

"Did it bother you!" said Dick mockingly.

"Yes, it was at the top of the shaft which you see over you."

Dick looked upwards. Above him in the glare of another electric bulb was a vertical shaft, some nine feet in height. Their breath, forming clouds of vapour, rose upwards into it. Dick asked:

"How did you get rid of the stone?"

"Flynn's bar was the answer," said Gigue. "You know that he is the only Englishman with a place promised on this tunnel. Well, if he had not stolen the bar from a lorry in the courtyard, I don't think we would ever have passed that rock. I will show you the bar later. We use it all the time. Barras and Cazaumayou worked upon the stone. It could easily have killed them, for it was as big as the shaft. They made a hole here to receive it. Then they worked underneath it for days, loosening it. It was touch and go. Finally they needed a long bar so that they could free it and escape from underneath it as it fell. At that point Flynn produced his bar. The stone fell one night while they worked, here, where you are. It shook the building. They escaped in time. Afterwards our work was simplified. You know, we had reached the floor of the chapel. Now follow me up the shaft."

Dick climbed upwards after Gigue on a skeleton timber scaffolding that had been erected inside the shaft. Below stood a helmeted Frenchman whom he left with a grin saying, *"Excusez-moi si je tombe sur votre tête."*

At the top Gigue disappeared again. Dick thought of Alice in Wonderland. Then he reached the top, looked over and reflected that he was not so far wrong. Gigue was lying in front of him completely blocking the view. Not a ray of light penetrated past him. He was struggling and panting as he moved forward. Dick waited patiently at the top of the shaft thinking, "They won't shift a ton this hour. We've put paid to that."

All transport of sacks had ceased. Beside him was a rope suspended from a wooden pulley above his head. The tackle carried the sacks down the shaft.

The puffing and blowing continued, growing more distant. Then Dick hear a 'Pssht!' and looked forward. Gigue's head appeared round a corner a long way off.

"Come quickly, Dick, you are occupying the place of one of our men who must handle the sacks."

Dick had already realised this.

Now it was his turn to push and squeeze, to twist and turn, to sweat and rest, wondering if he would ever see again the light of day. He squirmed himself forward eight yards under what was the floor of the chapel between heavy oak timbers which had been sawn through. At last he found himself in a large space, deeper than before, about two feet, but almost a living-room in other respects—about six feet square, in fact. Here Dick collapsed to recover his breath while a gentle rumble told him that the sacks had started moving again along the tunnel corridors.

"How did you get past those timbers?" asked Dick.

"They nearly finished us," said Gigue. "They are of oak, only six hundred years old, and forty centimetres square. We had to cut through seven of them, each twice, and our saws were made of German table knives!"

Dick felt the sweat clammy around his waist. He suddenly thought of something and asked Gigue:

"Did your fellows cut those seven beams in this freezing cold without getting pneumonia?"

"It was worse than that, Dick. It was very cold lying on those blocks of granite out there, you know, but they were not even allowed to catch a cold! We are under the chapel floor and a German in the church would think it funny if he suddenly heard a cough coming from the dead underneath his feet. We have had stooges always in the chapel when we worked underneath. They warned us if a Jerry came in."

"Pious chaps, I suppose," said Dick.

"Oh, yes! they were very pious. They held a retreat

which lásted for months. One after the other, for two hours each, they came to the chapel and prayed for our success. If a German came—well, you know, as we say, it is not prayer alone but good deeds also that count, so our friends did the good deed. They banged on the floor as they knelt, with their toes. There was not even a sneeze from the dead below after that."

"I suppose we are near your heading now?" Dick asked.

"No, we are not half-way," replied Gigue. "We are underneath the sacristy. You see the switchboard in the corner. That is where the electricity is branched off from the main chapel supply. Ah! here is Roger. He will explain all to you."

Madin's head appeared through a large hole in the floor of the tunnel some yards away. His pink face, appearing out of the ground, reminded Dick of a ferret. He had a long nose that looked as if it could smell out anything. His angular forehead was surmounted by a wispy crop of fair hair and he wore thick lensed glasses. His teeth were conspicuously undershot so that his huge triangular-shaped chin protruded outwards giving the impression of complete separation from the remainder of his physiognomy. He smiled on the least provocation and, when he did so, the sparkle in his eyes, enlarged by the spectacles, emanated humour and good temper as a fire radiates warmth.

"Hello, Dick!" he said pulling himself up higher out of the hole. "How do you like our tunnel? Not so bad, eh? Do you approve of it? I have just been checking the electric wiring."

Gigue said to Madin:

"Roger, will you tell Dick all about the electrical installation. I shall leave you—I must go forward to the digging face. Come along later, when you are ready. Au revoir."

He disappeared into the hole leaving Madin in charge.

"I must tell you how we obtained electricity for the tunnel," said Madin grinning above his large chin. "We should never have had it without the aid of our Curé Jeanjean. You know that the chapel was closed for a while after the morning service. Jeanjean protested he could not continue the spiritual instruction of his converts unless he was allowed to teach in the sacristy. He obtained permission for two hours a day. I was his principal convert! I worked on the wiring, and whenever a German came near the sacristy I was on my knees beside the curé praying hard or listening to his exhortations."

Roger was lying on his stomach, with his head resting in his cupped hands, chuckling away as he told his story: "Gephard came once and even tried to enter the room when wires and floor boards were lying loose all over the place. Neither the curé nor I have ever prayed so loudly, either before or since, in our whole lives. The curé gave Gephard such terrible looks that he had not the courage to enter and he left us in peace."

"Now, you see the power comes down from the sacristy to this switchboard," Madin continued, pointing to a wooden frame adorned with switches, fuses and lamps.

"The whole tunnel has electric lighting which serves at the same time for signalling. At the entrance there is a switch, and our stooges up above pass messages to the man at the entrance who passes them to everybody in the tunnel by means of this switch."

"When do you think the tunnel will be ready?" Dick questioned.

"We are working very hard to finish before the Germans remove us. You will take over, of course, if it is not finished in time. But we are near the end. We have only about fifteen metres to dig now in loose subsoil. You know how long the tunnel is?"

"No," said Dick.

"It is over forty metres long including the vertical shafts. The latter total up to eleven metres. The one in the corner over there which you will go down in a moment is the deepest, it is six and a half metres. We had to go underneath the main foundations of the Castle."

Dick was shivering again. The cold was intense. Movement was the only means of keeping warm.

"Take me down the mine, Roger," he said, "before I freeze to death here. You've been working but I haven't."

"Come along then," said Madin, leading the way. "After the next sack we will go."

A rope and pulley tackle was suspended over the hole and every few minutes a sack, appearing as if from nowhere, was unhooked by a worker who transferred it to the waiting sled. Empty sacks were also making their appearance from the other direction, heading towards the working face.

"Be careful to place your feet firmly in the prepared footholds," said Madin as he disappeared. Dick followed. The shaft was well lit and was about three feet square. It was lined with a timber framework, and a rope, attached at intervals to the frames, served to steady the climber. Dick descended warily, using the easily recognised, well worn footholds on the frames where the rock had been hollowed out so that the toes could take a good bite. A fall here would be dangerous. When he reached the bottom Dick looked up. The top seemed to be miles above him. A sack full of stones was swinging in mid air half-way up the shaft. Dick turned to Madin:

"I see now why you all wear tin hats. I wouldn't like to get a rock on my head from twenty feet, not to mention a half hundredweight sack."

The Frenchman who was hauling on the tackle grinned. He understood enough English to know what Dick was talking about. He remarked in French:

"Je ne permets à personne d'enlever les sacs sauf celui qui est là haut. J'ai plein confiance en lui!"

Dick nodded expressively looking upwards. He was wondering what it would feel like to walk in the open air again. Here in the bowels of the earth, surrounded by tons upon tons of rock, a sudden fear gripped him. He wanted to breathe freely and expand his chest but was cramped and confined by the forbidding walls closing in upon him from every side.

'Good God!' he thought. 'I'm getting claustrophobia.'

In spite of himself the thoughts recurred, 'One fall of

rock would be enough; we could never get out. The air in here would only last half an hour with all these bodies around. A self-made tomb in just the right place,' he muttered, 'underneath the chapel.'

He followed the tunnel forward. Madin had vanished. He soon saw why. There was a staircase ahead of him. He had to squirm himself round so that he lay on his stomach with his feet facing downhill. He descended steps, cut out of the layers of stratified rock, until he reached a new level five feet lower. Here he turned himself round again and crawled forward on his hands and knees. The tunnel was now of more spacious dimensions and he could kneel almost upright on the floor. Tunnellers could pass one another, and half a dozen men were hard at work filling sacks with rubble which was piled to the roof at one side as far as Dick could see. Madin was a long way ahead beckoning to him. Then he disappeared again.

Dick followed as quickly as he could, greeting the Frenchmen one after the other. They were working at top pressure filling the blue and white check sacks as fast as they could, then tying them with cords already sewn into the tops and stacking them ready for departure. They were dripping with perspiration and Dick asked one of them:

"Why don't you take off your shirts?"

"C'est dangereux," came the reply, "aussitôt qu'on arrète, même pour un instant, on attraperait froid si on n'est pas bien habillé."

Dick arrived at the end and found himself looking down another shaft. He counted. 'That's the third shaft in this tunnel,' he thought, 'not counting the clock tower. The place is just a rabbit warren.'

A large square wooden tub rose up towards him from the depths, hoisted by another pulley tackle. As it came to the surface the Frenchman next to him unhitched it, emptied it to the side of the tunnel, hooked it on again, and the tub descended. Not a word was spoken. Unseen hands worked the lift from below. The operation had become mechanical.

Dick followed the tub, descending carefully one foot at

a time. This shaft was not so deep, about eight feet, Dick estimated. He could see that he was nearing the working face. Rubble, earth and large rocks were cluttering up the passage, making progress difficult. Three men were at work filling wooden boxes as fast as they could, while a fourth carried them and emptied them into the tub on the lift. Dick passed them, caught up with Madin, and looked beyond him.

There was Gigue hard at work on the tunnel face in front. He was digging in comparatively loose earth and rock with a short-handled spade. It was coming away easily and he was working so fast that there were not enough wooden boxes to keep him supplied and he was piling earth up behind him, leaving it to his mates to clear away.

Gigue turned a sweating countenance towards them and flashed a broad smile at Dick. He wiped his face with a piece of towelling, "What do you think now, Dick? If we can get enough timber for the roof we shall finish in a week. The digging is easy, but it is dangerous too, without supports. It could easily fall in."

"I'm lost in admiration," Dick replied facetiously, "but not only in admiration. I've been up and down, backwards and forwards so often I'm lost in any other way you like to think."

"You see the tunnel just behind you. It's completely timbered—floor, walls and roof—you notice? Well, we had to do that. It is the most dangerous section of all. It is under very old foundations which are loose. There are some big stones above and there is not much holding them."

"Thanks for telling me. I shall move faster next time," said Dick feelingly. "Where exactly are we?"

"We are outside the wire and approaching the side of the valley which drops down to the stream in the wood. We should surface in about twelve metres."

"You deserve to have a break after all this," said Dick. "I've never seen a tunnel like it."

Gigue was patting affectionately a steel bar an inch and

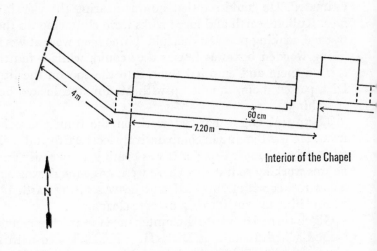

4m

60 cm

7.20 m

Interior of the Chapel

N

Electric lighting: taken from the Sacr

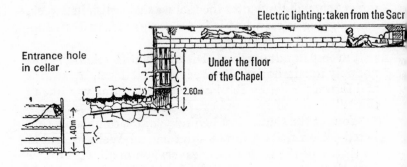

Entrance hole
in cellar

Under the floor
of the Chapel

2.60m

1.40m

THE FRENCH TUNNEL

This drawing has been traced from the original Plans made by the Germans a
the discovery of the Tunnel. The Plans were kept in the Escape Museum in
German Komandantur. When Colditz was relieved the Museum was found b
P.O.W. and Rupert Barry procured the originals

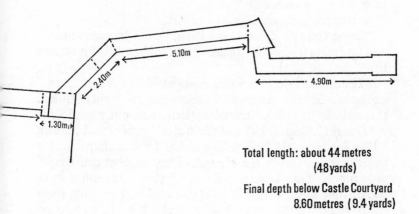

Total length: about 44 metres
(48 yards)

Final depth below Castle Courtyard
8.60 metres (9.4 yards)

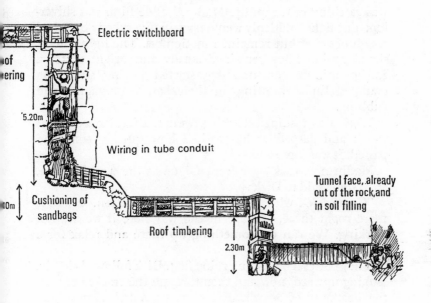

a half thick and four feet long. "Flynn's bar," he said. "The most useful tool we have."

At that moment the lights went out.

"Great Cæsar's ghost," said Dick, "what happens now?"

The lights flashed on again. Then 'off' and 'on' a second time.

"That means there is a German patrol in the courtyard," explained Madin. As he said the words, the lights blinked three times in quick succession then went out completely.

"Danger! Stop work! remain quiet!" whispered Madin. "The Jerries must be heading either for the chapel or for the cellar, probably the chapel. They suspect the chapel very much. They have heard our digging but cannot trace it. All they know is that it is in this region. I suppose their instruments cannot get close enough. We are very deep here."

They sat huddled in total darkness at the end of the tunnel for ten minutes waiting for the 'all clear'. Dick was catching cold rapidly. Madin, beside him, was shivering. The lights suddenly went on again. Everybody breathed a sigh of relief but remained motionless. The lights might signal again. They remained steady and bright. After a further minute, the tunnellers started moving, stretching cramped limbs, blowing on their hands, massaging and rubbing.

Work was resumed at full pressure. Dick looked at his watch and gasped as he realised how quickly time had passed. It was three a.m.

Madin now took over from Gigue at the working face, and Gigue said to Dick:

"Come back with me to the sacristy junction. There is more room there. We are in the way here if we are not working. We can eat something up there and relax for a moment."

They both set off, Gigue going first. Dick followed closely, looking upwards now and then through the cracks between the boards—bed-boards, of course, he noted, almost subconsciously—to see whether any large rock was about to

tear through the timber crushing him to pulp in its fall.
They passed the danger zone and retraced their steps to the
'junction' as they had come.

Dick breathed a sigh of relief as they reached it. He was
warm again from climbing and crawling, and he was feeling
hungry. He had come provided for this. Seated with his
back against one of the heavy chapel timbers, he removed
a bright yellow handkerchief, that had once been khaki,
from the pocket of his rugger shorts, and, unfolding it
gently, revealed a thick sandwich composed of two slices
of German bread enclosing a slab of Canadian cheese.

Gigue was not slow to follow him. His equally cumber·
some sandwich, however, did not contain cheese but a thick,
strongly smelling paste. They munched in silence for a
while. Then Dick's curiosity made him ask, "What's that
high smelling paste you've got, Gigue?"

"It's home-made *foie gras*," said Gigue. "I make it out of
everything that's left. It smell's good, doesn't it?"

"I'm not so sure," Dick replied. "If it tastes as it smells,
I think it should make excellent manure."

"You don't know what's good," said Gigue.

Together they sat for a while, each wrapped in his own
thoughts. Dick was reflecting upon the extraordinary twist
of fate that could bring about the present situation; a Lon·
doner, and a Frenchman from Marseilles a thousand miles
away, sitting side by side eating sandwiches in a burrow
underneath the floor of a fifteenth century chapel in a
medieval castle in the middle of Germany. How would it
end, this great upheaval of mankind all over the world?
Would he ever come out of it alive? Dick questioned and,
as always, reached the usual conclusion: 'Probably not. The
Nazis will see to it—the lousy bunch of gangsters.'

In spite of the cold he began to feel drowsy. The rumble
of the sleds and the pulleys was monotonous and the sacks
passed interminably before his eyes. Gigue was already
asleep. Dick dozed fitfully, shifting uncomfortably now and
then, growing steadily stiffer with cold and cramp. At one

point he awoke and noticed Gigue had gone. Then dozed again, as he thought, for five minutes. . . .

Madin was shaking him.

"Wake up, Dick, it's time to go," he said. "Follow me."

The shift had ended, and the tunnellers were filing past, one after the other, on their hands and knees. Madin and Dick joined the queue.

At six-thirty a.m. Dick found himself, once more, out on the landing at the top of the French staircase. It was all so strange. He felt as if he had been living for months in the tunnel and he had to pull himself together to realise where he was. In Gigue's dormitory he was given a mug of hot coffee. He drank it quickly, lay back on an empty bed and fell fast asleep.

Three days later the fate of the tunnel hung in the balance. According to the French, one of their own men, who had gone to Oflag IV.D., had talked too loudly or too openly about a French tunnel at Colditz which started on the top floor. The Germans were after it in earnest. Search followed upon search. Work on the tunnel had to cease completely with only five more yards to dig, to finish it. The situation was ominous.

Then there was peace for three days. Work started again —cautiously. But the Germans had not finished. Gephard made a surprise attack. He probed the long weight sleeves in the clock tower, he could see nothing as he flashed his torch down into the darkness, but there were men below. He sent a messenger out to the Kommandantur by the hand of the sentry who was with him. Had he heard a movement? A cough maybe?

Within ten minutes several Goons appeared with a small boy amongst them. A coil of rope was produced. The boy, a fair haired young Teuton, pale and trembling with fright, suffered the rope to be tied around his waist. He was led to one of the sleeves. With promises and blandishments he was encouraged to descend. He was lowered slowly through the sleeve into the blackness below. In his hand he carried a torch which he aimed at the floor beneath him. As he landed he flashed the torch around him and screamed in terror.

"*Hilfe! Hilfe! Hier sind Leute!*"

There were three Frenchmen in the chamber. Gephard was occupying the only exit. The Frenchmen knew of a last desperate way out. At one corner of the chamber, a comparatively thin wall, nine inches thick, separated them from a bathroom used by patients from the sick ward.

As the terrified youth, sobbing with fright and shouting, "Hilfe", was hauled up again through the sleeve, the Frenchmen attacked the dividing wall with crowbars like demons and, in five minutes, had battered a hole through it. The noise they made was deafening, yet the Germans above them were so occupied with the youth that, when they awoke to reality and sent search parties in frantic haste to locate the new hole being pierced with all the publicity of a battery of pneumatic drills, they were too late. The birds had flown.

A Belgian army Major, Baron Lindkerke, was peacefully reading a book, lying in his bath, when the earthquake started. The wall beside him began to pulsate and heave. Long cracks appeared, accompanied by earsplitting crashes from the other side. A brick shot out of the wall into the bath, landing on his stomach. 'It was time,' he thought, 'to evacuate. Something was under pressure at the other side and an explosion would occur at any moment.'

He rose from the bath and reached for his towel. Plaster was flying in all directions, and brickbats were leaping outwards splashing into the bath around him. A jagged hole suddenly appeared. Iron bars flayed the opening, enlarging it. As he stepped from the bath, a head and shoulders came through the opening. Then a half naked body scrambled over the bath on to the floor, bespattered, sweatstained and dirty. Another body followed and then a third, more bulky than the others. It had difficulty in squeezing through and fell into the bath.

Major Lindkerke picked up his belongings and rushed from the room shouting: "*Mon Dieu! Mon Dieu! c'est le*

comble!" Which translated means, "My God! My God!
this is the end!'"

Soon the whole Kommandantur was alerted. Squads of
workmen appeared with crowbars, pick-axes and sledge
hammers. The chambers at each successive floor were
broken into and the finger of fate pointed ever downwards
to the cellar.

For a time the French hoped that the Germans would not
find the tunnel entrance in the cellar; but alas! the scent
was now too strong. The Germans were hot on the trail.
The cellar was combed from end to end. Every inch of wall
was sounded. No camouflage could stand up to German
thoroughness indefinitely.

The next day the news came through: 'They've found
it!' That was all that was said. With those few words disappeared the hopes of more than a hundred Frenchmen.
So many dreams smashed, so much yearning for the sunny
lands of France; so many wives who would never hear the
sound of a familiar voice on the threshold; so many hours,
days and months of dangerous toil, for nothing.

And through it all came the voice of the French conscience: 'Was it our own fault? Was our stooging at fault?
Were we too confident?' Like the masters of the Titanic,
they had thought their ship could not founder.

CHAPTER VI

THE PARCEL OFFICE

THE French were still leaving. Throughout the Spring of 1943 the rumour persisted. They were repeatedly warned they were going. One day it was, 'Nous partons demain,'—the next day it was, 'Non! pas aujourd'hui, mais dans une semaine—certes—l'information est toujours juste par nos tuyaux.'

They packed and unpacked many times; their *convertures*, and rucksacks, their *valises* and portmanteaux, their *poussettes*—push chairs and prams. Some were glad to go, looking forward to the move as a relief from the overpowering walls of Colditz. Many of the French Jews saw the writing on the wall and were, quite legitimately, not so keen. Men like Gigue and Madin would leave with mixed feelings. They would have more opportunities in another camp—but not the same atmosphere. . . .

A dead Goon was found in the parcel office one morning. There was a bullet wound in his chest and his revolver lay beside him. The Germans said he had committed suicide. The question they never answered was: 'What was he doing in there, locked up for the night amongst the parcels belonging to the prisoners?'

The dead German was removed from the parcel office without ceremony and hurried out of the courtyard. Few prisoners were about at the time. The Germans chose their moment. The mystery was never solved and the reader, with this outline before him, knows as much as at least ninety-nine out of each hundred prisoners at Colditz. The odd ones are not talking. . . . The author is not one of them.

The office was naturally a focus of interest among the prisoners and many would have liked to have access to it. The entrance, however, gave straight on to the courtyard and on to the beats of two sentries placed there day and night.

During 1942, the British had been greatly troubled by the installation of an X-ray machine in the parcel office. Most valuable contraband material was lost, which, incidentally, never came in Red Cross parcels at any time throughout the whole war. The contents of other parcels, if in the least suspected, were passed across the X-ray screen which showed up secret cavities or metallic objects. The British quarters were a long way from the parcel office, and nothing much could be done about it. A burglar alarm in the guardhouse, wired from each of the two locks on the entrance door warned the Germans of any tampering. They installed it so secretly that the fact was not known for a long time. The Germans were obviously taking no risks.

Parcels were normally opened on a long counter behind a grill; suspected items were submitted to X-ray and then the contents passed to the recipient through the grill, which was opened for the operation and shut again immediately afterwards. The opening and shutting of the grill for every parcel was an unmitigated nuisance. The German N.C.O.s on parcel duty agreed with the prisoners on this point and occasionally became lax.

Some days after the dead Goon had been removed, the British were drawing parcels. Lulu was 'Parcels Officer' at the time. He had been planted there because contraband was expected. Bill Fowler, who had escaped from Colditz in September 1942 was, by this time, in France. Lulu's official duty as Parcels Officer was to be present at the opening of all parcels—a witness for the defence. The job was intriguing for the first twenty parcels or so and thereafter became steadily more boring until, at the end of a fortnight, 'one grew a beard' as the French would say.

John Hyde-Thomson stood in the parcel queue on this particular day because the parcel list, posted on the notice board outside the office, had his name upon it. He arrived in front of the open grill. An N.C.O., known as 'Nichtwahr' because of his irritating habit of ending every sentence with this ejaculation and who had the local reputation of being a Gestapo man, searched among the stack for John's parcel. It was unearthed and opened on the counter in front of him. Lulu stood beside him. His thoughts at that moment were in the Yorkshire Dales.

As the seals were broken and the maltreated cardboard cover burst asunder, there was a clatter of steel on the counter which brought Lulu's reverie to an end as conclusively as might a clap of thunder. John Hyde-Thomson was expecting warm woolly underwear and some good books. Lulu was not expecting the consignment which was on the counter at that particular moment. Wires had crossed somewhere.

He was not going to be outdone, however. Before the grill could be slapped down, he enfolded the parcel in his arms and was careering out of the office door as an astonished Goon held aloft a brand new pair of wire cutters, screaming, "*Halt! Halt!*" and struggling with the pistol in his holster.

Lulu was too quick for them all. He tore across the courtyard, as German banknotes fell like autumn leaves in his wake. Not a shot was fired. Up the spiral stairs he ran and collapsed at the top of seventy steps, shouting for help. Willing hands took over, and the contents were distributed and hidden within a few minutes—long before the pursuing rioting squad was able to mount the stairs and seal the doorways into the various quarters.

The spectacle in the courtyard after the meteoric passage of Lulu was out of the dream world of a prisoner in a high fever. The two sentries in the yard stood transfixed. They had never, in their whole careers as soldiers and P.O.W. guards, been given instructions as to what to do when German banknotes rain like confetti around prisoners of war, whose principal aim in life is to have enough money to travel as fast as possible out of Germany.

The notes were like manna from heaven. Prisoners, who had, one second before, been ambling aimlessly around the yard in their clogs and khaki overcoats, did not take long to realise, unlike the sentry, that they had witnessed a miracle and had suddenly become the chosen people. As Lulu disappeared through the staircase doorway there was a rush, and before the sentries could gather their wits together there was not a note to be seen.

A search followed, but nothing was found. The Germans were disillusioned. So many searches had yielded so little that searching had become a disheartening pastime. Since

Lulu Lawton

Priem's nocturnal visit in 1941 when his hatchet, tearing some floor boards asunder, had impaled a trilby hat concealed underneath, the Germans had had no luck. But the initial search after this episode would not be the end of the matter. A report would go eventually to the Gestapo. The Castle was heading for another ransacking, of this there was no doubt.

Lulu Lawton was removed from his post and sentenced to a month's solitary confinement. The contraband parcel contained everything that an escaper dreamt of, from wire cutters, files and dyes to cameras and photographic materials.

This kind of bull in the china shop operation, however, frankly disgusted Gigue. He had an advantage, of course, in that he lived in the French quarters over the parcel office, but, to be perfectly honest, he returned the compliment the British had paid his countrymen in connection with the theatre light well escape—with interest. As a parting gift before he left, in addition to the secret wireless set, he bequeathed to Dick his method of entering the parcel office.

Gigue had spirited seventy parcels out of the parcels office for his two wireless sets alone. He had caused no rumpus, no publicity, and had lost nothing.

First of all, he manufactured his own cruciform keys for the two parcel office locks. The cruciform lock is roughly equivalent to four different Yale locks rolled into one. While the office was open and in use, he had searched for, and discovered, the carefully concealed wiring of the burglar alarm system. This travelled, at one stage, along the ceiling under an electric light tube conduit. Gigue made a careful survey. Any civil engineer would have been proud of his work. Under the floor-boards of his own quarters, he pierced a minute hole through the plaster of the ceiling below, immediately over the alarm wires. He then tapped the wires and, manufacturing his own switch, he placed it in the circuit. He could thus control the burglar alarm system at will.

The method of operating his switch was equally ingenious. The switch was fixed under the floor boards which were replaced permanently and made to look as if they had not been touched for fifty years. A hole, about one-eighth of an inch in diameter, was pierced through the board directly over the switch, which was then operated through the board by employing a long thin electrician's screwdriver. When camouflaged, it was impossible for anyone to find this hole unless he possessed the secret of the measurements from two recognisable points in the floor.

Gigue's method of entering the canteen was simple

enough when carried out with a first class team. It consisted of providing distraction for the two courtyard sentries, while Gigue manipulated the keys with the help of two assistants at the parcel office door.

Dick initiated a team of his own into the secrets of the parcel office, and, when the French left in the summer of 1943 this team carried on successfully until the end of the war. The British had no further trouble in removing such parcels as they required, at will.

Dick's key assistant, in both senses of the word, was Vincent or 'Bush' Parker, an Australian and a Flight Lieutenant in the R.A.F. He might equally well have been called 'Fingers' Parker for his wits and his hands were as quick as lightning. He learnt to handle locks with consummate skill. Bush was a colourful character, which makes it worth digressing to shine the spotlight upon him. Colditz would not have been quite what it was if Bush had not been there, and his activities throw a revealing sidelight upon the life of the prison.

Bush was well knit and strong, a good athlete and an outstanding stool-ball player. Though not more than five feet seven inches tall, he was handsome with the features of a young Adonis and a winning smile which showed off his fine teeth. Black wavy hair crowned his classic shaped head. He had a charming manner which must have made him the complete lady killer in those happy far off days when 'Bush' was a Battle of Britain Spitfire pilot.

All that he could exert his charm on now was the sour, sensible Oberstabsfeldwebel Gephard from whom he could wheedle more of the rationed coal than anyone else in the camp. Gephard thought the world of him and the coal came in handy. Bush was one of the three directors of the British Distillery Monopoly, which developed by the natural process of free enterprise, unhindered by anti-cartel laws and appreciated by the drinking public because of the excellent service rendered.

Bush was definitely talented. He was an amateur card sharper of the highest professional standing!

One evening Dick sat in, as sixth player, in a regular poker school of five. The other players were 'Rex' Harrison of the Green Howards, head escape tailor, an indefatigable worker for the escapes of others and unfailingly good humoured; 'Bag' Dickenson, a Bomber pilot in the R.A.F., second director of the British Distilling Monopoly; 'Bush' Parker; Teddy Barton, the camp theatrical producer; and Scarlet O'Hara making up the sixth.

After a quarter of an hour's desultory play, Bush whispered to Dick:

"Watch this one carefully," as he started to deal.

Dick found himself, after the deal, with the Ace, King, Queen of hearts and two nondescript cards. The pool was opened with four players, Bush and Teddy Barton throwing in their hands.

Dick was watching Bush. He asked for two cards. Picking them up he found he had the knave and ten of hearts. A Royal straight flush—unbeatable!

Bag Dickenson drew two cards, Rex drew two and Scarlet three. The bidding started with Rex making the running. Dick tagged along and Scarlet soon fell out. When the 'raises' reached a hundred *Marken* (about £7) a time, Bag looked worried and said to Rex, "I warn you, I've got a power house."

Neither of them seemed interested in Dick who stayed in, and the bidding continued. Finally, coming to the fore, Dick raised another hundred, whereupon Bag said, "I'll see you."

But Rex was not satisfied. He began another raising spree —two hundred Marks this time—putting three hundred into the pool.

A few onlookers had gathered round the table. There were nearly two thousand *Lagermarken* in the pool. This was worth £140, which in Colditz was no mean kitty on a single hand.

Dick and Bag called a truce and 'saw' Rex who laid down on the table three aces and two kings.

"You're daft," said Bag, "raising like that on a full house. I've got fours," and he put down four nines. He had drawn a nine and another to fill three nines

Bag could see the *Lagermarken* already in his wallet— and began to pick them up when Rex asked casually:

"What did you have, Dick?"

Dick replied by firmly removing Bag's hand from the pile of notes saying, "Just hold everything, chaps, for one moment. I think you'd like to see this," and he laid down his 'Royal'!

All the prisoners in the room gathered around the table to see the hands as the immediate onlookers announced jubilantly to the world, "Boys, come and look! Dick's drawn a Royal Straight Flush!"

Bush and Dick roared with laughter as they saw the look of utter disappointment on Bag's face, and Rex sat back, stunned.

Bush spent much of his time teasing Bag and this occasion was a high-light. When he had pulled his leg enough about his four nines power house, Bush and Dick revealed the conspiracy and all the cash was refunded.

Not for one moment throughout the dealing and playing of the hand had the players suspected anything and Dick, who tried hard to see how Bush manipulated the cards, was none the wiser.

Dick could rest with an easy mind, assured that the parcel office keys were in good hands.

The others of the parcel office team were 'Mike' Harvey, a Lieutenant of the Royal Navy, Lulu Lawton, 'Checko,' the Black Marketeer, two stooges and Dick. They started the habit of sitting on the office steps to read and chat, so that, eventually, when the French left, sentries would be accustomed to seeing Englishmen seated where, formerly, Frenchmen had had the priority. The team-work was interchangeable among the four assistants who distracted the

two courtyard sentries, warned against patrols, and passed
the 'all clear' to Bush and Dick at the door. Bush performed
the opening and closing ceremony. Dick slipped inside to
seek out the parcel to be smuggled. The relocking of the
door was carried out in the same manner as the opening
and the complete operation usually required not less than
an hour, giving Dick twenty minutes inside the office.

CHAPTER VII

ATMOSPHERE

AN atmosphere can cling to a building just as cobwebs to its walls. It is intangible but it is there. In the years to come, man will, doubtlessly, invent instruments of such finesse that they will be able to pick up sound waves emitted in a room centuries before. The voices of great men of the past will be recaptured by detectors of microscopic accuracy, magnified and broadcast.

If man can measure the amount of heat radiated by a candle at a distance of a mile, if he can prise open the oyster of the atom, it is only a matter of time before he will hear the voices of the past talking in the present.

Dogs have been known to return home hundreds of miles across country; pigeons fly homeward across the seas. Animals can smell what man cannot smell, and hear sounds that man cannot hear.

The human brain is found to emit wireless waves; if it can emit surely it can receive.

The scientific explanation of the working of the refined senses, of instincts, and of the brain, is writ large inside a deep scientific tome of which this generation is now opening the introductory pages.

Certain of man's senses have been dulled. One of them is the ability to appreciate consciously the proximity of fellow beings in the present, not to mention out of the past, without the aid of the simpler senses which remain man's standby—sight and hearing and the nervous system.

Yet, dulled as the senses have been, something remains; an inchoate attribute by which man can sense vaguely what he commonly calls 'atmosphere'. Undoubtedly, much that provides the reaction in human beings which is often loosely termed the sixth sense, comes into the brain subconsciously through the other senses. The eyes, particularly, will take

384

in much more than is consciously registered by the brain and will perform unconscious permutations and combinations with memories much like a calculating machine. The answer is then handed over to the conscious mind which registers 'an atmosphere'. At the same time, almost certainly, this other indefinable attribute reacts within the brain.

Colditz had an atmosphere. Naturally a castle that had stood for centuries would. But it was not the atmosphere of antiquity, of the passage of history within its walls that struck every new arrival upon entering the courtyard.

Colditz had more recently been a lunatic asylum. There was a weird, bleak and depressing air about the place which struck the newcomer so forcibly that he knew, without being told, that the Castle must have been filled at one time by a great sadness.

It was not the place to encourage a sane outlook upon life. The high, dun coloured walls surrounding the tiny cobbled yard; the barred windows—even those opening on to the yard were barred; the steep roofs which hung precipitously overhead; the endless clack-clack of wooden sabots; the cacophony of voices in different languages and musical instruments in different keys, were not calculated to breed contentment or resignation. As a lunatic asylum it had never been a sanatorium where insanity might hope to be cured. It could only have been a home for incurables and a dungeon for the violent.

Into this prison the Germans threw the men who, of all the prisoners of war in Germany, were the most likely to chafe and strain and pine under the stifling confinement of its oppressive walls. Those who had found resignation were not for Colditz. Those who had broken their chains and would continue to do so, filtered into the Castle.

Colditz was a fruitful breeding ground for frustration and might easily become a prison full of mentally unbalanced men.

How easily it might happen is illustrated by the proportionately large number of officers who actually became unbalanced. The development of the malady could be seen and the symptoms usually followed a regular course. The process was known as 'going round the bend'. It started, commonly, with a passion for classical music, often followed by a demoniacal lust for physical training, after which the particular form of 'unbalance' of the individual developed —plain for all to see.

In one, it would be sheer violence and the officer became a danger to his fellows, but even more so to the Germans. A sentry was the 'red rag to a bull', and the demented prisoner would have to be held down by friends to stop him from hurling crockery, bottles, anything that came to hand, at the victim of his 'hate' complex. In another, it would take a suicidal turn. These two forms were the most trying for the community. The Germans were appallingly slow in taking action to remove the sufferers to a proper house of treatment and in the intervening months, a constant guard had to be maintained by the prisoners themselves which wore down resistance to a malady that almost became infectious.

Other forms of unbalance were as innocent as they were amusing, but their general affect was not to fortify the sanity of the other prisoners.

One would become eternally sullen and develop a baleful glare. It was disconcerting to a man, sometimes consciously aware of his own liability to 'go round the bend', to be fixed by this stony and hypnotic gaze. Thoughts of the fabled 'Old Man of the Sea' mingled with an uncontrollable desire to run. The glassy eyes could change their expression from mild to murderous without a flicker.

One officer of this type retained a devilish sense of humour, concentrating on the German sentries in the courtyard. He would approach one of them stealthily and fix him with his stare. The sentry was not aware of the attack until he turned and faced him. For a full minute their eyes met as the satanic hypnotist scowled at him. Then, with no warning, the insane one suddenly leapt high into the air and the unnerved Jerry jumped equally high in sheer terror.

The lunatic then walked off, quite unconcerned. Eventually, the sentries grew accustomed to this treatment. When they did, our man ceased to plague them.

Another 'leg-puller' type made a habit of puffing smoke from a filthy home-made cheroot in the faces of the same unfortunate sentries. Having done so, he flicked the ash off his cigar on to the cobbles in front of the sentry, then produced a dustpan and brush from behind his back, swept up the offending ash and marched off to the dustbins.

A soulful, melancholy type used to play the guitar for hours in the bathroom, seated on a stool with his head inside an empty suitcase. This officer was once removed to a hospital where he displayed remarkably good sense by denuding the hospital garden, in one night, of a good crop of ripening tomatoes.

Yet another type gave up washing and became so filthy that he was not allowed to eat at table. He sat cross-legged all day long on the top of a seven foot cupboard, occasionally eating from a bowl a nauseating mixture of his own concoction consisting of egg-powder and an inedible semidried vegetable, a German issue, called 'Rabbi' which the prisoners normally used for stuffing pillows and mattresses.

The Germans did nothing about the 'wackies' unless they were violent, and then only after several years. Others, they picked out, like the guitarist, as if they were picking an apple out of a basketful. There was no logic in their methods. One officer, who was not mad, pretended to be so following medical advice as to symptoms and behaviour. The 'fake' lunatic, after nearly a year, became discouraged and returned to normal. The attempt was known only to Dick Howe and a doctor. The community, as a whole, considered him a genuine 'round the bend' and were encouraged at the sight of a recovery.

Then there was the religious maniac of the proselytising variety who unlocked the staircase door in the dead of night and sallied forth into the lamplit courtyard where only the sentries monotonously paced their beat. Dressed in a flowing sackcloth robe and holding aloft a large wooden cross of his own manufacture, he recalled the world to prayer in loud, ringing tones, chastising the stolid sentries with his tongue, accusing them of dreadful sins and demanding their immediate submission and repentance.

*   *   *   *   *

Each prisoner had his own personal struggle and suffered his own fears. In the silence of the night, in fitful sleep, they rose uncontrolled to take on grotesque proportions. Waking from dreams of long unending tunnels, of the search for an opening that never appeared, tearing at stones with bare hands, lying prone in the clammy earth amidst worms and maggots, queer thoughts came univited. Waking from a nightmare race, thrashing the blankets, cursing, sweating and gasping for breath, fleeing for life, always uphill, with the Jerries close behind; hearing their shouts merge into the *crescendoes* of the proselytising preacher in the echoing courtyard, then melt away into silence; no! not peaceful silence, but another sound, travelling upwards through the windows, along the searchlight beams, the pad —pad—pad of the enemy—a sentry on his beat; at such a time a time men wondered if they were sane. The preacher in the yard might be funny no longer, the joke had lost its savour. Lying awake on his straw palliasse in the eerie half light a prisoner could see himself swaying on the tight rope of sanity, could visualise himself bearing down on the sentries with a cross or sitting like a buddha on the top of a cupboard.

Such moments were the testing time and much depended on the prisoner's reaction. A sense of humour was a healing balm of incalculable worth. If a man could laugh at the vision of himself seated cross-legged on top of a cupboard, it was as if he tore himself clear of the encircling tentacles of a strangling octopus. He promptly slept and woke up refreshed in the morning. If he did not laugh a red light glowed threateningly before him. Soon he would not dream his nightmares. They would begin to occupy the stage of his conscious, wakeful mind. He would rise in the morning nervous, irritable and depressed. That way lay danger.

Of all the qualities that make for sanity in such surroundings a sense of humour stands paramount. Thank God there was no lack of it at Colditz! It was small wonder that men returned in spirit to their boyhood days and took refuge in the antics of a schoolboy. What can be saner than a schoolboy!

The masters had guns instead of canes and might use them; the antics had a steely edge to their humorous side, but that way, nevertheless, lay sanity. The majority of the prisoners of Colditz instinctively found comfort and solace in the carefree, day to day psychological outlook of the schoolboy. It was another of the many secrets that the Castle held; a secret that the prisoners did not whisper about, for the simple reason that they were unaware of it.

CHAPTER VIII

THE COCOA 'V'

IN spite of a few deceptive spring-like days in February, winter took a firm grip upon the Castle in the early months of 1943; it was proving to be worse than the last. It was the winter of Fate for the Germans in Russia: the seige of Stalingrad.

There was less coal for the prisoners; fewer bed boards that could be removed with safety from beds for fire wood. Relief from perpetual shivering was only obtained by retiring under the blankets. Rations deteriorated further. The most plentiful food consisted of sugar beet residue, dyed red and brought into the camp in barrels labelled, 'Nur für Kriegsgefangene' only for P.O.W.s. It was issued as a jam ration and was uneatable.

In these conditions of cold and hunger the German Commandant decided to alleviate the lot of the P.O.W.s by purchasing a luxuriously complete and up to date equipment for the barber's shop. The finance was provided by what was known as 'The Commandant's Fund', which depended, for its revenue, on canteen profits.

One frosty morning, a decorator's van arrived, accompanied by a representative of the contractors, a civilian plumber, a fitter and four sentries. Such an exciting intrusion was a gala occasion for the prisoners. To look upon civilians, to see a civilian lorry, why! if a prisoner were to put his fingers in his ears so that he did not hear the clack-clack of wooden clogs nor the guttural sound of German voices; if he half closed his eyes so that he saw nothing beyond the lorry—neither the field grey nor the khaki around him; and if only he could stop shivering, why! he could imagine himself standing on the pavement in Regent Street beside a lorry drawn up at the kerb; a real live motor vehicle—a delivery van. Such a phenomenon was only seen in Colditz once a year, if that.

Enough of day-dreaming. There was work to do. The four sentries would require a considerable amount of skilful distraction. That merely meant a little more exercise for the talents of men like Scarlet O'Hara, Rex Harrison, Bush Parker, Peter Storie Pugh and Scorgie Price.

While the contractor and his men disappeared for a moment into the barber's shop, Rex and Peter, looking like Mutt and Jeff—Peter was not much taller than 'the medium-sized man'—on their way to commit a burglary, set about deflating one of the back tyres. They did not succeed because they were not meant to. Instead they started a loud argument in bad German with the two near-side guards protesting that they were only interested in the type of tyre and the shape of the wheel, which, they maintained with significant gestures, was not round. This brought the other two sentries over to the near side of the car which was the signal for redoubled angry protestations while, on the off-side Scarlet removed the road maps from under the driver's seat and Bush Parker disappeared with the tools. It was on an occasion similar to this, a year before, that 'Errol' Flynn, a Flying officer in the R.A.F., had 'won' the four-foot long crowbar which earned him a place on the fated French tunnel.

The contractor's men reappeared as Peter and Rex concluded their harangue and walked away exuding an aura of righteous indignation.

The workmen opened the van and began to off-load a highly polished adjustable barber's chair. Scarlet, returning to the scene, noted a hydraulic jack reposing on the floor of the van not far from the doors. The two sentries on normal duty in the yard stationed on the near side of the lorry, could see the open van doors. Rex and Peter were sent off to distract them, while Bush Parker and Scorgie Price took over the two sentries at the rear of the van.

The secret of the operation is synchronisation. It is impossible to distract a person and to keep an eye on three or four other people as well. It is difficult enough to look at one person out of the corner of an eye while concentrating upon a second, the sentry. Scarlet only has to watch one of the other four, namely Bush Parker nearby. Bush cannot see Scorgie at the far side of the van but only has to watch Rex, Rex watches Scorgie, Scorgie watches Peter, and Peter watches Scarlet. The circle is complete.

Peter, furthest away from the scene, starts the action upon a signal from Scarlet who then turns his gaze on Bush. Peter, facing so that he can see Scarlet, stops in front of his sentry who is momentarily standing at ease and begins talking to him mockingly about Stalingrad. The sentry is not supposed to talk, is confused and turns to march away which is what is required. Peter follows him still talking. Scorgie has now started work upon his sentry. He has a book in his hand. He is looking at a funny picture and roaring with laughter. His sentry can only half see the picture and is tortured with curiosity. Rex has seen the effect of Scorgie's effort and busies himself beside his sentry whittling a curiously shaped piece of wood. The sentry is intrigued. Bush then comes into action by showing his sentry a card trick. Scarlet vaults quickly into the van, seizes the jack, jumps off and walks casually away with it under his coat. The action is completed in five seconds. Peter has seen Scarlet walk off and retires. The others follow.

Later, when the balloon goes up, the sentries will all swear they never took their eyes off the van.

Having removed the jack, handle and all, Scarlet now contemplated 'winning' a wheel. He needed a heavy fly wheel for a lathe he was manufacturing. The rubber tyre and tube would always come in useful. The wheel brace was among the tools already taken. An offside back wheel would give his stooges an opportunity of practising their art upon the two sentries on the off side of the van.

The wheel nuts are loosened first. They are very resistant. A new distraction has to be brought into action at five minute intervals for each nut. The whole operation will take well over half an hour. . . .

The German contractor's representative, in a 'natty' suit, long green heavy tweed overcoat with a strap at the back and a dark green homburger hat, was busy supervising the unloading and transporting of his equipment into the room which was to be transformed into the palatial barber's shop. He did not become aware of the gradual disintegration of his lorry for some time. Then, suddenly, he missed the jack which he had seen not half an hour before. He gave tongue in no ordinary manner. He screamed with anger and his invective was aimed, mostly and quite rightly, at the German guards. He demanded that the security officer be fetched at once. Scarlet had to give up his task of wheel removing—with the job only half done. Four of the five nuts holding one rear wheel had been removed. Nobody noticed it. Scarlet thought it might be tactless to point out the fact.

"It would be more reasonable," he said, "if the Goonery let me finish the job. Then they would notice the wheel missing and put on the spare which is chained inside the van. It would save the back axle anyway," he continued. "I hate to think what's going to happen after a few hundred yards running."

Sadly Scarlet returned to the British quarters carrying under his coat three bricks on to which he was going to lower the brake drum. He had no intention of leaving the jack.

Hauptmann Eggers was apparently not available. Instead Hauptmann (Rittmeister) Lange, another security officer, arrived on the scene with another sentry. He and the irate civilian retired to the *Evidenz Zimmer*—the interview room—which had just been swept out for the day. The civilian, taking off his green homburger, put it on a table near the half open window. He did not remove his coat as it was too cold. The sentry stood at the door. A heated discussion took place. Rex Harrison took the opportunity to remove the hat with the aid of a long piece of wire passed through the bars of the window.

The civilian was gradually mollified by promises from

Hauptmann Lange that a search would be conducted and restitution made. He turned to pick up his hat and leave the room. He stood with mouth agape for several seconds, then raised his clenched fists above his head and turned his goggling eyes heavenwards.

"*Was ist?*" asked Lange innocently.

"*Mein Hut! Mein Hut!*" screamed the German, stamping his foot in a fury. "*Er war bestimmt hier—Donnerwetter—eine neue Schweinerei! Mein Hut ist verschwunden. Ich bien in eine Verücktenanstalt gekommen.*" He stormed out of the *Evidenz Zimmer*, shouting for his driver to come immediately and take him out of the madhouse while the lorry still had four wheels and an engine. The dramatic irony of his own remark was lost upon him.

By implication the solitary nut and bolt must have held the rear wheel for at least two days, because the workmen returned, albeit on foot, in the afternoon and all the next day to complete the installation. If the wheel had come off—the prisoners argued with reason—they would not have returned at all.

*   *   *   *   *

The big search was well overdue and everybody looked to his hide carefully and with some anxiety. It came, one morning as the first snow of the year began to fall. The Germans made the fatal mistake of 'letting slip' to the British, before the first *Appell*, that they were to leave the Camp for a day's outing. That was enough and every possible precaution was taken. The whole contingent, now nearly one hundred strong, marched off after seven a.m. *Appell*, across the causeway of the Castle and down into the town. They were accompanied by a guard of one hundred Goons and half-a-dozen Alsatian dogs.

The walk was greatly appreciated by the contingent although it lasted only ten minutes, hardly enough to warm up the body, ending on arrival at a building called the *Schützenhaus*. Upon entering the building after a roll call in the yard outside, the prisoners were delighted to see signs of a festive occasion. There, at one end of the *Schü-zenhaus* hall, stood a large canopied platform. It was already adorned with decorations and a long rosary of coloured electric bulbs. Outside the snow continued to fall gently.

Although some officers had set out with the intention of making a break, the weather was not propitious. The over-powering company of guards who took up their positions around the building did not serve to dispel that impression. Still, there was one vague possibility which was hawked around the hall by Dick Howe. The British were settling down for the day. Groups gathered around the few tables, and, on the floor in the corners, blankets were spread. Cards were produced, chess was soon in progress, Red Cross food appeared and the air grew heavy with tobacco smoke. Some-one obtained permission to boil water in an adjoining scullery and tea was served. With all this luxury in new surroundings Dick found only one officer sufficiently en-thusiastic to attempt an escape which had the remotest chance of success. Captain Geoffrey Munro Pemberton How, R.A.S.C.—alias Pembum—was prepared to have a go in spite of the fact that he had just received a new pipe from England; a treasure which would have kept him happy, even in Colditz, for many a long day. Pembum was renowned, among other things, for his voice which re-sembled that of a corn crake. Added to this, he spoke in staccato monosyllables. He had a ruddy face with a ruddier nose and, being somewhat older than the average at Colditz, he was looked upon kindly, as might be an uncle. Pembum wore, over his uniform, a British-warm which was a colour that could pass as civilian attire; like his pipe, it was brand new.

In the late afternoon, the order to return to the Castle was given. The British paraded in front of the *Schützen-haus* over a predetermined spot, a manhole cover in the yard. The snow had almost ceased and was melting into a slush on the ground.

It says something for Pembum that even when the man-hole cover was opened and a revolting slime revealed, his courage did not desert him. Down he went in a second, and the cover was closed on top of him.

The parade count was fixed. All went well and the company marched out of the yard, turning left along the road. Dick looked back as the column wheeled and was shocked to see a conspicuous cloud of smoke rising around the manhole cover.

"The blighter's smoking his damned pipe," he thought.

There were so many Goons in the yard that it was impossible the cloud would remain unnoticed for long. Within a few seconds and with the yard still in sight, the company was halted. An *Unteroffizier* returned, at the double, to the yard as one of the sentries at the rear, shouting a warning, called for assistance. The *Unteroffizier* lifted the manhole cover, saw Pembum, dropped it again and then jumped up and down on the cover several times whooping like a Red Indian war dancer.

Only the rear of the column saw Pembum removed and led off ignominiously, his brand new overcoat dripping with the grey brown filth from the walls of the manhole and his head bespattered with droppings from the underside of the manhole lid, the result of the pounding of the *Unteroffizier*.

Dick accused Pembum, on his return from a month in the cooler, of succumbing to temptation by smoking his pipe in the manhole. Pembum denied it and explained that the smoke was condensation in the cold atmosphere of the manhole rising with the air heated by his body. His explanation was correct, but in spite of protestations of innocence he took a long time to live down the jibe that he had sold an escape for a pipe of 'baccy.

The procession returned to the camp, but not empty handed. The *Schützenhaus* platform had lost its rosary of coloured lamps and the *Schützenhaus* itself was the poorer by a dozen electric lamp bulbs, several electric fittings and switches, some yards of cable, a useful length of lead pipe from the lavatories and some linoleum from the floor, window curtains of a good neutral tint, half a dozen chairs which had been converted into small firewood and, finally, the four legs sawn off a table and made into presentable logs, while the table top remained, leaning neatly against a wall.

The Germans discovered all these losses later in the evening, but they were by then disheartened. An exhaustive search of the British premises had been carried out over a period of eight hours that day, and the Germans had only some useless contraband—chicken feed—to show for their hard work. The quarters looked as if a bomb had burst in them, furniture and belongings lay in shambles all over the floors. The Dutch reported that immediately after the British contingent had left the camp with their escort, another company of a hundred Goons had marched into the courtyard headed by four bloated-looking Gestapo officers. They had filed up the stairs into the British rooms where heavy thuds and rumbles continued all day which Vandy described as "like the noise of many vindmills all turning round at vonce."

To consider a further search at that moment for electric light fittings and other paraphernalia, though admittedly enough to stock a reasonably sized jumble sale, was out of the question.

Where was the contraband hidden? The type and dimensions of hiding places varied enormously. The beams across the ceiling of one of the larger rooms were supported by simply designed cornices protruding from the vertical wall face. These plinths were of stone and mortar covered with plaster. The architect had omitted one, perhaps with his thoughts on the evil eye. Lulu Lawton, who was officer in charge of 'Hides', made good the architect's omission and the evil eye winked. The false cornice, with its trap door always repainted with plaster of paris and sprinkled with cobweb mixture after use, survived the war without a tremor. Other places, of course, had to be found for articles such as the hydraulic jack. Take a good look at a lavatory pan!

The French must have had the impression that the Germans were weary that night and would not be on the alert. Their notion was a good one. Two of their number, Edouard Desbat and Jean Caillaud, decided to attempt an escape over the roofs of Colditz, which they had been planning for some time. Snow lay on the ground though it was melting on the roofs. It would make the climb more difficult but there were signs of a mist coming up which was exactly what they wanted.

After the last *Appell* at 9 p.m. the British retired to their bunks and most of them were soon asleep.

Shots rang out in the stillness. Men stirred and turned over; some sat up. Scarlet O'Hara was heard to remark, "Coo! Did you hear that? Three grosse coups de fusil!"

More shots followed.

Blackout blinds were raised.* Lights went on in court-yard windows like patches in the quilt of night. Windows opened. There were shouts, orders, jeers, counter-orders and laughter. Windows shut again, blinds were lowered and the lights went out, one by one.

Only two Frenchmen, one, clinging by means of a lightning conductor to the vertical face of a chimney breast eighty feet from the ground, the other, perched on a roof ledge close at hand, knew what the shouting was about.

Desbat, hanging perilously from the conductor, knew it because he was being shot at, and Caillaud was taking the strain on the safety cord linking the two of them, ready to save his friend if he fell, wounded by the German attack.

Their objective was the outer edge of a roof ridge, from which they could descend two hundred feet in comparative darkness clear of the encircling wire and the ring of guards. The mist had failed them. They still might have succeeded, relying on the supposition that sentries seldom look sky-wards, and upon the fact that the chimney breast was in

---

* Although the outside of the Castle was floodlit, prison orders were to the effect that blinds must be drawn. It was a precautionary measure in the event of air raids, when the floodlights were always extinguished. The order was, needless to say, flagrantly disobeyed.

half-light, reflected from floodlight striking an adjacent building.

A loose piece of mortar was Desbat's downfall. His foot dislodged it, and it fell with a crash to the ground near a sentry in the outer courtyard. The sentry looked upwards. Desbat saw him out of the corner of an eye. He did not move. The German, accustomed to the glare of the lights, could see nothing at first. He called another sentry. Together they peered, shading their eyes, trying to pierce the gloom. They saw Desbat.

Shouts of "Halt!" were followed by three shots which loosened bricks around Desbat's head sending dust and splinters flying into his face. He yelled, *"Schiessen Sie nicht, ich ergebe mich"*—"Don't shoot, I give myself up" several times.

The guard was turned out. In spite of his yells which could be heard clearly below, fifteen more shots were fired at him. They may well have been warning shots, but the nearest hit the brickwork only three inches from his head and the volley was unnerving to say the least of it.

The alarm having been given, the sentries inside the prisoners' courtyard caught sight of Caillaud on his ledge and covered him, ordering him to descend.

The Jerries might have been tired early in the evening. They might justifiably have been in high spirits later in the evening at the recapture of two escapers. But they were ill at ease, jittery, uncertain of themselves and trigger-happy by midnight.

There was an atmosphere of 'Macbeth' abroad. Men slept restlessly. Dogs barked in the distance and would not settle down. The familiar tread of the sentries in the courtyard was not audible. They moved like ghosts in the snow, silent and unearthly. It was a night for witchcraft. Indeed Priem was plotting. With a mug of Schnapps beside him, he sat brooding in his office in the Kommandantur. He would have a revenge on the British after his own style.

At two a.m. he ordered an *Appell* for the British P.O.W.s. His heavy-booted Huns came striding through the dormitories, switching on the lights and shouting, *"Aufstehen—Appell! Sofort! Schnell!"* hardly giving the officers time to don overcoats over their pyjamas and stuff cigarettes and food into their pockets, before being herded without ceremony into the courtyard, now thickly carpeted with snow. They were met by a posse of Goons with their guns in the rabbiting position. This meant the Jerries were ready for trouble.

Priem himself appeared while the rooms were being cleared by his men. The floors were still littered with the debris from the search of the day before. Officers in pyjamas and Goons, tripping over their guns, were milling around the beds and tables in a glorious congestion of confused humanity. The Goons were shouting and the prisoners were all talking at once.

Harry Elliott, still lying in his bunk, yelled across the gangway to Dick, "What the hell's happening?"

Dick, struggling with one leg in his trousers, replied above the din, "Priem's on the warpath again."

Harry said, "Ask him what the devil he thinks he's doing."

"Ask him yourself," shouted Dick.

Harry jumped out of bed and strode off, in his pyjamas, in search of Priem. He found him on the staircase and said:

"Captain Priem, what the hell do you think you're doing? Go away and leave us alone."

Priem, saluting with mocking humour, replied, "Hauptmann Elliott, please go down to the courtyard."

"You go to hell!" said Harry, "I'm going to do a pee," and with that he marched back into the quarters and headed for the *Abort*. Harry relieved himself and returned to bed.

In the meantime, one of the German rifles had been stolen. The tempo of movement and the clamour redoubled. Guards charged around the rooms searching in the beds and under them for the missing weapon. Priem was sent for. He arrived as the scene reached a climax of pantomime chaos. He could not make himself heard. The more rebellious prisoners, who had not yet descended to the yard, were chanting all the songs they could think of at the top of their voices. Strains of the 'Siegfrid Line' mingled with 'B—— and the same to you.' Suddenly, Priem spotted the rifle inside an officer's pyjama leg. There was a mad rush of Goonery. The officer was completely smothered and then almost carried bodily out of the room under *"Strengen Arrest."* Jeers, whistles and catcalls rose to a deafening crescendo. The Germans were losing control and began to manhandle the prisoners towards the staircase with the usual, *"Los! Los! Schnell! Los!"*

Priem now took it into his head to visit the Dutch, living on the floor above. He mounted the stairs followed by a squad of Goons and, also, a party of British in pyjamas and overcoats; led by Rupert Barry, determined not to miss the fun. Sleepy Dutchmen rose on their elbows and blinked with astonishment at the incredible procession as it burst into their quarters. Priem was greeted with roars of laughter on all sides. Beside himself, he ordered the Dutchmen out of their beds, then turned to his soldiery and saw the cause of the laughter: a pyjama column of twenty Englishmen in attendance on the Germans, chatting innocently, grinning, waving to friends and generally awaiting developments. He emitted a bellow and went for Rupert, thumping him on the chest with his fists and screaming between the punctuating blows, *"Gottsverdammter englischer Schweinhund!"*

His squad were meanwhile pulling the blankets off the Dutchmen and turning them out of bed. Priem could not hold all the English. He was gripping Rupert with his two fists clenched over handfuls of pyjama and overcoat. The others mingled with the Dutch and the hubbub increased.

Within seconds the scene in the Dutch quarters became a repetition of the act in progress on the floor below. The shouting and singing, wafted up the stairwell, was soon drowned by a chorus upstairs.

Priem countermanded his order, screaming at the top of

his voice that the Dutch should return to bed. But, by now, they were all awake, enjoying the fun and had no intention of doing so. Priem sent in his men to force them and a steeplechase began around the clusters of bunks. The Dutch and British were indistinguishable in their night attire and the hide and seek continued fruitlessly until Priem, in despair, called his men off, and left the prisoners to sort themselves out.

Down in the courtyard everybody was singing. Blackout blinds were going up again and faces looked down upon the rioters below.

The *Appell* had been extended to the senior British officers from the theatre block. They descended, sleepily, one by one. The S.B.O., Lieutenant Colonel Stayner of the Dorsetshires, known as "Daddy" because of his grey hair and gentle, fatherly manner, walked into the yard. He looked frail and tired. He stopped for a moment under the lamp near the doorway, surveying the unruly mob before him, his tall, thin frame silhouetted against the darkness beyond. Wisps of hair straying from under his fore and aft cap, were caught by a swirling gust of wind which sent a myriad snowflakes pirouetting. He heaved a tired sigh, shrugged his shoulders and took up his accustomed place for the *Appell*, resigned to a long session in the cold.

The French and Dutch began booing from the windows as Priem appeared on the steps outside the entrance to the British staircase. Priem held up his hand, waving at the windows and shouting orders that nobody could hear.

His N.C.O.s must have understood him. They gesticulated warningly up at the windows as the rifles of the sentries came up to the shoulder. The French and Dutch wisely retired. There was a momentary expectant lull. David Hunter, a Lieutenant of the Royal Marines, could not resist the temptation. He yelled, *"Feuer!"*, and a salvo of shots echoed through the yard, as bullets flew into the night or embedded themselves in the walls. Slates rattled to the eaves.

Daddy Stayner remonstrated half-heartedly, "Hunter, don't do that again, you're aggravating the Germans."

He knew his junior officers well enough. He had no intention of attempting seriously to call for order. In fact, he was beginning to enjoy the fun.

A sly smile played about his mouth as he watched the German N.C.O.s, led by Gephard and the ferret, running around the yard demanding of the sentries, "Who gave the order to fire?"

Priem ordered the S.B.O. to command his men to form ranks for an *Appell*. Daddy Stayner maintained a stubborn ignorance of the German language and called for the British interpreter.

Flight Lieutenant 'Bricky' Forbes, R.A.F., the interpreter, was nowhere to be found. He had a Balaclava helmet well over his face and was determined to remain incognito. A German interpreter was sent for.

At this point a blackout curtain in the British quarters went up, and Harry Elliott poked his head out as far as he could to see the fun. Priem saw him and exploded. He bellowed orders at Gephard who headed up the stairs at the double with two sentries. He returned in five minutes without Harry. Harry was back at the window.

From behind the blinds in the windows of the French quarters a plainsong choir could be heard chanting. The voices rose and fell in monastic rhythm.

The French were intoning their usual litany:

"*Où sont les Allemands?*"

"*Les Allemands sont dans la merde.*"

"*Qu'ils y restent.*"

"*Ils surnagent.*"

"*Enfoncez-les.*"

"*Jusqu'aux oreilles.*"

Gephard reported to Priem:

"Hauptmann Elliott says he is too ill to parade in the snow."

Harry, it may be remembered, was cultivating a chronic jaundice at this period of his captivity.

"Escort him downstairs to the doctor's dispensary," ordered Priem. "He will parade in there."

Gephard clicked his heels, saluted and disappeared upstairs again at the double.

Bedlam continued in the courtyard. The prisoners were still singing and shuffling around in a turmoil of movement like a bubbling cauldron, with the legitimate excuse that they were trying to keep warm.

The monotonous chant of the French inside their building provided a background of continuous sound like seas breaking on a distant shore.

A German security officer appeared, accompanied by an elderly, wizened little German corporal who was to act as interpreter. The latter had obviously just been dragged out of his bed and was half asleep. What he saw on entering the yard made him blink, wondering if he was still dreaming.

Priem was at his wits' end. If he threatened again with the rifles of his men, a machiavellian voice would shout *"Feuer!"*, and he would be ultimately responsible if men were killed or wounded. He had lost the substance of power for a failing shadow—his voice.

Harry descended the stairs under escort and was greeted with vociferous cheering. He was led to the dispensary and locked in.

The Germans conferred with Colonel Stayner, then turned and faced the mob. The S.B.O. raised his hand, motioning for attention. Almost miraculously a lull descended on the unruly mob.

The intoning of the French could now be clearly heard and the quavering sound of Harry's voice—he did not see the S.B.O. from the dispensary—wafted into the yard rendering, to the tune of 'Mademoiselle from Armentières', an extempore composition:

> "...
> The Huns were hanged, one by one, parley-vouz,
> The Huns were hanged, one by one,
> Every b—— mother's son,
> Inky, stinky Hitler too."

The S.B.O. continued to demand silence as a wave of laughter threatened to bring new disorders in its wake. For a moment there was silence.

The German interpreter uttered in ringing tones his first words:

"All British are warned to mutiny."

They were his last.

A roar of applause greeted the announcement. Priem threw up his arms in despair, giving up the unequal fight. He turned to the S.B.O. and spoke to him.

Colonel Stayner turned towards the prisoners, "Parade, dismiss!" he shouted as loudly as he could. The order was greeted with wild cheers and the British broke up in high spirits. They had won a signal victory.

Gradually they filed back to their quarters under the sullen gaze of the bewildered sentries.

The courtyard emptied and the sound of voices dropped to a distant murmur issuing from the turret staircase door. The guards faced each other across the yard waiting for the order to 'fall in'. On the snow in front of them, where the British had stood a few moments before, was an enormous dark brown 'V'. An enterprising spirit had thought it worth the expenditure of iron rations—a tin of Bournville cocoa!

CHAPTER IX

FRANZ JOSEF

INTROSPECTION had little place in Colditz. On rare occasions a prisoner became interested in psychology. As a rule he went on—'round the bend'. Psychological studies, in fact, could be dubbed a third form of the initial symptoms of the disease; the other two being, as already mentioned, the inordinate passion for classical music and the untiring cult of the body—physical jerks.

The majority of the Colditz inmates seemed to prefer the more simple variety of self-examination; an occasional examination of the conscience. After all, it had the prestige of a few thousand years of beneficent usage, whereas the modern version achieved, in prison, sometimes startling, sometimes comic, but never satisfying results. The difference between modern psychological introspection and the Christian examination of conscience was described by a wag at Colditz as the difference between a Futurist nightmare and a Michelangelo masterpiece; only the canvas and paint were common to both, as the mind of man to the two forms of mental approach.

A new British escape scheme was afoot. There was little time, opportunity or inclination for the self-indulgence of morbidity. The project was big: it would involve the breakout of a large party. As usual it started in a small way.

One bright morning in April, 1943, Dick Howe was looking vacantly down from a window in the British dayroom at the sentries below. He was joined by 'Monty' Bissell, a six-foot Irishman who was a curious mixture of two temperaments. He had the temperament and the physique of a prize fighter and his bones must have been made of case-hardened steel. He had no fat on him whatever. Yet, although he was as thin as a rake, his weight remained well over fourteen stone. He charged everywhere with his head

down, like a bull. He could not walk slowly, with the result
that he frequently bumped into people. It was like being
hit by a shunting engine. He had black hair which fell over
his forehead and a long face with a beak of a nose and
hawk-like eyes. When he laughed, which he did at the most
incongruous moments, accompanied by a loud snort and a
satanic jerk of the head backwards, his mouth opened,
revealing yawning gaps where once had been a fine row of
teeth. Boxing had done that for him.

Monty had the soul of a poet. He would quote Shake-
speare and Yeats—in equal mouthfuls—lovingly, with the
tenderness and complete unselfconsciousness of one to
whom the music and the meaning of the words were ineff-
ably majestic, imposing and intuitive.

Monty leaned on the window sill beside Dick. Neither
spoke for some time. Then Monty recited with his huge
hand on Dick's shoulder:

> 'I've looked too long at life through a window
> And seen too often the freedom I crave.
> Yes, I've looked far too long at life through barred windows,
> But I'll look much longer at death from my grave.'

"Not bad, not bad, hah! What do you think, Dick? I got
it from Black Campbell. Didn't know he was a poet, did
you? Ha! Hm!"

A long pause intervened. Dick was in a reverie. Monty
might have been on the moon, but his heavy hand came
down again with a resounding thud on Dick's shoulder.

"What's all the thought about, Dick? Listen to this!"
and he intoned with almost fierce intensity:

> "Come,
> Close your eyes, see the graph of expression
> Traced by the pencil of Modernity,
> Watch those steep ascents and sheer declines
> Marking the course of enthusiasm
> Whose fire consumes itself and Phœnix-like
> Creates once more the spark of quick desire.
> These jagged peaks must needs record some trend.
> Dizzy heights and abysmal nothingness
> Can cancel out: but nothing cancels out.
> In Time all that does not move is stiller
> Than the still. We must progress or perish,
> And being able must progress yet more,

Else perish sooner. Man as yet unborn
Has all but solved the mystery of birth.
This Science cannot aimlessly suffice,
For one must know the 'I' to know the all.
To know this 'I' each age has creased the brow,
But ours of all the ages sets small store
Against the value of this seed of hope.
Philosophies, Religions, Mysteries,
Give way to stark Reality . . ."

"That's Humanity! Huh! not bad, eh! for a caged bird!
Black Campbell again."

Dick replied without looking up,

"I was thinking that, if we could change a sufficient number of the sentries on one side of the Castle, we could let out a large number of chaps through a prepared window and nobody would be the wiser."

"Eh? What's all that?" queried Monty, taken aback, "I was talking about Humanity."

"Were you?" said Dick and leaning again on the sill with his chin cupped in his hands he continued his reverie.

Monty did not go away. Instead, he elbowed Dick over to give him room so that he, too, could cup his chin and stare out of the window—out and then down. Thus they both remained, silent and absorbed in their own thoughts for a long time. Then Dick drifted away and Monty was left alone.

That was how the escape attempt started.

*   *   *   *   *

At the end of April, Monty Bissell and Mike Sinclair could be seen frequently walking together around the cobbled yard in deep conversation. Mike was back in prison circulation again after his long spell in solitary. He was looking, it seemed, paler than before, but then he had red hair and the sunless winter was only just beginning to recede before the onslaught of Spring.

Now, as they strode around the yard, Monty displayed, at times, great agitation, flinging his arms wide, slapping Mike on the back and walking at a pace that often brought his companion to a trot. Mike was of medium build, just about the same height as one of the German Guard Commanders, who was known in the Castle as Franz Josef.

Franz Josef was indeed the subject of their subdued discussion as they tore around the yard. It was not long before they buttonholed Dick.

One evening after the five o'clock *Appell* they approached him.

"Dick," said Mike, "we want to have a chat with you. Would you spare Monty and me half an hour in a quiet corner somewhere?"

"Come along to my room. We can sit on the beds. There's nobody there and we've got lots of time before supper."

They climbed the long spiral flight of steps to the room, where, in a secluded corner, well away from the door, was Dick's bunk. Nearby were the two-tier bunks occupied by Lulu Lawton, Rupert Barry and Harry Elliott. The room was long and the ceiling high but the windows were in deep casements which kept out much of the light. They sat or lay on the beds as the shadows slowly deepened in the evening light.

Mike began:

"Monty has an idea for an escape which, at first sight, appears pretty crazy, but we've talked about it a lot and I, for one, think it can be done. Roughly—without going into details—it's this: I dress up as Franz Josef and with two others, dressed as German guards, we get out of a certain window at the psychological moment. I relieve the guard below our old quarters, the ones that are empty. There are two sentries; the chap on the cat-walk and the fellow at the barbed wire gate. I send the real guards back to the guardhouse and my two men take over. Then, having the keys of the gate and having possession of that side of the Castle, you can send out a batch of say twenty chaps—more if you like—through another prepared window and the whole lot of us clear out as fast as we can."

"Hm!" said Dick lying back in his bed and appearing to examine intently the canvas palliasse and the bed boards of the bunk above him. "I see, Monty, you haven't been idle!"

"Eh, What! No! by Gad! I've been working up this scheme ever since you mentioned the idea, weeks ago. I think it's terrific—a cinch—I can't sleep at night for thinking about it. All we need are two more German speakers—three German uniforms—Teddy Barton fixes up Mike to look like Franz Josef—we cut the bars on two windows—the guards are relieved and off we all go—first class railway tickets to Blighty." A torrent of words flowed from Monty as he stood up excitedly and enacted the escape with his long arms.

"All right, Monty. That's all right, old boy. Sit down now and let's have a few details, quietly. First of all, this is how I see it. We'll have to do a long period of watching so that we know exactly what motions Franz Josef will go through on the particular evening assuming it will be in the evening—of the escape. Then, we must also do a lot of stooging so that we know which sentries will go on the posts we're going to relieve—we want dumb ones." He paused for a moment, thinking, then continued:

"We've not only got to make three uniforms complete, and mighty good ones—better than we've ever made before —but we shall have to make two rifles and a revolver in its holster for Franz Josef—also the two bayonet scabbards. Changing the guard means plenty of time for the Jerries to notice the uniforms and the lights may be on. Anyway, it's not at all like a couple of chaps, in uniform, marching past a sentry, in a hurry. That's how I see it. The answer is stooging—hours and hours of it, and the best uniforms we've ever made. Apart from that I'd like to see how Mike makes up as Franz Josef; and lastly which windows do you propose to work from?"

There was a moment's silence before Mike spoke:

"We'll show you the windows now if you'll come with us. I think Teddy Barton can fix me up as Franz Josef. I've asked him about it already and he's fairly confident about it. I'm the right height."

"You'll have to examine old Franz with a microscope for a couple of weeks at least, to pick up all his mannerisms. You've got to be word perfect," Dick interrupted.

"Yes, I know," continued Mike. "Have you any ideas for my two Goons?"

Dick thought for a second. "Where do you come in all this, Monty? You'll never pass as a weedy little tich of a sentry."

"No! I'm going to lead the storming party out of the second window," announced Monty with gusto. "What a show it's going to be! Hah!" and he threw his head back with a devilish grin.

"I thought, maybe, John Hyde-Thomson could be one of my guards," said Mike. "He speaks German well enough. I hadn't fixed on another yet."

"All right," said Dick rising slowly from the bed, "let's go and have a look at the windows. The idea's crazy all right, but if everything is word perfect—well—who knows! We must think about your guards and I'll talk to the C.O. about it."

They walked downstairs, across the now darkening courtyard and into the sick bay corridor. Monty led the way into the sick ward itself and they stood, huddled together, by a window. Monty then explained, in subdued tones, that this window was 'blind' from the sentries at night unless one of them walked the full length of his beat, and he could be expected to stand still for part of his duty period. Dick checked up and thought there was something in what Monty said. Two or three officers could be let down quickly out of this window, and, provided they were suitably dressed, they could walk away, round a corner, towards the next sentry without causing suspicion. The bars, of course, would have to be very carefully dealt with.

They continued their tour of inspection, to the window where it was proposed to let out the main body. This was on the park side of the Castle. The window was in quarters now vacated and in darkness, in which the British had once lived. Keys were employed to make an entry and here, beside the second window, Monty and Mike pointed out the two German sentries who would be involved in the escape.

One of the two sentries was stationed on a high catwalk surveying a long frontage of the Castle. The second sentry was posted at the barbed wire gate, for the keys of which he was responsible, and which opened on to the roadway leading downhill towards the park and the German barracks. The gate was also next to the deep tunnel-like archway leading into the Kommandantur courtyard; the one through which Mike and the Frenchman had sortied not many months earlier.

With the window bars prepared, if these two sentries could be relieved by ours, the way was clear for a rope descent by a large party.

The scheme was daring, to say the least of it.

Dick put the wheels of his organisation into action. Another 'Mike', namely Michael Harvey, R.N., one of the parcel office team already mentioned, kept a regular stooging roster on call for such eventualities. Dick arranged with Mike to put his roster at the disposal of Monty whom he charged with the task of obtaining sufficient data to be able to forecast with certainty, *three days* ahead of any given date, when Franz Josef would be on duty as Commander of the Guard; to map out his complete circuit and the frequency of his rounds with the time intervals between posts; the exact hours of evening guard changes; the times required for guards to regain the guardhouse from different posts, (a) if walking direct and alone, and (b) if in a squad on the circuit. The posts taken up by respective Goons were to be noted and particular Goons seeded out, leaving only dumb-looking ones in the running, whose tours of duty on the cat-walk and the gate were to be graphed with accuracy. It was a job the team were accustomed to, but it would necessitate at least a month of concentrated effort.

Dick required the *three days'* grace to provide ample time for completing the cutting of the bars of the two windows concerned. This was an operation which called for the greatest patience and for much experience. The work demanded such delicacy of touch that only saws made of razor blades could be used. The sick bay window would be comparatively simple, but the window opening in front of the sentry on the cat-walk was an extremely ticklish job. The escape depended on the success of both cutting operations, and the awkward point was that they would be the last part of the scheme to be completed. This work was put into the hands of Lulu Lawton and Bricky Forbes.

Two thirty foot lengths of rope were required. They were ordered from the marine department, Bos'n Crisp in other words. So much to begin with, but it was only a beginning.

Rex Harrison, blond, six foot two in his socks, with a long curling moustache, even tempered and patient, would have to produce three perfect German uniforms, one for a Sergeant. He no longer had Bill Fowler to help him expertly with the embroidery and cloth insignia, but there were other willing hands to fill the gap. 'Andy', Major W. F. Anderson, R.E., and Scarlet O'Hara were commissioned to produce two German rifles, two bayonet scabbards and a holster complete with revolver, and Scarlet was to deal also with the foundry work for buttons, badges, medals and belt clasps.

Finally, the principal actor in the whole drama had to be coached and transformed into the mirror image of Franz Josef.

The elderly and somewhat stout N.C.O. who was to be given a twin brother was not called Franz Josef for nothing. He was a living impersonation of Franz Josef, Emperor of Austria, King of Hungary and of Bohemia; ruddy complexion, puffy cheeks, grey hair, portly bearing and an enormous Franz Josef moustache which covered half of his face. Provided this could be faithfully copied it would, in itself, provide a magnificent mask.

Teddy Barton was one of the theatre past-masters. Besides producing shows and acting in them, he had the professional touch when it came to 'make-up'. His 'girls' on the stage had at once been the delight and the despair of theatre audiences. His male efforts could not have been bettered by Madame Tussaud. He and his principal aide, Alan Cheetham, manufactured fourteen Franz Josef moustaches before they were satisfied with their handiwork. The face, hair, and even the hands, were practised upon with like thoroughness.

Teddy Barton, Mike Sinclair and Alan Cheetham studied Franz Josef's gestures, facial expressions, manner of speech accent and intonation for a month on end. Franz Josef was dogged every time he entered the courtyard. He was engaged in long futile conversations while, unknowingly, he was scrutinised microscopically by three pairs of eyes that took note of every muscle he moved, every cough and splutter, every smile and grimace he made. Mike rehearsed, was criticised and rehearsed again and again, until he lived in the rôle of Franz Josef.

His moment was approaching. Two sentries had been chosen to accompany him. They were John Hyde-Thomson and Lancelot Pope. Both were good German speakers. They rehearsed with Mike the German words of command, and practised all the movements of guard changing according to the German routine. It was Pope's second effort of this kind. He had once marched out of Eichstätt prison with 'Tubby' Broomhall (Lt.-Col., R.E.), posing as a German General.

It was decided to prepare a first wave of twenty men to make the rope descent from the old British quarters immediately the guard had been relieved and was out of sight.

The factor, limiting the number in the wave, was the time it would take the first German sentry relieved, to march back to the guardhouse and report to his N.C.O., the real Franz Josef—Franz Josef I. Then the balloon would go up. This interval of time was checked repeatedly as a minimum of three and a half minutes and an almost certain maximum of four and a half minutes. Twenty men would, in this space of time, be able to drop down the rope and be well on the road to the park. If there was no violent reaction by the time the twentieth had descended the rope, more officers were ready to follow, but responsibility rested with their leaders not to lessen, in any way, by their action, the chances of the first wave. There might be German reactions other than from the guardhouse and much nearer the scene of the escape. Late departures might cause suspicion or an escaper might even be seen on the rope. This would shorten the start of the first twenty which, in all conscience, was short enough!

An escape of this calibre involved the co-operation of about fifty officers in its preparation. In addition to the month of preparation before the day of the escape, there had been the months of earlier work put in by the artists and the printers reproducing the maps, identity papers and passes carried by the officers who were to make the attempt. These personal credentials were now brought up to date and officially stamped. German money was issued. Each escaper, of course, had to produce his own civilian attire. In this task he was assisted by the expert advice and practical help of the tailors.

The team had gathered for briefing several times and at the final meeting, Dick wound up, with a wry smile:

"I'm sure you'll have an exciting time and plenty of fun. You can rely on it, there'll be some shooting, but keep your nerve and go on running. You know the password 'they can't shoot a British officer!' We have the advantage of darkness. Make for the three points indicated for climbing the Park wall, splitting up into your respective groups. And remember, once you're out, we don't want to see your ugly faces here again."

The main body was to make straight for the park at the double, followed closely by Mike—Franz Josef II and his two sentries. If a stray Goon appeared they were to keep running. Franz Josef II would give the impression of chasing the party and would intercept any such stray Goons and order them to run in the opposite direction, towards the Castle, with instructions to raise the alarm.

The revolver and the rifles were nearing completion.

Scarlet spent hours trailing the sentries in the courtyard holding sometimes a long piece of string, sometimes a ruler in his hand. When a sentry was stationary, Scarlet approached him casually from behind, then surreptitiously measured a particular section of the rifle. 'Andy' prepared the plans. Each measurement was recorded, the ruler providing the details in fractions of an inch. Then they set to work and made the dummies. The result was perfection. The rifles could pass close inspection in daylight. Contours, colours, shape and sheen were all correct. Only the weight would have given them away. Rifle straps were made to match. The revolver and holster followed the same high standard.

'D' day had to be fixed. Careful examination and discussion of the reports of Monty and Mike Harvey, resulting from their exhaustive stooging, settled the date, which was to be the 19th of May, and the hour was to be—immediately after the nine p.m. *Appell*. Franz Josef I would be the guard commander on that day and a particularly dumb-looking Goon was calculated to be on duty at the gate.

Among those remaining behind were Lulu Lawton, Dick's second in command, Bricky Forbes, Bush Parker who was to release the Franz Josef II party from the sick ward, and the stooging team for the event under the command of Mike Harvey. Monty headed the main escaping party.

Signalling was to be done by flashlight. It was laid on as a two-way code between three lookout points; one, at a window on the floor above the sick ward in charge of Bush Parker, with communication to the sick ward by tapping on a water pipe; a second, with the main body in the old British quarters; and the third overlooking the German guardhouse.

The most delicate operation in the whole scheme now had to be accomplished. The bars of the two windows in the different parts of the Castle had to be cut. Complete concentration and devotion to the job in hand was essential. Months of work and the desperate hopes of many men were at stake. Failure would involve much bitterness. For this reason, Dick chose the two men in whose conscientiousness, the whole British contingent had confidence. It could be said with conviction that if they failed to do the job, no other officer would have succeeded.

One window was 'comparatively' simple. The second window was in direct floodlight. 'Comparatively' is a relative term. In other circumstances the cutting might have been deemed very difficult, but, as bar cutting had, by now, become a stock in trade of the Colditz convicts, only the cutting of bars in full floodlight with a sentry immediately below attracted comment and a mild compliment from those who knew what was involved; the ear of a gazelle, a hand of iron controlled by a thread of silk, a heart of ice, a brain calm as a mill-pond and as quick to react as a trout flashing in the stream. During the five years Colditz was used as a prison, in World War II, the operation of cutting a bar in full floodlight was performed successfully only three times.

The bar cutting was accomplished successfully and camouflaged.

May the 19th arrived. The day passed slowly. There was suppressed activity everywhere, concealed by an overall air of casualness. The men taking part in the attempt were not beginners. What worried most of them more than anything else was the short start. If the first stage—the relieving of the guard—came off, that, in itself, would be tremendously exciting, but the real fun would start when twenty P.O.W.s were out, the first with perhaps a three minute start, and the last with less than a thirty second start, in front of the pursuing enemy. The hounds would be in full cry. Colditz had never known such an attempt before and the consequences were unknown.

Monty, six foot of heavyweight boxer, strode around the quarters all day like a rhino in search of a muddy pool in the Sahara.

Mike remained outwardly calm while the turmoil of

nervous anticipation was inwardly tearing at his entrails and gripping his throat.

Dick spent his time checking up on everybody's instructions, amplifying them, where necessary, to cover every possible hitch or misunderstanding. The escape was the largest and most daring so far attempted from Colditz. If it succeeded, it would make history. If it failed, 'Well!' thought Dick, 'it'll still make a good story!' He watched the final rehearsal of the guard-changing squad and thought they were word perfect. Franz Josef II could have walked out of the Castle with ease.

The hours dragged heavily towards the 9 p.m. *Appell.* Those in the escaping team lay on their bunks, trying to sleep. They yawned and stretched themselves nervously finding no relief for the tension around the heart or the nausea threatening the stomach, for the hot flush or the cold sweat. Then, when everybody least expected it, the siren began to wail. The show was on.

The *Appell* went off normally. Immediately afterwards, Bush Parker and the guard relieving party—Mike, John Hyde-Thomson and Lance Pope—faded off towards the sick ward. The second stooging contingent disappeared to their respective posts on the upper floor overlooking the guardhouse. The main escaping party with its stooges, led by Dick, Bricky Forbes, Lulu and Mike Harvey and followed by the members of the second escaping wave—altogether thirty-five strong—passed silently through locked doors into the dark unoccupied rooms of the old British quarters.

Dick looked down on to the sentry path below. "The ivory-headed Goon's at his post on the gateway—so far so good," he whispered.

Sounds of life in the Castle died down. Soon a deathly stillness reigned. Thirty-five men waited for the warning signals.

The first message came through:

"Franz Josef returned to guardhouse," Mike Harvey reported in an undertone. Then came, "All quiet in German Kommandantur."

That was the signal for Bush to act and release Franz Josef II and his party through the window, down the rope, on to the sentry path.

A silence, vibrant with tension, followed. Then, suddenly, Mike Harvey spoke in hoarse excited tones:

"Our guard party on their way—past first sentry."

A moment later, Dick, Lulu, Monty and Bricky Forbes, crouching near the window, heard the crunch of marching feet on the path and a loud heel click as a sentry, out of sight, saluted the passing patrol. Then they came into view, round the corner of the building. This was the crucial moment.

Franz Josef II followed by his two guards walked to the gate and spoke to the dumb sentry in German:

"Sie werden Ihre Wache diesem Posten übergeben. Gehen Sie sofort nach dem Wachtraum zurück, einige Gefangenen sind davon. Man braucht sie ——"

Lance Pope took up his post beside the gate. Franz Josef II mounted the ladder to the cat-walk and repeated his orders to the second sentry who started to descend. John Hyde-Thomson took over his post.

"My God!" whispered Dick, in a dripping perspiration, "it's going to work. Get ready!"

The cat-walk sentry had reached the ground and was marching off. Then Dick noticed the gate sentry had not followed. Franz Josef II was talking to him. Dick could hear the gist of it through the open window and repeated it to the others.

"The sentry says he's under orders not to move. Mike's demanded the keys. The sentry's handed them over . . . but he won't move. What the hell! . . . Mike ought to go. He's wasting time. The three of them can make it. He's getting annoyed with the sentry . . . he's told him to get back to the guardhouse. No! . . . it's no good . . . the dumb bastard won't budge . . . why the devil won't he move? Mike's getting really angry with him . . . this is awful. He's got to go! He's got to go! Mike's shouting at him." Dick was in a frenzy. "Good God! this is the end. The time's nearly up."

Mike was having a desperate duel with the ivory-headed Goon and the precious seconds were slipping away. He was thinking of the main party—he was determined that the main party should escape at all costs. He had cast his dice —it was to be all or nothing. He was sacrificing himself to win the larger prize.

As soon as he started to raise his voice Dick's stomach began to sink. The game was a losing one. He wanted to shout at Mike to make a run for it, but dared not interfere with Mike's battle. He was impotent, helpless, swearing and almost weeping with a foreboding of terrible failure. The scheme, within a hair's breadth of success, was going wrong. Mike might possibly have disarmed the offending sentry but it was too late for violence now with less than half a minute's start. If he had been disarmed at the very beginning it might have been different, but who would have done that when persuasion was the obvious first course. Alas! persuasion meant time and the precious minutes had flown. Four minutes had gone. It was nearly hopeless now.

The two British sentries stood their ground. John Hyde-Thomson was solemnly pacing his beat up and down the cat-walk.

Mike's voice rose to a typical Franz Josef scream of rage. Even as he shouted, there were sounds of hurrying feet and discordant voices shouting in the distance. A dozen Goons came through the archway near the gate, running fast with their bayonets fixed. At their rear, panting hard and bellowing commands, ran Franz Josef I. The game was almost up, but Mike was determined to play it to the end. He would challenge his rival; let the Germans chose between them. Franz Josef II outbellowed Franz Josef I and countermanded his orders. A scene of frenzied confusion ensued, in which the Germans obeyed first one and then the other —turned down the hill and then reversed—looked towards Franz Josef I and listened to Franz Josef II, seeing, yet not believing that Franz Josef had suddenly split into two violently opposed personalities.

The German sentry who had been relieved, was pro-

Mike Sinclair and the ivory-headed Goon

minent. He was yelling at his rival, pointing upwards and dancing with excitement, completely out of control. His substitute stood quietly at his post on the cat-walk looking down innocently upon the chaos below.

N.C.O.s ran backwards and forwards in a panic, waving their revolvers. They were no longer certain of the allegiance of the men they commanded. Lance Pope had mingled with the Germans and Dick could not distinguish him. In the alternate searing floodlight and darkness around the searchlights men who were dressed alike, looked alike.

Mass hysteria broke out. A German voice began screaming: "Armed mutiny! Armed mutiny!" which was taken up by a chorus, waving rifles in the air.

A shot rang out.

One of the Franz Josefs swayed and sank to his knees. A confused mob of soldiers gathered round him, all talking at once.

"They've shot Mike—I think it's Mike—I can't be sure," said Dick, turning to the men around him, "I can't see what's happening."

The panic and the hubbub continued for a moment, then subsided. Lance Pope was in the middle of the mob of Germans. John Hyde-Thomson was being pushed down the ladder of the cat-walk with a revolver in his back.

Dick spotted the Franz Josef on the ground. "It's Mike all right. I'm sure of it."

Monty at the window was shaking with rage, thumping one fist into the other and shouting, "Let me get at 'em! Let me get at 'em."

"The bastards!" said Dick, then turning to the waiting men, "they'll be in our quarters in a minute. Everybody clear out! Lulu see to the bars. Mike, signal to the others to return to quarters."

Then after a pause and another look through the window as Lulu carefully reset the bars: "They've left Mike on the ground. My God! The filthy swines aren't even attending to him!"

Dick and Lulu did not see the end. The *Appell* siren

was moaning and Germans were already in the courtyard. They had to leave the premises in haste, removing traces and locking up behind them.

For nearly ten minutes, Mike was left lying on the ground, bleeding profusely from a wound in the chest. His Franz Josef moustache had been torn off his face. A squad of Goons was standing by, evidently waiting for orders.

An N.C.O. appeared and Mike was picked up. He was semi-conscious—fainting from loss of blood. They carried him away to the Kommandantur.

In the courtyard feeling among the prisoners was running high. Many thought that Mike had been killed. There were struggles on the British staircase. David Hunter, shouting "Deutsche Mörder" at the top of his voice and resisting arrest was hustled off between four Goons with rifles and fixed bayonets in the rabbiting position, and thrown into a cell in his pyjamas.

Monty Bissell spotted the Goon who, he thought, had shot Mike. Shaking his fist in his face, he confronted him with "*Kaltblütiger Mörder! Deutscher Morder! Deutscher Schweinhund!*" He was promptly surrounded by another four Goons who manhandled him across the courtyard and pushed him into another cell.

There were fifty Goons in the yard waiting for the *Appell,* with their bayonets fixed and rifles at the hip. Priem had evidently learnt his lesson and was taking no chances. The guards were in an ugly mood. They had tasted blood. The atmosphere glowed hot and red with sparks that might start a nasty conflagration.

Oberst Pravitt, the German Commandant of the Camp, hurried into the yard. He spoke to the S.B.O. who called the prisoners to attention and announced amidst a frozen silence:

"Lieutenant Sinclair is wounded but out of danger."

Mike's time had not yet come.

CHAPTER X

UPLIFT

THE kitchen stove in the British quarters was naturally a centre of activity around which life hummed all day long and all night too. Then the distillers were at work. During the daylight hours a former Merchant Navy Engineer officer, Lieutenant Ernest Champion, R.N.R., more widely known as Ernie, constituted himself, like an Arabian genie, the guardian of the stove. He knew all about cooking as it should be done at Colditz because 'Bertie' Boustead, an ardent amateur, asked him, one day, when he had some pale looking potato rissoles on the fire, "How do you know when these are done?"

Ernie, who was sitting beside the stove, told him, "When they're brown they're burning, and when they're black they're finished."

Lieutenant John R. Boustead was a thin six foot length of Seaforth Highlander, who had been taken prisoner in June, 1940. He possessed unfailing good humour and, at the same time, somewhat hazy ideas about the mundane matters of everyday living. He was, at first, welcomed with great enthusiasm into the cooks' circle. They saw in his desire to cook a descent from an Olympian detachment.

Ernie was naturally anxious to help him so that when he saw Bertie, early one morning, stirring hot water in a small saucepan on the stove he asked him, "What are you stirring it for?"

To which Bertie replied with the enthusiasm of a pupil who was at last benefiting from his cooking course, "To prevent it burning, of course, you ass."

But Bertie never lived down the reputation he earned as a cook when he approached Ernie with a sizzling frying-pan in which an egg gaily cavorted from side to side. The

shell was brown in patches, black in spots and cracked all
over. He said:

"Ernie! I can't seem to get this egg to fry properly. Can
you help me?"

The kitchen stove would have told some soul shattering
stories if it could have spoken. One scandal which leaked
out, fortunately after the dish concerned had been greedily
consumed and appreciatively digested, concerned a delicious
curry. The chef was Derby Curtis, a Captain of the Royal
Marines. When his curry was only half cooked it took fire
without warning. With consummate aplomb, which was
only witnessed by a few onlookers, he lifted the frying-pan
quickly off the stove, put it on the floor and stamped out
the flames with his heavy booted feet. He then wiped his
boots off carefully on the edge of the frying-pan and continued to cook the curry.

In the evenings, when all meals were concluded, the stove
was taken over by the distillers.

The origin and early development of this industry dates
from the year 1941.* In 1943, however, an efficiently run
firm grew from small beginnings and eventually mastered
all competition and became a monopoly. The head of the
concern was a Dutchman, A. Van Rood, a Flight Lieutenant
in the R.A.F., who had been studying medicine in England
when the war broke out. He joined the R.A.F. and, as a
fighter pilot was shot down over St. Omer in 1942. Van
Rood was a good-looking blond type and was born to be
more than a doctor because he was an authority on every
subject known to man. His opinions were definite on them
all and he did not hesitate to expound his views at any
hour of the day or night, when given a cue and an audience,
in a loud voice in any one of the four languages—Dutch,
English, French or German—which his audience might
care to choose because he was fluent in them all. He became
a skilful brewer and was the chemist, as well as a Director,
of the Company. Scarlet O'Hara christened him 'Good

* See *The Colditz Story*.

'Time Charlie Goonstein' after the Damon Runyan character who ran a speakeasy off Broadway. The name stuck.

His brother Directors were Bush Parker who acted as the fuel contractor for the combine, and Bag or 'Ming' Dickenson. The latter came from Bristol, was also a Flight Lieutenant in the R.A.F., and before the war had been an engineer working for the firm of Rotol Ltd. He was shot down on a bombing raid over Germany. He liked to escape in an impromptu manner, on the impulse and alone. His best effort from Colditz was from the solitary confinement cells in the town. Returning from exercise, he stepped behind a door—it sounds so easy—and, while the guards marched upstairs to the cells, he marched downstairs, out, into the town, dressed as he was in mixed khaki and R.A.F. blue. Reaching Chemnitz, he thought himself conspicuous, so casually left his purloined bicycle at the kerb and entered the best hotel in the city. He walked into the lounge and over to a nice collection of coats hanging on a stand. He chose the best fitting one and walked out. Alas! The owner was not far behind him and that was the end of Bag's outing.

He was tall and thin, with a fair complexion and his temperament was essentially placid. He could not be ruffled— hence his alternative nickname, 'Ming.' When Bush was not hauling coal, playing cards or tasting liquor he was teasing the old Bag, but, in three years at Colditz he never succeeded in rousing him. Bag's placidity extended to his clothing. He disbelieved in the old adage, 'A stitch in time . . .' With a fatalism reminiscent of the East, when a button fell off, a shoe lace broke or a seam came apart, his shrug expressed the spirit enshrined in the words, 'Ins' Allah'—'Allah's will be done!' His equanimity reached distressing extremes when his bed caught fire as he lay on it. This happened frequently because he had a habit of dozing off in the afternoon with a lighted cigarette in his mouth. Scarlet O'Hara, who slept next to him, kept a bucket of water under his bed for the sole purpose of extinguishing Bag's fires—he may also have been tempted to use it sometimes when there was no fire. Bag would come to, soaked to the skin, while the acrid smell of burning hair mixed with smouldering straw and canvas dispersed itself through the room. Bag would stretch his long frame and rise slowly from the bed to say, between yawns, "Thanks Scarlet, old boy, but try and keep the water off my feet. You've soaked my only good pair of socks."

Bag was the Distilling Engineer. He was ever producing bigger and better stills at the expense of the Castle plumbing system. At other times he manufactured keys and tools of all kinds, beautifully finished and correctly tempered or case-hardened from pieces of iron bedsteads in the senior officers' quarters.

The three Directors ran their business on a barter basis and always had stock in hand to satisfy demands. An official exchange value, with a margin of profit, was placed on both sugar and raisins, and a given quantity of alcohol of any desired flavour handed over the counter for a given quantity of the two raw materials.

Flavour and colouring were the fruit of careful experiments under the direction of the Chemist. Very passable imitations could be purchased of gin, rum, crème de menthe and whisky.

Apart from the concentrated spirits, Good Time Charlie Goonstein and his mates displayed ingenuity in finding a use for the barrels upon barrels of almost uneatable 'jam' supplied by the Germans which littered the canteen and the camp kitchen. This was the stuff, already mentioned, made of sugar beet waste, dyed red, and distributed to prison camps all over Germany in barrels marked '*Nur für Kriegsgefangene*'.

The distillers transformed half a dozen casks into vats, where the 'jam' fermented, giving off a foul smell. The ferment was distilled to produce 'Jam-Alc'. Van Rood really deserved his nick-name for this 'speak-easy' alcohol. It tasted of old rubber tyres. The Company conscientiously tried to improve its quality, but, experiment how they would, even after three distillations, 'Jam-Alc' still tasted of rubber.

In spite of this gastronomic disability it had a ready sale,

at a low rate of exchange—for instance, three bottles of
Jam-Alc for a bucket of coal—among a clientele who seemed
able to stomach it without immediate undue ill effects. One
gay party, however, which began on Boxing Day, 1943, as
a fancy dress party, continued until February 29th, 1944.
Undoubtedly Jam-Alc played a part in the celebration of
such a happy and glorious anniversary as the fourth New
Year spent in a Nazi prison.

Coming round from it, after a debauch, was unpleasant.
So much so that the sufferer was tempted to return to the
comatose condition, rather than face the horrors of the no-
man's land which lay between him and sobriety. Jam-Alc
then became known as 'the needle' after the hypodermic
variety. One reveller spent New Year's Day sprawled on
the floor with his head in the lavatory pan. The cisterns
had been arranged to flush automatically as soon as they
filled. Every time a cold douch of water poured over his
head, he raised himself a few inches on one elbow to splutter, "Thanks ver' much, old boy—ver' kind of you," then
dropped his head again, ready for the next two gallons.

*   *   *   *   *

As 1943 dragged out its endless repetition of daylight and
darkness and as the significance of the capitulation of Stalingrad slowly sank into the reactionary recesses of the Teutonic mind, German morale became noticeably poorer.
Like the weeds which show themselves when a soil is badly
cared for, so the German temperament sprouted corruptive
practices when the selective weed-killer of propaganda lost
its force and hold upon the people.

Nineteen forty-three saw the birth and growth of the
corruption of the Colditz guards. In 1944, it grew to such
proportions and involved such a large quantity of the con-
sumable Red Cross foodstuffs, cigarettes and tobacco that
even a casual observer could deduce that the prisoners were
not obtaining value for money. There was undercutting,
throat cutting, Dutch auctioning and blackmail. There were

rings, cabals, cartels, subsidiaries, commodity monopolies, short and long term contracts and financing houses.

In the midst of this tumultuous sea rode 'Checko' in an unsinkable boat. Flight Lieutenant Ceňek Chalupka, R.A.F., was, metaphorically, made of cork. In the hey-day of Neville Chamberlain he flew for his country—Czechoslovakia. After Munich he flew for Poland; after Warsaw he made his way to France; and after Paris he flew for England. He was decorated by every nation for which he fought.

He was tall, dark and handsome and full of vitality. He spoke English with a catching accent in a manner that would rival Maurice Chevalier. How the women must have fallen for him!

He was the only prisoner in Colditz who could claim to have kissed a girl while imprisoned there. It happened in 1944. Checko was escorted to the dentist in the town for treatment. One look passed between him and the pretty German receptionist. It was enough. The next day she contrived to deliver to the camp a muffler Checko had 'inadvertently' left behind! She persuaded the Guard Commander to send for Checko to come to the prison gates. There, through a tiny grill in the massive oak, no bigger than the palm of a man's hand, the muffler and Cupid's dart passed simultaneously, and a pair of rosy lips presented themselves for their reward.

Checko was an adopted godson of Eric Linklater. Indeed, his was a character that would fit admirably into this famous author's portrait gallery; puckish, virile, humorous, dynamic, uproarious and explosive. Checko, in the course of 1943, flooded the Colditz market with maps, files and hacksaw blades; dye stuffs, photographic materials and coloured inks; stamps, identity papers and time tables; tools of every description, paints, plaster, cement and chemicals. He had rivals and he had difficulties. Racketeering among the French—until they left—was reaching alarming dimensions, and, whereas he concentrated as far as he could on the accessories of escape, he was up against firms that worked only for the bodily comforts of prisoners. Extra food and

fresh food, eggs, butter, cheese, vegetables and fruit, commanded high prices and threatened, at times, to run him
out of business. For a while he sailed with the wind, keeping his head, and gathered allies to his cause until public
opinion in the camp was eventually roused and came to the
rescue of those seeking escape, as opposed to luxury.

All this, however, did not happen in a day. Not until
December, 1944, did order develop out of chaos. David
Stirling—the tall Scotsman whose exploits as the Commander of 'L' Detachment, Special Air Service Regiment,*
are written in war history— was detailed by the S.B.O. to
co-ordinate and to regulate the Black Market activities of
Colditz. Prices came down with a crash, distribution became orderly and goods remained plentiful. In addition, by
way of bonus with every exchange, 'pieces' of Military
intelligence were collected. When these were all put together they solved the jigsaw puzzle of the local German
Command; the division of responsibility between Wehrmacht, Gestapo and Landwacht, the pressure groups and
personalities, the weight of weapons and military supplies
and the local forces that could be deployed. But this is
jumping ahead in time and sequence. . . .

Returning to the spring and early summer of 1943, when
racketeering was still in its infancy and the Goons were not
demoralised, one of the principal aims of the Colditz convicts was, naturally, to try to demoralise them by every
means possible. Goon baiting is a self-explanatory term. It
meant simply baiting the Goons. This activity, like distilling, gained impetus and attained dizzy heights in 1943.

There were few officers at Colditz who had not, at one
time or another, faced court-martial charges. There was,
generally speaking throughout the war, at least one officer
languishing in a solitary confinement cell under sentence
of death.

* 'L' Detachment eventually became the 2nd S.A.S. Regiment. The
S.A.S. should not be confused with the Long Range Desert Group, which
was under the command of (then) Lt.-Col. R. A. Bagnold until August,
1941, when it was taken over by Brig. G. L. Prendergast. Later, in 1944,
in Italy it was commanded by Lt.-Col. David Lloyd Owen.

Appeals took a long time and the first appeal was not usually successful.

No death sentence was, in fact, carried out from Colditz, but this did not lessen the heavy toll of suffering inflicted on the unfortunate ones imprisoned for years, alone with their thoughts and with the shadow of the shroud spreading over them. To die or not to die—that was their question. It was worse than knowing the final outcome because, during the eternity of months, there was hope manacled to frustration and utter impotence on the part of the prisoner to help himself. It is one thing, for instance, to struggle madly against death in the depths of the sea, but it must be a far worse agony to lie, pinioned and helpless, in the depths in a submarine, dependent on the help of others that may never come or which may, when it comes, be ineffectual.

The situation in which some of the prisoners thus found themselves became almost intolerable. They were spirited men of fine character, expiating no crime and the strain told heavily on their nerves. Some indeed were insane before they were finally reprieved. As far as is known, they have recovered.

Goon baiting was not therefore a pastime to be undertaken lightly. A little surreptitious baiting here and there was always good fun and the risks attached to it added to the excitement. But there were some who attached a more serious view to this side of prison life. Goon baiting was a weapon—of some potentiality in the prison 'cold war.' If wielded systematically and with perseverance, in a campaign extending over several consecutive months, its effect on the morale of the German garrison could be gauged. There were results. It paid dividends.

The waging of this cold war involved risks. The danger of a court-martial death sentence, with its accompanying anguish, was already real and proximate. In the heat of an argument with a German officer, the laying of a restraining hand upon the officer's sleeve was interpreted as 'a personal attack', punishable with death; the raising of an accusing finger close to his face became an insult, a menace; and if it touched his face it was 'an attack' punishable by death.

Happily for the prisoners, there was Lieutenant Alan Campbell, R.A., known as 'Black' Campbell. He had been training for the Bar before the war and devoted himself at Colditz to the defence in court-martial charges brought by the German High Command. Black, the heavy eyebrowed, black-haired sleuth with the hawk-like nose gave the German legal pundits no relaxation. When Black himself relaxed, it was to play the piano and write poetry. He had escaped from Tittmoning in broad daylight by climbing over the wire, while twenty-six assistants diverted the sentries armed with machine-guns.

The Germans would not supply him with a copy of their Army Code. He arranged for one to be ghosted out of the Kommandantur. He burnt the midnight oil over this frightening document, written in the heaviest of legal German, a language which, even in its simplest phraseology, lends itself to alternative translations. German is a tortuous language. Its meaning can be twisted and Black learnt, in time, to make good use of this flexible faculty. He quoted, for the benefit of the German barrister defending, usually a Dr. Naumann, passages of the Code which the Germans omitted to mention and he shook their confidence by his ability to beat them at their own game of weighting interpretations of text in their favour.

Altogether, he defended forty-two court-martial cases, including thirteen in which the charge was high treason and the sentence death; the plaintiffs being Czech officers flying for the R.A.F. He saved them on a point of International Law. It should be of interest to many and to legal circles in particular to read, one day, the story of his long, arduous battle of wits against the German High Command. He fought to ensure that a prisoner had access to his legal advisers in order to prepare his defence. At one period of the war, the number of acquittals he secured on account of his incisive verbal duelling, so incensed the Germans at Colditz that they packed him off to another camp—Span-

genberg. Within six months he had been caught under a
bridge at night, on his way out of his new prison. Sentries
shot at him with the aid of spotlights and he was only saved
by feigning death. He was returned to Colditz.

Among the many colourful characters he defended was
Flying Officer Peter Tunstall, R.A.F., who, in the course of
his sojourn in Germany, underwent five courts-martial with
an endless round of appeals and re-trials and paid the price
of four hundred and fifteen days of solitary confinement for
his convictions with regard to escaping and to the value of
Goon baiting. His last sentence of nine months, for 'insult-
ing the German nation,' was awarded too late for him to
carry it out. 'Pete,' a Hampton bomber pilot, was of medium
build, fair, with good features and pale blue eyes that had
a warning light. His mouth had a humorous curl that could
also convey defiance.

In one court-martial, Pete was offered honourable acquittal if he would state that there had been a misunderstanding between himself and the German N.C.O. concerned.
The case was one of assault with his index finger! Pete refused to make the statement, adding that the N.C.O., witness for the prosecution, was lying. A re-trial was ordered
and took place at Leipzig. The N.C.O. fainted during cross-
examination. Pete quickly seized a carafe of water off the
judge's desk and administered it to him, asking the judge,
a German general, not to press the poor fellow too hard
with awkward questions. Although the prosecution attempted to tamper with the written evidence of defending
British witnesses, the court awarded an acquittal. The only
spur that drove the Germans to show a semblance of justice
was the existence of the protecting power—Switzerland—
and the threat of 'Nach dem Krieg! After the war!' Black
insisted on handing all his briefs to the Protecting Power
representatives, when they visited the camp towards the end
of the war.

Scorgie Price, one of the said British witnesses, went to
Leipzig with intentions far removed from the simple resolution to see that justice was done. He went with the idea

of making a break. Although the opportunity never presented itself and the expedition was, as far as he was concerned, a failure, it is worth recording what he did.

He wore a standard army officer's service dress uniform
on which had been sewn sky-blue, silver embroidered
épaulettes; sky-blue collar badges and two, broad, sky-blue,
silver embellished stripes down the trouser legs. Rex Harrison and Scarlet O'Hara had gone 'all out' to produce a
'variety show' costume. A Frenchman had given him flam-
boyant, gilded aiguillettes to which he added red tassels.
His service dress cap was adorned with silver and blue
edging. Over this exotic uniform he wore a simple khaki
overcoat.

The German Regimental Sergeant Major, in command
of a heavy guard accompanying the court-martial party,
looked askance at what little of the uniform he noticed
under the bottom of the overcoat and on Scorgie Price's
head. But it was too late to remonstrate. Scorgie had timed
matters carefully. The team had to catch a train at the
station a mile from the camp. Senior German Staff Officers
would be waiting impatiently at Leipzig. Lieutenant Price
was a principal witness in the trial. Besides, the Sergeant
Major was assured that British officers always attended important functions in full dress uniform—if they possessed
it. Lieutenant Price's uniform was the correct ceremonial
dress of his regiment, the Gordon Highlanders. The Sergeant Major could check it, if he liked, but there was the
train to catch. . . .

The most important parts of Scorgie's outfit were not
visible even when he removed his overcoat. They consisted
of the credentials of a high ranking Hungarian officer on a
tour of inspection of frontier patrols. The *pièce de résistance* was a letter of introduction, beautifully forged, completed with the embossed crest of the German Foreign
Office and signed by none less than Baron von Neurath,
German Ambassador to Hungary.

The cortège returned from Leipzig with mixed feelings.
The acquittal of Peter Tunstall was a victory but the return

of Scorgie Price was a defeat. Scarlet O'Hara ruefully conceded where his allegiance lay, when he was heard to remark disconsolately, addressing his question to the heavens, "Is there no justice in this God-forsaken country!"

*   *   *   *   *

It must have been the advent of the horse-drawn fire brigade which put ideas into the heads of some of the Goon baiters. The German Commandant decided to hold a fire practice in the Castle courtyard. It was a ludicrous performance consisting merely of the entry into the yard, at a hearse-like pace, of a hearse-like fire engine drawn by two chestnut horses which looked as if they had pulled gun carriages in the First World War. Hoses were uncoiled. Orders were issued to shut all windows, whereupon weak jets of water rose towards the second floor while the firemen were soaked to the skin by cascading jets which spouted in all directions from the leaking canvas coils.

The rehearsal was quickly terminated. Amid hoots and jeers the fire engine retired. The prisoners could, obviously, seek no succour in that direction if a fire broke out. The fact that all windows were barred was a little discomforting —but thoughts of fire soon disappeared—ousted by rival and more congenial thoughts of the possibilities of water.

Peter Tunstall was among the first to use the water weapon. An identification parade was in progress in the courtyard, one morning, in the chilly early hours, after a major escape. The Dutch were lining up before a table at which sat Hauptmann Eggers—security officer, the official German interpreter, and a feldwebel behind a tall pile of files, card index forms, paper, pencils, ink, pens and blotting paper. A bucket of water was poured from a window high up in the wall, behind the seated officials. It drenched the Jerries and left the table a slippery mess of ink pools and sodden paper. Unfortunately for Peter, Hauptmann Priem was also in the courtyard and caught a sidelong view of the face of the culprit. He was 'clapped into jug' and, later, produced for court-martial on charges of: assaulting a superior in the course of his duty; causing a superior to take cover; causing confusion on a roll call parade, and breaking a prison camp rule prohibiting the throwing of water out of windows.

A sentence of two months' solitary—to run concurrently, did not prevent him from doing it again. On the second occasion he used an oversize water bomb. It was high summer and the German Camp Commandant appeared in a spotless white duck uniform, followed by five Germans in the brown uniforms of Nazi politicians, with massive leather belts encircling their paunches, their left arms swathed in broad, red armbands carrying the black Swastika in a white circle. Their shoulders, collars and hats were festooned with tinsel braid like Christmas trees. They were Gauleiters from Leipzig and Chemnitz.

The *Gefreite* called 'Auntie' ran ahead of them, up the British staircase, and burst into the mess room. Prisoners were having their tea and his shouts of "Achtung! Achtung!" were received with the usual compliment of 'raspberries' and rude remarks. Tea continued and his more frenzied "Achtungs" were ignored. The Commandant walked in at the head of the procession. He had expected everyone to be standing glassily at attention. Instead he had to wait three minutes; the time it took for the more ardent tea drinkers to note his presence 'officially.'

Benches and chairs scraped, mugs and plates clattered and men rose slowly to their feet wiping their mouths and blowing their noses with large khaki handkerchiefs in a studied display of insolence of finely calculated duration.

The Gauleiters raised their arms in the Nazi salute with their arms bent—Hitler fashion. The salute was returned by the members of one table including Scorgie Price and Peter Tunstall in a manner which appeared to please the Gauleiters. The prisoners saluted with a variation of the 'V' sign in which the fingers were closed instead of open and the thumb facing inwards. The Gauleiters, happy to think that their importance was appreciated, saluted again, and the salute was acknowledged again but with greater vigour.

As the procession passed between the rows of men standing
to at their tables, the cue was taken up and prisoners everywhere gave the new salute, which was acknowledged punc-
tiliously at every turn by the Gauleiters.

They turned, retraced their steps, saluting and being
saluted, beaming with smiles at their pleasant welcome and
finally left the quarters.

A water bomb just missed them as they emerged from
the British doorway, but spattered the Commandant's duck
uniform all over with mud. He shouted for the guard, hurried his visitors through the gates and returned alone. A
posse, despatched upstairs at the double to find the culprit,
was not quick enough. Pete was learning; nothing could be
pinned on him. The Commandant left the courtyard followed by cries of *"Kellner! Bringen Sie mir einen whisky
soda!"*

His exit signalled the arrival of the riot squad. Windows
were ordered to be closed; rifles were levelled upwards at
those delaying to comply with the shouted commands.
Scarlet O'Hara, sleeping peacefully beside an open window,
awoke from a siesta in time to hear the tail-end of the shouting. Poking his head out as far as the bars he cautioned the
squad: *"Scheissen Sie nicht,* my good men, *scheissen Sie
nicht!"* all to no avail. A bullet zipped through the opening
and he closed the window from a kneeling position cursing
the ill manners of the "uncouth b—— Huns." The word
he had pronounced was *scheissen,* not *schiessen.*

The Commandant never appeared again in his white
duck uniform.

*   *   *   *   *

International games of stoolball between the British and
other nationalities had not been popular in the early years
of the war. The game had no rules and no referee and the
Continentals were frankly not attuned to such a form of
competition.

Then the camp had decided, in 1942, to hold an Olympic
games. Stoolball was not included in the competitions. The

Olympics were a great success and it was thought, generally, a pity that stoolball had not been included.

The upshot was that some British officers conferred together, invented a few rules and produced a referee. British teams were pitted against one another, and the rules modified until they dovetailed with the circumstances and surroundings of the game. Then they were codified and published.

Once more the game was to become international. By that time, however, the Poles had gone, but the French started practice matches of their own with a British referee. Teams consisted of seven a side; scrums were broken up after a few minutes if there were signs of a deadlock and the ball thrown into the air; as before, the ball had to be bounced every three steps or passed in any direction.

A team was composed of three forwards, one half back, two full backs and a stoolie.

International matches soon became a monthly feature, and heavy betting took place on the results. For the British, the three forwards were chosen from Peter Storie Pugh, Checko, Dick Howe, Colin McKenzie and Howard Gee; the half backs from Allan Cheetham, Bush Parker and Peter Allan; the two full backs from Lulu Lawton, Willie Elstob and Sydney Hall—a Channel Islander, lumberjack and strong man of Colditz who, with one arm, once lifted an Australian orderly, Archer—a grandfather in the 1914–18 war, by his coat collar and hung him on a peg. The stoolie was usually Bill Goldfinch. Rupert Barry was the recognized international referee. The French team always included Edgar Barras and André Almeras.

The last international match of all, just before the French left Colditz in the early summer of 1943, was the most exciting game ever held in the courtyard. The whole camp, and a large number of Goons, turned out to watch it. The game resulted in a draw at four all. The Jerry spectators were as excited as the rest, some yelling for the British, others for the French.

Although stoolball was the excuse for a 'rough-house,'

played in a cobble stone courtyard, nobody hurt himself
seriously; Checko is recorded to have once broken a finger
during a dive for the stool over the top of a large scrum.

When the French left, enthusiasm for the game waned,
it was gradually replaced by basketball—known in Colditz
as 'dolleyball.' It lacked the verve and the rough and tumble
excitement of stoolball but was very fast. Bill Scott, a
Canadian captured in the Dieppe raid, had represented
Canada at basketball in Olympics before the war. He undertook coaching and was the moving spirit in popularising
the game. A league was formed. It provided scope for the
laying of odds, which the camp bookies, principally Hector
Christie and 'Screwie' Wright, were not slow to appreciate.

The bars on the courtyard windows saved them from
breakage by wide flung balls during the more hectic
moments of stoolball, but the Gothic chapel windows were
only protected by wire netting which was not tough enough
for the job. They were consequently often broken. The
Germans did nothing about it, preferring to replace the
broken panes on rare occasions rather than go to the expense
of stronger screens.

One day, shortly after the French farewell international
stoolball match, the courtyard gate opened to allow the
entry of a little man in grey overalls, known as Willie, carrying a long ladder and accompanied by the usual sentry to
look after him.

Peter Tunstall happened to be ambling across the courtyard at the time. He was rather at a loss to know what to do
with himself since the Franz Josef escape attempt in which
he had been one of the participants. The weather was fine
and warm. Spring had turned to summer and some
prisoners had even started sunbathing in the square of sunlight that carpeted the yard at noon.

Pete's normal relaxation, 'Goon baiting,' also seemed to
have 'hit a low' since the climax of the water bombing. He
was on the verge of one of those vacuums in a prisoner's life
when several months may pass in a procession of painfully
slow days, at the end of which the prisoner, waking up, can-

not account for the passage of time. There are no signposts and he appears to have been dreaming through a long, fitful slumber.

Pete sat down absent-mindedly on the stone steps near the canteen and idly watched Willie, an ordinary little workman, carrying a wooden rule, who now slowly climbed his long ladder which he had leant against the wall beside one of the chapel windows. Absent-mindedly Pete's gaze turned to the sentry who stood nearby.

"They're all alike," he muttered to himself, "can't pick out one in a hundred—wonder who thought of the name 'Goons'—just what they are."

Little Willie took measurements, climbed slowly down the ladder again, spoke to the sentry, and walked off towards the courtyard gate.

Peter saw him disappear, wondering vaguely why he had gone away. 'Suppose he's gone to fetch the glass.' Then his eye roamed once more towards the sentry. The latter was standing stolidly on guard five yards from the ladder and facing the courtyard.

The reaction of a well-trained 'Kriegie' was instantaneous. Peter rose; the vacuum had filled. There was a glint in his eye. He returned hurriedly to the British quarters and buttonholed the Weasel (Don Donaldson), who in turn shouted towards a far corner of the almost empty room.

"Heh!—come over here, you browned-off eagle—I want to talk to you—quick."

Bag Dickenson yawned and slowly rose from a bed in the corner. "Are you addressing me?" he queried, tucking his shirt into his trousers as he walked over. He sat on a bed opposite the other two. "You've upset my sleep quota, you rocky mountain buzzard."

. . . A few minutes later they descended together to the courtyard where they separated.

Don sat down on the cobbles. There was nothing unusual about that. He sat near the sentry, upright, against a wall and facing him. He started playing with his hands. Looking

wide-eyed into the sky, he made his hands climb Jacob's
ladders; he played churches and people and the preacher in
the pulpit; he made his hands into mice which chased each
other all over his body, behind his back, round his neck,
under his shirt and up his trouser legs; he counted his

Peter Tunstall and Bag Dickenson remove the ladder

fingers and started all over again. He not only attracted the
gaze of the sentry but that of a small group of mildly amused
spectators whom he had to motion away so that the Goon's
view was not obstructed.

In the meantime, Peter Tunstall and Bag Dickenson removed the ladder which they carried into the porch at the
bottom of the British staircase, behind the sentry's back.

They started to climb the spiral steps but found that the twenty-five foot ladder would not circumvent the curves.

It became securely wedged. There was only one solution which did not require much thought. While the browned-off eagle fetched a saw (made out of gramophone spring) from his tool kit, which was the best in Colditz, Pete returned to the courtyard and signalled the Weasel to carry on. This was asking for something because Don was not prepared for a long solo act. Pete could see his mind turning over as his eyeballs rolled, following the juggling motion of his hands. He left him to it and went back to the staircase, where Bag and he were soon engaged in an argument as to how much of the ladder should be sawn off. Bag was playing for safety while Pete insisted on running it close. They compromised at five feet from one end.

It took ten minutes to saw through both legs of the ladder, which they did to the accompaniment of generally encouraging, but sometimes very rude, remarks from passers-by navigating the obstruction on the stairs.

Pete was wondering what the Weasel was doing and how soon Willie might return. He was delighted to see, when he descended to the courtyard with a five-foot length of ladder under his arm, that the little fellow had not yet come back and that the Weasel's knot of spectators had grown. Don was finding great difficulty in clearing a view for the sentry who was genuinely intrigued by his efforts to scratch his left ear with his right foot.

Pete leaned the five foot length of ladder where the twenty-five foot one had previously reposed and retired to a distance to view the effect. At that moment little Willie was let into the courtyard again, carrying a large square pane of glass carefully in his arms. Don, seeing that his act was no longer required, stood up with a final handspring and walked off hurriedly to the French quarters. The knot of idlers was dispersing when the new focus of attention presented itself. The sentry and little Willie stood, side by side, gazing incredulously, with jaws dropped, at a transformation of which Lewis Carroll might have been proud.

The prisoners started to laugh. The sentry shook his head slowly from side to side and Willie looked up and down the chapel wall. They faced each other and Willie asked, *"Was ist geschehen?"* A crowd was gathering and the laughter was growing. The sentry answered, shrugging his shoulders and looking frightened as if he had seen a ghost. *"Ich weiss nicht. Sie war bestimmt hier. Ist da veilleicht ein Poltergeist?"*

Little Willie laid the pain of glass against the wall, took out a large handkerchief, mopped his brow and blew his nose to recover his composure. It was not easy. There were faces now at almost every window, and laughter was echoing round the courtyard. He and the sentry were the only figures on the stage, playing before a large audience.

He approached the five-foot ladder, picked it up, turned it over and adjusted it under his arm. The sentry, crestfallen, picked up the glass, fell in behind him and, in single file, they marched forlornly across the courtyard through a gangway formed between cheering prisoners.

CHAPTER XI

THE FLYING DUTCHMEN

ON June 7th, 1943, the Dutch contingent received orders to pack up and leave at twelve hours' notice. This did not perturb them as they had known of the move for a week through information passed inside the camp. Their contraband was safely stowed in prepared suitcases. One Dutchman packed his suitcase for the last time in Colditz. He had packed it every morning and unpacked it again every night for two years.

The Dutch were bound for Stanislau, in Poland. Their departure would mean the end of a long chapter in the story of Oflag IV.C; a story of close collaboration with the British, of unfailing understanding and generosity, of courage and good humour. They would be missed everywhere in the camp. The smartest 'turn out' on parade, and in chapel; their divine contempt of the Germans; the Hawaian orchestra would be no more; Vandy's inimitable personality would disappear from the Castle and only his ghost would haunt the corridors in the minds of the men who remained. Soon, even those memories would fade, but, for all who knew Vandy and his Dutchmen well, they can never fade entirely. A pleasant aura surrounds them to this day, and an honoured place remains for them in those inner recesses of the mind where narrow distinctions fade but a deep impression rests. As the tracks left by a stream of vehicles which pass along a sandy road twist and intertwine and eventually merge into two great ruts, so the mind recollects an episode, a chapter, an era that has long since passed.

The whole camp turned out to see them off.

"We'll miss you, Vandy," said Dick.

"I'm *rather* sorry to go," replied Vandy, who was obviously deeply moved. "Ve may haf a chance to escape on the vay. I haf many men prepared. Good-bye, Dick. Ve had good times together. In Colditz ve haf shown those Huns how to behave themselves."

"Yes!" said Dick, "it's funny, isn't it, how well they've behaved in Colditz considering the hell we give them."

"Ach! Dick, that is the secret. You must alvays give them

Vandy

hell. If you do not you are finished. The Hun, he vill sit on you and sqvash you and bully you to death, unless you bully him. He only understands that. I was in camps before I came to Colditz. There I saw vot happened. Germans despised the prisoners and gave them hell. Here it was otherwise. You vere all brave men—you had proved it—and you gave them hell from the virst days. So, they respect you and are afraid to bully. It is a simple qvestion of domination by vorce of the character. Do not vorget! Good-bye, Dick . . . and Gott bless England! . . ."

So, the irrepressible Vandy, the officer in charge of all the Dutch escapes but never of his own, departed.

Hardly had Vandy left the courtyard with his men, to be searched in the Kommandantur before entraining, than he gave expression to his deep convictions with regard to the Germans. His large suitcase was a maze of secret pockets, and had a false bottom filled with escaping contraband. The Germans took from the open suitcase an army over-coat, the collar of which Vandy had altered and dyed for civilian purposes. Speaking German fluently and with a fine colloquial vocabulary, equal to that of any *Wehrmacht* sergeant major, he seethed with indignation, mounted a stool and harangued the whole room. He would not move without his coat. He would lie on the floor and they would have to carry him. How right Vandy was! The Germans knew that he would lie on the floor. They knew that bayonets would not move him. It was 'vorce of character' all right. The major in charge gave in and his men were sufficiently subdued by Vandy's oratory and by his deter-mination, not to look further into his belongings.

The fifty-eight Dutchmen voyaged for four days in two old-fashioned railway coaches, crammed together like sar-dines. The Colditz guards, numbering thirty-three, under the command of a Hauptmann, stood at the windows of the compartments and along the corridor. The windows were plastered with barbed wire. On the evening of the second day, near Feschen on the Polish border, while water bottles were being filled at a stop, Baron van Lynden, a cavalry lieutenant and an aide-de-camp of Queen Wilhelmina, escaped. He was soon missed, and the German Captain of the Guard, stopping the train at Krakau, refused to con-tinue further without guard reinforcements from the local garrison. Twenty more guards were piled into the coaches on the third evening and remained with them until they reached Lemberg (Lwow). The party reached their destina-tion, without further incident, at the end of the fourth day.

Stanislau is an industrial town in the province of Galicia, in the South East of Poland. The camp to which they were conducted was two miles from the railway station. It had once been an Austrian cavalry barracks and later a Polish prison. On their arrival at the station they were met by a German officer with a bicycle. The Colditz Hauptmann flatly refused to escort the prisoners to the camp without adequate supervision; thirty-three guards were not enough. Again, reinforcements arrived from the prison. The fifty-seven Dutchmen were then marched, in four squads at intervals, surrounded by a total of fifty-six guards and eight N.C.O.s and led by two officers, along the Adolf Hitler Strasse, the main street of Stanislau. Silent, sympathetic Poles, clustered on the pavements in small groups to watch them pass. They arrived at the camp singing patriotic Dutch songs and were delighted to see Dutch faces at the windows to greet them. They were all officers and cadets of the Dutch forces who had remained in Holland on a bogus *parole* at the beginning of the war. In May, 1942, one hundred of them had been shot for underground activities and about two thousand had been transported to Stanislau. Their morale was not good, but the influence of men like Vandy changed the atmosphere of the prison within a matter of weeks.

Vandy had his showdown with the Prussian Abwehr officer of Stanislau immediately on arrival. The latter was showing off in front of the Captain and the guards from Colditz and began browbeating the prisoners. He 'went for' a lieutenant in Vandy's platoon and 'caught a packet' himself for addressing a junior officer in the squad under the command of a more senior officer. Vandy took the opportunity, with righteous indignation on his side, to explode with anger and concluded by appealing in German to the Colditz Hauptmann who was handing over his assignment. The Colditz sentries thoroughly enjoyed the situation.

"Herr Hauptmann, is it not your experience from Colditz that we prisoners have always behaved with correctness and decorum because the German officers have treated the prisoners in the same manner?"

The Hauptmann could only answer "Yes", although he was still smarting under the loss of one of his prisoner contingent.

This collusion left the Stanislau Abwehr officer at a loss. Vandy believed in attacking from the start and never letting go, once he had the advantage.

To emphasise the contempt in which the Dutchmen held the Germans of Stanislau, and the Abwehr officer in particular, three of the the Colditz party escaped from the first floor of the building within an hour of arrival. The windows overlooked a drop of twenty feet and beyond that a garden and the highway to Hungary The drop, was, nevertheless, too much for two of the three who twisted their ankles in the fall. A window collapsed with a crash of splintering glass at the psychological moment and gave the alarm. Otherwise all the Dutchmen would have disappeared within ten minutes.

The two men with twisted ankles were recaught immediately, but the third, Van Lingen, was free several days before he was recaptured in the Carpathian mountains, having asked for food at the farm of a *Volksdeutscher*, by mistake.

Van Lynden, who had escaped from the train, was recaught after some days at Görlitz, and returned, at first, to Colditz much to the amusement of the inmates. He remained in the cells for a week before removal to Stanislau.

Vandy was soon recognised in the camp as 'Escape Chief.' Among the younger officers, and especially the cadets who had been incarcerated in 1942, there was a feeling that they had been duped, by their seniors in Holland, into betraying their country by giving them *parole*. They had little confidence left in those around them. The advent of the Colditz diehards caused a spiritual rejuvenation among them, and the blood of patriots began to course, once more, through their veins.

The camp was separated into two halves; the officers

being kept apart from the cadets (aspirants). Vandy placed one of his most trusted cadets, Aak Hageman, in charge of escape matters in their barracks. The morale of the whole camp rose steadily throughout the summer and autumn of 1943.

On November 30th, three more Dutchmen escaped. One, travelling alone, made his way to Hungary and later to London. The other two, former Colditz men, Charles Douw van der Krap and Fritz E. Kruimink, nicknamed Beer by the English, reached Warsaw, where they disappeared into Bor Komorowski's underground. Beer was eventually despatched to Paris where he fought with the French Resistance and took part in the relief of Paris.

Van der Krap and an Englishman were stopped by a German sentry, one evening, on a bridge over the Vistula in Warsaw. He demanded their papers. While he was examining Douw's, the Englishman gave him a right to the jaw which sent him over the balustrade, into the river and through the ice. The next day the Germans found the body under the ice and Douw's papers lying nearby. The Poles thought it was time he moved. With typical *sang froid* they sent him as a fireman on the engine of a German military train which carried him back to Holland. Van der Krap took part in the Battle of Arnhem and was rescued with the few survivors of the Airborne Division who were helped back to the Allied lines.

Then came the 'big move' on January the 10th, 11th and 12th, 1944. It was public knowledge when it came and was, in fact, considered to be rather late in the day as the Germans in Stanislau were terrified of a Russian advance long before January. This time the move was to a huge camp at Neu Brandenburg in Mecklenburg, a hundred miles north of Berlin, housing Americans, French, Poles and Serbs in different compounds.

Vandy and his second in command, Lieutenant Dames, made the escape preparations and gave Hageman the assistance he needed to organise the cadets. In general, the intention was not to make a break on the journey unless a reasonable opportunity presented itself; the new camp was reputed to have good possibilities. However, before leaving Stanislau, there were several escape schemes on hand, to be put into immediate action.

Vandy and Dames first concealed twelve men under the floor of their theatre auditorium. Secondly, they equipped six others to re-enact the escape of Douw and Beer in 1943, which had depended on the help of Yugoslavian orderlies. Four of the six were Colditz men, the fifth non-Colditz, and the sixth, a Dutch Rear Admiral. Thirdly, among the cadets, four men, of whom two from Colditz, were also concealed in the camp before departure.

The move was organised by the Germans, in three batches, one on each of the three consecutive days.

The cadets departed on the first day. Before leaving, the Abwehr officer made a speech. He said that it was no use trying to escape because: (a) it was mid-winter with snow everywhere, (b) their boots would be removed on the train, and (c) he had transported thirty thousand Italians from Italy without a single escape. This incredibly tactless approach was enough for the cadets.

When they arrived at Neu Brandenburg there were sixty-eight missing. Many more had escaped but had been re-captured at various stations and put on the train again. A German sentry, who spent hours shooting at the cadets as they escaped, said afterwards that the men leaving the train reminded him of a game of Tiddlywinks.

On the second day the Senior officers left. One escaped on the way to the station and hid in a culvert. He was seen by a guard who fired twice into the culvert, wounding him seriously. He was transported back to the Stanislau camp.

On the journey, the same guard shot and killed another Dutchman who had made a hole through the floor of his wagon and lay between the tracks waiting for the train to move off after a stop in the open country.

A third officer jumped the train, fell and remained un-conscious on the track. A train, passing in the other direction, cut off both his legs. In addition, forty-four others escaped.

The next day, the third batch, including the Colditz group, travelled. Thirty escaped. On the way, the third train, like a trawl net, picked up those recaptured after escaping from the first two trains. The Dutchman who had lost his legs was taken on board. His case was given up as hopeless by German doctors, but a Dutch surgeon attended him in Neu Brandenburg, day and night for a week, and saved his life.

The move was a major disaster for the Germans. When they counted up the totals at the end of three days, one hundred and fifty prisoners were missing.

A special alarm was broadcast covering Germany and Poland. Hitler was advised of the escape and Himmler's minions were set to their work of extermination. The code name for the order was known to the Gestapo as the order 'Stufe Drei.'

It was many a day before Vandy could add up the final score of this escape. It went somewhat like this:

1. The twelve who were hidden in the theatre had to give themselves up after a week as the camp remained fully guarded though empty. They followed the main body to Neu Brandenburg.

2. Of the six who escaped (including the admiral) two, the Admiral and Diederik Baron van Lijnden (ex-Colditz) reached Roumania with identity papers and exit and entry visas supplied to Vandy through his wife from the Dutch underground. They were freed by the Russians and sent to England. The other three (ex-Colditz), including Captain Veenendaal, R.N.I.A., and Lieutenant Donkers, R.N.I.A., reached the Dutch border where they were trapped. The sixth was recaught on the Czecho-Slovak frontier. They were all later forwarded to Neu Brandenburg.

3. Of the four cadets who hid in Stanislau before the move: one reached Hungary, was released by the Rus-

sians and found his way to England; one was recaught
and sent back to Stanislau where he disappeared, and two
ex-Colditz men, Hans von Seydlitz, Kurzbach, and Aire
Ligtermoet escaped to Russia, where they were imprisoned along with Germans. Ligtermoet, who died in
Odessa in 1947, was awarded a posthumous decoration.
Von Seydlitz is still missing.

4. Ten officers including the officer wounded in the
culvert and the cadet from 3 above were submitted to
'Stufe Drei', and one officer was shot dead under the
train.

5. In spite of the snow on the Carpathian mountains
and the absence of boots on their feet, seven men reached
Hungary.

6. Three more arrived safely in Holland and two
reached Switzerland via Vienna.

Totalling up: one hundred and sixty-four men attempted
to escape, of whom fifteen made home-runs, eleven were
murdered, one had his legs cut off, two died in Russian
prisons, and one hundred and thirty-seven were recaptured.

*   *   *   *   *

Within eight days of arriving at Neu Brandenburg, on
January 22nd, the first escape, organised by Vandy and
Dames, took place. Twelve men, seven of them from
Colditz, disappeared from the camp. One, ex-Colditz, named
Fraser, reached England via Sweden; one is missing; one
was executed, and the remainder returned to Neu Braden-
burg.

These men were incorrigible.

A new block of eleven solitary confinement cells had to
be constructed beside the old, rotten, timber frame Barracks in which they were housed in this camp. The cells
remained fully occupied into the autumn of 1944.

In September 1944, many of the older officers were moved
to a camp at Tittmoning, not far from Salzburg in Austria,

owing to the damp, unhealthy conditions existing in Neu Brandenburg.

The record of Vandy's sixty-four officers and cadets, mostly of the Dutch East Indies Forces, who were sent from Holland in 1940 to Colditz via another camp—Juliusburg, is here set down.

Thirteen made home-runs; two others reached Russia, one is dead, one missing; and, in addition, this company can lay claim to twenty-six 'gone-aways.'

CHAPTER XII

ROUNDABOUT

THE summer was in full course when the French, at last, after several false starts, received orders to pack in preparation for a move. They were going north-eastward to Lübeck where the Poles had gone. The move was to include the Belgians but left behind, temporarily, a second batch of eighty French for whom there was no room on the first train. The second batch also included a few de Gaullist Frenchmen who, eventually, remained permanently.

Shortly after the departure of the main French body, sixty-five British Officers arrived from Oflag VII.B, Eichstätt. This raised the total of the British contingent to about one hundred and sixty souls.

The Eichstätt mob, as they were sometimes called, comprised the men who had broken out of their camp by tunnel on the night of the 3rd–4th June.

The tunnel was well engineered and was about forty-five yards long. Unfortunately, none of the sixty-five who escaped made the home-run.

After completing their bout of confinement, during which three made another break, they were despatched to Colditz in several parties. The three who made the second break were Gordon Rolfe, D.S.O. (Major, Royal Canadian Signals), Bill (Dopey) Miller (Lieutenant, Royal Canadian Engineers) and Douglas Moir (Lieutenant, Royal Tank Regiment). They did not travel far and soon turned up at Colditz.

Among those who arrived from Eichstätt were: Mike Edwards (Lieutenant, R.W. Fusiliers), George Drew (Lieutenant, Northamptonshire Regiment), Charles Forester (Lieutenant, Rifle Brigade), Bill Scott, M.C. (Lieutenant, Essex Scottish, Canada), John Penman, M.C., Lieutenant, Argyll and Sutherland Highlanders) and Lieutenant

Colonel C. C. I. Merrit, V.C. (South Saskatchewan Regiment). Captains, the Lord Arundell of Wardour (Wiltshire Regiment) and the Earl of Hopetoun (Lothian and Border Horse), were also Eichstätt tunnellers who trickled into Colditz.

Others who arrived at about this period were Charlie Upham, V.C. and bar, the New Zealander, Tony Rolt, the motor-racing driver, and Michael Burn, M.C., *The Times* reporter who had been captured at St. Nazaire.

The opportunity offered by the move of a large party was not lost upon the old hands in the camp. When the Poles had left in 1942, Bertie Boustead had changed places with Count Felix Jablonowski.

Bertie Boustead was tall and thin and exchanged with Felix Jablonowski who was of small build. Boustead knew no Polish but learnt off by heart his Polish prison number. During the departure proceedings, each time the name Jablonowski was called, he stepped forward and, in reply to whatever the German interpreter asked him in Polish, he said, "*Trzysta Pięcdziesiąt Siedem*"—which was Felix's prison number—357. It did not matter what the interpreter asked. He always obtained the same answer. The Germans made a habit of asking for the prisoners' numbers, so that Bertie managed to 'get away with it' on the final parade and again in Lübeck, the camp to which he was sent with the Poles.

After a week, Bertie's name was called out at *Appell*. The Germans wanted some information about a parcel addressed to Jablonowski. The interpreter asked in Polish, "What are the contents of the parcel?"

Bertie replied, "*Trzysta Pięcdziesiąt Siedem*." The interpreter asked him a second and a third time, but always received the same answer: "*Trzysta Pięcdziesiąt Siedem*." The comedy could not last long. The Germans checked up on Jablonowski's particulars and Bertie had 'had it'.

At Colditz, Felix was soon busy answering a string of awkward questions in atrocious English. He was 'rumbled' and an exchange of prisoners took place causing the Goons much annoyance. Neither Felix nor Bertie managed to escape on the journey, which was the purpose of the whole subterfuge, owing to the number of guards employed—an N.C.O. and two sentries to each prisoner.

This exchange had now passed into history. The only memory which remained vivid was that of Felix Jablon-owski sitting up in his bunk on his first morning in the British quarters wearing a hair-net. He had to be told that the practice might make him conspicuous.

When the Eichstätt British arrived, Dick immediately prepared an exchange with some of the French still at Colditz who were due to leave any day. The faces of the 'old lags' were too well known to the Germans, but some of the 'new boys' might be exchanged successfully.

Lieutenant Cazamayou and two other Frenchmen quickly responded to the idea and three promising-looking British officers among the new arrivals were picked out. They were Lieutenant T. M. Barratt, The Black Watch (R.M.R.) of Canada, commonly known as Jo-Jo the Dog Faced Boy, who took the place of Cazamayou, and Lieutenant D. K. Hamilton, R.A., and Lieutenant C. E. Sandback, Cheshire Yeomanry.

These three left Colditz with the last French contingent. They had no opportunities for escaping *en route*. They arrived at Lübeck, where there was a huge French camp, and were soon lost in the crowd. They began reconnoitring for an escape. It was high summer—July. The weather was fine and dry, most suitable for a long trek across country but, within four days, Hamilton and Sandback were un-earthed, evidently from the Colditz end. The discovery would have come about through photograph identity checks on the Eichstätt men in Colditz, which were due in any case.

Peter Barratt, however, appeared to have a respite. He knew it would not be for long, so he arranged with one of his French colleagues from Colditz to make a further ex-change if his name was called. The next day it was. Sous-Lieutenant Diedler presented himself as Lieutenant Barrett, and was whisked back to Colditz with Hamilton and Sandback.

Barratt was caught a few days later leaving the Lübeck camp under a pile of sacks in a cart. He was escorted to the Kommandantur, where he gave his name as Diedler and was marched off to the cells.

The next morning he was cross-examined about his attempted escape, and the German-French interpreter began to think he was dealing with a moron. Barratt knew well enough how to say, *"La plume de ma tante,"* but his French lessons at school had not provided for the present contingency.

He was soon unmasked.

The Germans were confronted with a problem. They had already disposed of a Lieutenant Barratt under the alias of Lieutenant Cazamayou. Now they had a second Lieutenant Barratt under the alias of sous-Lieutenant Diedler. They even began to have misgivings as to the seriousness of the name Diedler. It had an ironic, Anglo-Saxon ring. They unravelled the mystery eventually, but it annoyed them considerably, just as it amused the Frenchmen at Lübeck, to know that the prisoners were playing with them.

*   *   *   *   *

The companionship of men like Gigue and Madin, of the French stoolball players, and the French language teachers was badly missed in Colditz, but their memory was kept alive by the wireless set the French left behind. Dick took over the control of the secret studio. Lulu Lawton and Hector Christie, together, organised the stooging teams required for the periods of news reception and the routine camouflaging of the secret entrance to the studio.

Michael Burn, adept at shorthand, became the first news reporter. He was known as 'The Scribe'.

The operation of entering or leaving the studio took five minutes. Stooges were posted on each of the four floors of the building, two more in the courtyard and one at the entrance to the upper attics where the studio was concealed. The last stooge held the key and was responsible for the door through which passed the operator—Dick, the scribe —Mike, and the camouflage-man—Lulu. The three crossed two more attics. Lulu went to work at a point where the roof beams and the attic floor joined. Floorboards were removed, then a sawn length of timber joist, then a four-inch depth of under-floor rubble and, finally, more boards. The operator and scribe descended into the studio. Lulu replaced all camouflaging as he worked, and then retired. The heavy layer of dust over everything in the attic was a great bugbear and necessitated careful treatment. A knocking signal at the end of fifteen or twenty minutes warned the stooges that the news reception was over. The process would be repeated to extract the two officers from the studio. Mike then retired to a quiet nook, enlarged on his shorthand notes and prepared his bulletin. When this was ready he called together his assistant news reporters from their various quarters and copies were made from his original.

As the Allied pressure increased from 1944 onwards, news bulletins were demanded ever more frequently and the work became too much for one team to carry out efficiently. The studio operation, in fact, was carried out so frequently that the danger of over-confidence or staleness on the job became very real. The team consisted of no less than eleven officers. Dick decided to institute a second team. He trained Jimmy Yule as operator. Jim Rogers, who had been studying shorthand furiously as soon as he saw his principal joy in life being taken from him by a news reporter who was proficient in this art, was appointed scribe of the new team, to his intense satisfaction. Norman Forbes undertook the camouflage work, Hector Christie trained a second team of stooges.

In the event of being trapped in the attics or studio, two methods of escape were available, depending on where the Germans were.

When the French tunnel had been discovered, the ropes which had been used by the French for the disposal of their tunnel debris were removed, leaving the long cylindrical sleeves from the top of the tower to ground floor empty. There was access to the sleeves from the attic.

In effect, the radio team of three had a fast-descending lift at their service. A piece of iron plate reposed over the sleeves at each floor level. If an alarm was given when all three were in the attic above the studio, they waited until the last moment, in case of false alarms. As soon as they heard the German keys in the attic lock (and having checked that the iron plates were in place!), they dropped, one after the other, down the cylindrical sleeves, using their arms and thighs as brakes. An exit was, nowadays, conveniently provided by the Germans two floors below—they used it for inspection purposes. All three could, thus, descend two floors in a matter of seconds and sortie by the exit into their own quarters. The safe descent of the sleeves required practice, because, if the braking was not sufficient, the body accelerated downwards and a heavy fall could result. Of course, if the iron plates were not over the holes there was the prospect of a vertiginous descent, out of control, to the ground floor.

If the operator and scribe were ever to be actually trapped in the studio there was a last line of retreat. The studio reposed, partly over the solid outside wall, partly over the ceiling of the (now) British quarters. The joists and ceiling lathes were exposed in the studio and the latter could be broken in an emergency simply by jumping on them. The operators would then fall into the room below. In the event of surprise, they could, at least, save the wireless set by the emergency exit. Fortunately, this method of evacuating the studio never had to be used. The sleeve self-propelled lift, on the other hand, was frequently employed as the Germans made surprise searches of the attics. Although its existence was known, the whereabouts of the wireless set remained a secret from the Germans until the end of the war.

The electric power for the receiving set was tapped from the Castle mains. The supply was 220 volts d.c., that is, direct current. The set was manufactured to work on 110 volts d.c., and a dropping resistance had, therefore, to be employed in the circuit. The mains supply was switched off by the Germans at night, but this obstacle was circumvented by tapping the positive lead, using it as supply, and by earthing the negative lead to a lightning conductor.

All went well until the R.A.F. and the U.S.A.A.F. set about obliterating the power stations. Then, for long periods, there was no power at all.

The prisoners had to have their news. Dick and the scribes were in a quandary.

Officers used to mess together in groups of between seven and ten, depending upon how many could be conveniently seated around the various-sized kitchen tables which were provided. A group seldom remained more than a few months together. The petty exasperations that pass in everyday life were liable to accumulate, to combine and become distorted into grotesque catastrophes, causing major upheavals in the stifling conditions of the prison. One group alone is known to have remained constant throughout the war. Its members were Padre 'Dicky' Heard, Harry Elliott, Kenneth Lockwood and Dick Howe. They formed a durable nucleus at their mess table around which others gyrated, sometimes attracted, sometimes repelled. It was to be expected that the variety of topics of conversation was gradually exhausted as the war continued until, among the old guard when at table, there was scarcely any object in conversing. It was as if each could read the mind of the other.

Even mannerisms were so well known that their subconscious motivation was understood. Questions could be answered before they were asked. When Dick Howe stroked his nose he was given a cigarette, because that was what he would have asked for in a few seconds' time. If Harry twirled his moustache with one hand and stared momentarily into space, his table companions sat back, wondering which of his many funny stories Harry was about to tell. If he stroked his moustache with both hands, the question was, 'Which Goon has got your back up this time, Harry?' because, indeed, that was what he was going to disclose. When Padre Heard coughed gently twice, it meant he wanted 'A pinch of salt, please,' and he was given it, usually, before the words came to his lips. When he gazed fixedly out of a nearby window overlooking the chapel it was understood by his colleagues that his remarks, in a few minutes' time, would concern the chapel organ and he would relate how the Germans never repaired the bellows nor the missing keys and stops.

The association of ideas—the sequence of thoughts that fill up the mental activity of man is like the pathway in a labyrinth. New openings and news paths appear at every turn, tempting the mind to travel along them. Concentration is, presumably, the art of not being deflected, or of consciously noting the deflection so as not to take the wrong path a second time.

Dick Howe was certainly not concentrating when he sat, one day, at the mess table mentally bemoaning another power cut that had ruined the whole day's news bulletins. He was staring vacantly in the direction of Dicky Heard who, in turn, was staring fixedly out of the window. Dick was suddenly thinking about organs and then about bellows, then about electric motors and then generators. At this point there must have been a short circuit somewhere in his mind because Dick jumped as if he had been electrocuted and banged the board in front of him with his fist. "I've got it!" was all he said and left the table.

He repaired to the chapel, mounted the miniature spiral staircase that led to the choir loft and examined the electric motor that worked the bellows that worked the organ.

'If the Jerries won't repair the bellows,' he thought, 'we may as well, at least, make use of the motor.'

Electricity supplied to an electric motor turns it. If an electric motor is turned by other means it can supply electricity. Upon this simple principle Colditz wireless news reception was made independent of a mains supply of current. The prisoners built their own power station!

Dick 'borrowed' the organ motor. It was wired into a closed circuit through the ordinary wiring of the camp in such a way as to feed the radio. The motor, when required, was produced from a hiding-place and bolted on to a firm platform. Bos'n Crisp provided a rope pulley belt, fifty feet long, which fitted the 'V' section rim of the motor

The Treadmill

pulley. A large wooden, collapsible, driving-wheel was manufactured. It was five feet in diameter, made in three segments, bolted together, and it was mounted on trunnions attached to a cupboard which was laid flat on the floor in the dormitory. When not in use, the cupboard resumed the vertical and the wheel was dismantled. The trunnions and wheel segments were transformed into shelves, angle-pieces, back boards and loose, nondescript pieces of wood.

The wheel was known as the treadmill and it amply

deserved the name, because the reduction gear ratio to the generator pulley was, as might be expected, not sufficient to provide the generator speed necessary for the current required, without immense exertion on the part of relays of the camp's strong men. The power plant worked well. The background interference of the unsmoothed current was noticeable, though not disturbing. Its volume depended on the steadiness of the output which depended, in turn, on the freshness of the slaves.

After severe bombing raids the slave-gang, consisting of men such as Checko, Charles Lockett and Mike Edwards, was called out for work on the treadmill in order to provide the camp with the 'news' and the Radio Parson's bulletins, precious links with the outside world and with reality. What would the Radio Parson think! What might have been his thoughts had he known, as he came over the air, that men were sweating at a home-made treadmill to turn a chapel organ motor in order to feed a wireless set so that they could hear the gospel he was preaching! Could he have heard the swearing and the groaning of the perspiring slaves! Could he have seen the glow of the tell-tale lamp in the parallel circuit as it rose and fell, accompanied by the voice of the foreman of the slave-gang—now cautioning "Slower!" then urging, "Faster! Faster!" and ending with, "Steady at that speed!" as the intensity of light indicated the strength of current being produced.

There were several reasons why the men in Colditz went to such pains to ensure that no news bulletin was ever missed, but it may be revealing to mention one reason in particular. It was imperative that no report of the capture or surrender of any town to the Allies should be overlooked. Large sums of money were involved for the lucky holders of winning tickets in the continuously running 'Town Falling' sweepstake.

CHAPTER XIII

WALLY AND TUBBY

NEWS concerning the men who escaped successfully from Colditz in 1941 and 1942 trickled into the camp slowly and was sketchy when it arrived, to say the least of it. Nevertheless, when it came, it boosted the prisoners' morale considerably. A first wave of elation started about a week after an escape, when, with the continued absence of the escapers and glum reactions from the Germans upon questioning by the S.B.O. as to their whereabout, it was reasonably safe to assume that the men were out of enemy territory, provided they had not been killed *en route*.

Reliable confirmation arrived by various routes: sometimes a picture postcard slipped through the censor's net, written in a disguised hand from a fictitious character, but leaving no uncertainty in the mind of the recipient as to the meaning of the seemingly innocuous phrases in the text.

Hank Wardle, often called Murgatroyd by Rupert Barry, had thus written to him from Switzerland in November, 1942:

> '*We are having a holiday here (in Switzerland) and are sorry you are not with us. Give our dear love to your friend Dick. Love from*
>
> *Harriette and Phyllis Murgatroyd.*'

'Harriette' and 'Phyllis' with the H. and P. heavily emphasised, were obvious cover-names for Hank and Pat.

The successful exits of Colditz escapers leaked into the camp during the spring and summer of 1943. Details of the escapes never reached the prisoners, and the stories which they would have given much to hear were left untold until years later.

On the other hand, inaccurate reports, rumours and half-truths became rife, sometimes even leading men astray by causing them to concentrate their efforts on doomed escape routes. For instance, one conclusion reached by some of the Colditz escapers in 1943 and 1944, was an unfortunate one, though deduced from a sound premise; sound, in that, as the rate of outflow of escapers from Switzerland across German-occupied France to Spain and England from November, 1942, onwards, was woefully slow, men argued it was better to seek other frontiers; unfortunate, in that other frontiers presented all the problems of the unknown, whereas, in Colditz, there reposed the secret of a well-documented frontier crossing into Switzerland, which had proved successful on repeated occasions.

Bill Fowler reached Switzerland safely in the early hours of September 13th, 1942. He reached Spain on January 30th, 1943, and was in England on March 27th, over six months from the time of his arrival in neutral territory. Billie Stephens took even longer. He arrived in Switzerland in October, 1942, and landed in England a year and eight months later. Men who escaped to Sweden were back in England in a matter of days, but, along the escape routes from the camps to Sweden, the casualties could be counted in tens, if not in hundreds. The old adage, 'Better safe than sorry,' was applicable in so far as safety can ever be held to apply to escaping: 'Slow but sure' suffers from the same inexactitude. Perhaps 'Better slow than sorry' is the answer.

Although the escapades of Wally Hammond and Tubby Lister, free in Germany like a couple of Don Quixotes, took place in December, 1942, titbits of information concerning their adventures reached Colditz only by the summer of 1943.

Going back a little in time, what happened was this:

One day, at the end of November, 1942, Wally asked Dick Howe what he thought was the best remaining way of escaping from the Castle and Dick's reply was of crystal clarity. He answered, dryly, "The best way, Wally, is through the main gate." Dick's accompanying grin conveyed an ironical twist to his dryness.

Wally and Tubby were both Engine-room Artificers. The former had been rescued by his captors from the Submarine H.M.S./M. *Shark,* on July 6th, 1940, and the latter from H.M.S./M. *Seal,* in May, 1940. Wally was small in build with a barrel chest. He dressed neatly and gave a clear-cut impression. His features stood out distinctly against a sallow complexion of uniform tint from his neck to his deep-furrowed forehead. His eyes were sharp and watchful, like those of a bird. Tubby was very much his opposite: taller, much heavier and inclined to run easily to fat, with a rosy complexion, a big nose and a casual air. He would accept life as he found it, with one proviso—that he never lost an opportunity of improving his lot if it came his way. But he would not go out of his way to find it. Wally provided the initial driving-force and, once roused, Tubby displayed all the ingenuity of a sleuth.

They made a formal application to the German Camp Commandant to be removed from Colditz and to be sent to their rightful camp—they were not officers; they were chief petty officers. Dick engineered a demand from the S.B.O. to the Commandant to the effect that the officers objected to their presence in the camp. An interview took place. They expressed the opinion that they did not want to live with officers.

The Commandant's dictum was:

"You escaped with them—you must live with them."

To which Wally replied, "The only reason we escaped was because we had nothing to do."

In parenthesis, they had been caught in Hamburg with a number of Naval officers tunnelling their way out of another camp—Marlag Nord.

"Are you prepared to work for Germany?" asked the Commandant.

"Yes," was the answer.

A few weeks passed. Then, at an hour's notice, they were given the order to move. They were ready: completely equipped by Dick with papers made out for Flemish Engineer Collaborators, money and a mental picture of the

Swiss frontier crossing. They survived the search before departure by the means prescribed at Colditz, which is better left unmentioned. Accompanied by three guards, they set off for a troops' camp at Lamsdorf.

At Leipzig main station they supplied the buffet attendant with Red Cross tea while she, a war-worn blonde, provided the boiling water. Prisoners and guards sat down together to enjoy a brew of good, strong English 'char'. The combined charm and carefree friendliness of the two E.R.A.s was difficult to resist. The Goons, returning hospitality, bought a round of beer. Cigarettes were offered by the prisoners.

The buffet was crammed with German uniformed men of different ranks and services. Many were intrigued, stopping for a moment to gaze upon the unaccustomed sight of men in khaki and field grey, chatting together round a table in jovial conviviality. Wally was enjoying himself. Unaccustomed to the sound and movement of a busy hub of life, he sat, for a moment, surveying appreciatively the scene before him. He noticed a very old man threading his way amongst the crowd, picking up cigarette butts from the floor and out of the ash-trays on the tables. He wore the medals of the 1914–18 war.

As he approached the table where the prisoners and their escorts were now busy over tall glasses of lager, Wally pushed a newly opened packet of Player's cigarettes, which lay at his elbow, in his direction. The German veteran raised his eyes, poignant with the sadness of a long disillusionment, to look at his benefactor, clad in the uniform of the enemy. Grasping the cigarettes, he came smartly to attention and saluted Wally Hammond. The echo of his heel-click sounded painfully loud in a room where the hum of conversation had suddenly ceased. Eyes turned incredulously towards the scene of an act of treason. But the veteran profited by the pause and disappeared from the restaurant before a movement was made to accost him.

The two prisoners arrived in the R.A.F. section of Lamsdorf prison just at the moment when the P.O.W.s were having their hands tied behind their backs with Red Cross string, in retaliation for the tying of German prisoners taken by our Commando raiders on the Channel Islands. They were thrown into the same compound and suffered the same fate. Thus they remained from seven a.m. to nine p.m. daily, with an hour's freedom for lunch.

Within a week, however, early in December, 1942, Wally and Tubby succeeded, with the help of a Regimental Sergeant Major named Sheriff, in having themselves drafted to a working party in the gasworks at Breslau. One hundred British P.O.W.s were working there, but none had as yet, according to report, escaped.

When they reached Breslau, Wally and Tubby carefully studied the route they travelled—by tram—to the works. Their plans were maturing. They had gathered some useful information about the possibilities of making a break from the gasworks. They were handed over by the Germans to the N.C.O. in charge of the working party, Sergeant Brown, and, wasting no time, they began sounding him to find out his reactions.

He was the right type, as far as they were concerned; enthusiastic, anxious to help and thoroughly knowledgeable as to the routine of the works. He advised them to lie low for a few days and to study the lie of the land while he set about procuring some necessary articles of· civilian clothing and equipment for them. In the meantime he allotted them the task of shifting coal from one dump to a second, which was within the reach of an electrically powered rail-mounted grab engaged in loading it into railway trucks. They began their first day of toil amidst the hum of industry. The gasworks was a maze of railway sidings. Shunting engines whistled and belched smoke and vapour, marshalling the clattering wagons. White puffs of escaping steam rose from a hundred points around and above the grime-covered brick buildings.

Every time an engine passed near Wally and Tubby, the electric leads of the grab crane were across the tracks.

During the first day's work, to the accompaniment of sparks and sheets of flame, they were mangled out of all possible service.

The evening saw a small heap of coal shifted six yards. During the second day the heap was shifted another six yards in a direction at right angles to the first move; the crane was out of commission. On the third day the heap was moved a further six yards again at ninety degrees and, on the fourth day, the coal was returned to its original location by this indefatigable team of coal hauliers. Before the fourth day's work was over, an old poverty stricken couple appeared with a cart drawn by a starving horse. They were old age pensioners, allowed to appear at regularly defined intervals to remove dross, the only fuel permitted them for heating their homes. Wally and Tubby took charge of the horse. No foreman was in sight. They halted the cart between their coal heap and an extensive pile of dross nearby and loaded the cart with coal. The aged couple stood by, looking on appreciatively, but with fear in their glances. When the cart was full and the coal covered with a layer of dross to pass inspection, they proferred surreptitiously, a packet of German cigarettes which the two prisoners accepted. They would be useful camouflage on the forthcoming journey.

The cart trundled away.

Towards the end of the week, after loading the remains of the coal on to a wagon, they were instructed to tidy up, collect the remaining coal dust together with a lot of rubbish in the vicinity and shovel it on to the existing pile of dross. On Saturday, December the 12th, 1942, before knocking off work, they carved out of the slack a long mound representing a newly filled grave. A cross made of two pieces of wood nailed together was placed at the head and in large letters in the coal dust, plain for the world to see, was inscribed 'ADOLF, R.I.P.'

They planned to move that night. Wally describes their preparations in these words:

'For a Colditz incumbent the getaway was a cake-walk; the filing of a few bars, the cutting of a few wires, the timing of a few patrols, obtaining some civilian attire, and we were ready.

'With the help of Sergeant Brown and two soldiers I gathered together a pair of large brown and grey check flannel trousers, a dark grey jacket and a fawn raincoat with the initials F. L. inside which I could not remove, so I added a P. to make it P. F. L. as the name I was travelling under was Pierre Lebrun. I also wore one of those caps that grandfather wore, very small, with a button in the centre. Tubby had a dark blue pair of trousers, a heavy woollen jacket and a Trilby hat that had been folded and hidden for years. All the steam in the world would not remove the creases. Later, the rain and sleet improved it. But his coat was the funny piece, a despatch rider's wind-jacket, treated with boot polish. If it was not a Saville Row fit it nevertheless kept the rain out. Tubby carried his toilet gear, boot brushes and food in a small suitcase and I contented myself with a large size briefcase, in which I carried, amongst other things, needles and cotton and a small bottle of concentrated cough medicine: the latter in case I might get my smoker's cough at an awkward moment.

'We both smoked pipes, of German meerschaum design. Our pouches were filled with Bulwark Strong underneath and covered with a layer of mixed French and German tobacco. We also flaunted the German cigarettes.'

But Wally and Tubby had not reckoned with a stooge. On Saturday night, for the first time in two years, a Goon sentry was placed on their projected route. They were undaunted. Packing away their civilian kit, they let it be known widely that the show was off until Sunday night. At the same time they resolved to try an alternative route during the early part of the next day, Sunday. They volunteered for the routine chore of washing out the Sunday dinner soup cauldrons. Quietly they collected their escape equipment and hid it in the cauldrons. They carried these to the washhouse which had an exit into the gasworks proper. They changed their clothes in the washhouse, walked into the works and left again through the manager's garden. They encountered little difficulty and there were no alarms. Taking a tram to the railway station, they bought tickets for Dresden, their first hop, to regain the Colditz escape route, and by nine-forty p.m. were trundling towards freedom. Wally's papers were signed by Willy Wants, after the variety artist! They were stopped and questioned on two occasions but their papers carried them through. Once a police officer retained their papers an unusually long time and their anxiety grew acute. Then the officer returned to them and apologised, saying he had to be on the look-out for escaped P.O.W.s. He added reassuringly that he had caught two the previous day. Wally accepted his apologies and expressed the hope that he would catch a few more before long. "They are a *verdammte* nuisance to the honest hardworking citizen," he said feelingly, in German, as they parted.

They reached Dresden, and then Nüremberg, travelling standing all the way in packed railway coaches throughout Sunday night and Monday. *En route*, at Chemnitz, a sympathetic German soldier bought them each a glass of beer. From Nüremberg their journey continued during another night and day towards Ulm. They were on tenterhooks, because Ulm was the death trap for many a Colditz escaper before them. It was to be avoided if at all possible, yet, like Rome, all roads seem to lead there. They found, arriving at nine p.m. on Tuesday evening, that there was no connection for Rottweil until the next morning. They were stuck in Ulm for the night.

They had to make a decision quickly. To remain in or near the station was suicidal. The weather could scarcely have been worse. Sleet had been driving against the carriage windows as they drew into the station; the temperature

was now below freezing and a high wind was blowing snowy
guests into the booking hall. It was no night to spend out
in the countryside. Besides, Ulm was a big industrial town.
They would spend most of the night walking to the country
and, to find a sheltered hiding place where they would not
freeze to death was, virtually, impossible in the darkness.
Walking anywhere after midnight was dangerous. Police
patrols would stop marauders abroad in the late and early
hours. They had to find cover somehow and quickly. A
cinema was no solution. There was only one answer.

As they hesitated for a moment under the archway at
the main entrance to the station, peering into the snow-
laden blackout beyond. Wally said in an undertone:

"How about it, Tubby? We're in it now up to our
necks. We can't stay here."

"The only sensible place to be to-night is in a warm
bed, my feet don't belong to me any more. Our papers are
pretty damn good. Why not try a cheap hotel?"

"Our German lingo's not good enough."

"Yes it is. You've managed fine so far, and aren't we
Flemish anyway!"

Wally turned to a passer-by.

"*Bitte, gibt es ein gute Hotel hier in der Nähe—aber
billig?*"

"*Jawohl!*" replied the stranger, "*zwei Minuten von hier,
links da oben ist das Bahnhofshotel. Es ist nicht teuer.*"

"*Danke schön,*" said Wally as the stranger disappeared
into the darkness.

They followed, pressing against the wind and holding
on to their hats. They turned left, crossed the road and
proceeded slowly looking at the doorways one by one until
they saw the sign of the Bahnhofshotel faintly outlined
above them.

"Here it is," said Wally, "it's all or nothing now. Once
inside, if the Jerries examine our papers and don't like 'em
they'll catch us with our pants down—good and proper—in
our beds, as like as not."

"It's a fair risk," said Tubby, "my feet say so!"

"O.K. Here goes!"

They pushed through two pairs of heavily curtained swing doors and found themselves in a long hall furnished in Victorian style with plenty of gilt. A lounge opened out to the right and a staircase ascended at the far end. On the left were the offices, the cashier's desk and the Hall Porter's lobby. The whole place needed repainting, but there was an air of cleanliness about the floors and furniture.

The weather outside was an excuse for the two men to remain muffled up, concealing their shabby suits. Wally asked for a room in his elementary German and a well-dressed man behind the cashier's desk asked in perfect English:

"Do you speak English? I see that you are not German. Perhaps you understand English?"

Wally was completely taken aback. He was on the point of saying, "Yes of course," when his wits returned to him. "Just a leetle, speak veery slow, please. I can understand Eenglish a little better than German. Ven you speak fast I understand not."

"Tell—me—exactly—what—you—want," pronounced the man behind the counter slowly and distinctly. He spoke in an educated manner with an air of authority. Wally accepted him as the manager, which he was.

"*Ach!* that ees good. Vee weesh one small room with two —*zwei* beds—vone great bed eef not, yes?"

"Yes, I can give you a room with two beds."

"How much, please?"

"Seven marks fifty with fifteen per cent. *Ablösung.*"

"Vee shall take it," said Wally relieved. At eight marks to the pound he had expected the price would be higher.

"Fill in these forms, please," said the manager politely. "Here your name, here your occupation, your nationality, where you come from, where you go to; and your reason for travelling."

"Vee are Ingineers—diesel—nationality Flamsche, go to Rottweil, vee come from Stuttgart. Vee haf important reparations to do in Rottweil." Wally reamed it out slowly in pidgin English as he wrote his particulars down.

He noticed Tubby spelling 'Engineer' with an 'E' in the English way and nudged him meaningly, pointing with his pen to the word on his own form. Tubby dropped a blot of ink on the 'E' and started again with an 'I' in the continental fashion.

The manager looked up the railway timetable and confirmed that their Rottweil train left at ten a.m. the next morning. Being Flemish workmen, though not understanding a word of that language, Wally and Tubby felt it appropriate to exchange a few broken sentences in Maltese which they knew in a scrappy fashion. This made a good impression on the manager who smiled and said:

"I will give you room fifty-two. Let me have your papers, please."

They handed in their identity papers which were pinned to the forms they had completed and they were escorted upstairs. The lift was not in use. Two comfortable beds in a warm cosy room greeted them.

"Do you wish for anything to eat or drink?" asked their conductor.

"Noting, *Danke*," replied Wally—with Tubby echoing the words a split second after him. As the door closed, Tubby went to a basin in the corner and turned the taps. After a minute he exclaimed, "Hot water by G——!" and began stripping off his boots and socks as fast as he could.

Within ten minutes they were fast asleep, tucked into their beds between clean sheets enjoying more luxury than they had ever had since they left their submarine base in 1940.

They awoke next morning thoroughly refreshed but with hunger gnawing at their vitals. They had not eaten for nearly forty-eight hours. It was now Wednesday morning. Tubby produced German bread, margarine and sugar from his suitcase and they sat up in their beds chewing in silence. The evening before, they had not felt so hungry. That was the effects of weariness after the severe nervous

tension. Fatigue alone, if sufficiently intense, can suppress
the pangs of hunger. Two major primitive forces seem incapable of taking possession of the human frame both at
once. One or the other is uppermost and claims the whole
consciousness until it is satisfied. The hackneyed expression
tired *and* hungry is inaccurate unless the sufferer is neither
very tired nor very hungry.

As the pangs of hunger ebbed, nervous anticipation
began to assert itself. Their pulses quickened as thoughts
came unchallenged and their hearts pounded. Wally expressed their mutual anxiety:

"Do you think we'll ever get our *Ausweise* back?"

"They're probably examining them with magnifying
glasses at the police station at this moment," said Tubby
with nervous jocularity. "If they're not downstairs I'm not
waiting for them."

"We'll never get far without 'em," said Wally. He jumped
out of bed and went to the window pulling back the curtains. Outside the snow had turned to sleet again and the
roofs were glassy grey under a sombre sky.

They shaved and dressed hurriedly and packed their
belongings.

"All set?" asked Wally, opening the door of the bedroom. Tubby nodded. Then they noticed a beautifully
polished pair of military high boots reposing outside a
door on the opposite side of the corridor.

The anxiety of the moment faded into the background
and a gleam of devilment came into Tubby's eyes. He
glanced at Wally and met his gaze.

"No! not that," whispered Wally. "Just plain water. Fill
the chamber pot." Tubby was back in the room in a twink-
ling, filling his bedside pot with water from the basin tap.

"Steady!" said Wally, as Tubby appeared again with the
brimming pot, "don't spill it near our door for hell's sake."

Gently, they tipped the water into the boots.

"Not enough," said Wally, "quick another!"

The corridor was empty. No sound issued from the other
side of the door. Quickly another pot-full was tipped into

the thirsty boots filling them, and a faint trickle of water appeared from underneath the soles. They closed their own door quietly and walked downstairs. It was eight forty-five a.m.

At the cash desk, Wally asked for the bill and the identity papers. The manager was obviously short of staff. He was in his shirt sleeves and had been cleaning the lounge, but his grey hair was carefully brushed and he had shaved. He asked if they had had a good night and "Will you not have breakfast?"

"Vee haf no coupons," said Wally biting his lip and feeling he would like to run straight out through the swing doors.

"You must have some coffee then—*ersatz* coffee. It is very cold out this morning," said the manager almost forcing them towards a small table in an alcove of the lounge. They sat down. Then, suddenly, rose in their seats ready to take off. A German officer was coming down the stairs and he was not wearing jack boots. . . .

He passed them with a *"Guten Morgen"* and did not stop at the desk. Wally and Tubby relapsed into their chairs, sighing audibly.

"What the hell made you do it?" whispered Wally hoarsely.

"It was your idea," said Tubby, "you distinctly said water!"

"My godfathers! now we've got to sit here for half an hour drinking filthy coffee." Wally grimaced and resigned himself to fate. What they had done could not be undone. Their papers were not yet forthcoming. The *ersatz* coffee seemed to be waiting for the acorns to grow and, at any moment, screams of rage would issue from the stair well. They fidgeted uneasily in their chairs.

After an agonising wait of ten minutes the coffee arrived in two large, steaming mugs. More sighs were followed by subdued curses. The coffee was far too hot.

"We've got to drink some of the blasted stuff," said Wally eyeing the staircase. Tubby promptly poured most

of his mug into a flower pot of aspidistras where it formed
a cloud of vapour around the plant.

"For crying out loud!" said Wally, pouring half the
contents of his mug into Tubby's empty one. "Let's get out
of here quick before the place blows up."

Together they vacated the alcove and approached the
desk again.

"Tank you, *Danke schön*," said Wally to the manager,
now seated behind his desk. "Ze bill, if you please. Vee must
hurry."

"But your train does not go until ten o'clock, you have
plenty of time!" said the manager with exasperating
accuracy.

"If you please, vee vish to buy zom tings bevore," Wally
replied with painful care. He was hypnotised by the stairs
and could not keep his eyes away. He spoke now, deliberately facing the staircase, ready to turn about and run at
the first bellow from above. "Hurry please, and do not
vorget the *Ausweise, bitte*," he murmured as beads of perspiration appeared on his forehead. Almost in a trance he
noticed Tubby edging towards the swing doors.

At last the bill was ready. Wally fumbled—much too
nervously, he thought—for the German notes in his wallet.
He paid the bill; still no shouts from the direction of the
staircase.

"The *Ausweise* please?" he questioned. He could see
them nowhere on the desk.

"*Ach* yes! of course, forgive me. Here they are," said the
manager apologetically, bringing them out from under a
counter.

"Good-bye! *Auf Wiedersehen!* Tank you!" Wally said
clutching the two papers with soaring relief registering on
his countenance. "I 'ope vee shall kome again zoon to visit
Ulm."

Tubby repeated "Good-bye, tank you!" and opened the
swing doors.

Outside, they both gasped as heavy sighs filled their lungs
with cold air. They quickly disappeared into the crowd

hurrying towards the station. They muffled their coats around them as they scurried along, and the first streaks of a storm of sleet carried on a biting wind, stung their faces.

In the shelter of the station they paused for a moment to recover their breath and their composure.

"Phew! we're well out of that," said Wally.

"I 'ope the R.A.F. vill kome again zoon to visit Ulm," mimicked Tubby grinning. "Vone German officer kan use his boots to put out ze fires *nicht wahr?* I'd give a lot to go back and see the fun, wouldn't you?"

"Sorry, Tubby, we've not got time—let's telephone the manager from Switzerland instead. Come on! we've got to get the tickets to Rottweil. There may be a queue. The train goes in half an hour," said Wally, and they headed for the booking office.

There was a queue and they waited nervously for fifteen minutes before their turn came. Wally did not wait to be asked for his *ausweis*; he pushed it in front of the girl issuing the tickets saying, "*Zweimal, dritter Klasse, Rottweil, bitte*," and tendered his Reichmarks at the same time. The tickets and change appeared without a word.

They hurried off to the train and found the platform without difficulty. Seeing a 'Raucher' (smoking) third class carriage, they climbed in and were soon smoking their pipes with evident satisfaction and more at ease than they had felt since they awoke that morning. Several other passengers entered the carriage just before the train departed.

As it gathered speed, leaving the grey windswept atmosphere of Ulm behind, Wally noticed that one middle aged unprepossessing female passenger was obsessed with Tubby's despatch rider coat. Tubby had finished his pipe and was feigning sleep. Wally saw her curiosity growing and spreading as she gazed up at his crumpled hat, then studied, it seemed, the texture of his coat, and continued downwards to his boots. There was only one answer to this. Wally stared at her—long and intently—with his sharp eyes. It was not long before she became visibly self-conscious. He continued the grilling until she was so confused that she forgot all about Tubby. He kept it up until she reached her destination half an hour later. She left the carriage blushing crimson as she stumbled over Wally's

Wally stared at her—long and intently

feet to reach the door, still followed by his burning and pseudo-lecherous gaze.

They arrived at Tüttlingen at four p.m. where they broke off their journey to Rottweil. This was the Colditz route as followed by the author and others from the Castle before them. Tüttlingen was only fifteen miles from the Swiss frontier, whereas Rottweil, reached by another line, changing at Tüttlingen, was much further away, and for that very reason a less suspicious town to be heading for. I wait for the Rottweil connection gave passengers a legitimate excuse to leave the station. Wally and Tubby took the precaution of drinking water from a cast iron fountain in the station before they walked past the barrier showing their tickets.

Before they had walked half a mile, they encountered a police patrol. They were ready. The officer questioned them and searched their wallets, their pockets and Wally's briefcase, all the time with one hand on his pistol. He said:

"Warum fahren Sie nicht nach Rottweil?"

"Wir warten auf dem Zug nach Rottweil um sechs Uhr fünf und dreissig," answered Wally. *"Wir sind seit zwei Tagen im Zug—wir machen jetzt einen kleinen Spaziergang. Könnenwirirgendwo ein Bier kaufen?"*

Wally continued volubly. His German vocabulary soon exhausting itself, he carried on in broken German with words of Maltese, pidgin English and some French thrown in. He and his mate were going home to Belgium for Christmas when the order came for the rush, breakdown job at Rottweil. If the police officer did not believe them he only had to telephone the *Arbeitsführer* (works foreman) at Rottweil. They would be quite happy if the police officer could put them up for the night, provided he 'phoned the *Arbeitsführer*.

The officer was slightly taken aback by this frontal attack. He said simply, *"Komm,"* and they set off together, not as a party of prisoners with their gaoler, but amicably, side by side. After twenty minutes they reached a large house standing back from the road. They followed the officer inside and discovered that they were in a 'pub.'

There were a dozen country folk and two soldiers in the saloon and the officer told one of the latter to keep an eye on the two strangers while he went to the telephone. The officer was calling their bluff. They looked around casually but with their eye on the door. A 'getaway' might be managed, but Wally had plenty of fight in him still. He could continue to bluff in spite of the 'phone call. Within five minutes the officer returned; handed them back their papers; led them outside and told them how to find their way back to Tüttlingen station.

Wally said in German, "But we have had our walk. Now it is time we had a drink."

"*Ach so!*" replied the officer, "then go back and have your beer and return to the station afterwards. *Gute Nacht,*" and he left them standing at the pub doorway.

Tubby and Wally looked at each other. A sly smile spread over Wally's face and Tubby winked. They re-entered the pub and ordered beer. They drank one each quickly and ordered seconds. The other occupants of the bar were friendly and talkative. A large flabby looking man with a bald head and staring pale blue eyes approached them asking, "*Sind Sie Flamen?*"

"*Jawohl!*" they answered with mock gusto.

The large man then recounted what seemed to be a long story in a language they had never heard before in their lives. At last Wally and Tubby were listening to the throaty tones of the language of their adopted birthplace! So this was Flemish they thought and exchanged bewildered glances. They were definitely 'up against it.'

The large man stopped, smiled jovially and fixed them with his glassy eyes. For a second there was stony silence. Then, with one accord, Wally and Tubby started to laugh. They laughed loud and long—not forgetting to drink their beer between guffaws. The large man began to laugh too. This gave them a chance to stop. When he ceased, they began again. Their beer finished, they put down their empty glasses and, still roaring with laughter, they shouted "*Gute Nacht! Gute Nacht!*" to the Flemish linguist and the assembled company and backed out of the room as quickly as propriety allowed.

"Phew! Lumme!" said Tubby, as they stepped outside, "that was a near one. Who would have expected to hear that lingo on the Swiss frontier. Do you think it really was Flemish? Perhaps he was having us on and that's what all the joke was about!"

"He was speaking Flemish all right or perhaps Dutch. I could pick up a word here and there," said Wally, and added as an afterthought, "that was two near ones, not one! You've forgotten about the policeman and the 'phoney telephone!"

"He seemed quite happy about it. We must be expected at Rottweil after all! What was your next move going to be, Wally? I was ready for the door, if he'd come back looking glum."

"If he'd come back suspicious," Wally answered, "I would've told him to 'phone again and let me speak to the *Arbeitsführer* about the Diesel breakdown job. That would've stumped him long enough for us to think up the next one."

They walked quickly, continuing along the road they had come, then, approaching some woods, they left the road, skirting along the fringe of the trees. They travelled by compass all that night and the next, making very slow progress across country, and lying up in the daytime in dense woods. In the early hours, after the second night's tramp, in spite of the walking, they began to feel the cold. They were stopping frequently to check their direction and at such moments the sweat on their bodies chilled and made them shiver. They came upon a woodman's hut. The door was locked. By climbing on to the low roof and re-moving a few tiles they were able to drop inside. They made ready to spend the day there with suitable precautions. Wally detached the lock on the door and held it shut with a piece of string while Tubby cut out knots in the pine wood boards of the walls with his jack-knife providing spy holes in all directions.

They found some boards in a corner, spread them out on the floor over the damp earth and slept fitfully until morning. From dawn onwards they took turns at the spy hole watch. They were in a clearing and would make a run for it if anyone approached the cabin.

During the day they reviewed their trek of the previous night, established their position with a fair degree of accuracy and made plans for the frontier crossing. At midday they ate the last of their food. They suffered badly from thirst and during a rainstorm they tried to collect water in a bowl under the hole they had made in the roof. The rain did not last long, but they captured a few drops which they lapped up like dogs. It no more than moistened their tongues.

Not a soul approached the cabin all day. At dusk they departed leaving a five mark note under the broken lock which they placed carefully in a tool cupboard in the hut. They walked, at first, due west along a railway line in the forest until they reached open country. Then they turned south, skirting the trees for an hour before hearing the sound of traffic using the road they were heading for. They lay down near it and began timing patrols.

At this point, about five miles west of Singen the road passed within half a mile of the frontier. Across the road were fields inclined to be marshy, and the bottom of a wooded hill sloping towards the east beyond the fields was their target. A deviation of two hundreds yards to the right or left of the bee line from where the men lay to the edge of the wooded hill would find them back in Germany and probably into the arms of a sentry.

By midnight they were ready for the 'off.' The moon was shining brightly and had been helpful so far. Now, for the last lap, it would be a hindrance. It would help others to see them when they least wanted to be visible. There was a low ground mist on the other hand which would be useful if they chose to drop suddenly at an alarm.

They waited for a motor cycle patrol to pass with flashing headlamps, counted three minutes and crossed the road. Wally went about twenty yards in front of Tubby. They timed the crossing well, as a large cloud began to cover the face of the moon. They carried jack-knives in their sleeves. After twenty-five minutes of fast going, with the mist enveloping them up to their waists, they approached the trees at the bottom of the hill. Suddenly a torch was flashed on Wally before he had time to drop, and there was a shout, "Halt! *Wer da?*". He approached the sentry in a roundabout way. Tubby had dropped and had not been seen. Wally forced the sentry to turn with him as he advanced until his back was facing the direction where Tubby lay. The moon re-appeared, bathing the scene in an unearthly light. The sentry had not unslung his rifle. It was a good omen. Then. Wally distinguished the outline of his Tyrolean style cap, and his buttons gleamed showing up the Swiss cross. He looked beyond the sentry and saw the form of Tubby appearing out of the ground mist. He was much nearer than expected and Wally caught the glint of his knife as he moved noiselessly like a shadow. "Stop! Tubby, for God's sake!" he shouted over the guard's shoulder, "he's Swiss."

Tubby masked his knife and fell on the astonished sentry's neck as he turned. Keyed at one moment to the pitch of killing his enemy. Tubby was so overcome at the next that he found himself hugging the sentry shouting, "Swiss, Swiss, good old Swiss!" The sentry accepted the greeting good humouredly. He spoke a little English and contented himself with establishing that they were prisoners of war who had escaped, accepting their statements at face value. He shouted to another sentry in the darkness of the woods and then escorted them, talking cheerfully all the way, to the village of Ramsen. They were handed over to the Commander of the guard post who promptly produced bowls of soup and sent them to bed with four army blankets each in the 'off duty dossdown.' The time was two a.m. on Saturday, the 19th December.

They arrived in Berne for Christmas and for a reunion party that will be long remembered by the participants. The others were: Ronnie Littledale, Billie Stephens, Hank Wardle, Bill Fowler and the author, all ex-Colditz inmates who had escaped during the autumn.

*   *   *   *   *

The Colditz group in Switzerland was growing into a colony. The escapers were packed off by the Military

Attaché for a time to Montreux, then to Wengen and later to Saanenmöser in the Bernese Oberland. They all learnt to ski on the comparatively deserted slopes, first of the Kleine Scheidegg and then of the Hornbeg and in a matter of two months had regained much of their former strength and energy.

The invasion of North Africa in November, 1942, by the Allies and the subsequent entry of the Germans and Italians into Vichy France upset all the recognised ways of travelling to Spain. With the Germans present, new and much more clandestine 'tourist' routes had to be organised.

Bill Fowler and Ronnie Littledale were the first of the colony to leave. They crossed the Swiss frontier into France on January 25th, 1943. Bill set down his record of the journey to Gibraltar on his arrival in England and it is reproduced here as he wrote it—a straightforward account fresh with vigour and the simplicity of understatement which was so typical of this fine airman who, as his companion Ronnie too, was to meet his end before the war was over.

'On the 25th of January, 1943, Ronnie Littledale and I went to Geneva, where we were given French identity cards and introduced to a Belgian called Jacques. We were told that our journey must be left entirely to him.

'We were taken then by car a short distance, to a point near the French frontier, west of Annemasse. Here we waited in a yard while Jacques made a reconnaissance. In a few minuts he came back and told us to follow him, so we walked till we came to a small stream, where we were joined by a French girl about twenty years old. We crossed the stream, which was shallow, and were helped out of the water on the other side by a French customs official in uniform. We waited hidden behind a wall for a few minutes, and then Jacques led us down a deserted road into Annemasse village. He took us to a house where we dried our clothes, had some food and met a man in a ski-ing suit, who, Jacques told me, would be our guide for the next part of the journey. He and the French girl left us.

'We went to bed and very early next morning, with our new guide, we walked to a garage, passing some Italian soldiers on the way. The guide left us here, arranging with a man to drive us in a car to La Roche, where we arrived at eight a.m., and went to a hotel. We slept most of the day in a corner of the lounge, interrupting our dozing to eat a good lunch, at which our guide rejoined us.

'At four p.m. he led us to the railway station, where he gave us a hundred francs each and told us to book separately to Chambery. We boarded the train—arriving at Chambery at about 9 p.m., where we changed. The guide bought tickets to Perpignan, where we arrived after an all night journey, at 9 a.m. on the 27th of January. We took a tram to the Hotel St. Antoine. We spent the 27th and the 28th very quietly in the hotel, only going out once to have our photographs taken for our fake identity papers in the back room of a small shop close by.

'On the 29th of January our guide handed us over to a Spaniard and then departed. We took a bus to Elne, arriving there in the evening. The Spaniard insisted on our buying our own tickets and sitting separately in different parts of the bus. At Elne we met a French boy about nineteen years old who said he was coming with us.

'Darkness descended upon us as we walked along the railway line southwards and crossed the River Tech by the railway bridge. We continued across fields until after an hour's trek the guide said he was lost. I directed him towards the south by the stars and we eventually came to a goat track which the guide said he recognised. We followed this and arriving at a cave, we lay down and slept for some hours. At 6 a.m. the following morning (30th January) we set off again. We marched the whole day, reaching the La Junqueras-Fiquaras road at 4 p.m., and, while crossing it, we were arrested by Spanish soldiers who were patrolling the district in a lorry and picking up the numerous refugees in the neighbourhood. They seemed familiar with this routine and were not even armed.

'The lorry took us to La Junqueras, where we were locked into a cell. We were not searched. Later we were interrogated in French by a Spanish officer who said he supposed we were Canadians. We told him we were British officers who had been captured in France (following our instructions). I gave the name of John Parsons, while Ronnie gave his name as Bighill (opposite of Littledale). The military authorities then handed us over to the jurisdiction of the civil police.

'Our guide was put into a separate cell, and the police telephoned to Madrid about him. They found out that he had been a Red in the Civil War and beat him up properly in the next room apologising afterwards to us for the nuisance caused, saying that the man was a "Red murderer" and deserved all the treatment he got. While waiting in the cell, we burnt our papers. The police searched us and questioned us again. The Chief of Police promised to treat us well and to send us to a hotel. He asked us what we thought of General Franco and what was our opinion of the Bolshevists. We said we thought Franco was a grand fellow and that we admired the Russians, who were our Allies. At every opportunity we demanded permission to see the British Consul and always received the answer, *Mañana.*

"On the 1st of February we were marched off to a central prison in Fiqueras, where our heads were shaven and we were inoculated under dirty, unhygienic conditions (I was tenth in line for the same needle), and thrown into the filthiest gaol I have ever seen in my life, and I have seen quite a few! All that has been written in the war about Spanish prisons is correct. We were jammed in with fourteen other men; some of them criminals, mostly Spanish, and two of them awaiting death sentences, in a disgusting, dirty hole, measuring four yards by two. In this cell we spent twenty-three days without blankets or even straw, sleeping on the damp stone floor huddled together like sardines and crawling with vermin. The only window was bricked up leaving a six-inch aperture, and as it was mid-winter long hours were spent in total darkness. The cold was intense. For all natural functions, a pail was placed in the middle of the cell and removed once every twenty-four hours. It made the atmosphere so foul that prisoners were sick intermittently all day long. Two men died during our incarceration and their bodies remained propped up in the corner for two days before the guards removed them. A tureen of gruel a day was all the food we were given. The only hope of maintaining life was to pool valuables and to buy, at exorbitant prices, extra food from the guards. My only asset, a wrist watch, went.

"We were visited, once, by a representative from the British Consulate, and, as a result, on the 22nd of February, a Spanish army sergeant conducted us to Barcelona, where we reported to the British Consul and were sent off to a hotel.

"We were given civilian clothes and stayed there till the 18th of March, when I parted company with Ronnie.

"A Spanish air force officer took me to Alhama de Aragon, where I met several men of the R.A.F. and U.S.A.A.F. We were well treated here, and, on the 24th of March, I set off with six R.A.F. personnel, mostly Canadians, to Madrid; and thence to Seville, where we spent the night. The next day we motored to Gibraltar, stopping on the way at one of the principal sherry towns, where the British Consul, a Spaniard, happened to be a wine merchant. He conducted us over his cellars. We sampled varieties copiously and, on our departure, he presented each one with a bottle of sherry 'for the road.' One of the Canadians admired the Madonna lilies in his front garden so the Consul pressed an enormous bunch on him. The sherry lasted us as far as La Linea, on the north side of the neutral zone separating Spain from Gibraltar. Here the Canadian, with the lilies climbed on the bonnet of the car, swearing he would kiss the first British citizen he met in Gibraltar. At the north gate of Gibraltar, a sentry challenged the convoy, whereupon the Canadian climbed unsteadily from his perch, solemnly kissed the sentry on the cheek and presented him with the huge bunch of lilies. The party were escorted to the guard room, led by the Canadian. The sentry, carrying his rifle under one arm and the madonnas in the other, followed. He seemed to regard the incident as an everyday occurrence, evidently accustomed to the arrival of service 'tourists' from captivity."

CHAPTER XIV

THE GHOSTS

DICK HOWE, in his capacity of Escape Officer, played an important rôle in the black days of Colditz, in the darkness before the dawn. Always encouraging, never despairing, he fostered, cajoled and counselled.

*　　*　　*　　*　　*

When Scarlet O'Hara was allotted a bed in the first floor quarters over the parcels office where the French had formally resided, he browsed around the rooms for several days and then took to measuring. What he carried out was a miniature trigonometrical survey. It was certainly three dimensional and soon wound itself up around the spiral of the staircase in the turret leading up to his dormitory.

Between the first floor and the ground floor, beside the spiral, he calculated there was an uncharted space sealed off from all directions. He set to work and in a matter of six weeks of patient toil he had worked through a couple of feet of masonry and found his secret chamber. He quite expected to find some treasure, hidden there centuries before, but there was nothing. Dick helped him to build a camouflaged entrance weighing a hundredweight and turning on pivots like the French tunnel entrance.

Then Dick left Scarlet to his own devices, to choose his own team of workers and carry on with the job. 'The Job,' of course, was tunnelling downwards through the stone, mortar and concrete of the massive staircase foundations.

The point in favour of Scarlet's scheme was that he could tunnel in almost any direction. The Germans might hear his sledge hammer at work—in fact they did—but for a long time they could not find his working.

His team consisted of senior officers, none below the rank of major, which accounts for the title conjured up by Don

Donaldson. 'Crown Deep' was the name and it stuck like glue.

Tunnelling continued for many weeks. The dull thuds of hammer blows reverberated up the stairs, rivalling the sounds of heavy excavation that used to emanate months earlier from the nearby French tunnel. The Jerries listened and probed and searched in vain.

Scarlet approached Dick periodically.

"I want you to come and have a look at the working," he would say, and both of them would descend through the hinged opening into his chamber. Scarlet would light up his lamp.

"I've been driving a heading in this direction, see?" and he would point to a depression in the foundations about the size of a small hip bath. "That represents three blasted weeks work! It's heading in a good direction, out between Gephard's office and the chapel. It starts off fine aand dandy and then it gets tougher and tougher. It leads you up the garden path good and proper and lets you down good and proper."

Both the scene and the occasion were familiar to Dick and he would look wistfully round the chamber at the other holes. One after the other, as his gaze travelled round, he recollected Scarlet's grumbling phrases. Grudging defeat, painful susceptibility at his own impotence, dogged refusal to accept fate, and a nonchalant sarcasm that veiled the suffering.

"And where do I go from here?" Scarlet would ask pathetically, kicking the rubble under his feet in a fruitless gesture as he followed Dick's gaze.

"Why not try heading inside towards the courtyard, you might pick up the drains again," or "Have a go over there towards Monty's hole. He's heading for the old French tunnel and two different entrances would have many advantages."

Dick's counsel always encouraged Scarlet to start off again and the familiar thud of his working would waft up the medieval turret once more. It was a reassuring sound to the men who climbed, daily, up and down the winding stairs. Comments passed from mouth to mouth.

"Crown Deep's at work again."

"Yes, never heard it last week. Couldn't think what was different about the place."

"Life's not the same without it!"

"It's like a heart. When it stops throbbing, there's a death in the house."

The Germans were bound to react violently eventually. Their sound recorders must have been working overtime. Crown Deep never had a real chance. As they could not find the entrance, in desperation, one day, they brought in their own team of navvies and set to work on the staircase. Their action savours of the rival mining operations that were carried out between the German and Allied trenches during the First World War. In this case, fortunately, Scarlet had no high explosive or he would certainly have used it. The Germans wielded their pickaxes, sledge hammers and wedges and discovered his concealed chamber. Crown Deep passed into the catalogue of Colditz failures. Only the name survived; an epitaph without a grave.

*   *   *   *   *

It is one thing to be incarcerated alone in a stone cell like the Count of Monte Christo; to have only bare hands with which to hammer against the walls and finger nails with which to scrape away the mortar. To have company in such a situation is another matter. It is a mixed blessing.

Prisoners can commiserate together, they may also grow to hate each other. They can help one another and they may be wildly jealous of each other. There can be order or anarchy; an outstanding character can seize the helm and hold the course; moral weakness and the absence of leadership breed bad blood and lasting enmity. The elemental forces in man's nature are scarcely veiled; they lie under a veneer of civilised custom which grows tenuous. They can burst into fury as a spark becomes a roaring furnace. All the physical constituents, the infinite monotony; all the mental anguish, the panoply of tyranny and the atmosphere for revolt, are present.

The stage was set for heroism or violence in the stifled community life which existed behind the walls of Colditz. The majority of the inmates lived for escape. The decision, for most of them, taken long ago, was irrevocable. It was too late now to turn back. There was no road behind them. Instead, if they turned, beneath them was a yawning chasm. They stood giddily on the brink. It was the pit of despair threatening to engulf them in a mad, suicidal fall. Scarlet O'Hara's Crown Deep was an instance of men beating their fists against walls of solid rock. Monty Bissell's hole was another, and the glider, in a different sense was, probably, the last. Here was resolution for its own sake. This way lay sanity for active, courageous men who were determined not to look back.

A few, very few, attained Nirvana; they deliberately faced the yawning chasm, gritted their teeth, steadied their swaying minds, clung to the edge and slowly stepped backwards into tranquillity and resignation.

*   *   *   *   *

The ghosts were in a bad way. In spite of all the tender care that Monty Bissell expended on them they were definitely wasting away. Like a mother hen looking after its chicks, Monty saw they were fed and kept warm before he ever thought about himself. But their trouble was disturbing. It was not so much physical, as mental. Their morale was at rock bottom.

Not that their chains were heavy. They did not have long sessions of clanking; on the contrary they were quiet ghosts. Their job was to be silent and to be inconspicuous. In fact, they were not supposed to appear at all. Naturally, under such conditions the morale of any ghost could be expected to go to pieces.

The reader will remember that the ghosts, two of them, were hidden in Monty's hole in the Chapel. Their appearance or disappearance—take your choice—had coincided with the escape of Rupert Barry and his French companion down the theatre light well in November, 1942. Dick had decided, on that occasion, to be reasonable as to the number. Volunteers were called for and Jack Best and Mike Harvey had been chosen.

Monty Bissell, at the time, was busy digging a tunnel under the steps leading to the pulpit.

Jack Best thought that, by becoming a ghost and going to ground, he would be free to help Monty and to work to his heart's content, and Mike Harvey thought so too.

Monty looked after them well. They were his first, and almost continuous, charge to the exclusion of other activities. He attended to their every need, brought them their food and all the titbits he could muster. He saw that they were warm, regaled them with news of the activities of the camp and of events taking place in the world outside. The ghosts for their part repaid Monty's care and attention by tunnelling quietly and leisurely forward.

They had a few tins of Red Cross food laid in as a reserve, but Monty thought it would be a good idea to lay in a stock of staple diet for them as well. Bread would go mouldy in a day. There was nothing else save potatoes; they were better than nothing and, thought Monty, they would prevent starvation. Thus, if the chapel was closed by way of a reprisal for some 'offence against the Reich' for a month or longer, the ghosts would survive long enough for Dick and Monty to evolve a plan to extract them and at the same time obviate their disclosure. Dick thought this a wise precaution and set about obtaining the potatoes.

He went to the mess kitchen in the British quarters one Sunday afternoon to find Goldman, the cockney Jew orderly. Goldman was there, seated at the kitchen table, poring over a letter he was writing home. His blond, curly hair fell over his forehead and a pencil protruded from the corner of his mouth. The table was littered with postcards and letters, on paper of many different colours.

"Goldman," Dick said, "I want to talk to you."

"Yes, Captain 'Owe," said Goldman standing up and transferring the pencil from his mouth to behind his ear.

"Could you scrounge me a small sack of potatoes?" Dick continued, "I want them for the ghosts. They must be absolutely sound—no bad ones—because they may have to last some time."

"Why, Captain 'Owe, that ain't so difficult, and you know I'd do anything for you anyway. Come along wiv' me. De Jerry cook and me, we're pals. 'E's comin' to visit me after the war an' see de family."

They descended the stairs to the courtyard and headed for the cookhouse. The door was locked. It was two o'clock and a Sunday. Cooking for the day was finished. Goldman was not deterred. He opened a small serving hatch near the door, stretched his arm through and slipped the lock of the door on the inside. Dick and Goldman walked into the kitchen and shut the door quietly after them.

Silence reigned in the deserted cookhouse, but from around a corner, in an alcove, wafted a sound of gentle snoring. The German cook corporal was sprawled over a desk fast asleep, with his head on his folded arms. Goldman crept over to him, then bawled at the top of his voice, "*Achtung!*"

The German N.C.O. came to his feet as if a thousand volts had been shorted across his terminals and stood rigidly at attention before Goldman's cheery "Wat yer, cookie!" brought him to his senses and relaxed his galvanised frame. Goldman grinned airily at him. "That's right, cookie, you can stand at ease now, but don't go to sleep on dooty again, see!"

The German, a comparatively young man, retired from the Russian front on account of wounds, was, rather naturally, in a surly mood. He and Goldman wrangled for several minutes. Finally the grumbling ended with Goldman showing the corporal all the photos of his family in Hackney, in return for which extraordinary favour, the Jerry felt it his bounden duty to hand over thirty pounds of potatoes. Goldman and Dick turned to leave the cookhouse with the sack

Jack Best

hidden under a jacket. The German, as docile as a lamb, accompanied them to the door and closed it politely after them.

"You see 'ow it is, Captain 'Owe. It gets you anyfink you want."

"What does?" asked Dick.

"Charm," replied Goldman.. "It's charm wat does it."

The ghosts now had their reserve of cooked potatoes.

Three weeks of confinement in a black hole under a chapel are not warranted to lift morale and the ghosts, in spite of Monty's nursing, began to wilt. The atmosphere was not of the best, either physically on account of the curious smell which could hardly be described as the odour of sanctity, or spiritually, because of the indefinable proximity of the dead. The dead had died many, many years ago, but their spirits seemed not far removed from their decayed coffins under the chapel floor. It was ironical that the ghosts should be so affected by the company of their elders, if not their betters. The fact is the chapel was 'plain spooky', in the dead of night.

After three weeks it had become obvious that the ghosts should be relieved of the strain and given some fresh air. The excitement and hubbub of the light well escape had died by Christmas, 1942, and it was considered safe to let them out of close hiding provided they were protected by stooges from being seen face to face by a German who might recognise them.

The French tunnel was discovered within two months of their taking up residence. Work had to cease completely for a time. Then they began once more in a new direction with a view to connecting up with the French tunnel and making use of it again.

Sound detectors were known to be installed all around the Chapel. They had to proceed at a snail's pace.

By the summer of 1943 work on the Chapel tunnel had to stop. Monty and his ghosts had reached the French tunnel, but the Germans had laid a trap. Sound detectors must have been left hidden it it. Every time the British tunnellers entered it the Germans appeared to know, and a squad would enter the Chapel, search it and leave a sentry posted there for twenty-four hours (relieved, of course, periodically). Progress came to a standstill.

Grismond Davies-Scourfield made a break during the summer. He was 'gone away' for seventeen days before recapture at the Dutch frontier. His story cannot be told here, but during his absence Mike Harvey stood in for him on *Appells,* with the result that when the German Commandant was informed by long distance telephone of the recapture of a Colditz prisoner he replied, "It can't be so. We had an *Appell* two hours ago and the count was correct."

Mike promptly went back into close hiding until the tangle was sorted out!

For the period of less restricted confinement, Monty, still looking after his brood like a mother hen, instituted the stooging system that made it safe for his chicks to sortie at all times, except, of course, during roll calls when they went to ground again. He had a team of stooges working for him, including Keith Milne, known as the 'City Slicker,' one of the most charming, unassuming and gentle characters it is possible to imagine, and handsome, dair-haired and black moustached into the bargain. Be that as it may, he was noticed later one evening at his look-out post by Lulu Lawton.

"What are you up to Slick?" he asked.

"Stooging for Monty's ghosts," came the reply.

Lulu said nothing, but it was eleven o'clock and he suspected something. He searched high and low for Monty and could not find him. Then he happened to pass Monty's bed and there he was, tucked up nicely, fast asleep, with only his forelock showing. Lulu shook him.

"Huh! ... Hm! ... Oh! ... What? No! What the hell do you think you're doing?"

"What time did the ghosts go to ground?" asked Lulu.

"Hours ago. Has anything happened? Are they all right?"

"What time did you put them away?"

"Six o'clock. Why? What the devil's up with you anyway, Lulu?"

"Nothing, nothing at all, Monty! only the City Slicker's going to be a bit browned off."

"By the holy Saint Patrick!" shouted Monty, leaping from his bed. "I forgot to lay him off." He looked at his watch, "That's five hours ago," and he rushed in his pyjamas to release the faithful sentinel.

Stooging hit a low spot at that moment, but Monty could be said at least to have erred on the right side. Stooging also had its high spots and reached a peak in Dick's plan for the escape of Bush Parker and Mike Harvey.

The Australian airman and the English sailor had a notion that a door in the wall of the Castle halfway down the first causeway led somewhere. The door was marked 'Luftschutzraum'—air-raid shelter, and was being used fairly frequently these days for its allotted purpose. Although it was impossible to estimate with certitude—as the door was not visible from the prisoners' windows, frequent observation during air raids gave the impression that there was a second way—in or out—of this air-raid shelter.

Bush Parker was determined to find out and he wisely chose Mike Harvey as his partner for the attempt. Mike, being a ghost, was at the top of the escape roster.

Together they buttonholed Dick about it.

"Mike and I," he said, "have been watching the causeway during air raids now for a couple of months and we are as certain as we can be that there is a second entrance to the Luftschutzraum."

"How do you make that out?"

"We've counted the bodies going in and then the bodies coming out. They never agree."

"H'm, where have you watched from?"

"From the window in the Saalhaus (theatre block) on the second floor which overlooks the causeway and is immediately above the air-raid shelter entrance."

"But you can't see the door from there," said Dick.

"No, I admit that, but by looking downwards from the

top of the window there's only about a yard of the causeway which is blind. We can't be absolutely certain but we're nearly certain. If there's a second exit, it's beyond the sentry on the second gate. Once past this gate we have a good chance of bluffing our way past the others. It's worth a try, Dick, if you'll O.K. the idea and help us."

"Wait a minute, now, what's the rest of the plan?"

"Well, Mike and I drop from our *Saalhaus* window by rope right in front of the door. I can bring some keys which I know will open it. I've studied the lock carefully every time we've walked by the door, going down to the park. We get into the cellar, kit and all and find our way out."

"With three sentries looking at you all the time!" commented Dick.

"No!" replied Bush. "Only two for certain. The third would not worry us very much if properly stooged."

"I reckon all three will have to be properly stooged. It's just about impossible, Bush. Look! where have you got to put your stooges to cover the beats of the three of them? . . . you see? They have to be miles apart in different rooms. So you'll need a string of supplementary stooges to pass on the signals. That means seconds wasted and I can see right now this is a job of split seconds. You're in the direct beam of searchlights all the time."

"Once I can get into the air-raid shelter doorway," interrupted Bush, "I've got some deep shadow to help me. It's about nine inches inside the wall face. If I hug one side I might get away with it for a few minutes while I open the door.'"

"That's a fair risk I agree," said Dick, "but the stooging is the trouble. You'll need all the stooging in any case while you cut the window bars. That'll take you ages. No! you go away, Bush, and have another think about it. I will too."

Dick kept his promise and produced what he christened 'The electric stooge'. Five stooging posts were necessary to follow the movements of the three sentries directly concerned and also stray patrols. Dick manufactured five 'make and break' press button switches. These he fixed at the five stooging posts, connecting them all in series through the Castle wiring along with a tell-tale shaded lamp installed at the corner of the window where the 'job' was to be performed. When all buttons were pressed down the light went on. This signal meant work could proceed. If one stooge only saw danger, he released his button and work stopped instantaneously.

The cutting of the window bars by Bricky Forbes took many days of the most patient labour. Absolute silence was essential. The saw used was made, as usual, of razor blades. By the time the window was ready, however, the even more hazardous operation of letting the two bodies down in the full searchlight glare within the vision and easy hearing of the three sentries, one only fifteen yards away, could be tackled with some confidence.

Incredible as it may seem Dick and his colleagues succeeded in letting Bush and Mike down to the causeway where Bush picked the air-raid shelter lock. As he did so a sentry saw Mike, fired at him, missed, and ran to the alarm bell. Bush and Mike disappeared through the door, which was not solid but made of wooden slats. As a posse of Goons dashed out from the guardhouse, Bush put his hand through the slats, relocked the door and removed his key. The two men disappeared down a long flight of stone steps into the recesses of the air-raid shelter.

The Jerries searched the area for an hour, but never thought of unlocking the door of the air-raid shelter. However, Bush and Mike were unlucky. There was not a second exit. They were in a cul-de-sac. The escape was, to all intents and purposes, from the moment of that discovery, doomed. Although dressed in German fatigue overalls, they would have to walk out of the air-raid shelter doorway into the glare of searchlights and in full view of three sentries. Not only that, they had, within ten yards, to ask one of the sentries to open a locked gate, which required a password. If an air raid had occurred while they were in the shelter they might have had a chance, but they could not budget for an

air raid in advance, and that night there was none. The two
men therefore remained hidden in the shelter until the next
day. They then tried to pass the sentries, but were
trapped. . . .

Months of difficult work for nothing; the escape was a
failure and a complete anticlimax.

The same evening over their supper, Dick's table were
holding an inquest on the escape. Harry Elliott said it reminded him of a story that his uncle George used to tell.
Twirling one end of his moustache, he began:

"This old Uncle of mine, you see, lived for a long time
in India, Uncle George was his name. He always talked
about snakes as serpents, and he had a habit of telling stories
without any point at all. There was one story of his in particular which we, as children, always loved, and we could
always be certain of getting it by asking him, 'When you
were in India, Uncle George, did you ever see any snakes?'
to which he would reply, 'Serpents, my boy, serpents! Well
as a matter of fact I did see one, very close too. When I was
in Poona and your Uncle Edward was staying with me, we
were walking together in the compound when we saw a ser-
pent of the species *cobra de capello* coming towards us. It
came to within a few feet of us and then disappeared down
a hole.

"'I clapped my hands and the servants came running. I
ordered chairs to be brought and had them placed one on
either side of the hole. Your Uncle Edward sat in one chair
and I sat in the other, and though we waited there for
several hours, we never saw the creature again'."

The ghosts had doubles. Mike Harvey's double was
Lieutenant Bartlett (Royal Tank Regiment), who looked
rather like him. As soon as Mike was caught he posed as
Bartlett and Bartlett went into hiding. Unfortunately, when
Mike set off to the solitary confinement cells the German
sergeant in charge looked at him closely and said, "You are
not Bartlett!"

He could not make out who the stranger was, but he put

him in the cells, nevertheless, for safety. It took the Germans two days to sift out the mess this time. A security officer came to Mike's cell with his correct papers and that was the end of Mike as a ghost.

Jack Best carried on.

CHAPTER XV

THE TERRACE

DICK was sunbathing on one of the rare occasions when he found time to do so and during that short period of the day when the sun stared almost vertically downwards into the deep pit of the courtyard. It was sultry August weather. Roughly a third of the yard reflected the dazzling white glare of the sunlight, while the shadows deepened to black around the sides.

He lay on a blanket stretched over the cobbles, naked, except for a pair of pants, and was deeply engrossed in 'Gone With the Wind.' His eyes followed the printed words and his thoughts soared on the magic carpet of fiction, upwards and outwards, far beyond the walls, beyond the horizons. Over the blessed gardens of oblivion he floated happily setting his course towards the mountains of the past. What a Godsend books were; like cool water upon the fevered brow; like the caress of a loved one!

Dick was brought back to earth through the sudden covering of his open page by a blanket which descended seemingly from nowhere. He looked up.

"Sorry, Dick," came a cheerful voice as the blanket was whisked away and spread more carefully beside Dick's own. It was Gordon Rolfe, the Canadian. The sunlit patch of cobbles in the courtyard was filling up with bodies. Soon no cobbles would be visible as row upon row of sunbathers formed up for an early afternoon siesta.

"Getting like Coney Island around here," said Rolfe.

"Palm Beach!" protested Dick. "Put on your rose tinted spectacles—look at those two lovelies—just flown in from Hollywood this morning." Dick nodded towards two particularly skinny angular, almost nude figures wending their rickety way amongst the recumbent forms.

Rolfe grinned and sat down cross-legged on his blanket.

"Dick," he said, "how about you taking me for a Cook's tour around the Castle. It'll save me a hell of a lot of time. I'm trying to find a way out the same as everyone else, but if I can build on your knowledge I might, with a pair of new eyes, hit on something that hasn't yet been thought of."

Dick thought for a moment before replying.

Among the Eichstätt tunnellers there were many outstanding escapers, men who had broken bounds more than once before but who had not made the home-run. Gordon Rolfe and Dopey Miller; Frank Weldon of the R.H.A. and J. Hamilton-Baillie, R.E., the two leading tunnellers of Eichstätt; others like Hugo Ironside and Douglas Moir of the Royal Tank Regiment, and Tom Stallard; Phil Pardoe and Tony Rolt of the Rifle Brigade.

Dick said, "The Old Lags have looked out of the same windows for so long that they've got permanent squints. I'll take you round all right with pleasure, but if it's to be a Cook's tour how about half a dozen of you new chaps coming along together?"

Dick mentioned some of the names he had thought of.

Gordon Rolfe agreed:

"I'll get hold of them, Dick; they'll be only too glad. What's the best sort of time? We don't want to look like a bunch of tourists."

"Oh, sometime in the evening is probably best. How about after the five o'clock *Appell*?"

"I'll fix it—sorry for interrupting your reading." Rolfe sprawled over his blanket and Dick returned to the realms of the Southern States and the times of the Civil War.

They met again in the cool of the early evening after the roll call. Rolfe had gathered quite a party, including Dopey Miller and Tony Rolt. He led them, first of all, once the *Appell* guards and N.C.O.s had retired, through the doorway opening from the cobbled yard into the corridor leading to the sick ward. He walked over to a small window in the north wall of the ward beside a round turret at the north-west corner of the Castle, and beckoned the others to look out and downwards, pointing:

"Have a look down there," he began. "Through this window—you can see where the bars have been repaired—Bush Parker did his stuff with Mike Sinclair, Hyde-Thomson and Lance Pope in the Franz Josef escape. . . ." He went on, describing to them how the escape had been engineered. He told them how Mike had hung on, trying to get the second sentry to move, how the two Franz Josefs had faced each other and how Mike had been wounded. At the end Rolfe asked:

"Why didn't Mike make a break with his two men—he should have, don't you think—instead of hanging on?"

"Many people have asked that question," said Dick, "to be quite candid I've taken the can back for it. I left the final decision to Mike himself instead of giving him a specific instruction to quit at the slightest sign of obstruction. What some chaps argued afterwards was that, knowing Mike, I should also have known that he just wasn't the type who would quit and I should, therefore, have given him an order."

Walking back once more into the corridor he pointed to Gephard's office and they looked through the window at the end of the corridor down on the sentry footpath. "Six men went out there to the right, from the building known as the clothes store, starting off with a hole underneath Gephard's desk. They were dressed as German N.C.O.s and Polish orderlies. Two of them—Bill Fowler and a Dutchman—got to Switzerland. Underneath where we're standing is a cellar where the French tunnel started; it ran under the chapel towards your right heading for the park."

They returned to the courtyard. Dick stopped outside the doorway, looking up at the clock tower. "The French used the tower," he explained. "Their entrance was at the top and they hid fifty tons of stone and rubble in the attics mostly over the chapel. In the chapel at the moment," he went on, "there is a working, run by Monty Bissell. We're hiding a ghost in it. Don't do any snooping in there without letting me know first."

The party walked casually across the courtyard and into

the dentist's room on the east side of the Castle. Dick gathered them once more at a window and pointed out through the bars. "You see that buttress over there to the right. Well, it's hollow—it was a medieval lavatory. Vandy and half a dozen Dutch and British got down to the bottom of it from the third floor. It was on rock. They tried tunnelling but were caught. Just round the corner, beyond the buttress and above us, is the window where we had the team ready to go out if the Franz Josef bluff had worked." He led them through several small low-ceilinged rooms, unlocking two doors on the way with his master key.

They found themselves in the barber's shop. "Under this floor there is still a whacking great hole left by Pat Reid. The Jerries have never found it. If anyone has ideas for starting up work again here, they're welcome. There are several snags but nothing is impossible. You might have a think about it." He led them next to the canteen in the south-east corner.

"This area's vulnerable," he explained, "and may give you something to think about. We had a tunnel here in 1941 which led out under the canteen window and under the grass lawn beyond. Fourteen of us were caught. Several efforts have been made by Poles and Frenchmen to get out of the window—unsuccessful. Up above, there's a sealed room which we reached by a snow tunnel. It connects with the German quarters. On another occasion a team got into their quarters through a hole in the German lavatories which backed on to one of our dormitories. There's hope of doing something up above on the roof—it might be possible to have another crack at breaking through the gable of the Kommandantur and entering the German attics . . . let's go and have a look at the cookhouse."

Germans and orderlies were still at work and they could not approach the windows overlooking the German court-yard to the south. Dick contented himself by standing inside the doorway and explaining:

"This is where Reid, Ronnie Littledale, Hank Wardle and Stephens got out into the courtyard, then over the

sentry's beat into the Kommandantur and out to the moat
and away; four home-runs. Above the kitchen, Frenchmen
have tried the roofs and chimney stacks, so has Peter Storie
Pugh. It might be tried again, but it's not a cake walk.
Don Thom and Donaldson have had one shot also along
the lean-to roof just under the stacks—you've got to be an
acrobat to get there because it's an overhanging roof, though
nearly flat, once you're on it."

Someone asked 'out of the blue': "Why don't you ever
try to escape yourself, Dick?"

"I suppose because I'm a b—— fool," was the response,
"but you can't do my job and try to escape as well. The two
just don't add up. I know everybody's plans. It would be too
easy to pinch someone else's idea and use it myself. Even if
I had an idea of my own—nobody would believe me. I
might have retired some time ago and asked someone else
to take on the job—but now—at least I can't do it until you
fellows are well stuck in. Then one of you might take over."

In the courtyard again, he showed them the de-lousing
shed. "In one corner of the shed," he said, "there's a tunnel
shaft—it was found by the Jerries but the working has been
used again. The Poles, before they left, made a tunnel, from
their quarters over the canteen—which were once ours, too;
joining up with the drains. The drains run just beside that
corner of the de-louser and they linked up. They continued
outside the courtyard, under the main gate. The escape is
in hand at the moment and Duggie Bader's in charge of it.
He could do with help—it's a stinking job—every cut
festers."

They next trooped upstairs to the theatre where Dick
told his audience the story of the light well escape. Then
pointing to the stage, he said:

"Four men got out from under the stage—Airey Neave
was one. They went through a narrow corridor, over the
main gate, into the German guardhouse and walked downstairs and out—in German uniforms, of course. Two made
home-runs to Switzerland. A couple of Poles also got into
the guardhouse from the building opposite this theatre

block, by walking along a four inch ledge, forty feet above the cobbles. They made too much row climbing down their rope on the outside. A Jerry officer popped his head out of a window. They were only then about a hundred feet above the rocks at the bottom, hanging on to the rope. The Jerry pointed a pistol at them and shouted 'Hands up!' I'm told the Poles laughed so much they nearly let go."

Looking downwards from one of the theatre windows facing due west he showed the group where Bush Parker had dropped in the searchlight beams on to the causeway. Finally, the tour ended in the British quarters overlooking the terrace which also faced westward and were situated just to the south of the turret where Dick had begun.

"Some weeks ago," he told them, "Don Thom took the bull by the horns. He's an Olympic diver, incidentally. He's as tough as nails and a bundle of springs. I think he was browned off by all the effort we put into Bush Parker's escape which fizzled out. We've got another job on hand at the moment, too, and I'd ask you chaps to leave this area alone until it's over. If I tell you of Don Thom's effort you'll see that we're up against a very tough proposition."

"Have you a large scale plan of the Castle?" Gordon Rolfe asked. "I'd like to study it for a while to get my bearings."

"Yes, there is a plan," said Dick, "it's a series of plans really. It gives the state of the buildings from about the seventeenth century onwards as a matter of fact. The one thing I can't tell you is how we got it. I'll show it to any of you who want to examine it. Lulu Lawton will get it out of its hide after dinner."

"What happened to Don Thom?" Tony Rolt asked.

The group had relaxed. Some were lolling on the beds, others were looking out of the window down upon the terrace. The bars prevented them from having a clear view directly below them. Nobody was in a hurry.

"Don Thom's escape was a Douglas Fairbanks show-piece," Dick began. "Don first of all earned himself a month in the cooler—that was easy. Then, during the hour's exercise on the terrace you're looking at below you, he just leapt

for it. It's the most daring escape recorded here and more
death defying even than the Park escape of Mairesse Lebrun, the French cavalry officer. Mairesse at least had the
assistance of one other officer and was exercising in the park
under vigilance. There have been many escapes from the
Park, incidentally, which you'll hear about. Don Thom
dared four sentries in broad daylight, one of them—you can
see from that window—with a machine gun. I know exactly
how he must have felt because I'd never have the guts or
suicidal courage—call it what you like—to do it myself.

"The men in the cooler inside the Castle are usually
taken out under guard to the terrace through the guardhouse itself. They come out through that small doorway at
the south end. The terrace wall drop, from the outer balustrade, forty feet to the garden below. The far edge of the
garden is protected by the low parapet wall which you can
see, and by the nine-foot barbed wire fence. On the far side
there's a precipitous drop which descends into a welter of
rocks and concertina wire about fifty feet below. The cliff
then levels out into the back yards of a few houses alongside the road which borders the river.

"Bag Dickenson, Van Rood and Don were all doing solitary together. One morning, the same as any other as far as
solitaries are concerned, the three of them were escorted for
their daily exercise, one sentry in front, one behind—regular daily routine—through the courtyard gate, into the
guardhouse, down a few curving steps, and out on to the
terrace.

"A sentry went first, and Bag next, through the little
doorway into the open air. Don Thom was third. As he
passed the door, he took off his jacket, dropped it in the
corner, and vaulted the parapet; a clear forty foot drop—
just like that! Don's tough, but still, forty feet is not the
kind of jump to be contemplated when rifles and machine
guns are going to open on you as soon as you land. As he
dropped, he gripped the bars of two windows, one under
the other, to break his fall. You can't see the windows from
here, they're below the terrace in the guardhouse wall. He

was seen by four sentries, including the one following Van Rood, and the fifth—the sentry in front of Bag—turned round when his mate shouted. Five sentries tried to hit him as he ran. Bag and Van Rood jitterbugged into their two sentries on the terrace and managed to upset their aim. But a machine gun post in a pagoda and two other sentries opened fire without hindrance.

"Don Thom ran to the fence. He probably saved his life by turning to the right when common-sense dictated he should go to the left. He scaled the nine foot wire with the bullets whizzing around him. He was forced to slow up by the climb. Then he dropped out of sight down the cliff below; hit or unscathed nobody could tell. He wasn't yet out of danger. Two sentries, who could still see him, potted away. He must have been moving fast at the bottom, tearing his way through a weak point in the concertina wire. But he couldn't make it. His clothes were ripped to pieces and he got tangled up; he had to put up his hands and they stopped firing. The nearest bullet took a piece out of his scalp."

There was a long pause when Dick finished the story. Then Tony Rolt asked:

"Did you say, Dick, that another escape was being planned from the terrace?"

"Yes, Mike Sinclair and Jack Best are going to have a crack, at dusk though, not in broad daylight. They have to start inside the Castle, of course. The only other way to get out on to the terrace is to do what Dom Thom did and that means a daylight job."

There was a long silence. It was broken by the sound of a raucous voice in the corridor shouting: "Char up! Char up!" As if waking from a dream, the men rose and ambled out silently one by one to the mess room.

*　　　*　　　*　　　*　　　*

Jack Best, of the R.A.F.V.R., the boy from Stowe, the Empire builder with a farm in Kenya, was becoming desperate. He had been a ghost for almost a year. The tables were turning upon him and he was beginning to look like a haunted man. Jack, at thirty years of age, had the patience of Job. It was the reason why he had been accepted when he volunteered for the uneviable task of becoming a ghost. But it was plain that the job was beginning to tell on his health. Don Donaldson had, not without reason, christened him the 'unfledged eagle'. Now his downy feathers were drooping; his hair was looking thin and bedraggled, ready to fall out in a high wind. His long beak of a nose was losing flesh. The bridge was standing out prominently and the tip would soon meet his chin as his mouth receded. His dark eyes, with the fire of the eagle within, were more sunken than ever, and looked like two coals burning into his skull. His tall angular frame was hunched. The protruding shoulders and arms looked as if they should sprout feathers at any moment.

The only way by which he could break the vicious circle in which he found himself and retain his self respect was by escaping, because he was no longer officially recognised as a prisoner. He had escaped, but into another prison inside the prison instead of outside. If and when he escaped properly, another officer could take up his ghostly manacles. If he made a home-run the arithmetic would, in his case, be simplified; it would have caught up with him. From the German point of view, the sum would add up correctly. But if he was re-caught the Germans would have to use algebra, beginning with 'let X be the officer who escaped in November, 1942. . . .' If Best was re-captured after some days of freedom there was one series of possible solutions. If he was caught at the camp, there were other solutions, including the possibility that he was entering the Castle—gun-running—a possibility not so far-fetched as it might appear at first.

Although Jack had a tremendous sense of humour, he lived on his nerves. He had seen the funny side of living like a mole underground at Sagan—Stalag Luft III—while he tunnelled himself and his friend, Bill Goldfinch, outside the wire to mark up a 'gone-away' and earn them both a place at Colditz. He could still see the funny side of being a

ghost—up to a point, but, by November, 1943, the joke was
wearing thin.

Mike Sinclair was planning his next escape. A duel of
wits of his own conception was to take place on an old
battle-ground: the terrace where Don Thom had sailed
gaily over the parapet as if he had been performing in the
high jump at his annual school sports.

Mike selected Jack Best as his partner for the break.

The time at which the perimeter searchlights were
switched on was tabulated and graphed as a matter of routine. What Mike was looking for was a short blind interval
at dusk; blind in two senses: firstly, on account of the
approaching gloom and, secondly, coinciding with a change
of the guards, taking them from their points of vantage. He
posed the problem to Dick Howe and indicated when he
thought the short interval of time might occur.

Regularly, over a period of four months, Dick, Lulu
Lawton and Mike watched the changing of the guard in the
terrace area; in the pagoda; on the cat walk; in the garden
(an orchard), and in the corner turret. Jack Best could not
help them in this, being a ghost.

A machine-gun sentry post, an outsize crow's-nest, situated on an elevated scaffolding, reached by a ladder, in the
garden beneath the terrace, commanded the whole wall face
of the prison on that side, including the outer wall of the
German guardhouse. It was known as a 'Pagoda,' and was
manned day and night. Another type of scaffold, providing
a long elevated corridor with timber balustrades, was known
as a 'cat-walk.' One such was built close to the outer wall
of the guardhouse where the garden narrowed, and at one
end it jutted out over the precipice below. The sentry post
at ground level in the garden and the machine-gun post in
the turret under the prison walls were only manned at
nightfall, when it became difficult for the machine-gun post
in the pagoda to command the walls fully, owing to deep
shadows cast by the searchlights at certain angles. The garden sentry also replaced a sentry on the terrace itself, who

was useless at night, standing directly in the glare of the searchlights.

The turret sentry and the garden sentry came on duty at the nearest regular guard change coinciding with nightfall. With this pinpoint of knowledge, culled by simple observation, Mike Sinclair opened an oyster.

The first essential that the three watchers deduced, was that, between the time when the pagoda sentry at dusk left his post and was replaced and the first turret sentry had gained his position, there was a blind spot of sixty seconds duration. The second essential for the escape was the seasonal advent of a period when the searchlights, governed, as was discovered, by a routine schedule depending mainly on the time of year and hardly at all upon the state of the light on any particular day, were switched on just after a regular guard change. 'Just after' was the important point, so that the sixty seconds coincided with the maximum darkness possible. Not until the end of November, 1943, were all the conditions favourable for the attempt to take place.

Sixty seconds! Perhaps seventy seconds. Perhaps only fifty! Dick, Mike and Lulu were not prepared to argue over ten seconds either way. The job to be performed was one that would require the services, under peace-time conditions, of a team of workmen for a day with long ladders and several tool kits; an industrial safety inspector, and a merger of Lloyd's insurance brokers. Mike Sinclair and Jack Best, dispensing with the anomalies of peace, reckoned to do the job in sixty seconds.

The bars of a window in the British quarters on the second floor of the Castle, thirty feet above the terrace, had to be cut by way of an opening gambit. This was done in the same manner as for the Franz Josef attempt.

Bo'sn Crisp prepared no less than ninety feet of the best rope he had ever made from strips cut out of the blue check cotton sleeping bags and tested at every splice.

The civilian clothing, the maps, the money, the home-made compasses and the identity papers were forged with minute accuracy.

Mike Sinclair selected his wire-cutters. He preferred the pair made by Bill Goldfinch to the factory-made pair smuggled into the camp.

The four of them discussed the launching ramp.

"You'd better use the long table," said Dick, "and give it a thorough rub down with sand-paper. The long one will take the two of you lying flat, end to end, and you can be shot straight through the window opening, holding on to the rope."

Mike said, with a curious air of finality, "I want you two, Dick and Lulu, to do the launching, nobody else. I don't want anyone else to do it."

"Mike will go out first," Dick explained, "with the wire-cutters strapped to his leg. When he's dropped to the terrace he takes the rope end with him and jumps over the balustrade, Don Thom fashion. Now, Jack, if you don't hustle after Mike, you'll find yourself suspended in mid-air over the terrace when he takes the rope with him over the second drop. Everything's got to move together. Lulu, you must let the rope out as fast as Mike needs it, but keep it fairly taut all the time. Jack, you've simply got to be on the terrace by the time Mike goes over, so you must slide down the rope following Mike like streak lightning down a moving escalator. Get me?"

Jack intervened, "What about the brief-case and the second length of rope all attached to the end of the main rope?"

"When you've finished with the main rope, that is, after the second drop, unhitch them both—they'll be on a slip-knot—and carry on. Now, Lulu, this is where you come in. As soon as the tension is off the main rope you must haul in like mad! Jack, don't forget to keep a firm hold on the rope or you'll find your food and kit disappearing upwards. Let go only when everything is clear. After that the rest is up to you and we can't do much more for you."

When the two escapers reached the bottom of the second drop they would have to run thirty yards diagonally across the garden, cut a gap in the barbed-wire perimeter fence, tie the second rope to a post and drop down the rocky cliff below, a matter of fifty feet. This was the cliff over which Don Thom had thrown himself, clinging to jutting crags as he hurtled down in broad daylight with rifles blazing at him. On the new assault, Mike and Jack hoped to tie their rope and disappear over the edge before they were seen. To this end, of course, silence was invaluable.

At the bottom of the cliff they had concertina barbed-wire to deal with before they were finally 'gone-away.'

*   *   *   *   *

The stage is set for the escape of sixty seconds. It is a cold afternoon at the end of November, 1943, with sleet and a biting wind which augurs well for a murky evening. The day wears on. The two bars of the window have been cut by Bricky Forbes and Bill Goldfinch. The stooges are placed as the gloom of evening begins to creep over the Castle and their intercommunicating code system is checked. The signal, 'all clear,' will come from the accordion of the master stooge at a window directly above that at which the operation is about to take place. Dick will give the final order, 'go'....

Zero hour has arrived and zero minute will soon be here. The wind has dropped, which is a pity. Mike and Jack will need all the self-control they can muster to avoid making a noise and giving the alarm on the last lap.

In the dormitory there is silence as the shadows deepen. Along the smooth table the two escapers lie. Jack Best is dead still. Mike is fidgety. The cutters strapped to his leg are uncomfortable. They may give trouble. Dick is readjusting them.

High up in a corner, sitting on the top of a wardrobe, is John Watton, the camp artist, with his drawing-board, pencils and chalks. He is working furiously in the gathering dusk, his hand and brain alive to the terrific tension as he tries to translate the suspense of the moment on to the flat medium of paper. He stares downwards. His eyes gleam in the fading light and his hand circles upon the paper.

"Three minutes to go," says Dick, in a hushed voice, "providing the sentries behave themselves. Keep dead calm. Remember it's a cinch. Go quietly as you drop and move."

The two men lie still, stiffening against the fierce heave that will project them along the table out into the twilight one after the other, like rockets from a launching ramp; that will shoot them out of the window in a headlong swoop which they must check before landing. The rope is laid out straight beside and behind them. Mike holds it coiled around his right arm.

All the actors on the stage who may approach the window have blackened faces, and the two escapers, in addition, wear long dark stockings over their shoes. Their two forms lie stretched, like beasts on a sacrificial altar, ready for the moment when the high priest will raise his arm aloft and pronounce the words of doom.

"One minute to go," Dick intones in a low voice, clear for all to hear in the grim silence.

Two strong men stand rigid beside the window, waiting, ready to grip the bars and twist them out of the way at the signal. The whites of their eyes flash out of their blackened faces.

Derek Gill and Mike Harvey stand by the rope, to pay it out, to prevent it tangling and to take the weight of the descending bodies.

Dick and Lulu, the priests, stand over the table while Dick leans towards the window, listening intently, peer-downwards.

Mike is jittery. He is complaining the cutters are too tight around his leg. Almost like a child, he is whispering to Dick, "They're too tight! They're too tight! I must have them looser—help me quickly—looser—quick—— No! Dick, there's no time now. It's to late. There's not enough time, stop."

The accordion starts to play.

Dick looks at his watch and raises his arm, counting audibly, "Four—three—two—one," and then drops it at "go!"

The two strong men at the bars clench their teeth and heave with the strength of devils, twisting the bars inwards and sideways in a slow, quivering movement fraught with the tautness of muscles and the wracking of sinews. Hell breaks loose. The spirit of action like an unholy demon takes possession of the room.

Lulu and Dick grip Mike bodily, one on either side, and hurl him through the window feet first. He shoots horizontally outwards. Another tremendous heave and Jack Best

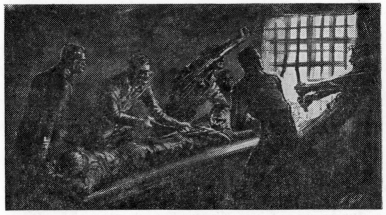

—Go!

slides forward, rockets out and disappears from view. Gill and Harvey feel the rope tearing through their hands. They let it out to the first marker knot, lean back, take the strain with the rope twisted round their forearms. There is a tremendous jerk, followed by a thump. The rope holds. The two are down on the terrace, thirty feet below.

The rope pays out again, uncoiling like a cobra, weaving, snatching and turning, as Mike races across the terrace.

Dick, at the window, raises his arm again in signal. Gill and Harvey take the strain once more on the rope. Mike and Jack are over the terrace and dropping down the second forty-foot descent.

The guardhouse door is opening. A shaft of light breaks through the gloom along the terrace. A German N.C.O. walks out, advancing slowly along the terrace. He seems momentarily blind.

"They must free the rope!" hisses Dick. "Good God, he can see it! It's straight in front of him. For Pete's sake, Derek! heave it in, heave like mad!"

As he speaks the light blue rope slackens. The German leans on the balustrade. He looks over the parapet. At that instant the rope whistles past him, upwards, not a yard away. He has heard something; he whips out his revolver, but seems not to have seen the rope. He shouts: *"Hallo! Hallo!"* There is no answer.

A scurry above, as the rope is hauled through the window, makes the German look upwards for a moment, puzzled. Then he turns towards the garden as a distinct 'ping' is heard from the direction of the wire below. Another loud 'ping' and the German shouts again, *"Hallo! Hallo! Was ist los?* and peers into the shadows below, shading his eyes with his hand, and with his revolver cocked.

Mike has crossed the garden and is cutting the wires underneath the pagoda where the new sentry has taken up his position. Mike appears to take no notice of the guard who has come out on to the terrace. He has not seen him. The sentry above him answers the N.C.O.: *"Ich weiss nicht."*

Jack is in the shadow under the terrace wall. He can see the German above him and dares not move. He cannot warn Mike. A third 'ping' is heard clearly by Dick and Lulu in the window high above.

The German walks slowly along the terrace near the parapet, looking outwards. The night sentry in the garden has reached his post and is standing fifteen yards away. This is Jack's chance; he creeps to the end of the wall and then across the garden among the fruit trees and the deeper shadows to where Mike has already fixed the rope for the last drop. Mike drops over. Jack follows, but lies on the edge of the drop, trying to close the wire gap behind him. He looks up and sees the German on the terrace staring straight towards him with his pistol at the ready. That is enough. He drops out of sight, sliding down the rope over rocks and bushes, fifty feet, to the bottom. The N.C.O. turns slowly away.

There is more barbed-wire below—coils upon coils of it.

"We can't get through there," whispers Mike hoarsely; "we must crawl along to the end."

They do so, slipping and stumbling on the steep incline, ripping their clothes on the wire at every move until they reach a narrow path.

Here Mike tackles the wire again. 'Ping! Ping! Ping!" Bill Goldfinch's home-made, five-to-one lever wire-cutters do their work. They crawl through.

But a woman in a nearby cottage has heard the scrambling and comes to the window, looking out. "*Was ist los?*"

Silence! as the two men lie prone, their hearts pounding, she moves away and they are off again.

They are dripping with sweat, winded and breathing painfully. Their civilian clothes are badly torn. Seventy seconds ago they were prisoners in the impregnable fortress. Now they are free. . . .

*   *   *   *   *

As they moved off into the countryside at a slow trot, Dick stood motionless at the window high up in the Castle.

The German N.C.O. had returned to the guardhouse, walking slowly with hesitant steps, frequently turning round, obviously worried and uncomprehending.

Dick gazed outwards over the fast darkening countryside, out into the gloom towards the river where he knew his two men were heading. He was tingling all over with nervous elation. Then, as he peered, he felt his legs weaken under him and he gripped the window sill to steady himself. Gall rose in his throat and a sudden revulsion turned his stomach. His eyes misted over. He closed them quickly, gripping the sill tightly. The nausea continued for a couple of minutes as he fought against the urge to vomit. . . . The crisis passed slowly and he opened his eyes.

The searchlights came on with a blinding flash around the Castle and all beyond turned as black as pitch.

"They've gone· away! They're safe by now!" said Dick thickly, turning to Lulu and the others, and mopping his blackened brow with the flicker of a smile spreading over his face. There was silence again. He glanced at his companions, noting at once he was not the only one whose stomach had turned over. After the fever of the past two minutes, they were stunned. For a few seconds they had all been escaping with the two who had disappeared. Now they stood, silent, wondering, almost inexplicably, why they had not gone, why they were still in the room within the oppressive walls. There were no words that they could say.

Watton climbed down from his perch, shaking with the excitement of the action. "Fantastic, simply fantastic!" he shouted, waving his drawing-block wildly around his head.

"I'm glad you like it," said Lulu drily. "I'll appreciate a signed copy of the result, if you don't mind."

Dick said simply, talking to them all, "Thanks for a pretty piece of team work. You've made escaping history to-night—I think." And, as they went about clearing away the signs of the escape, Dick turned once more to the window, staring out into the blackness beyond the searchlight beams.

He stood, motionless, with the reflection from the blazing arcs outside accentuating his worn, haggard features, still streaked with black theatre paint; the strong chin, the drawn lines of the skin and the sunken eyes. His thoughts had suddenly been turned inwards. He was trying to answer the question that had flashed through all their minds when they stood silent and perplexed a few moments before. "Why were they still there? Why had others gone?" There seemed to be no general answer. "Many are called, but few are chosen," he thought, "might not be far off the mark."

It was more than a question of plain guts. For this kind of escaping a man required a will of iron and a calculating, cold-blooded courage that was not commonly found. There was a deep sense of duty behind it all, too—but that applied to all of them.

'All over the world' Dick thought, 'men are fighting and falling. To be impotent—a prisoner—helpless and unable to help, is a degrading state, hard to bear.'

At least these men were doing something. They could hold up their heads and keep their self-respect. They were thinking of the future and not necessarily of their own. They had not Milton's excuse. 'They also serve who only stand and wait' was not for them. They were not blind.

For several minutes Dick stood at the window, then, turning slowly, he came out of his reverie.

"I thought Mike was a bit jittery to-night, not quite his usual self," he said to Lulu. "I wonder why the Goon chose to come out on to the terrace at that precise moment?"

"Most inconsiderate of him," was Lulu's comment as they walked out of the room together.

CHAPTER XVI

CHINA TEA

TONY ROLT was one of the sixty-five Eichstätt tunellers. From the day they had arrived, in July, 1943, these tunnellers had been known as 'the new boys.' The name clung to them and, the English being a conservative race, they were still new boys at the end of the war, by which time they had been indistinguishable from their blood-brothers, 'the old lags,' for nearly two years.

In self-defence the 'new boys' invented 'the men of spirit' —a term which they applied to any and sundry among the 'old lags' who, either by innuendo or direct attack, tried to inculcate in them a sense of inferiority. They were not to be browbeaten and the sarcasm behind the appellation had its effect.

Undertones and rumblings, disturbances from the intrusion into Colditz, echoed around the camp and slowly died away. Like the spilling of one lake into another when the weir gates are raised, the two waters clashed, shot up in spray, sent waves dashing to the shore, swirled in eddies, rippled, merged and gradually subsided into one, still, homogeneous pool, deeper than before.

The new boys were under a disadvantage: the disadvantage suffered by all new boys throughout the world. They did not know the ropes, they did not know the old boys, they were in strange surroundings and sometimes at a loss —humiliating, under any circumstances. But they brought with them some new ideas which the old boys eventually acknowledged—grudgingly to begin with—and later with enthusiasm. The scorpion's lash of 'the new boys' lost its sting.

Tony Rolt was one among the many whom the old boys would have liked to claim towards the end of the war, as one of the 'men of spirit.' This term also, like an old, well-worn, ugly pair of shoes, became 'cosy' from long usage.

Rolt, in his early twenties, was an amateur motor-racing driver who had achieved fame before the war. He was a lieutenant of the Rifle Brigade. He was dark and clean-shaven, almost streamlined, like one of his cars, and he had a serious yet lively nature; at one and the same time, painstaking yet bubbling with enthusiasm.

He could not drive a delicate, highly-tuned racing car out of Colditz, even a heavy tank would not have gone far. He used to lie for hours on his bunk, exasperated by the frustration, stung by his own impotence and goaded to action by the blackness of the escaping outlook. He wondered how some highly technical *flair* could be brought to bear on escaping; there was any amount of scientific talent in Colditz. It was clear to him that only the most desperate action would succeed in these days. The last two escapes which had put British prisoners outside the perimeter wire were cases in point. When men were taking to leaping over forty-foot walls in broad daylight, braving the machine-guns, rocketing out of windows attached to ropes, weaving between sentries in mad, second-splitting escapes, it was time to be original, and in a big way. To Rolt's way of thinking there was no hope of success for anything in the least mundane. The Jerries had all that taped, tied up and sealed irrevocably.

He brought together and crystallised the gleanings of weeks of cogitation one day in December, 1943. He sat brooding over a morning cup of acorn coffee, made palatable with powdered milk and a saccharin tablet.

Rumours were abroad that Mike and Jack Best had been recaptured. Pessimism was on the prowl again, looking for victims.

He spoke first to Bill Goldfinch, who was sitting opposite to him munching a piece of German sawdust-bread thinly coated with the remains of a Canadian Red Cross butter ration.

"Quite a tribute, I thought, the way Mike Sinclair took

your home-made wire-cutters in preference to the factory-made variety. You're a bit of a wizard with your hands, Bill. Where did you learn it?"

It was not a coincidence that he should be talking to Bill Goldfinch. It was part of his thinking—this morning, it seemed, everything had come to a head. Bill Goldfinch was sitting there. The time was ripe.

Bill was speaking.

"There's nothing to it, Tony. I just got the habit of tinkering when I was a kid, ever since the family went out to Rhodesia. My old man was an engineer. I suppose that had something to do with it. He sent me to work in the Salisbury City Council engineering department. I'm not happy unless my hands are at work."

"What made you join the R.A.F.?" Rolt asked.

"I got mad keen on flying and aircraft design. That sent me into the R.A.F.V.R. when I was twenty-one. It must have been about 1938. That's how I'm here now. I got called up when war started and was trapped in the Greek evacuation. My Sunderland flying boat crashed at Kalamata. If I hadn't been spitting blood I'd've been evacuated. Instead they operated on me—found nothing wrong—only mouth bleeding. But before my operation wound healed I was a prisoner. I met up with Jack Best in the hospital."

As he listened, Tony was thinking, 'This is the man all right. I'm sure he'll do it. . . . I bet he will.' Aloud he said, "Bill, I've got an idea. I'm going to tell you something that'll make you think I'm going round the bend. I'm not though—not yet."

"Go ahead, I'm listening," said Bill quietly, in a reassuring voice. He was like that, reassuring, with a touch of kindliness. His fair complexion, his mousy hair and his pale blue eyes, made up a picture of an unassuming, even shy nature. His inner strength, the peculiar tough fibre which has nothing to do with physical strength, but a lot to do with mental equanimity, only made itself felt after long contact with his personality. He was the type of man who would survive alone in a lifeboat after weeks of exposure, long after all the other occupants had gone overboard.

"I'm not an engineer, you see, Bill," Rolt continued, "but I know enough about mechanics and, I think also, enough about aerodynamics to imagine that what I'm thinking about is not complete nonsense.

"I seriously think a glider could be built that would be able to take off from one of the roofs of this castle. Don't think me crazy yet—listen—let me finish. I've been thinking about this idea for months. There's a long roof overlooking the river—the one over the old French quarters. It's so high that the ridge is completely out of sight from all the sentries below. In fact, you can only see the ridge if you go down into the town or away, over the river. Look!" Here Rolt produced a piece of paper from his pocket. He unfolded it and spread it before Bill Goldfinch.

"You see—there's a cross-section of the castle to scale with the sentries at their posts. Their lines of vision run from the roof gutters straight up, skywards. They can't see anywhere near the roof ridge. We could make a flat launching ramp like a saddle, built in sections, to sit on the roof ridge. It's twenty yards long."

"You mean," interrupted Bill, who was becoming curiously excited in spite of himself. "You mean, the glider would be catapulted then?"

"Yes, that's it. I've already got some ideas for the catapult, but let me finish. The glider would have to be built in parts, with dismountable wings. I don't know how many persons it could take. That's where you would begin to come into the picture. What do you think, Bill? I can't do this myself, but with one, or even two, professionals, I'm sure a glider can be built. I'll do all the donkey-work, everything I can possibly do, but I don't know enough about aerodynamics, and I'm not a highly skilled craftsman."

"A glider isn't so very hard to build, you know," said Bill, becoming involved and beginning to fall for the idea. "What it requires is tremendous patience. I only wish Jack Best was around. He's just the man for this. He's got the patience of Job. A glider consists of literally thousands of parts, all the same—like the wings of a bird—thousands of feathers all the same shape. If I made a few prototype parts and some templates, you could carry on."

"Does that mean you'll seriously think about the idea?" asked Tony.

"Yes," said Bill, "I'll think about it," and that was all Tony Rolt could extract from him at that sitting.

During the next two weeks Rolt continued to badger Bill Goldfinch until he had the latter sitting down in front of a home-made drawing-board with pencils, paper, rulers and rubber. From that moment Bill Goldfinch was lost. He found himself starting upon a course which would lead him he knew not where, but quite likely to a 'sticky end.' He was at the top of a steep hill, sitting astride an infernal machine of his own making, without brakes—or engine. He was gaining momentum, out of control, and the end of the hill was just round the corner.

*   *   *   *   *

While the new boys were still new, it goes without saying that they had their legs pulled.

Harry Elliott was recounting to a few of the newcomers, some time after their arrival, the history of the several continental contingents which had come and gone from Colditz. He talked glowingly of the Poles; humorously of the French and Belgians, warmly of the Dutch, and, to make sure that he lost nothing in effect, he reminded his listeners of the Yugoslavian officers, the Indian doctor and the North Africans, and introduced them forthwith to a Bedouin sheik who was, at the time, a resident in Colditz. Nobody quite knew, and least of all the Bedouin himself, how he had filtered down to Colditz. He had been mixed up in some mêlée in North Africa and had been captured. Nobody understood what he said, and he could not understand what anybody else said. One misunderstanding led to another, until the smiling sheik, with the features of an Orient King and the character of a humorist in perpetual adversity, arrived at Colditz, where it seemed he would not have much opportunity to strike his tent or silently fade away.

"What a collection of nationalities!" exclaimed one new boy in respectful admiration. "What a pity there are no Chinese!" said another with a slight hint of sarcasm.

It was enough for Harry. He would shake them.

"Oh! but haven't you met the Chinese naval officer?" he said.

"No! Where is he? Do introduce us. This is terrific!" The hint of sarcasm had gone. Now there was only astonishment and unconcealed wonder.

The Chinese naval officer was in the sick bay, explained Harry. He was not very well but he would try and arrange an introduction for the next day.

Harry lived in the sick quarters himself at that time. He was working hard at his own escape plans. His jaundice had given place to duodenal ulcers. These were having marital complications with a genuine form of arthritis, which he was nursing successfully into a galloping paralysis. He had, unfortunately, failed to discover an appropriae disease that was highly infectious—one which would help him back to England quickly and not into a 'Klim tin'.

Two Dutch Colonial officers, one of them a naval lieutenant, had remained behind in the sick ward long after the main Dutch contingent had departed. They occupied beds near Harry. He confided to them that he was committed to produce a Chinese naval officer on the following day. They agreed to carry it off with him. The Dutch naval Lieutenant was sallow-skinned with an Asiatic type of head and definitely oriental eyes, which, of course, accounts for the mental vision that had goaded Harry on. This Dutchman would be the Chinese officer; the other Dutchman Steenhouwer by name, would be his interpreter. They would speak 'Chinese'—in reality Malay, and hope none of the British would understand.

Harry returned to the charge next day, telling the new boys that his Chinese naval officer friend was feeling well enough to pay an official call on the British in their quarters. He suggested after tea that day as an appropriate time and explained that the Chinse officer could, of course, only speak Chinese, but that, fortunately, a Dutch officer in the sick ward knew a smattering of that language and had kindly offered to act as interpreter.

Tea-time arrived. The senior ranking officer of the quarters, Captain Lord Arundell, posted himself near the door as he heard the visitors mounting the stairs. There were thirty officers scattered around the large room, some sleeping, others reading, smoking or studying, others seated round the tables chatting over empty tea-mugs. They had been warned of the arrival of the visitor. Harry entered the room first and spoke to John Arundell, who called the room to attention, announcing the arrival of "a representative of our brave Allies, the Chinese." Harry whispered his name as the Chinaman and his interpreter came through the door and Arundell repeated in ringing tones: "Lieutenant Yo Hun Sin of the Chinese Navy." Arundell stood his ground, while the Chinese Lieutenant advanced, bowing towards him and towards the company in turn. He was wearing a dark blue naval uniform with brass buttons and an anchor insignia. An exchange of greetings took place— the Dutch officer interpreting in Malay for the benefit of his confederate.

The occupants of the room began to lose interest. A hum of conversation arose. Arundell called for silence. Attention turned towards the party again, and the Chinese officer gabbled a few sentences of Malay, in a sing-song voice, at the assembled company. Steenhouwer, the 'interpreter,' translated:

"The Chinese officer sends greetings and wishes of long life to his English friends."

Then the Chinese officer bowed slowly and stiffly down to his waist. The Dutchman followed suit, but not quite so far and a few of the Englishmen, rather self-consciously, thought they had better do something, so they bowed too.

Arundell said: "Please give our greetings to the Chinese

officer and say we are glad to welcome him as representing our staunch Ally."

Steenhouwer translated. There were more bows and then some handshakes also, for good measure. The Chinaman spoke further phrases, which were interpreted as:

"Great honour to be fighting as Ally of British people,

The Chinese naval officer was introduced to Captain Lord Arundell by Harry Elliott (extreme right)

China and England, together, are invincible and will win war, perhaps, after many years."

This piece of laconic Chinese realism, rather shaking to British P.O.W.s, was received with pained smiles.

John Arundell then asked the visiting party to join him at his table. Cigarettes were produced. Officers began to gather around, and the interpreter was inundated with questions.

"Ask him if he knows Chiang Kai-shek."

Malay sentences passed between the two; then beams and smiles and much nodding of heads.

"In case you do not know, Chiang Kai-shek is a great General," was the reply.

"Good Godfathers! what does he think we are!" was the English reaction.

"I say, ask him if they've got heavy tanks in China."

More sentences in Malay, then out came the answer:

"Yes, they have got very heavy tanks in China."

"Ask him have they finished the Burma road yet?"

"Where was he taken prisoner?"

"How is the Chinese Navy doing?"

"How did he get to Germany?" Questions were reeled off and the two men were hard put to it, to keep up with their Malay.

The answers were repeated into the crowd who had gathered in the background.

"I say, did you hear that, they *have* got heavy tanks in China."

"The Burma road is nearly finished."

"He blew up a Jap warship and then got blown up himself."

"The Chinese Navy has a secret weapon."

There was a pause and the Chinese officer seized the opportunity to rise to take leave. He spoke some more words in Malay. The interpreter recorded faithfully: "The Chinese Naval Lieutenant wishes, before departure, to sing his National Anthem."

Unfortunately, many of the prisoners, by this time, were back at their private occupations. John Arundell had to call for order again—banging on the table.

The Chinaman was standing with his hat on his head, looking very solemn.

An awkward moment of embarrassment followed; the British not knowing whether to stand or remain seated, to put their hats on or stand at attention without them.

The Chinese officer began in a pale, quavering voice,

snatches from a Malay fisherman's song that he happened to know.

The British stood stiffly to attention and, when the Chinaman saluted at the conclusion, they acknowledged the salute—a little sheepishly.

Someone said: "Hadn't we better sing 'God Save the King'?"

With doubtful enthusiasm and some self-consciousness officers persevered with the lines, and finished the anthem with a major effort.

The Chinaman now bowed in all directions, moving backwards slowly towards the door, followed by his cortège who had to edge out sideways, so as not to get in front of his bows.

The door closed behind them, and the curtain dropped upon the incident until the next day when the new boys spent the morning telling the old boys what the Chinese Naval officer had told them. "They've got heavy tanks in China. Got it out of that Chinese Naval officer—decent type, I thought," and the old lags would say:

"What Chinese officer? We've got 'em all colours, but take me to a Chinese!"

Then someone began to smell a rat and soon the story was all over the camp. The new boys took a few days to live it down. The man who enjoyed it most, of course, was Harry, who laughs to this day when he talks of it.

*   *   *   *   *

Harry Elliott may have had an even earlier cue for his practical joke about the Chinese Naval officer. In fact, he was not the first in the Chinese field and the Colditz story would not be complete without the episode (it happened in 1942) of the British officer who taught Chinese to a Pole for several months.

Cyril Lewthwaite, of the Royal Warwicks, was an unforgettable character. He hailed from Bromwich and was one of the first escapers of the war. On a solo effort from Laufen, Oflag VII.C, in October, 1940, he escaped in the middle of the pig-swill cart. On reaching the off-loading place, Cyril rose out of the swill with a scream as he received, in the fleshy part of his leg, the full force of a sharp fork aimed at a recalcitrant heap of rotting potatoes under which he grudgingly reposed. Within a matter of minutes he had the whole village of Laufen chasing him in full cry. He ran gamely in two senses of the word, and then found himself cornered in a sharp bend of the river Salzach. He took to the water in the style of Walter Scott's stag with the hounds baying behind him, but, unlike the stag and coming from the Midlands, he had forgotten in his youth to learn to swim. He was soon up to his chin and going deeper. At this tragic point he was recaptured and marched back to the prison. He was escorted by the whole village in a pitchfork procession in which, as the chief object of veneration, he made a sorry spectacle, dripping from head to foot, filthy, with the slime of half a ton of pig swill upon him and smelling to high heaven as he slopped along the village street accompanied by the jeers, hoots and screams of a population that had nearly tasted blood.

When Cyril arrived in Colditz, he became involved in languages. He had only one language to sell, that was English. He wanted to learn French, German, Italian and perhaps Russian also. He could, of course, select a different teacher for each language he required, and teach them, each in turn, English. But English bored him stiff. He could speak it, but he could not, for the life of him, explain how he spoke it or why. He would have preferred Latin for that. His best French friend had already another English teacher. It was all rather difficult until he found the way out. Then it was plain sailing. He was talking, one day, to a Polish officer who was a barrister. The Pole recounted a story in which a Chinese business man had fared very badly at the hands of the Polish law-courts because nobody in the country understood Chinese. The Polish barrister spoke French well. Cyril seized upon this and suggested filling the gap in the Polish legal fence by teaching his friend Chinese. The Polish barrister took the bait, hook, line and sinker; gave up teaching French to his other pupils and agreed to concentrate on Cyril alone, in exchange for Cyril's Chinese.

Cyril did not know a word of Chinese but he was un- daunted. He started his lessons quite simply on classical lines. He outlined the notions of Chinese declensions; he said there were twenty, thinking that would give him plenty of breathing space. He spoke of the various tenses and emphasised that the Chinese, living as they do without much reference to time, and the passage of history, spoke of everything in the present tense unless it was about a thousand years old in which case it went into various forms of imperfect, ultimately ending in the perfect past. As for the future, unless it would take place after a thousand years it was also in the present. This paved the way for Cyril. He was able to explain with graphic illustrations why it was that the Chinese always spoke that peculiar tongue known as pidgin English. He would then quote an old story he knew, about a Chinaman who fumed at a railway station cloakroom attendant searching for his luggage, screaming as his train left without him: "Pretty damn seldom how my bag go. She no fly. You no fit keep station than God's sake." He would explain, "You see, everything is in the present tense unless it's very, very old."

He continued with conjugations and thought it wise to have lots of those too, Chinese being an ancient language.

He started the Pole off with a Chinese version of amo, amas, amat. It was! Mo, mao, maoto, pronounced in a decidedly oriental manner. Cyril thought he ought to change the meaning, so 'mo' meant, 'I eat,' and so on. He gave him a few other simple verbs to learn as well.

To increase his vocabulary, as the declensions, Cyril said, were so complicated, he would teach him the first declension and with the nouns of other declensions he would permit his pupil, for the time being, to speak pidgin Chinese. It would increase his 'word power' rapidly. He gave him the equivalent of 'mensa, mensa, mensam . . .' to study.

It went like this:

Soya, soya, soyo. . . . It meant, a bean.

I eat a bean: mo soyo. The Pole made progress. In fact, he was much too quick, because Cyril found that, instead of learning any French, he spent his homework hours trying to keep up with his frighteningly assiduous pupil. He struggled on for several weeks until, one early morning, when he was on mess orderly duty, as he queued up in the grisly dawn outside the German kitchen, wooden clogs on his feet, his head swathed in a long balaclava, bare legs showing beneath his dressing gown, a tattered French khaki cloak, he suddenly heard a voice beside him.

"Hokito tao yen yosh inko?"

He knew the voice only too well. He could bear it no longer. Besides he did not know what on earth the man was saying, and to be caught out like this, at an early hour, was just the last straw—speaking Chinese in his underpants! Cyril prided himself on his military turn-out, and rightly so. In the normal light of day, he was one of the smartest looking officers in the camp.

"Yoshinka yen?" continued the voice solicitously. "Mao cha pani undu yoyo." It was the 'yoyo' that finally choked Cyril. He remembered teaching some quite fantastic participles, which ended with yoyo, weeks before. Only a progidy could have remembered its meaning now. With a weary sigh he pulled himself together and looking his pupil in the eye, he said solemnly, placing his hand over his stomach;

"Mo chu la beri-beri suyu."

To which his pupil replied, "Munchi sunya! munchi sunya!"

Between them there was a bond of perfect mutual comprehension. Cyril fled upstairs and his pupil gazed touchingly after him before returning to the copybook over which he diligently pored.

That was the last Chinese lesson Cyril ever gave.

CHAPTER XVII

THE WRITING ON THE WALL

WHEN Mike Sinclair and Jack Best had escaped over the parapets, Dick Howe had no ghost to cover the absence of Sinclair at the evening *Appell*. He laid on the 'rabbit' instead. An air-raid that night also gave Dick the opportunity to repair the window bars while the searchlights were extinguished. He expected that the Germans would notice the hole in the wire and the dangling rope in the morning. His fears proved groundless. The hole, hidden under the structure of the pagoda, remained undiscovered for two days.

Upon the discovery, Lieutenant Barnes, who was Jack Best's double, went into hiding. At the *Sonder*—i.e. special —*Appell*, Mike Sinclair and Barnes were declared to be absent.

At this point there were no more volunteers to undertake the unhealthy job of being ghosts. Jack Best had been haunting the Castle for just one year!

Mike Sinclair was missing. The *'Rote Fuchs'* had escaped again! Military and Gestapo telephone lines began to hum. Heads began to swim and a special inquiry was set up. The German Commandant appeared before the High Command at Leipzig, where he had to make the ignominious confession that he did not know when the escape had taken place.

The two escapers had ended up their hair-raising descent of the east cliff wall, on that fateful evening, with their clothes ripped to pieces by the barbed wire. They found a small path at the bottom of the cliff, and followed it. In the friendly darkness of a wood, half an hour later, they sat down to repair their damaged clothing, threading their needles by the light of a burning cigarette.

Three days later they were captured by civil police in

the small town of Reine twenty-two miles from the Dutch frontier.

On this occasion they had not headed for Switzerland. The trouble was that men who escaped to Switzerland had been filtering much too slowly out of that country, with the result that escapers were tempted to try other routes with the chance of a quicker repatriation to England. Knowing the Colditz route by heart, they should have had a much better chance of crossing safely into neutral territory. It was a pity they were biased by information which, though correct at the time, should not have been allowed to out-weigh their better chance of freedom.

An astute police officer at Reine thought he recognised Mike from a photograph published in a police broadsheet circulated daily throughout Germany. At the same time he did not like the look of Best; "not Germanic enough," he said later. The police officer arrested them both while they were walking together along the main street of the town.

The two men were escorted back to Colditz guarded by an N.C.O. and four soldiers—a small tribute to the esteem in which they were held.

The German High Command were in a quandary. The Red Fox had escaped at an unknown date. Positive evidence as to the Fox's presence in the camp went back several weeks. They were bewildered and angry. All they knew was that there was a large hole in the perimeter wire and that, in the hours of darkness, prisoners might have used it as a rabbit run. How many had gone out? How many had come in? Nobody really knew. The Colditz inmates were playing hide and seek with them. The High Command had to consider the possibility that the Allied secret service might be at work, that the wire had been cut from the outside—nobody had been seen cutting it inside—and that prisoners were being removed or exchanged 'ad lib'. The Commandant was made to look very foolish, and his senior officers let him feel the whip of their scorn. The Germans were convinced that the British were up to no good. Mike was a dangerous man, known to have had contacts in Poland before he came to Colditz. A veritable underground movement was forming under their noses. They could not keep the scandal away from the Gestapo, who, as far as the prisoners' intelligence service could estimate, took charge of Colditz men, recaptured while escaping, from that day forward.

Jack Best, immediately upon recapture, knew his part and posed as Barnes. On his return to the Castle he was allowed back into the camp pending his sentence. The question then arose: should Barnes or Jack continue as the ghost? Jack thought he himself should because Barnes, at least, could then remain Barnes, though he would have to do a month's solitary for Jack! Jack, on the other hand, would always be in difficulties roaming the camp as Barnes. However, it was decided the other way.

The Doctor Jekyll and Mr. Hyde comedy continued for several days. But the Germans, under the prodding of the Gestapo, were forced to probe the mystery of the Red Fox's escape. They must have reflected upon the case of Mike Harvey and his double.

A long drawn-out identity parade was held at which Jack appeared as Barnes, but the Germans pondered a long time over his record sheet. They suspected he was not the man whose photo was before them, but they let him go.

The next day they pounced again. Jack was removed and his finger prints were taken. They were not those opposite the name of Barnes!

The game was up. Jack continued to bluff until he saw that the Germans suspected he was Flight Lieutenant J. Best. They were awaiting his records which had gone to Berlin when Jack confessed his real identity.

The end of this story is that Jack was sentenced to a month's solitary for escaping and to a further month for . . . 'being absent from one thousand, three hundred and twenty-six *Appells*, including three Gestapo *Appells*.'

Lastly, Dick found out, months later, how it was that a German N.C.O. had opened the guardhouse door and walked out on to the terrace at the same moment as Mike and Jack dropped from the parapet. Jack, climbing over the balustrading, had accidently pressed an alarm bell button which had immediately summoned the N.C.O. to the very spot where the escape was taking place!

III

1944

THE YANKEES ARE HERE

AMERICANS were trickling into Colditz in 1944.
Colonel Florimond Duke of the U.S. Army was taken prisoner in Hungary. He had been parachuted into that country on a special mission and had, after some weeks of activity, been captured by the Gestapo. He was treated according to the Gestapo routine, travelled in chains to Colditz, and was released into the Castle more dead than alive. A brave man, who fought in the U.S. Air Force in the First World War, nothing could keep him away from the hazards of the Second, and he 'stuck his neck right out'. He was handsome with a dark brown military moustache, stood over six feet in height and was a quiet retiring individual, with a consoling personality. In civilian life he was the advertising manager of the magazine 'Time'.

A member of Colonel Duke's team who ended up at Colditz was Captain Alfred Suarez of the U.S. Army Engineers, commonly known as Al. He was another who loved adventure and, being originally of Spanish descent, he had fought in the Spanish Civil War of the thirties. After this episode, it came about as a natural sequel to his career, that he found himself parachuted into Hungary. He was a gay daredevil with a great sense of humour.

Another member of Duke's team was Colonel W. H. Schaefer, U.S. Army, who was less lucky than his two colleagues. Although he reached Colditz, he was kept there in solitary confinement pending court-martial. He was sentenced to death and remained isolated while appeals were made continuously on his behalf up to the time of the liberation of the Castle. This happy event saved his life.

None of these Americans had any opportunity to escape. For Schaefer, even the most recalcitrant Colditz convict would have admitted there was not a hope. As for Duke and Suarez, there was another very good reason why they should not 'stick their necks out' any further than they had already done. Their necks were, metaphorically, hanging on to their bodies only by the thread of sufferance. A queer twist of the Gestapo mind had saved them from extermination. Even these brave men realised that they had had their day.

*　　　*　　　*　　　*　　　*

The 'Prominenten' were a class of prisoner set apart by the German High Command for special treatment in Colditz. They consisted of prisoners who had connections with important personages on the Allied side by virtue of birth, or of fame, either their own or that of antecedents. By the same token they possessed special value for the Germans. It became plain to all, as the war progressed in favour of the Allies, that they would ultimately be used by Hitler as hostages and this is, in fact, what Hitler, through his lieutenant, Himmler, attempted to do when the time of the great holocaust approached.

Such prisoners were not maltreated. On the contrary they were allotted small cell-like single bedrooms giving them some privacy and elementary comfort. But they were most closely guarded. During the day they could mix with the other prisoners. At each roll-call they were counted separately. At ten o'clock each evening they were escorted from the general quarters to their rooms by special sentries and locked in.

A guard was maintained outside their cells all night. They were only released again at breakfast time in the morning. The door of each cell had a shuttered spy-hole fitted in it, and the sentry patrolled regularly throughout the night, flashing a torch through the open shutter to see that the prisoner was up to no mischief.

There was Giles Romilly, Winston Churchill's nephew. A young man with a misleadingly sulky expression because he was unfailingly cheerful with a kind disposition. A wave of dark hair flopped over his forehead; he had strong features and he had heavy lidded blue eyes and was small and stockily built. He had left England with the Narvik expedition in 1940, as a newspaper correspondent and had been captured by the Germans. He tried, once, to escape from Colditz, without success. At the end of the war he tried again and succeeded, but more of that anon.

Captain the Master of Elphinstone, a nephew of Her Majesty the Queen (now the Queen Mother), arrived in Colditz in 1944. He had been captured near Dunkirk in 1940.

Other Prominente who arrived earlier from Eichstätt, most of them having escaped from its famous tunnel, were: Captain the Lord Arundell of Wardour, Wiltshire Regiment (already mentioned); Captain Lord Haig, son of the Field-Marshal; and Lieutenant Lord Lascelles, nephew of King George VI; Captain Michael Alexander, cousin of Field-Marshal Alexander; Captain The Earl of Hopetoun, Lothian and Border Horse (already mentioned), a son of the Marquis of Linlithgow; and Lieutenant Max Duhamel, a relative of Winston Churchill.

Charlie Hopetoun was one of the three star theatrical producers of Colditz. He produced 'Gaslight' by Douglas Hamilton in October, 1944, which played to overflowing houses in the Colditz theatre and, later, he wrote a play which received quite an ovation.

While on the subject of theatrical productions, which became an important part of camp life in 1944, it is worth recording the versatility of Dick Howe who found, in conditions of semi-starvation, the energy and the time to carry through major theatrical productions, run the escape nerve centre and control the wireless news service of the camp.

Dick produced 'George and Margaret,' which had run in England before the war, in June, 1944, and 'Jupiter Laughs' by A. J. Cronin in November of that year.

The third outstanding producer, and the peer of the trio, was Teddy Barton. He produced 'Pygmalion', in February, 1943; 'Rope' in January, 1944; 'Duke in Darkness' in March, 1944; and 'Blithe Spirit', in April, 1944, with Hector Christie of the Gordon Highlanders, acting superbly the part of Madame Acarti. Other leading lady parts were excellently performed by Alan Cheetham, a Lieutenant of the Fleet Air Arm. In May, the theatre was closed by way of reprisal for an offence against the Germans; in June, 1944, Teddy produced 'The Man Who Came to Dinner'. 'Hay Fever' and 'To-night at 8.30' followed, and several Noel Coward compositions occupied the theatre until the end of 1944, when productions ceased.

The scenery for the theatre was painted mostly by the master hands of John Watton and Roger Marchand on newspaper glued to wooden frames. Roger Marchand was a French Canadian who had somewhere in his travels picked up a 'Bowery' accent. He was asked one day what he was painting and his reply was, "A'm paintin' a scene for dat guy Ot'ello."

Dresses were manufactured out of crêpe paper. There was plenty of Leichner make-up provided by the German Y.M.C.A. A carpenter's tool kit was accepted, on *parole*, but the prisoners soon dispensed with it, preferring to use illicitly manufactured tools, equally good.

Hugo Ironside was invariably stage manager. The electricians were: a Dutchman, Lieutenant Beetes, and later Lulu Lawton, who performed wonders in lighting effects. And the litany would not be complete without mentioning the manufacture of stage props., such as a highly polished concert grand piano for 'George and Margaret', an ugly looking brass festooned coffin for 'The Man Who Came to Dinner', out of old Red Cross boxes by Hugo Ironside, Mike Edwards and George Drew.

The superior productions of 1944 were a far cry from the early days when a handful of British gathered together in their quarters on Christmas Day, 1940, to hear Padre Platt sing:

> "Any old iron, any old iron, any any any old iron!
> You look sweet, talk about a treat!
> You look a dapper from your napper to your feet,
> Dressed in style with the same old tile
> And your father's old green tie on,
> And I wouldn't give you tuppence for your
> Old watch chain.
> It's iron, old iron!"

Let it be said that our popular padre sang it with an unforgettable éclat. His false teeth took off from his mouth at the crescendo enunciation of the finale 'Tuppence' and clattered to the floor amidst roars of laughter from the boorish audience.

The possibility of a general reprisal on the camp theatre was always uppermost in the minds of the theatre actionaries. Until the curtain rose on the opening night, nobody could ever be sure a production would take place; there was so much clandestine activity in progress that might be unearthed at any moment, and the closing of the theatre was always among the first acts of retribution carried out by the Jerries.

A cinema show once came to Colditz, but only once; that was in 1943. Scarlet O'Hara remarked loudly after the performance, and in the close hearing of Hauptmann Eggers, who understood English well, "If that's the b—— sort of film the Jerries put up with, no wonder they're losing the war."

His remark closed the theatre for a month and no more films came to Colditz.

No 'privilege' lasted long. Two games of Rugby took place on the Colditz village green in the winter of 1943/44. On two occasions in the summer of 1944, a batch of prisoners was escorted down to the river for a bathe. On one occasion a party of officers went to the cinema in the village. These outings constituted 'privileges'. They were all '*parole* jobs', that is to say, prisoners had to sign a promise not to make an attempt to escape during the excursions.

Privileges were extremely rare. Suspicion was mutual. On the one hand, the Jerries thought that frequent repetition would ultimately prove to the advantage of prospecting escapers. On the other, *parole* savoured of the thin end of the blackmail wedge and the Colditz inmates were nothing if not diehard. The number of prisoners willing to sign *parole* passes dwindled remarkably after the first outing.

Douglas Bader, the air ace, indulged in a different kind of *parole*. He demanded *parole* walks on the grounds of his inability to exercise properly in the Castle precincts owing to his physical disability; namely, that of having both legs missing. The very ludicrousness of a legless man demanding *parole* walks is reminiscent of the defiance of this great airman.

During the summer and autumn of 1944, he had his way. He gave his *parole*—promising not to make any attempt to escape or even to make preparations to this end. What he did not promise to eschew was the continuation, outside the camp, of the cold war campaign which he relentlessly carried on against the Germans inside the camp. He would continue to break German morale by every means in his power.

So, insisting that he had to be accompanied on his walks, in case his tin legs gave trouble on the hills, he usually obtained permission for Dick Howe or another to go with him. Together they would load themselves with Red Cross food. With internal trouser pockets elongated to their ankles and filled to the brim and with their chests bursting outwards, they would set off to demoralise the country folk with food and luxuries they had not seen for five years; English and American cigarettes and pipe tobacco, chocolate, tinned meat and ham from the four corners of the earth. Bader and Dick gave generously, asking for little in return; a few eggs, maybe, or fruit or lettuce. They naturally started this campaign on the accompanying sentries. When they had the latter in their pay by the simple process of bribery followed by blackmail, the way was clear for the major offensive. At first lone farms were visited, then the attack approached the fringes of the town of Colditz itself. The enemy fell like ninepins for the subtle, tempting baits. German morale in the countryside bent under the attack.

CHAPTER XIX

MUTINY

AS early as the autumn of 1941, Harry Elliott had studiously learnt the symptoms of a common and unnerving stomach trouble—duodenal ulcers, and had applied carefully the lessons he learnt. He complained of pains. He lost weight. He had warning prior to being weighed, so he started off with bags, full of sand, hanging down inside his pyjama trouser legs, supported at his waist. Thereafter he lost weight regularly by off-loading a few pounds of sand at a time. He painted the skin round his eyes with a mixture of carbon and yellow ochre so regularly that it became ingrained and would not come off with washing. Harrowing pains and the loss of two stone in weight succeeded in sending him to a hospital, Elsterhorst, in February, 1942. Here he found two stalwart Indian doctors captured in Cyrenaika in 1941 who 'fixed' blood in his various medical samples. All was ready for a breakout with his Belgian confederate, Lieutenant Le Jeune, when the night before the 'off', the latter's civilian clothing was found.

The Germans were nothing if not radical and, knowing the Colditz reputation, they acted judiciously. The whole Colditz contingent at Elsterhorst was returned, lock, stock and barrel, under heavy guard by the 4.30 a.m. train the next morning, to their natural home.

Harry lay low for a while, then started a chronic jaundice. By 1943, Harry's back began to trouble him; the result of a fall when he was trying to escape in France, after his capture in 1940. Arthritis set in and showed on X-ray plates, but Harry had cooked his goose, as far as hospitalisation was concerned. Nobody would take any notice of his serious and troubling complaint. He was becoming a cripple.

'If the Goons won't swallow it one way, they'll jolly well

have to swallow it another way,' thought Harry. He decided to start up his duodenal ulcers again. This time he had to travel far to make the grade. Already as thin as a rake he had to lose two more (sand) stone. After several successive weighings he ran out of sand and still the Jerries would not transfer him. His face was the colour of an ash heap at dawn, but the German doctors were unsympathetic. Harry decided he had to starve. He ate nothing for a week, could scarcely stand upright and the Germans gave in. He returned to Elsterhorst hospital.

There were several English doctors working in the hospital, including a Radiologist, whom Harry made his particular *confident*. The result was some really juicy ulcers on an X-ray plate which had his name attached to it. All this time Harry was suffering the real pangs of arthritis which was turning him into a crippled 'old man of the sea'.

Harry's ulcers flared up and died down in the traditional manner of the really worst type, and the X-ray plates showed the legitimate and pitiable arthritis mingling with cleverly transposed awe inspiring, if not terrifying, ulcers in such a picture of blended medical misery that expert opinion considered he was, at last, ripe to appear before the Mixed Medical Commission.

Harry was returned to Colditz as an incurable case with not long to live and a ticket of recommendation for interview by the Commission.

The Mixed Medical Commission was a body formalised by the Geneva Convention for the examination of sick and wounded Prisoners of War with a view to their repatriation. It was composed of medical officers divided equally between nationals of one belligerent power and nationals of the Protecting Power of the other belligerent. The Mixed Medical Commission which, at intervals, toured around Germany consisted of two German doctors and two Swiss doctors. Doctor von Erlach was the best known of the Swiss delegates. Although the war had been going on for over four years, the Commission had never been allowed to put its nose inside the gates of Colditz.

Now, in May, 1944, the miracle happened and the new Senior British Officer, Colonel Tod, was informed of the forthcoming visit of the Commission to the *Sonderlager* of Germany. Germany was surely losing the war! Colonel Tod had recently taken over as S.B.O. from Tubby Broomhall of the Royal Engineers, who in turn had taken over from Daddy Stayner in 1943.

Harry realised it was all or nothing. The Commission was due next day. He and another officer, Kit Silverwood-Cope, who had thrombosis in one leg, spent the night walking up and down the circular staircase leading to their quarters—a matter of eighty six steps—at twenty minute intervals. They were still alive when the sun rose and took to their beds in the sick ward as bona fide stretcher cases.

Unfortunately this was not the last ditch. The Gestapo had the final word. Silverwood-Cope had been loose, too long for the Gestapo's liking, in Poland, after an escape and knew much that they would like to know. They had already submitted him to torture in a Warsaw prison without success but were not courageous enough to go the 'whole hog'. At the same time, in the camp records, he had a red flag opposite his name: '*Deutschfeindlich*'—an enemy of the Reich. It was almost certain they would not let him go.

The other cases submitted for examination included: Major Miles Reid, an M.C. of the First World War; Lieutenant 'Skipper' Barnet; 'Errol' Flynn and Dan Halifax of the R.A.F.; in addition, two French de Gaullist officers. De Gaullists, captured fighting in various parts of Europe, were now arriving in Colditz replenishing the French fire which had added much to the spirit of the prison through the earlier years.

The camp, as a whole, was resigned to the rejection of the case for Silverwood-Cope. But when, at the last minute, the High Command, through the instigation of the Gestapo, began quibbling over the repatriation of the two Frenchmen, they came up against trouble.

The names of those to be examined by the Board for repatriation would be called at the morning *Appell* and the Gestapo decisions would then be known.

The roll call sounded and the officers paraded. After the count had been checked by Hauptmann Eggers, Hauptmann Priem read out the verdict of the High Command.

Major Miles Reid, Captain Elliott, Lieutenant Barnet, Flying Officer Flynn and Flight Lieutenant Halifax were named, and after that . . . silence. The silence continued, palpitating ominously, fraught with meaning. *"Danke!"* shouted Priem in a forced stentorian voice. This was the German signal for the British S.B.O. to dismiss the parade. No order was given. Nobody moved.

Then something happened which under other circumstances would have caused chuckles of laughter in the ranks. But another mood had gripped the waiting men. They had seen the incident, funny but pathetic, often enough. At this moment, its occurrence spoke worlds more than any words. An officer, who had gone round the bend and who should have been repatriated long ago, appearing from nowhere, advanced towards the German officer in the middle of the open space in front of the parade. He was dressed in a tattered blue tunic, his bare legs protruded from beneath a dirty pair of khaki shorts and on his feet were old plimsolls. He wore a paper cap of his own design like a French képi on his head. It resembled, vaguely, the headgear of a French Foreign Legionary. A white handkerchief trailed from the back and the hat was coloured red and grey. Slanting over his left shoulder he carried a long piece of wood—his rifle. He came to attention in front of Priem, saluted smartly with his rifle still at the shoulder, then fumbled in his tunic, produced a piece of paper and handed it solemnly to the German. Priem unfolded it, turned it over and held it open, loosely, in his hand. It was blank on both sides—a helpless, mute appeal. The French Legionary saluted again and marched briskly along the stationary ranks, reviewing the parade before returning to his place in the rear.

'Why was his name not on the list too?' The silence

shouted, echoing the unspoken question and, of course, there was no answer. The Germans did not explain their actions in the mad-house of Colditz.

Eggers, speaking in English, addressed Colonel Tod, the S.B.O.:

"Parade the walking cases in front at once, Herr Oberst. Stretcher cases will be inspected later."

The tall, grey haired Royal Scots fusilier, standing alone in front of his men, replied coldly: "Herr Hauptmann, this action of the German High Command is despicable. It is dishonest, unjust and cowardly. The Frenchmen must go. I will no longer hold myself responsible for the actions of my officers. The parade from this moment is yours. Take it!" and with that he turned about, marched back to the ranks behind him, turned again, and stood at attention—at the right of the line.

Eggers, speaking in English, started to harangue the parade:

"British officers, you will remain on parade until those ordered for examination by . . ." His further words were lost as, with one accord, the parade broke up in disorder and men stamped around the courtyard, drowning his voice with the shuffling of boots and the clatter of wooden clogs on the cobbles.

This was mutiny. Priem hurried to the gate and spoke through the grill. Within seconds the riot squad entered the courtyard. The two German officers, surrounded by their men with fixed bayonets and followed by three N.C.O. snoops with revolvers drawn, forged into the crowd before them in search of bodies. Their scheme was to identify and seize the men approved for interview, take them out of the courtyard by force, bang the gates behind them and leave the prisoners to nurse their wounded feelings in impotence.

The German officers and their snoops peered, now to the left, now to the right, into the sullen faces around them. Suddenly there was a shout and a pointing finger was levelled:

"*Dort ist Oberst Reid, schnell! nehmen Sie ihn fest!*"

Four guards charged at the man, surrounded and held him fast by the arms and shoulders awaiting further orders. *"Sofort zur Kommandantur! Rechts-um! Marsch!"* Reid was frogmarched out of the courtyard, the posse forcing their way with jabbing bayonets through the swarming, obstructing prisoners, shouting as they went, *"Los, los! Weg da! Los!"*

The search continued, but the other walking cases could not be found.

The mêlée in the courtyard continued for fifteen minutes. The Swiss members of the Commission were in the *Kommandantur* waiting for the proposed repatriates. They became impatient and demanded to be allowed to see the Senior British Officer. The courtyard was, by now, in an uproar with jeering, booing, catcalls and singing competing for the maximum volume of sound. The Swiss could hear the riot in progress. The Camp Commandant was spotted from a window giving orders outside the gate. He dared not enter. Priem left the coutryard for several minutes, then returned. He sought out Colonel Tod and spoke to him. Tod mounted the steps of the Saalhouse and raised his arms calling for silence. There was an immediate lull. He announced:

"The German Commandant has agreed that the de Gaullists shall go forward for examination."

The whole camp broke into a tremendous cheer. Within a few minutes, the two Frenchmen were produced and, together with the rest of the walking cases who appeared also, as if from nowhere, they were escorted out by the German guards, marching through a lane formed by the cheering mob.

The German capitulation was complete and Allied solidarity, aided by the Swiss Commission outside, had won a memorable victory. The German arrogance of 1941 and 1942 was changing and from this day in May,. 1944, onwards, the Prisoners in Colditz began to feel solid ground once more beneath their feet.

The episode was an important turning point. The

prisoners knew that Hitler and his minions intended to use them as hostages in the hour of defeat. Here was a gleam of hope. The camp Commandant would have to square his action over the de Gaullists with the Gestapo, but the fact remained he had countermanded their orders, obliged to do so by the combined pressure of the prisoners and a neutral power, and was evidently prepared to cross swords with them. What had been done once for two de Gaullists might be repeated. In the hour of Germany's defeat, the signpost for action pointed towards defiance.

The Mixed Medical Commission passed for repatriation all those they examined, including Harry. They took one look at him and wrote his name down on the list.

*   *   *   *   *

Most of the repatriates, including Harry, remained in Colditz until July when, one evening, they received orders to pack, and the next morning at 5.30 a.m. in the grey light of dawn they bade farewell to Colditz for ever. The departure arrangements were so sudden that Harry as he walked through the gates, thought he was dreaming. It was difficult, almost impossible, to believe that he was, after four years, really on his way home, that he would not wake up and find himself lying on his palliasse inside the walls and the barbed wire. A curious feeling took possession of him. A few heads popped out of windows as they filed out, hands waved and voices shouted good-bye. It was all a dream. He had seen it happen before. He would wake up soon. Another part of him felt suddenly guilty; he was disloyal to the men who were shouting those pathetic good-byes behind the bars; and, more peculiar than anything else, was the sensation of tearing himself away from something that had become a part of him—the Castle itself. Could he be having regrets? Yes! He was feeling sorry. Something was being wrenched from him. He was hugging his chains, and would feel lost without them in the strange world of freedom.

The repatriates marched down to the station with the German guards and, as the dawn came, Harry looked back over his shoulder and upwards to the towering outline of the Castle showing pale and faintly luminous in the first light. Only then did he realise he was not dreaming. A sudden fear gripped him and his skin contracted. He was, indeed, outside the walls but they were reaching out to seize and envelop him again. Now that he could see the Castle's forbidding exterior, the ghostly horror of its greyness, fear came upon him—he wanted to run from the loathsome prison before he was trapped.

The party arrived at the station and boarded the train. Only as it steamed out of the station did Harry begin to feel safe. He was filled with a great exaltation and a surge of revengeful elation; he cursed the Castle, as it faded, growing paler and paler in the morning haze, cursed it again and again in a queer uncontrolled frenzy...

He had defeated his bitter enemy, the Castle; he had escaped from Colditz. Those who remained, facing nearly another year behind the bars, would talk about his exploits and his humour until the end of the war, and long afterwards too. They would never forget his 'Battle of the Dry Rot'* which was waged unceasingly until the day he departed. They would miss his excursions up the stairs, into the attics, with his faithful band of followers manned with buckets of water—water which they thereupon poured through cracks in the floors until the ceiling seeped, dripping upon the occupants of the rooms below. How the Dutchmen swore when they returned to their bunks at night to find soaking pillows and blankets below the weak spots in the ceiling! They never found out where the water came from. For years they thought it was caused by leaking water pipes and holes in the roofs. They employed a different staircase, and, consequently, never saw Harry at work. His 'razor blades in the pigswill' campaign* was over. There would be no more Chinese officers; no more sand-bags jettisoned along the road of the years; no more ulcerous landmarks on the patient uphill climb which eventually led him out of Colditz. He had reached the top of the hill and looked

* Described in *The Colditz Story*.

once more over the sunlit plains of freedom. He was going home again to his beloved England. He would be missed back there, behind the grim walls, where a gay heart and an unquenchable spirit were like sunshine in the early spring.

* * * * *

'Dopey' Miller (Lt. W. A. Miller, R.C.E.), a Canadian and a born escaper, who thought of nothing else all day, escaped from Colditz in June, 1944, at the time of the Normandy invasion. His was a lone effort. The route out of the Castle was the beginning of that route used by Ronnie Littledale, Billie Stephens, Hank Wardle and the author in 1942. Dopey and his helpers cut a bar in the window in the camp kitchen facing the outer courtyard. On a favourable night, during an air raid, he climbed out of the window, over low roofs and dropped to the ground in a dark corner. He hid underneath the chassis of a lorry that was parked every evening in the outer yard. During the daytime, the lorry was used on haulage work for the camp, in the village and the surrounding districts.

Early the next morning, the lorry driver started up his engine and drove out of the camp. Dopey was hanging on, underneath. There were no alarms at the outer gates.

He was never heard of again. It is assumed that he was recaptured and that the Gestapo submitted him to 'Stufe drei'.

Within the camp, of course, none of this was known or thought of at the time. It was hoped that Dopey had chalked up another 'home-run' from the impregnable fortress. As the days passed into months, however, and there was no news of him, uncertainty as to his fate left an uneasy feeling in the minds of those who knew him. He was not the kind of man who would leave the camp in ignorance if he had succeeded in reaching the Allied lines.

CHAPTER XX

THE RED FOX

AS the autumn days of 1944 shortened and the second front in France settled down, the prisoners of Colditz gritted their teeth once more to stand another winter behind the bars, hoping for relief in the spring. The prisoner contingent numbered about two hundred and seventy at this time, of whom two hundred were British, the remainder French de Gaullists and a sprinkling of every other Allied nationality. They had hoped for freedom in the autumn but it was too much to expect and they knew it. An air of sadness and depression spread over the camp: the eternal optimists had little enthusiasm left for the victory that was always 'next month' and 'just around the corner'! They were nearly played out. The winter of 1944–45 was, for Colditz, the grimmest of all the war winters. The incarcerated men made what little contribution they could to the war effort. They had done everything possible behind the bars and had given of their best. They had pinned down a German battalion. The Landwacht were afraid of them. They had made Colditz a by-word in the offices of the German High Command. The Gestapo loathed the mention of the name.

Patience in the camp was at the sticking point. As runners, reaching the last lap of a marathon, feel their hearts being torn out of their bodies, unable to drag their legs another pace, yet knowing they must still race hundreds of yards before they pass a finishing line which, in the mist of perspiration before their eyes, they despair of ever beholding, so the escapers of Colditz struggled in a motionless marathon of the mind to retain their equilibrium to the end. The last lap was the toughest endurance test of all.

In such an atmosphere Mike Sinclair decided to try again.

The Red Fox

His indomitable spirit could not be tamed. He would finish the war in harness. The Red Fox had to be free.

This time he planned a lone and desperate break. Surprise was the essence of it. He would repeat the escape of the Frenchman Pierre Mairesse Lebrun who, in 1941, had been catapulted over the barbed wire fence in the recreation pen in the park beneath the Castle. Mike planned the break alone so that no other man could be blamed if a hand or foot slipped or the timing went wrong. Lebrun had dared the sentries to shoot him, dodging as the bullets whistled past and jumping to safety behind the park wall with a volley as a send off. Dick Howe would not have to take the blame on his broad shoulders this time. He would not have to 'take the can back' as he had done for the Franz Josef affair. Mike was seeing to that. He told nobody.

On September the 25th, 1944, Mike went down to the recreation ground and walked the well-trodden path around the periphery inside the wire with Grismond Scourfield.

In half an hour the guards had settled down. They suspected nothing. This hour of recreation would be the same as the hundreds that had gone before it.

At the most vulnerable point in the wire, Mike stopped suddenly, turned and shook hands with Scourfield. "Goodbye, Grismond," he said quietly. "It's going to be now or never."

He was ashen pale. Even the gigantic courage of his spirit could not conceal from his own brain the awful risk he was about to take. The subconscious reactions of the nerves and cells of his frail body rebelled and would not be controlled. His hand trembled as he grasped surreptitiously the hand of his friend. His whole body seemed to quiver. His eyes alone were steady and bright with the fire of a terrible resolve.

In the next instant he was at the wire, climbing desperately, climbing quickly, spreadeagled in mid-air. To those nearby, his progress seemed painfully slow, yet it was fast for a man mounting those treacherous barbed strands. He had reached the top and was balanced astride the swaying wires when the Germans first saw him. They began shouting: "Halt! Halt!" and again, *"Halt, oder ich schiesse!"* came echoing down the line of sentries.

He took not notice. Freeing himself from the top strands he jumped down to the ground and stumbled at the nine foot drop. He picked himself up as the first shot rang out. There were shouts again of "Halt!" and then a fourth time "Halt! Halt!" He was running. The hill was against him. He was not travelling fast. He dodged once, then twice, as two more shots rang out and he ran straight for the outer wall. But the Germans had his range by now and a volley of shots spattered around him. He dodged again. He could still have turned and raised his hands. He was nearing the wall but he was tiring. Another volley echoed among the trees of the park and he fell to his knees and a gasp of horror rose from the men watching behind the wire. Then, slowly, he crumpled forward amongst the autumn leaves.

He lay still as the sentries rushed forward, swooping, on their prey. He did not move when they reached him. A sentry, bending down, turned him over while another quickly opened his shirt and felt with his hand over the heart. He was dead.

The Red Fox had escaped. He had crossed the last frontier and would never be brought back to Colditz again a recaptured, spent, defeated prisoner. He had made a "home-run". He was free.

*   *   *   *   *

Seven months later, the Castle was relieved and Mike would have been freed—alive. That freedom would not have been of his own making, nor to his own liking. He had reached that stage in the humiliating mental struggle of a prisoner of noble stature when, to desist from trying and to await freedom at the hands of others, would seal his own failure, scar his heart and sear his soul. His duty would have remained unfulfilled.

The sermon that follows was delivered by Padre Platt at the memorial service in the Castle.

"Mike came from an Ulster family living in England. He was at school at Winchester, went up to Cambridge, and joined the 60th just before the war. He fought at Calais, was taken prisoner, was sent to Laufen and then to Poland. There he made his first escape in which he crossed the frontiers of the General Government, Slovakia, Hungary, Yugoslavia and was caught getting into Bulgaria. He tried to escape on the way back through Czechoslovakia, was recaptured, held for a time by the Gestapo, and finally sent on here two and a half years ago.

"Since then his life has been practically one attempt after another to escape. On different occasions he has got as far as Cologne,* the Swiss Frontier, the Dutch Frontier. You know better than any congregation in the world what that means. About a hundred of you have got right away from a camp once, only about twenty more than once—let alone a frontier—and this is the 'Escapers' camp.

"He didn't himself take foolhardy risks, but when he went with others and risks were unavoidable he took full share—and more. You remember his escape as Franz Josef. And in his last and riskiest attempt he went alone. Whenever the story of escaping in this war is written, Mike Sinclair's name will be there, high up on the list. And he deserves it because he had qualities that really ultimately matter.

"When he'd made up his mind upon a thing he was absolutely determined to carry it through. He made mistakes, as we all do, but he learnt from them and had a conscience about them. Most people's reaction to failure is to wipe it out of their memories and be comfortable. Mike's was NOT to forget it—and at times it made him very depressed—but to go on trying till he'd made up for it. That is the kind of character that really matters in a soldier —the kind of quality that made Wellington and Sir John Moore great.

"On at least two occasions while he was here, he made escapes that any soldier would be proud of. When he and

* An escape carried out from Colditz early in 1942.

Jack Best went through the line in the orchard, the scheme
—and it was largely Mike's scheme—was about the most
brilliant there's been here. It came off, so we took it for
granted, but it was a grand piece of work. The other occasion was on his earlier 'Franz Josef' escape, then he was
nearly killed by a guard losing his head. Mike took the lead
in the preparations and the escape itself—he spent three
months on it. With two or three people it was a 'certainty',
with the members he agreed to include—well, not likely
to succeed. At one stage in the escape it was clear to Mike
that to get the main body out was going to be a much more
dangerous and difficult job than expected, but that, by forgetting about them, he, Lance and Hyde-Thompson could
walk out and get clear away. That's a testing moment for
a man's character, and we know how unhesitatingly he
chose the unselfish way.

"Finally, Mike was a believing Christian, and one who'd
known suffering and turned it to use. That's why, although
his death is a tragedy for his parents, it isn't just a wasteful
tragedy of a life. We say in our Creed that we believe in the
Resurrection of the Dead and WE KNOW that Christ's
promises are sure. Mike was the kind of man who wouldn't
be confident about himself, but we, who knew him, know
that he is all right, and that he's met up with his younger
brother, who fell at Anzio, and the countless others who, in
their country's service, have gone before us on the way that
leads through death, but comes out in a brighter eternal
world."

CHAPTER XXI

THE GLIDER

BY the autumn of 1944, the construction of the glider was under way in a secret workshop. Assembly had not yet begun but tall piles of wing sections lay carefully stacked and docketed ready for the great day when they would be threaded on to the spars.

Jack Best had long ago been incorporated in the team; a fourth member, stooge Wardle, the submarine officer, had also joined them.

Jack Best had come out of solitary confinement after the terrace escape in the early spring of 1944. By that time, Bill Goldfinch and Tony Rolt had made a little headway with the glider plans. Tony had remembered Bill's remark, when they first discussed the glider, about how useful Jack Best would have been on such a scheme. Jack was only just out of solitary when Tony took the bull by the horns and proposed he join them.

"It's asking something I know, Jack," he had said, "you've probably had a belly-full of escaping and solitary just recently and want nothing more than to be left alone for a while."

"Tell me some more about it," Best had said.

"We've already started making parts," Tony explained. "Bill has a lot of drawings and whatnots. He has plans, elevations, sections and detail part drawings and he's made some templates. I've been working on the manufacture of parts using the templates; but we need help. The going is slow. You're the chap we need. You're good with your hands and some of the parts are going to require a lot of workmanship and patience, more than I've got."

"Have you mentioned the scheme to Dick yet?"

"No, I think it's time we did. If you'd agree to join us,

564

that would count with Dick too, and I think he'd see we got all the help possible."

"Show me the plans and some of the parts you've made," said Jack.

Tony had led him over to the corner of the dormitory where his miniature workshop, consisting of a small table and a cupboard were situated. He spread some engineering drawings out on his bed and showed him bits of wood already taking shape as wing ribs. He had a pot of glue, and a primitive wooden press weighted with bricks.

"How long have you been at this?" asked Jack.

"Over a month."

"You'll never get anywhere at that rate," Jack had said. "It's all too cumbersome. Where do you melt your glue? Where do you hide the parts? You must have a proper workshop—you need space to build a glider. It can't be built on a bed."

"I know that only too well," said Tony. "What about it?"

"Let's have a talk with Dick," said Best. "We need room and a place where we can work undisturbed."

"I'll find Bill Goldfinch, and we'll tackle him together."

So Jack Best had fallen for the scheme and Tony had again won his way.

Bill Goldfinch had been working for a long time on the design when Jack Best joined them. He was beginning to wonder whether the machine would ever materialise or merely remain a dream child—perfect on paper.

Tony's introduction of Jack Best into the scheme gave him new zest and enthusiasm for the work.

Dick was tackled and listened, incredulously at first, and then with growing interest as the three men laid before him the details of the plan. What sounded preposterous to begin with became feasible in Dick's mind as he looked over the drawings and realised that the entire machine would be constructed from wooden bedboards and floorboards, cotton palliasse covers, and a large quantity of glue. Goldfinch and Best were, probably, the two finest craftsmen in the camp. Jack Best had manufactured, years ago, a complete tool kit of tempered chisels, saws, planes, augers, bits and brace. The two men had infinite patience. They were meticulous and persevering. If anyone would ever succeed, they would, thought Dick, and Tony Rolt could be relied on to whip up the necessary enthusiasm among the stooges and recruit unskilled help when required.

He gathered together the sheaves of paper on which Goldfinch had drawn his stress diagrams and made his aerodynamic calculations.

"Have you checked these?" he asked.

"I've been over the figures three times," said Bill, "but they should be checked by someone else. Lorne Welch could do it. He's a gliding expert."

"Right! Get him to run through them carefully and give them back to me afterwards. I'll have a third opinion also, and, if all three agree that it will fly, then go ahead, and we'll find a proper workshop for you.

"I suppose the dumb cluck who wins the toss will have to take off in it?" he remarked as an afterthought.

"The glider is designed to take two passengers," said Goldfinch calmly.

Dick turned to him in astonishment, "Blimey O'Reilly! you'll need some catapult to launch that weight safely!"

"Yes," said Goldfinch, "we'll need a bathful of concrete."

"Go on," Dick chuckled, "what then?"

"As I see it," continued Goldfinch, "we'll fix a pulley at the far end—the launching end—of the runway; you know —the flat tablelike pieces saddled astride the roof ridge. The glider will be pulled forward on its skid by a rope passed around the pulley returning the full length of the runway underneath it, passing over a second pulley at the starting end, and there attached to the weight."

"Do you mean," intervened Dick, "the bath filled with concrete?"

"Yes. The bath will have to be free to fall a distance equal to the length of the runway, that is sixty feet."

"How do you release the rope from the glider?"

"Simple enough. We'll use the same type of automatic release hook as all towed gliders use. It's foolproof. Better still, we could make a light trolley for the glider to sit on and fix the rope to that."

"Provided the glider calculations are O.K. and it's airworthy," said Jack Best, "I'm sure the take-off will be all right. Holes will have to be made in all the Castle floors, as far as I can see, down to ground floor level. That should give the full sixty foot drop required for the bath."

"I propose," said Goldfinch, "to use the bath tub, you know the one, on the third floor under the attics. We can suspend it over the holes and let it go when everything's ready. You've got plenty of cement, Dick. Will you let us have enough to mix up and fill the bath?"

"Yes, if you ever get that far," said Dick. "There's tons of sand and gravel and rock up in the attics from the French tunnel. You can mix that with it and make a respectable concrete. Where are you going to build the glider?"

"Ah! now this is where I come in," Tony interrupted. "Jack Best says we've got to have a proper workshop where we can work undisturbed. I'm afraid I agree. Otherwise it'll take years. I've only made a few parts, so far, to Bill's designs and it's taken me ages. It's not so much the actual work, but all the alarms and the hiding of parts and the stooging and so on that wastes the time. If we could fix up our jigs on benches and not have to dismantle them: if we had a permanent stove handy for the glue pot; if the tools did not have to be hidden all the time, then we could get somewhere."

"Well, there you are!" exclaimed Dick. "You've posed the problem that I was just going to raise. What are you going to do about it?"

"I've been thinking about it a lot," said Rolt, "and I have an idea. We might be able to wall off completely a section of the top attic over the chapel without the Jerries being any the wiser. If it was done, say, in one night and made to look exactly like the original wall at the end, they might never notice the shortening of the attic. It's long enough as you know."

"What do you think, Dick?" said Bill and Jack together.

"Quite canny," Dick agreed grinning, tickled at the prospect of the Jerries regularly patrolling the attic with torches to see there was no monkey business going on while a whole workshop was set up under their noses. "The French tunnel debris is going to be put to good use, I see! Let's go and have a look at the attics."

The four of them, together, examined the uppermost attic carefully. The west end of it was ideally situated for the workshop because it abutted the roof ridge above the old French quarters along which it was proposed to launch the glider.

If this end of the attic were sealed off, the machine could then be constructed and assembled where it would be used. When ready for launching, a large hole could be pierced in the west wall just at the level of the roof ridge outside. Unseen by prying eyes, the saddles would be posed and interlocked forming a runway two feet six inches wide; the machine taken through the hole; its wings attached outside; the rope fixed around the pulleys, and the machine would be ready for the "take-off".

The attic was long and dark. There was no ceiling; only the timber roof trusses and the boarded floor, and the faintest glimmer of light entering between the layers of tiles.

A properly constructed false wall, built to look like the existing end wall, immediately under one of the trusses would give no clue as to the existence of a space beyond, unless measurements were taken to check the lengths of the floors at different levels.

The four men agreed the idea had a fair chance of success.

"The problem as I see it now," said Dick, "is to get the wall built and camouflaged to look like the old one before a Jerry interrupts us. That means it's got to be done in one night. Can you see it being done?"

"I think so," said Tony Rolt. "If you'll give the O.K., we can get enough volunteers. With about a dozen men working all night it should be possible. We'll make a sketch of the old wall and reproduce it again in three ply and cardboard as near as damn it. We can prepare the wall in sections beforehand."

"That'll do as a foundation," said Dick. "What you want after that is to tack canvas on to the wall; you can use the palliasse covers from the beds in one of the unused dormitories and apply a coating of plaster on to the canvas. I'll show you how to prepare it. The French used it on the tunnel doors very successfully. It turns out exactly the right colour when it's dry. To be expected—I guess—as the original plaster was obviously made from local ingredients. You sift out of the tunnel debris a fairly fine grit about one-eighth of an inch diameter—no more. You mix that with the clay and sand from the tunnel—there's tons of it round the corner—and make a puddle. You smack this on to the canvas about a quarter inch thick and let it set. We'll try a sample out right away and check it. How about the framework for the wall?"

"There's some good floor boarding around here," said Tony. "It's thick stuff—a good seven-eights of an inch and five inches wide, that should do. It's what Bill proposed to use also for the main wing spars of the glider."

"How long are the wings to be?" Dick asked, beginning to pace out the width of the attic.

"Each wing is sixteen feet long and five feet wide," said Bill, "but that includes the aileron—fourteen inches."

"Good," said Dick, "they'll just fit nicely into the width."

"Just a minute—" interrupted Bill, "the fuselage is longer. It's eighteen feet without the tail wing and rudder."

"Well, I make the width thirty feet," said Dick checking again. "It should be ample, even allowing for dead space where the sloping roof meets the floor."

"That'll do," said Bill, "the tail and rudder are separate and fit on afterwards."

"Good! Now, what about the width of the room—where

shall we build the wall? About twenty feet should do. That brings us. . . ." Dick said breaking off his sentence as he measured again. . . . "That brings us just under the second truss. What do you think?"

"Twenty feet should do," Bill replied, "if we take too much the rest of the attic will look suspiciously short. We've got to squeeze a bit. We can always break a hole in our own wall to help push the fuselage out, if necessary, on the day."

"The next thing you want is lighting, leave that to me," said Dick. "Lulu Lawton and I can fix up a branch circuit from below. We'll do that when the wall's finished. Now, about getting in and out? How about that corner over there, where the flooring's already off. You could get in by ladder from the lower attic and we could make a trap door. Yes," Dick ruminated, "let's go down below and have a look at that corner."

They left the upper attic, locking the doors as they went and descended to the lower attic which was unoccupied and lit by dormer windows. Dust was everywhere as it had been above, but at least there was daylight, and some pretence at turning the attic into a room had been made. The gable walls and also the low walls beneath the dormer windows had been whitewashed and the ceiling was of plaster.

They walked over to the corner where Dick had suggested making the entrance.

"Yes," he said, "I think this corner will do nicely. There's some plaster already fallen down on the floor here. That makes the job easier. Jack," he said, turning to Best, "I'll arrange for Lucy Lockett and Andy to make the trap door. You'll have to help. But they'll do the actual trap; they're experts. Fit it so that the laths are cut behind the plaster and show nothing from below. You can support the plaster from above. I'll give you some cement for it. That hole where the plaster's down already will do nicely. It's near enough to the gable wall to lean a short ladder against and a man can climb up, get through and take the ladder with him. You must be damn careful always about this loose

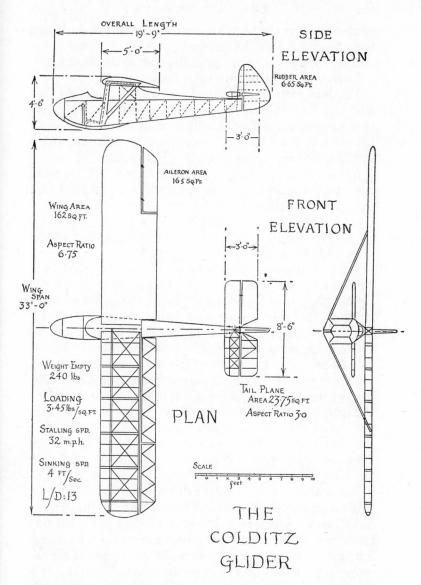

OVERALL LENGTH
19'-9"

5'-0"

SIDE
ELEVATION

RUDDER AREA
6·65 SQ.FT.

4'-6'

3'-0"

AILERON AREA
16·5 SQ.FT.

FRONT
ELEVATION

WING AREA
162 SQ FT.

ASPECT RATIO
6·75

3'-0"

WING
SPAN
33'-0"

8'-6"

WEIGHT EMPTY
240 lbs

LOADING
3·45 lbs/SQ.FT.

TAIL PLANE
AREA 23·75 SQ.FT.
ASPECT RATIO 3·0

PLAN

STALLING SPD.
32 m.p.h.

SINKING SPD
4 FT/Sec.

L/D:13

SCALE
1 0 1 2 3 4 5 6 7 8 9 10
feet

THE
COLDITZ
GLIDER

THE GLIDER PLANS HAVE BEEN COPIED FROM THE ORIGINAL DRAWING MADE
AT COLDITZ AND NOW IN THE POSSESSION OF JACK BEST IN KENYA

plaster lying on the floor. See that it's always left dusty and no footmarks must be left around."

A stooge put his head round the door of the attic:

"Jerries in the yard," was all he said.

The four men retraced their steps to the door. As they left, Jack Best, the last in line, spread a heavy dust mixture over suspicious marks on the floor with the aid of a small bellows which he carried for the purpose. It looked like a small beehive smoker and was effective in action.

In the dormitory below, Dick continued, "If you need any paint or whitewash, I've got some. You can collect all the cobweb mixture you like yourselves and also a few pounds of soot and dust will help. We'll need a hell of a lot to cover the false wall. When do you think the wall sections could be ready?"

"We can produce them in about a fortnight," said Jack. "There's a big area to cover and it's all got to be prefab."

"All right then," said Dick, "other things being equal let's prepare for to-day fortnight—after the last *Appell*. I'll produce a sample of the plaster beforehand. Then you can get weaving on producing it in bulk. I can lend you five volunteers and Lulu and myself, making seven for the building operation: you'll collect the rest between you. Don't forget the stooges, Tony, I guess you'll see to that. Provided the design—the calculations and so on—are checked again and found O.K. the escape is on, as far as I'm concerned. I wouldn't dream of taking off with you, of course, but then I was brought up in a Tank and I get scared moving in anything weighing less than ten ton."

A fortnight later, all through the night, a dozen men worked furiously with shaded lights to assemble the dummy wall! Screws were used to fix the framework to the existing roof truss. All had been carefully measured up beforehand. The prefabricated sections, covered with a layer of canvas, were then screwed into their predetermined positions. Towards morning, the plastering began, with the thick puddle prepared according to Lulu's prescription. It stuck well to the canvas but the droppings created a problem for the camouflage men who followed. Damp marks on the floor at the foot of the wall could not be covered easily.

By dawn the wall was finished and professional touches had been applied. But, as the morning light pierced through the chinks in the tiles, they showed up a wall which did not look in the least like the original. The colour stuck out like a sore thumb. It was dark brown, uneven, and patchy with sooty streaks. Too late to do anything now; the team departed to clean up and rest for an hour before the seven a.m. *Appell*. They were depressed.

Dick felt badly about the result of the night's work but he was sure the cause of the trouble was the moisture. If only the Jerries would keep away for twenty-four hours, he thought—the crisis would be past. He watched the Germans all day with apprehension. Towards evening he breathed more freely and together with Lulu Lawton he paid a visit to the wall. It was already much better in appearance but still damp. Another day would improve it out of all recognition.

During the next day the Germans paid a routine visit to the attics. They must have flashed their torches cursorily. There were no alarms. All that day, Tony Rolt and Jack Best paced the courtyard nervously, longing to mount the stairs every hour to register any toning down in the colour of the wall. But they had to possess their souls in patience— no good could come of too frequent visits. It was wiser to keep away.

Towards the evening, just before dark, Dick and Lulu went to the attic along with the glider team. Stooge Wardle (the submarine lieutenant), recently added fourth member of the team, who had helped in the wall construction was there. As they opened the door a broad smile showed on Dick's face. The change in the colour of the wall was remarkable. The tint was not yet perfect, but, to anyone who had seen it twenty-four hours before, it was clear that it would be perfect in a matter of another twelve hours. The stucco had now turned an old sandy grey, like Sussex or Cotswold stone and would be a lighter colour by the morning. It was almost indistinguishable from the surrounding walls even to those who had worked on it.

Dick turned to Jack Best and said, wryly:

"Jack, you'd better think about fitting that trap-door mighty quick. The ball's over to you and you're holding up the proceedings. Get on to Andy and Lucy. Thanks, Lulu," he added, turning to him, "you've a better eye for colour than I thought a few hours ago."

"Don't be a damn fool," said Lulu, "anyone in the wool trade knows about allowances for moisture. It's a question of judgment. There's nowt to be afraid of."

"So you concocted that b—— awful mixture!" said Stooge, turning to Lulu. "I thought we'd all been having our legs pulled. Now I must say . . ." he looked at the wall critically, ". . . it's not bad; not bad at all for an amateur job."

"Any more cock from you and I'll make you walk the plank," retorted Lulu cheerfully.

A load had been lifted from their minds. They locked the attic door and returned to their quarters talking animatedly of the next stage in the venture.

The attic was vacated entirely for a week in order to watch Jerry reactions. Patrols unlocked the doors, and controlled the attics almost every day. They noticed nothing unusual. After the week had elapsed Best completed his trap-door and the team took possession of their workshop. The construction of the glider began in earnest.

A work-bench was set up, and tables for the jigs and templates. There were no windows in the workshop, but Dick and Lulu produced electric light. Dick also provided the glue which was melted on a stove, using as fuel a mixture of any kind of fat that could be found, including boot polish. The glue came, mostly, through the channels of Checko's black market. Racks for the tools soon made their appearance. The four men spent the greater part of every day at their work and continued, sometimes, late into the night. Then they had to use heavily shaded lamps to prevent light showing through cracks between the roof tiles.

The myriad component parts of the glider piled higher and higher upon the floor and hung festooned from long pegs on the beams awaiting the final assembly.

Their carpenter's kit consisted of the following principal tools:

A side-framed saw, the handle of beech bedboard, the frame of iron window bars, and the blade of gramophone spring with eight teeth to the inch.

A minute saw for very fine work, with gramophone spring blade, twenty-five teeth to the inch.

A square, made of beech and gramophone spring.

A gauge, made of beech, with a cupboard bolt and a gramophone needle.

A large plane, fourteen and a half inches long with a two-inch blade, bribed from the Goons, the wooden box made of four pieces of beech screwed together.

A small plane, eight and a half inches long, with a blade made from a table knife.

Another plane, five inches long.

Drills for making holes in wood were made of nails; a five-eights inch drill for metal was obtained by bribery.

And lastly there was a set of keys, including a universal door pick, forged from a bucket handle.

The two wings of the glider were each made up of seventeen aerofoil section frames or ribs, manufactured out of deal and beech bedboards, which were cut into long strips of cross-section, half an inch by three-eights of an inch. The ribs were put together in jigs, dovetailed, glued and gussetted where necessary, using three-ply wood stripped down to two-ply, nailed in position. The underside of the wing was flat. The curve on the upper leading edge was reproduced on the aerofoil sections partly by bending the wood strips and partly by making a series of small saw nicks along the outer edge to give pliability.

The aerofoil sections were assembled by threading on to the spars and tacking into position. The main spar of each wing was a solid floorboard eighteen feet long of section five inches by three-quarters of an inch. A secondary spar at the trailing edge of the wing, of section two and a half inches by three-quarters of an inch, provided the surface on to which the ailerons were hinged.

The aileron ribs were of uniform construction from one end to the other; they were fourteen inches wide. Ten ribs and two spars, smaller than those of the main wings, were required for the tail wing, made in one piece, to fix above the rear end of the fuselage.

The fuselage itself was constructed from floorboards cut into strips of section one and a quarter inches by three-quarters of an inch. The two side trusses were curved in both the vertical and horizontal planes and were strapped together at the bottom by short, straight ties and at the top by longer hooped ties, all gussetted where necessary. A raised head-rest, behind the pilot's seat, provided the pillar which supported the wings. Light wooden struts nine feet long were also used underneath the wings. A wide skid of well-planed board shaped like a ski was hinged to the fuselage at the front end. It was also highly polished with french chalk and lead. The top of the fuselage bellied upwards, which gave it a streamlined, airworthy appearance. It was not unlike the body of a Spitfire. The controls—stick, rudder-bar and rudder—were of conventional pattern, lightly constructed. The control wires were made from field telephone wire which the Goons had used for electric lighting in certain rooms.

Prison sleeping bags of blue and white check cotton were employed for the "skinning" of the glider. Wrapped around the leading edge of the wings, they were stretched tightly back to the trailing edge, where they were sewn together. Doping was the next process and, for this, German ration millet was ground fine and boiled in water for four hours, forming a paste. This was applied hot to the skin. When cool and dry, it produced a smooth, glossy surface, shrinking the fabric at the same time, so that it became as taut as a drum.

Apart from the light two-ply gussets and thin sheet metal capping-pieces used all over the machine, parts requiring greater strength and solidity were made from straps and bars taken from some of the iron bedsteads used by senior officers in the *Saalhaus*. Such parts were the root fittings, stout metal straps with steel dowels, two at the inside end of each wing-spar, which linked the wings together through the fuselage immediately behind the cockpit.

The four members of the glider team knew that only two of them would eventually take off in it. They agreed not to make the selection until the machine was ready, thereby ensuring that all four would continue to put their whole effort into the labour of construction.

Normally all four of them were in the workshop together: three at work and one stooging. The stooge sat on a cross-beam in the apex of the roof above the heads of those below. He raised a tile, propping it up with a wedge. Through the slot provided he could see a window in the British quarters on the third floor in which a second stooge was posted. The second stooge surveyed the courtyard and the entrance to it. He employed four signals: a white towel which, placed prominently in the window, meant 'all clear,' a blue towel, which meant 'Silence—Goons in the building —stop smoking,' a green mustard-pot, which meant 'stand by for danger—silence—take precautionary measures to quit workshop,' and a larger red-painted metal jar containing salt which meant 'quit workshop at once.'

The safety of the team depended greatly on the common ·sense of the window stooge. To quit the workshop, camouflage the entrance and conceal the ladder took a good five minutes. The stooge had to divine when the Germans really meant business such as a snap *Appell* and when they were just snooping, for which the green signal would suffice.

The above stooging system was not enough. Circumstances might arise in which the stooge might not be able to give his signals. This would occur, for instance, if the Germans raided his room and prevented him from acting. A secondary system—another electric stooge—was brought into play if the window stooge failed.

The Glider Workshop

Germans, entering the room in which the stooge worked, had to pass through an ante-chamber. In this lobby sat another stooge. As soon as a Goon entered the lobby he lifted a small piece of iron mostly covered with rubber which lay at his hand, against a corner of the window-sill. The action broke an electric circuit. Upstairs, a long way off, in the glider workshop, a light promptly went out. In case this was not noticed (with other lights on) a long nail fell at the same time from an electromagnet into a tin basin which acted like a gong.

The complete stooging system, organised for work over an extended period of time, involved a personnel, consisting of twelve principal stooges, known as 'the disciples,' with forty assistant stooges.

During the ten months which it took to construct the glider, there were some thirty red alarms—wearing on the nerves, and every day's work included at least one or two 'greens'. The most nerve-wracking 'green' alarm the team experienced occurred when three German N.C.O.'s spent over an hour in the attic. They remained motionless while the Jerries probed the floors and even sounded the false wall, but discovered nothing. Old plaster on walls often sounds hollow! That fact probably saved them. The Jerries were after the hidden wireless set.

Work continued on the components and on the assembly of wings, fuselage, rudder and controls and on the runway saddle boards, pulleys and ropes through the winter of 1944-45. Construction had started seriously in May. The take-off was scheduled for the spring of 1945. By that time, it was estimated that air raids over the Berlin and Leipzig areas of Germany would be sufficiently intensified to provide ample black-out cover at night in which to break out the hole in the outside wall; set up the launching-ramp and take-off without being heard by the sentries below or seen by observers farther afield in the village. By the spring, too, the winter floods on the meadows flanking the far side of the river below the Castle should have subsided. They would provide an excellent landing-ground for the glider, over three hundred feet below the launching-ramp and two hundred yards away.

The stage was being set for the greatest escape in history. Would the spring of 1945 see its fruition?

IV

1945

CHAPTER XXII

THE END APPROACHES

IN January, 1945, the camp held about three hundred British officers from England and every part of the Commonwealth. A recent arrival was Brigadier Davis of the Ulster Rifles, who had been parachuted into Albania. There were the three Americans, the twelve Czech airmen in the R.A.F., some Jugoslav officers, a company of de Gaullist paratroopers from North Africa, and a number, growing daily, of other Free French officers.

Early in February, Prominente began to collect in Colditz from different parts of Germany. Five French Generals arrived from the east led by General Denny. A sixth should have arrived, but was detained and 'Klim tinned'—never heard of again.

General Bor-Komorovski, the head of that courageous, almost suicidal, band of Polish patriots who kept the heart of Poland beating throughout the blackest years of the war, arrived, accompanied by five Polish Generals and other Staff Officers. The Warsaw insurrection was the culminating point in the General's underground career. He survived, though war, treachery and murder had threatened to engulf him each day. He possessed hostage value in the eyes of the German leaders, which fact undoubtedly saved his head.

A man of infinite courage and resource, he won the hearts of all who knew him by his simplicity and cheerful friendliness. He was every inch a hero, yet with the modesty of an æsthete, saintly in his detached outlook upon life. His head was partly bald and reminded one of a tonsured monk. Of slender physique, medium in height but wiry, he had direct, searching, hazel eyes under dark eyebrows. A neatly trimmed moustache, beneath an aquiline nose, set off his sensitive nostrils.

In March, twelve hundred French officers were dumped

into the prison, six hundred more parked in the village. They had been marched eighty-five miles from their camp east of the Elbe in the face of the Russian advance. Overnight, Colditz became a crowded refugee centre. Men slept everywhere, on straw laid out on the floors. The Castle theatre became a large dormitory choked with human beings. It was calculated that if everybody assembled in the courtyard at once there would be three officers per square yard of cobbles. The invasion heralded the end of an era—the end of normal camp life. The closing days of the war were at hand.

The French, many of them old friends from the early days of Colditz, were starving and there were a large number of sick and dying hospital cases amongst them. They had had no nourishing food for months. The British took them gradually in hand, sharing food and clothing, while the S.B.O. and the French generals fought with the German Camp Commandant for extra medical attention, which was produced, and for medicines, which never materialised.

Heavy air-raids, centred on the Leuna oil refineries south of Leipzig, became a nightly performance. By day, the tactical Allied air force began to make its appearance.

The tempo of events quickened and the daily wireless News Bulletins issued in the camp showed that the end was approaching.

The race was nearly finished.

It had been described in a German propaganda leaflet, distributed in English to British prisoners and others in Germany, in the following terms, as early as September, 1944:

'In 1944 they (the Allies) started a grand offensive, and at the same time Stalin, in the east, threw in all he had. It was certainly impressive. But why was this sudden terrific outburst of energy necessary? Why all the hurry?

'Because Churchill knew something. A year and more ago he knew something which most of the Germans at that time had no idea of. Mr. Herbert Morrison knows something about it, too. Remember how he warned the House of Commons recently about the "Frightful things" which Germany had in store for Britain.

'This vast Allied onslaught against Germany is not a sign of strength. It has been caused by their deadly anxiety and intense panic. They must get to Germany and defeat her before she can use her new weapons.

'Think of a race between two motor-cars. The Allied motor-car, although it has been fitted up with a reserve petrol tank, has now got to go all out. The German machine, which had been left far behind as its juice ran out, has in the meantime filled up again. And it is racing ahead. Its tanks are full with special fuel.

'Germany's victory, the final victory, is not so very far away....

The German V1's were well known by September, 1944, when this article was published. The V2's were about to start their work of indiscriminate destruction. But Hitler had another weapon nearing completion. His scientists were working frantically on the heavy-water bomb—the hydrogen bomb.

Lieutenant John Winant Junior, of the U.S. Army Air Corps, arrived in April. Being the son of the American Ambassador to the United Kingdom, the Germans treated him as a Prominente. He had been shot down in a Flying Fortress raid over Munster. A fair-haired young man with steel-blue eyes, and a strong, though sensitive, character, he went to war straight from his university.

Early in April, Dick Howe's wireless communiqués began to speak of General Patton's and General Hodge's armoured spearheads, moving like shafts of lightning and driving deep into enemy territory.

Colonel 'Willie' Tod, the S.B.O. of the camp, came into his own as the man to be relied upon in a crisis. He was recognised as the senior officer of the whole camp and represented all nationalities in their routine dealings with the

Germans. He watched the mounting tide of chaos around the Castle with cool detachment, and, having the confidence of his own officers, he was able to handle the Germans with skill. He was all that a soldier should be.

Aged about fifty-four, Willie Tod was a regular officer of the Royal Scots Fusiliers, tall, grey-haired and good looking, with strong features and bright blue eyes.

Dick Howe always remembered a short conversation he had had with him; it must have occurred in 1943. He had lost his son—killed fighting. The news had come to him, a helpless prisoner in Colditz. Dick had said, sympathetically, after some casual conversation:

"I'm sorry, Colonel, about the news you've just had."

Tod replied simply, "It happens to soldiers." There was a moment's pause, then they had continued their discussion.

Almost forgotten, as the tornado of world events swept across the globe and the Allied armies from West and East dashed headlong to meet each other in the heart of the German Reich, the Colditz glider was made ready for flight. Discussion centred around the use to be made of it. Dick had recently been criticised for allowing the building of the glider to proceed. Some senior officers criticised it on the grounds that it was completed too late for use, saying that a better estimate of the time required to build it should have been made. They were correct in that the glider was finished too late to be of use for an escape, but they were speaking after the event. Others maintained it was a waste of good time and material from the very beginning. The answer to this was a simple one. None of the men even remotely connected with its production regretted what they had done. As for others, did it concern them?

Nobody could foresee when the climax and conclusion of the war would occur. If it had not occurred in the spring of 1945, but months, perhaps even a year later, which was by no means impossible, then the glider would have undoubtedly been launched. Those who built it were prepared to fly in it. They were certain it would take off.

Colonel Tod did not criticise. Even if he had wanted to,

the discipline of a soldier forbade the criticism of junior officers who had been allowed to build the glider with the help of his own staff and with his own knowledge. On the contrary, Tod foresaw the possibility of a last and desperate use for the glider and issued his instructions accordingly: 'The glider is to be held in reserve in strict secrecy until the Castle is liberated, or until you have further prior instructions from myself or my successor in Command.'

On Tuesday, April the tenth, came a new sound; quite different to the familiar 'whoof' of bombs which had been falling every night on Leipzig and the Leuna synthetic oil plant not twenty-five miles away. There was the distinct crump of shell bursts, and the evening clouds glowed on the horizon with vivid infected spots as the dusk came down.

Dick found it difficult to throw off the feeling of unreality that surrounded the events taking place. This untoward intrusion into the normality of the camp was deeply upsetting. Here was a routine that it had been sacrilegious to break during five years, now going overboard in a day. *Appells* almost ceased. The S.B.O. was repeatedly in conference with the German Camp Commandant, and not inside the prison, but outside, in the Kommandantur. A world was coming to an end. It was an eerie feeling and upsetting.

There were maniacs at the helm in Berlin. The prisoners of Colditz were hostages. They had known it for a long time. There were so many imponderables in the atmosphere surrounding them and in the kaleidoscopic nightmare of events taking place in Germany. Anything might happen. 'Thank God,' Dick thought, 'there's a cool head looking after our interest. Tod will handle the situation if anyone can.' The same thought was in the minds of many. Their lives were literally in his hands.

Tod had their confidence because their discipline showed it. His responsibility was so much the greater. He must save their lives at all costs and, in these hours, life was being held cheaply by the Germans. An S.S. Division had moved into the village of Colditz overnight. He had information that the remnants (those who had not died of starvation or illness) of four hundred Jewish slave prisoners, in a camp three miles from the town, had been murdered already by the newcomers. Four only survived to tell the tale, having remained hidden under piles of dead until nightfall.

Tod saw clearly that he had to temporise, yet show no weakness. The German Commandant was terrified. His own Wehrmacht High Command had moved to Dresden. Underneath his window were the S.S. and the Gestapo. The mention of the Russians, who were closing in from the east, made him shiver. Hodge's Task Forces from the west were advancing quickly—but how quickly would they reach Colditz? They might be checked. The Commandant would run with the hare and hunt with the hounds as long as he possibly could.

The murder of prisoners on the spot was the first danger. A time might come when it would be advisable for them to make a mass break-out and run for the Allied lines. But there was no front line, properly speaking, at the moment, within two hundred miles. Over that distance, the Stormtroopers and the Hitler Youth were running amok, well armed and merciless. Tod was not going to lose half his men that way if he could help it. Then, close at hand, was the S.S. Division in the village and in the surrounding district. The prisoners might not make their escape quick enough to pass even this initial obstacle, and their break-out might precipitate the very mass murder from which they were trying to escape.

The second danger which the S.B.O. had to combat was the removal of the prisoners to the redoubts in which the Nazi fanatics would make their last stand. Hitler's own redoubt was known to be in the Tyrol around his beloved Berchtesgaden. Here he would bargain for his life and those of his immediate entourage, employing as many Prominente prisoners as he could muster as his hostages. His minions, the S.S. and the Gestapo, would similarly use officer prisoners and even the rank and file, wherever they could seize and hold them in last-ditch defences and mountain fortresses.

Tod's strategy, therefore, was to turn to the best account the value of his men to the Germans as live prisoners; while, at the same time, stalling and delaying any attempt to move them away from the advancing Allied columns.

There was a third danger which Tod had to envisage in connection with which he issued his orders concerning the glider. It was to be a standby in case the Commander of the S.S. troops in the surrounding district had a dangerous brain-wave. He might take over the Castle itself and use it as a stronghold for a last stand on the lines of the siege of the Alcazar in the Spanish Civil War of the thirties. The prisoners would not, in that case, be compelled to move from Colditz, which was the order expected and which Tod was prepared to resist. There was a danger that the Germans, in desperate straits, might turn upon him and say, "All right, if you will not move for us and with us, then we shall move into the Castle and you will remain too, as you so wish it, and as our hostages!"

In this event, the glider could come into its own, to send emissaries from the prisoners, like carrier pigeons, in the hope that they would reach the Allied lines, conveying perhaps vital information at a crucial stage in the siege, or even the plans for a combined assault, from outside and from within.

In the early afternoon of April the tenth a messenger arrived at Colditz from the Wilhelmstrasse, in Berlin, carrying an offer to General Bor Komorowski. The Commandant conveyed to him the instructions of Hitler, to the effect that he should be freed at once along with his staff, who included General Petczynski, his Chief of Staff, and General Chrusciel, Commander of the Warsaw garrison, on condition that they helped Germany to form an underground army to fight against the Russians. It was the third time the offer had been made and, for the third time, General Bor rejected it.

Wednesday, April the eleventh, passed quietly within the Castle. The sentries around the perimeter remained at their posts. In the distance the thunder of battle continued. Ominously, in the foreground beneath the Castle, could be seen feverish preparations for the defence of the town. The bridge across the river Mulde was mined, ready for detonating. Tanks and motorised artillery rattled through the streets to positions in the woods around. Houses on the outskirts were taken over by troops and barricaded for defence.

The unreality of it all continued to obsess the minds of men, like Dick, who had looked down upon the quiet town without ever noticing a change during five and a half weary years. The scene had become so permanent, so indestructible, that nothing could change it; only in their dreams and reveries had the scene ever altered. When they awoke it was always there, the same as before, unchanged.

They had imagined bombs falling on the houses; Allied artillery flashing and shells raining into the town; the rattle of machine-guns; then the advance into the streets; British Tommies, armed with hand-grenades and tommy-guns, creeping stealthily or dashing forward from doorway to doorway in the wake of Mark IV tanks. The dreams of years had never materialised. Could it be different now? Why should it be different? The sound of the guns in the distance might fade to-morrow. The Germans would bring up reserves. They would drive wedges into Hodge's advance. The wireless news would alter, at first subtly, letting the listener down very gently, then the Allied retreat would begin. The S.S. would leave Colditz once more . . . to its former peace. The distant rumble of bombing in the great cities would alone remain a reality. That had gone on for so long now, it was part of their lives, but it altered nothing. 'To its former peace . . .!' A quiet, like that of the solitary confinement cell, where the thud of the heart, beating in futility, is the loudest noise, would descend again.

Dick shivered at the prospect and his skin crept. If the guns were to retire, now that they were so near, perhaps, real after all; if the 'crumps' of exploding shells died away now, it would be much harder for him to live and bear the silence. To raise the hopes of a despairing prisoner, then to drop him back into the slough of despondency, is one of the more refined tortures that mankind has invented.

Dick dared not hope. He lived a suspended existence, numbing his virile senses with a self-imposed stupor.

He slept feverishly that night. The gunfire had ceased and he asked himself repeatedly, 'Will it begin again in the morning?' It was always at night that thoughts took their own course and the will was at its weakest. He longed for the reassuring sound of the guns.

Thursday, April the twelfth, dawned. As the prisoners sat at their tables over a breakfast of acorn coffee and German bread, news came through from the wireless-room, which was continuously manned, that the Americans were at Leuna. They were only twenty-five miles away. A cheer went up at the announcement, and the fears of the night gave way to a reassurance which buoyed the spirit through the daylight hours.

The defence preparations continued around the village more furiously. Slit trenches could be seen everywhere, thrown up, like mushrooms during the night, in the fields on the higher slopes and bordering the woods. Boys and girls of all ages could be seen at work with spades and pick-axes alongside their elders in uniform. The Germans looked as if they were going to make a serious stand in the country around the Castle.

Keith Milne, the City Slicker, known also as 'the Breed' because he came from Saskatoon, had, in the course of the years, manufactured a couple of good telescopes, making use of spectacle lenses. They were in high demand, more so than Rex Harrison's telescope, the lenses of which had been made by grinding down glass marbles. Scarlet O'Hara swore the Castle would not be relieved until the pearl handles on General Patton's own pair of pistols could be seen through a telescope.

Towards evening, Colonel Tod was called to the Kommandantur. Lance Pope, of Franz Josef fame, accompanied him to interpret in case of difficulty. Oberst Prawitt, tall and emaciated, standing beside his desk in the plainly furnished office, looked at the Commander of his prisoners. There was no softness in the answering glance. Tod stepped forward over the soft pile carpet and took from Prawitt's hand the letter which he held out. It was a letter from Himmler's Headquarters, addressed from Himmler personally, but unsigned. It contained the marching orders for the Prominenten. They were to be removed that night to an unknown destination. Two buses would be waiting at the Kommandantur entrance at midnight. Oberst Prawitt would be answerable with his life if any of them escaped.

"This is an outrage, Herr Oberst. The order must be disobeyed," said Tod.

"I cannot. I am under orders, even though I might wish to disobey them," was the reply.

"Our guns are on the horizon and you still have the temerity to dare to carry out this act? Herr Oberst, you must reflect. You will have to answer for the lives of every one of the men on this list which I see attached to the order," said Tod, flinging the papers on the desk.

"You must also reflect," said Prawitt. He looked very old, tired and haggard, and his white hair was bedraggled. He was no longer master of the situation. He was merely a tool in the hands of men who used the blackmail of life or death to impose their will. "If I overrule this order which has come through the local S.S. Headquarters, they will enter the Castle and see that it is carried out. I shall not even live to see it done. There will be many deaths throughout the camp and still the Prominente will depart. What will you have achieved?"

"Have you no sense of justice, Herr Oberst? If you will not face matters now, you will have to face them later, before an Allied court-martial."

"I would far rather face an Allied court-martial," said the Commandant with a sigh of infinite weariness. He was played out. The future that he saw before him was a violent death, sooner or later, and he preferred it later. The thin thread which held him to life was still precious, old as he was. Time was his only hope and a poor hope at that, but he would try the course that gave him time.

The dangers of the situation presented themselves clearly enough to Tod. If the Commandant would not act, the S.S. would, with bloodshed that might end anywhere. It was not the moment for heroics by unarmed men—unless—and he thought of the last resort, but, looking at the Commandant he could see, almost before he said what was in his mind, that it was useless.

"Will you either hand over the garrison inside the Castle and the armoury to me, or will you, at least, help me to hide or get away the Prominente from here?" he asked.

"It is more than my life is worth. If the men escape they will not get far. It is better to temporise."

"You are certainly not a hero, Herr Oberst!"

"I am old but not yet ready to die in a suicidal attempt to save the enemies of Germany. In fact any such attempt by me will merely precipitate their end."

Tod saw the relentless logic behind his words. They were both confronted with a vicious enemy who valued life at nothing. He, too, must play for time. Time alone could save the Prominente.

"What is their destination?" he asked.

"I do not know."

Tod was not sure that he was not lying.

"I insist on knowing their destination," he reiterated.

"I can only do one thing," said the Commandant. "As some of my personnel will accompany them, I can instruct that they bring back here a message from your men. From that, you should know where they have gone."

The conversation was at an end.

The S.B.O. was escorted back to the prison, where he found that extra guards had already been mounted over the quarters of the Prominente. An *Appell* was held just before dusk and the Prominente were then locked into their cells.

Colonel Tod was allowed to speak to them. He told their senior, Captain the Master of Elphinstone, of his conversation with the Commandant, of the position with regard to the Castle and warned him, at all costs, to fight for time, wherever they might find themselves. "The situation is changing hourly and in our favour," he concluded, and then gave them a final word to cheer them, saying: "I've foreseen this eventuality for some time. You will not be deserted. The Swiss Protecting Power Authorities have had specific warning and requests to watch this camp and to follow the movement of any prisoners. They are in close contact with German authorities in Berlin, who are in the know. You will probably be followed by a representative in person or, if not, your movements will be known in their Legation. You are being carefully watched. Good-bye and good luck to all of you."

Nobody else was allowed near them. At eleven-thirty p.m. the order came for them to move. They were roused from their beds and given two hours to dress, pack and make ready. At one-thirty a.m. they were escorted through a lane of guards to two waiting buses. Bor Komorowski was there with twelve of his most senior officers. John Winant appeared. There were seven British: Captain the Master of Elphinstone, Lieutenant Lord Lascelles, Giles Romilly, Captains, Charles Hopetoun, Michael Alexander and Earl Haig and Lieutenant Max du Hamel. The prison windows were crowded with faces. There was a chorus of good-byes! and good lucks! The twenty-one men filed through the gate. Outside two buses were waiting to take them to an unknown destination. . . .

There was really not much difference between those who left and those who remained. They were all going to be hostages; only the Nazi *Herrenrasse* believed in classifying them, under the delusion that the Allies would bargain for the lives of men as if they were cattle, pedigree cattle being worth more than others.

As the buses, escorted by a light armoured vehicle, tore out of Colditz and into the night, Giles Romilly, in the British bus, said suddenly, breaking the silence,

"I thought you'd all like to know that to-day is Friday, the thirteenth!"

CHAPTER XXIII

HITLER'S LAST REDOUBT

D URING the course of Friday there was a lull within the Castle. Two important items of news, only, came into the camp: one, from the guards returning after taking the Prominente to their destination, the second from the secret wireless receiver. In their wake, the story of Colditz divides naturally into two separate trails, which it were better the reader followed separately to avoid becoming lost. The first trail leads away from the Castle.

A written message was handed to Colonel Tod, signed by Elphinstone, saying the party had arrived safely at the Castle of Königstein on the river Elbe; the same from which General Giraud had escaped to rejoin the Allies earlier in the war. Two of them, he added, Hopetoun and Haig, were seriously ill. They had been ill before they left, as the authorities knew well, and the journey had made their condition worse.

On Saturday, the fourteenth, in the afternoon, the Prominente were moved under heavy guard as before from Königstein, through Czechoslovakia, to Klattau on the borders of Bavaria. There they spent the night. Hopetoun and Haig were left behind at Königstein being too ill to move. The German Commandant had to obtain permission from Berlin to leave them.* The sound of Allied guns could be heard as the two buses and the armoured car left Königstein heading for Hitler's redoubt in the mountains.

Sunday morning, in bright sunshine, the Prominente were moved again. Now they headed towards Austria. As evening drew on, they arrived at Laufen on the river Sal-

* See Author's note on page 622.

zach that divides Austria from Bavaria. They stopped out-side the barracks, once the palace of the Archbishops of Salzburg, and also the prison where the story of Colditz began. The barracks, which, at the beginning of the war, had been Oflag VII.C, was now a civilian internee camp.

Elphinstone as head of the British party refused to disem-bark. He was suspicious. The camp was not under Wehr-macht control and responsibility for any outrage might be difficult to trace. Where he was, he was definitely under Wehrmacht control, facing an Army Colonel who would pay with his head under Himmler's orders if his prisoners escaped and who would also pay with his head under Allied retribution if they disappeared by other means.

The German Colonel in charge agreed to take them to another camp at Tittmoning, ten miles away, occupied by Dutch Officers.

It was nearly dark when they reached Tittmoning. They were marched into the prison, another castle perched on a hill, and in the presence of the German Commandant, were introduced to the Senior Dutch Officers. Giles Romilly could hardly contain himself. Who should he see in the group standing before them but Vandy, grinning all over his face and with the usual devilish twinkle in his eye. Giles was the only one in the British group who had been a contemporary of Vandy in Colditz. The others had all arrived after his departure.

The Commandant of the camp commended the party to the care of the Dutch officers and left them together in order to organise extra precautions amongst the guards. Himm-ler's orders were clear. German officers responsible for the prisoners would pay with their lives, if any of the prisoners escaped.

As soon as they were by themselves, Giles approached Vandy and the two men shook hands warmly.

"I am zo glad you haf come here. Ve vill look after you," said Vandy ubiquitously. "How strange to meet you again in such circumstances."

"Tell me how you got to this camp," said Romilly, "and then I'll give you all the news from Colditz."

Vandy looked at him.

"Come with me. Virst you must haf a hot coffee and something to eat."

He led Romilly through the echoing corridors, to a mess room where a meal was in full swing. They sat down together and as Romilly ate hungrily, Vandy went on:

"I vas sent here in January because the Germans thought to get rid of me. I vas a damn nuisance, they said. I vas *Deutchfeindlich*. They knew I organised all the Dutch escapes and zo they sent me here where there are only old officers and many sick ones—none who vish to escape. Zo they thought, but again they are wrong, vor I haf now some men here ready to escape!" Vandy chuckled with glee. He was looking older and his face was deeply lined but his eye had not lost its sparkle.

Vandy introduced Giles to the officers in the refectory and they talked for some time. Then he escorted him to a dormitory prepared for the five British and the one American Prominente, John Winant. The Polish Generals were entertained by another Dutch officers' mess in a different part of the Castle and slept in a separate dormitory.

The Prominente stayed at Tittmoning for several days.

On Thursday, the nineteenth of April, Vandy had news through the German guards, some of whom were in his pay, that Goebbels and Himmler had been seen in cars, passing through Tittmoning at high speed, in a whirlwind of dust, taking the road to the redoubt built near Hitler's Berchtesgaden. On the same day the Prominente were informed they were to be moved to Laufen. There was little doubt as to the implications of this move. At Laufen, out of the control of the Army, Himmler's thugs would take charge of them.

A secret conference was held at which Vandy produced a plan of campaign. He was nothing if not resourceful, but he was not only resourceful, he was far-sighted. He had a method of escape prepared for two of his own officers which could be used in an emergency such as this. The escape could take place the next day, the twentieth. He proposed that three officers, of whom one should be Romilly who spoke German fluently and the other two, his Dutchmen, should escape by his projected route. But he had not finished. He proposed to wall up the other five (including Winant) in a secret radio room which he had prepared for a clandestine wireless set. They would have food and water for a week, and the Germans would think they had escaped with the three.

The Prominente had only to listen to Vandy for ten minutes, after which they placed themselves entirely in his hands.

The twentieth of April was Hitler's birthday. The escape was planned for the evening. Romilly was equipped along with Lieutenant André Tieleman and a young officer Cadet, both of whom had come to Tittmoning by mistake, as they were neither elderly, nor decrepit, nor sick, nor dangerous like Vandy.

First of all, the five men were walled into the secret radio room with their food reserves. Then, as the moon rose, Vandy and his assistant for the escape, Captain van den Wall Bake, escorted the three escapers to a doorway in the castle from which, one at a time and with suitable distraction of the sentries by helpers in the castle windows, they were able to make a quick dash into the shadows immediately underneath a pagoda sentry box inside the prison perimeter and beside an eight foot wall, bounding the castle. On the other side of the wall was a seventy foot drop to a water meadow. Vandy had the rope. He climbed carefully up the pagoda framework to the top of the wall and secured the rope firmly to a timber strut. The sentry was ten feet above him, on the platform, inside a glass shelter with a veranda around it. Vandy helped Tieleman to mount and then eased him over the edge for the long descent. Dutchmen, in their mess rooms close by, were playing

musical instruments and keeping up a continuous cacophony of laughter, music and singing. Romilly and the
Dutch Cadet came next. Romilly lay flat on the top of the
wall and gripped the rope. As he lifted one leg to drop over,
he hit one of the timber stanchions a resounding whack
with his boot. The sentry came out of his pagoda and leaned
over the balustrade. He saw two men standing on the wall
and a third lying along it. He had left his rifle inside the
pagoda. He yelled "Halt!" and ran to fetch it. In that instant Romilly disappeared over the edge and Vandy whispered to van den Wall Bake, "Quick! Quick! on to the
wall." Van den Wall Bake had not been seen in the shadows.
The next moment he was lying on the top beside Vandy.

The sentry had rung the alarm bell and now dashed on
to the veranda again, aiming his rifle over the side at the
three men and shouting: *"Hände hoch! Hände hoch!"* The
Dutchmen complied as best they could without going over
the edge down the seventy foot drop. The guard was turned
out, arrived at the double and arrested the three men. The
sentry reported he had caught them in the act and had
spotted them in time, before anyone had escaped.

They were led before the Commandant, who treated
them jocosely, in conformity with the state of the war at
that moment.

"How silly of you to try to escape now! What is the
point? The war is nearly over. You will be home soon. I
have told you that General Eisenhower has issued strict
orders by wireless that prisoners are to remain in their
camps. They run excessive dangers of being killed by
moving about alone in the open country at this time. I
suppose you just wished more quickly to see your wives and
sweethearts?"

The Commandant was elderly, grey haired and formerly
a retired senior ranking army officer. He was not an arrogant
personality.

Vandy replied in German,

"Of course, the Commandant has divined our intentions
correctly."

"Very well, the matter is closed. I must, according to regulations, hold an *Appell*. I am sorry, but, please remember, it is you who have caused this trouble and not me."

The whistles blew and the floodlights were switched on. The Dutch officers assembled, and the Polish Prominente assembled. . . . There was a pause as the German officers, with horror-stricken incredulity, surveyed the ranks before them. Hurriedly and nervously the count was taken. Six Prominente and one Dutch officer were missing. A second count was taken. The result was the same. It was reported to the Commandant in his office. The elderly soldier's hair rose from his scalp. He had thought he would spend the last years of life quietly and peacefully. Now, in a moment, all had changed and he saw his head in the noose, the gallows below him and felt the sickening drop. No! he thought, as his eyes started from his head, it would not be like that. Instead, he felt the handkerchief round his eyes, he could hear the fire orders and then one rending crackle. . . .

He sat up in his chair behind his desk. His junior officers were awaiting orders. He would have to give them. He would be signing his own death warrant. He must stall. It was his only hope. He ordered his officers to search the camp at once and to continue until he issued further orders.

Searching continued for two days in the camp. Nothing was found. The Commandant had to report and give himself up. He was arrested, summarily court-martialled and sentenced to death. The order of execution remained only to be signed by Himmler, as being the Head of the Organisation which, under Hitler's authority, had issued the original commands. Himmler was not easily accessible. He was already in hiding in the mountains. In the meantime, the search continued desperately, outside the camp. Three thousand Germans scoured the countryside without avail. The Polish Prominente were removed to Laufen. On the fifth day, perhaps information had leaked out, nobody could tell, they began to search inside the camp again; knocking down walls, removing floors and attacking the ceilings.

Eventually, they came upon the secret hide and unearthed four British officers and John Winant.

This discovery occurred on Tuesday, the twenty-fourth of April. What followed is best told by the Master of Elphinstone himself in a report which was published in *The Times:*

'Under very heavy escort we were taken to the internee camp at Laufen. Here the German general commanding the Munich area visited the camp, and in the course of an interview finally gave me his word of honour that we should remain there until the end of the war—a promise repeated in the presence of the Swiss Minister by the German Kommandant next day. The latter, however, could, or would, give no information as to the reason for our detention apart from all other officer-prisoners, except that it was ordered by Himmler.

'All remained quiet until the fall of Munich, and then, with the Americans once more rapidly approaching, the orders were given that we were to move at once—in spite of promises given—into the mountains of the Austrian Tyrol. Two officers, an S.S. Colonel and a *Luftwaffe* major—were sent by Obergruppenführer and General of S.S. Berger to conduct us. At six-thirty a.m. we entered the transport, with the colonel, fingering his revolver, watching us, together with a somewhat sinister-looking blonde woman who accompanied him in his car. This was possibly the most trying of all the moves, as the whole scene had a gangster-like atmosphere. We drove through Salzburg, past Berchtesgaden, and finally stopped at a Stalag in a remote valley in the Tyrol. We were allowed no contact with the prisoners, who included representatives of most of the allied nations, but were isolated in the German part of the camp.

'The representative of the Swiss Legation (Protecting Power), with admirable and very reassuring promptitude, followed us and visited the Kommandant within a very few hours of our arrival. Later the Swiss Minister and his staff started on the series of interviews and discussions with the leading German Government figures who were in the neighbourhood. This work, which they carried out with such wonderful patience and success, was of the utmost difficulty, as the leaders were scattered in remote mountain hamlets, and all roads were choked with army vehicles and personnel.

'Finally, S.S. Obergruppenführer Berger, chief, among other things, of all prisoner-of-war affairs, agreed to hand us over to the Swiss and allow them to conduct us through the lines. He did this on his own responsibility, and warned the Swiss that other elements in the Government would, if they knew, resist his orders and lay hands on us. He therefore sent to the camp a special guard under an S.S. Colonel, armed with every type of weapon, to guard us against the "other German elements" during this final night of our captivity.

'Berger himself came to visit us and in a long and theatrically declaimed speech reiterated, probably for the last time, many of the well worn phrases of German propaganda together with several revelations of the complete break-up of the German Government and people. He then informed us that owing to this break-up he felt he was no longer in a position to safeguard us properly and had agreed to hand us over to Swiss protection. On leaving, he turned, theatrical to the end, to the German officers in charge of us and, having given his final commands, said: "Gentlemen, these are probably the last orders I shall give as a high official of the Third German Reich." We were due to leave at eleven next morning. The Swiss Legation attaché who was to accompany us in his car arrived early, but for more than three rather tantalising hours there was no sign of the German trucks which were to take the party, a fact which caused some anxiety in view of Berger's warnings. At length, however, two other trucks were secured locally, thanks once again to the perseverance of the Swiss attaché, and finally at about five p.m. we set off, each vehicle draped with the Swiss flag, along the densely packed roads. Accompanying us was an S.S. medical officer as personal representative of General Berger.

'At about eleven-thirty p.m. this officer stopped the convoy in a small village in the mountains, saying he had orders from Obergruppenführer Berger to see that we had food and drink in his headquarters here. We entered a house filled with S.S. troops, many of them intoxicated, and were shown into an upstairs room where some food and much drink were laid out. In the middle of the meal the Obergruppenführer himself once more made a theatrical entry, played the expansive if somewhat nerve-strained host, and again poured out a flood of propaganda and explanation. After some time he gave an order to an S.S. adjutant, who handed him a scarlet leather case. After yet another speech he turned to me, as senior of the British-American party, and handed me the case, as "proof of his good feelings." Inside was an elaborately ornamented pistol of ivory, brass and enamel, with his own signature engraved across the butt.

'After this strange interlude we set off once more. At dawn we passed successfully through the last German post, and shortly afterwards were halted, to our joy and relief, by American tanks. A few hours later we were most kindly and hospitably welcomed by an American Divisional Headquarters at Innsbruck. It would be difficult indeed for our party adequately to express our gratitude to the Swiss Minister and his staff for all that they did to make this release possible."

The Polish Prominente were released in the same convoy. It is interesting to note that Colonel Tod's last cheering words to the Prominente before they left Colditz were not said without avail. The Swiss Minister to Germany was on their trail and caught up with them at Laufen on the 25th of April.

Giles Romilly takes up the thread of his own last escape from the castle at Tittmoning in an article he wrote for the *Sunday Express* of May 6th, 1945. He says:

'My legs were dangling over the wall. The drop was seventy feet down to the moon-whitened grass, and it looked terrifying.

'I gripped the rope, let myself forward and began to go down faster than expected.

'I knew I should grip with my feet, but never once managed it. And the rope was tearing my fingers. About halfway I remember thinking, "This parachute should open soon."

'At the bottom, already down, was the Dutch officer, Lieutenant André Tieleman.

'We tramped down lonely side roads, star-guided. It was a grand night. And it was Hitler's birthday. And we were free; precariously free—but still free.

'That was eleven days ago.

'We were Prominente, and I heard the word in Dachau horror-camp.

'In Dachau there were thirty-two thousand prisoners—and forty Prominente. Two of the 'Proms' were English. One was Lieutenant Colonel McGrath, brought there for refusing to form a "Free Irish" corps.

'The other, I believe, was Major Stevens, captured on the Dutch frontier by a trick in the first months of the war.

'A few days before the U.S. troops moved in the "Proms" were moved to Schloss Ita, near Innsbruck in the Tyrol.'

The Prominente were, indeed, all moving in the same direction. From camps all over Germany, the great trek had begun to bring Hitler's hostages into his spider's web, cast in the Austrian mountains.

Romilly and Tieleman managed to reach Munich in three days, after some adventures. On one occasion, they were held for questioning at a police station but their papers, prepared by Vandy, were found to be in order. The officer in charge received an urgent telephone message while they were standing in his office, concerning the escape of important prisoners from Tittmoning. He hurried them out of the office immediately, saying he had an urgent assignment and politely wished them a pleasant journey.

In Munich, the two men lived as Germans, quietly and inconspicuously in a cheap hotel, awaiting the American advance. They reported themselves to American Army Headquarters as soon as the latter entered the city during the last week of April. Romilly was back in England by May 2nd.

Vandy had not completed his duty as a soldier and an ally. Not satisfied with having delayed for five days the execution of Himmler's orders, perhaps saving the lives of the Prominente thereby, he risked his life by leaving the camp in the dead of night as soon as the Americans had entered Tittmoning, and contrary to American Army orders. There was a severe curfew in operation. Anyone seen on the streets was liable to be shot at sight. He appeared at American Headquarters where he reported the transfer of the Prominente including John Winant and was able, moreover, through his own German sources of information to give details as to the route they had taken into the Tyrol from Laufen.

The cataclysm that swept over Germany and Austria in April saved many lives. Communications were severed, the roads were clogged with refugee traffic, and the precious signatures of Hitler's hierarchy were not forthcoming. Hitler committed suicide in the Berlin bunker on April 30th; many executions were stayed and many a happy man to-day owes his continuing life on this globe to a missing black scrawl on a sheet of white paper; among them is the German Commandant of the Dutch Camp at Tittmoning.

CHAPTER XXIV

FINALE: THE RELIEF OF COLDITZ

BACK in the Castle: Friday, the thirteenth of April, an unlucky day for the Prominente, brought good news to Colditz through the secret wireless receiver. Hodge's spearhead, south of Leipzig, was advancing again after a slight check during the day of the twelfth. The Americans were twenty miles away at dawn and, by the evening, they were in the Colditz area, invisible but there, nevertheless. Shells fell in the town as the dusk approached and, in the distance, machine-gun fire could be heard. Desultory firing continued through the night.

The next morning, Saturday the fourteenth, at dawn, the battle for Colditz began. The Allied Air Forces had possession of the sky. An American reconnaissance plane zoomed overhead. A few shells followed, dropping into various parts of the town. The artillery were ranging.

Colonel Tod was called again to the Kommandantur, where Prawitt faced him.

"You are to move the British out of the Castle towards the east under guard. I have orders from Dresden."

This was Tod's chance. Twenty-four hours had just made the difference. The S.S. had their hands full. To-day, they were under attack fighting a battle, and they could not possibly deal with three hundred British prisoners not to mention a thousand Frenchmen. They could not even spare the time to come into the camp and shoot them all. Tod seized the opportunity.

"The British refuse to move," he said. "You will have to turn them out with the bayonet and the British will fight. This is not mutiny. It is self-defence. You are sending them out to their death. Tell Dresden we shall not move."

Tod was recalling another occasion, a long time ago,

when the Commandant had shown he was less fearful of his superiors when they were a long way off. Those nearby were heavily engaged which came to the same thing.

The Commandant weakened.

"I shall 'phone my Headquarters," he said, sitting at his desk and picking up the army field telephone. He spoke to a couple of exchanges in turn, using German code names. Then he was speaking to the General. He reported the position at Colditz, leading up to his interview with Tod, ending with, "and the British refuse to move."

There was an explosion from the other end. A guttural German voice was yelling blue murder at the Commandant who held the receiver far away from his ear. Gradually the rasping died down. Oberst Prawitt was at last showing signs of courage. With remarkable calm he addressed his senior:

"I cannot move the prisoners without shooting them and they will then resist. Their Commander will disclaim mutiny on grounds of self-defence. Will you take the responsibility if I use my weapons and prisoners are killed?"

"No!" came the answer, shouted down the telephone.

"Neither will I!" said the Commandant and banged down the receiver. . . .

Even the few marker shells dropped into Colditz by the American artillery were having a surprisingly salutary effect on the conduct of affairs within the Castle walls.

The prisoners did not move.

Heavy shelling started in the afternoon and buildings were soon on fire in many quarters. The noise of gunfire increased to a crescendo. To the onlookers in the Castle, no orderly plan appeared to be unfolding. There was only destruction, smoke, flames and noise, the tearing scrunch of shells, the whine of splinters, the acrid smell of burnt explosive and chaos.

Half a dozen shells landed in the Castle, splintering glass everywhere and leaving ragged holes in the roof. Nobody was seriously hurt. Duggie Bader was knocked off his tin legs. The prisoners were ordered to the ground floor.

The Kommandantur fared worse and a dozen shells tore large gaps in the building, wounding several Germans. Nevertheless, the general shelling appeared to be avoiding the Castle.

In the early afternoon, Colonel Tod had another session with Oberst Prawitt. The Commandant, judging by his appearance, had probably received information, though he did not say so, that the S.S. would not retreat into the Castle and make a stand in it. His face showed immense relief. He was wreathed in smiles and almost fawning on Tod as he told him that he would surrender to him the inside of the Castle on certain conditions: the S.S. were still in the town, and no sign must be given to them that the Castle had been surrendered; no national or other coloured flags to be in evidence: no white flags of surrender to be visible at the windows; appearances to be kept up by leaving the sentries at their posts around the exterior; a guarantee to be given by the S.B.O. that he, Oberst Prawitt, would not be handed over to the Russians.

Tod refused to give any guarantees. He thought for a moment, realising the value and importance of access to the armoury in case of need. He decided to take a risk. He compromised on one point, making a counter proposal. If the interior of the whole Castle were handed over to him, including the armoury, if and when he so desired so that he could move his officers freely within the Kommandantur area, he would instruct them not to show signs of surrender outside the Castle. He added that he would see the Commandant was treated with justice, that was as far as he could go. Tod was becoming master of the situation. He would move his officers about and would obtain arms if he wanted them though already he felt the danger from the S.S. receding. He ran the risk that the Americans might take it into their heads to blow up the Castle not knowing who was inside. He would like to have put out flags. He used his judgment. The shells, he considered, which had entered

the Castle were 'off target'. The Americans were now pouring high explosive into the town. He was sure that they
were avoiding the Castle and for no other reason than that
they knew there were prisoners inside. Finally, Tod considered it wiser to keep his men within the inner courtyard,
unless the situation deteriorated. If the S.S. decided to move
into the Castle he was to be informed in time. The Commandant was not treacherous. He himself with a small
staff would keep their eye on developments from the
Kommandantur.

The Commandant accepted the terms with some alacrity.
As Colonel Tod walked back to the prisoners' courtyard
to assemble his staff officers, the first American tanks were
spotted on the horizon through Keith Milne's telescope.

All through the night of the fourteenth to the fifteenth
the battle for Colditz continued. There was an electric
power cut in the whole district, and the slave gang was hard
put to it, to keep the wireless receiver in action. The searchlights went out. Instead, a pale moon suffused the Castle
with ghostly luminosity. Its belfries, buttresses and towering
walls stood out grimly against the skyline. Unearthly lights
and shadows flickered across its surface, cast up from the
flames and the smoke in the valley. Like an evil witch, it
hovered over the steaming cauldron of the town, applying
fuel to the fire underneath as the bright flashes of exploding shells sent dark clouds into the air and new fires licked
around the bowl.

Nobody slept much during the night. The moon cast a
grey light into the dormitories and the very air seemed
feverish. Men tossed and turned, straw palliasses rustled
interminably. Explosions shook the buildings and air blast
whoofed through the wide open windows, tinkling the panes
of glass. The rasp of machine-guns increased as the moon-
light faded giving place to a dawn that streaked layers of
grey and gold across the sky from the east. The rattle of
muskets drew nearer. American light bombers droned overhead and dropped their shattering loads on the railway
lines and the roads.

Sunday, the fifteenth of April, saw the culmination of the attack. The weather was fine and the sun shone in a translucent spring sky. American shellfire was heavy all through the morning, yet the Castle was not hit. It was now obviously being carefully preserved. The town was being reduced to a mass of burning timber, rubble and twisted steel.

One of the five French Generals who had recently arrived, General de Boisse, of the French 62nd Division, chose this morning to have his portrait painted in pastelles by the camp artist, John Watton. A jagged white chalk streak on the picture, underneath the General's chin, which he would not allow to be removed, records to this day, the moment when the Germans tried to blow up Colditz bridge.

It was their last despairing effort to delay the Americans before retreating with their tanks, a beaten enemy, towards the southeast.

The blown bridge did not collapse. Piers were damaged but the roadway held, and the Americans were not stopped. By eleven o'clock in the morning the tanks were seen in the town. One after the other, with long intervals between, they trundled carefully into the main street, splaying out fanwise into secondary roads and lanes as they reached them. Moving warily in front and around the tanks could be seen the mine removal squads and the infantry. The latter, covered by the tanks, advanced from house to house amongst the ruins, breaking in the front doors where they remained standing, and disappearing inside. From the windows, white sheets would appear, one after the other, in token of surrender.

Underneath the walls of the Castle, a tank rounded a street corner. Lying in the gutter, not fifty yards away, a fairhaired Hitler Youth, of scarcely fifteen years, opened up on it with a machine-gun. A woman, probably his mother, screamed at him from an upper window in the house nearby. Another machine-gun crackled angrily, and the boy rolled over. American G.I.s appeared from behind the tank and began taking over the houses, one by one, on either side of the street.

Half an hour later, the gate into the prisoners' courtyard opened, and an American soldier stepped into the spring sunshine in the middle of the yard. A tall, broad-chested G.I. with an open, weatherbeaten countenance, his belt and straps festooned with ammunition clips and grenades, a sub-machine gun in his hand, he stood and, looking upwards, slowly turned around. His gaze toured the full circle of the steep roofs above him, the massive walls, the barred windows and, finally, the cobbles at his feet.

There were many officers in the courtyard at the time. For fully a minute they watched him, incredulously. Some were walking around the yard. They stopped and stared at him blankly. Some were chatting in groups. They ceased talking and looked, quizzically, in his direction. A few, unperturbed by the march of events, were sitting on benches, reading. The sudden silence made them raise their heads. They stared with mouths agape at the strange intruder standing in the sunlight. Faces at the windows remained motionless like wax masks without expression.

Dick Howe saw the G.I. enter. A brainstorm momentarily paralysed the normal currents of his mind. His memory played tricks upon him, and switched, suddenly, to a scene which floated past his inward eye. He saw himself standing on a dusty road outside Calais in 1940, unarmed and a prisoner. A German soldier was passing and he shouted, *"Für Sie ist der Krieg beeudet. Wir fahren gegen England, Sie gehen nach Deutschland."* Now the irony of the words struck him. "For you the war is over." That was five years ago. And the German? He was probably dead long ago.

An officer, standing near the gate, advanced with outstretched hand and shook the hand extended by the American, who grinned at him and said, cheerfully, "Any doughboys here?" The spell was broken.

Suddenly, a mob was rushing towards him, shouting and cheering and struggling madly to reach him, to make sure that he was alive, to touch him and from the touch to know again the miracle of living, to be men in their own right, freed from bondage, outcast no more, liberated by their Allies and their friends, their faith in God's mercy justified, their patience rewarded, the nobility of mankind vindicated, justice at last accomplished and tyranny once more overcome.

The blown bridge did not stop the Americans

Men wept, unable to restrain themselves. It was not enough that the body was free once more to roam the earth. Feelings, pent up and dammed behind the mounting walls of five successive torturing, introverted years, had to erupt.

They welled up like gushing springs, they overflowed, they burst their banks, they tumbled unhindered and uncontrolled. Frenchmen with tears streaming down their faces kissed each other on both cheeks—the salute of brothers. They kissed the G.I., they kissed everyone within range. The storm of emotion burst. The merciful rain descended. The grey clouds drifted from the horizon of the mind, borne on fresh salt and moisture-laden breezes across the unchained oceans of memory from the far off shores of love. Home and country beckoned, loved ones were waiting. Wives and sweethearts, mothers, fathers, and children never seen, were calling across the gulf of the absent years.

Man was at his finest amidst the grandeur of this moment of liberation. A noble symphony arranged by the Great Composer had reached its thunderous finale and, as the last triumphal chord swelled into the Hymn of Nations, man looked into the face of his Creator turned towards him, a vision of tenderness, mirrored for an instant by the purity of his own unrepressed torrent of joy and thankfulness. At such a moment, mountains move at the behest of man, he has such power in the sight of God.

CHAPTER XXV

CODA: THE CLIFFS OF DOVER

THE celebrations upon the relief of the Castle began in earnest on Sunday afternoon, the fifteenth of April. Food reserves, laid in for a siege, were broken out and the Americans brought wine and beer from the town. Colonel Tod wisely kept the prisoners inside the Castle until the first exuberance at their deliverance had worn off. It was better they should become accustomed in their minds to the idea that they were free before they were actually let loose upon the world. They were, be it remembered, 'the men of spirit'.

Tod had already organised officers into squads with specific duties and instructions, varying according to the different eventualities that he could foresee. In the circumstances, as no fighting was required of his men, only the squads with technical duties came into action. Before they did so, however, he held a conference with the American officer commanding the troops who had captured the town.

Lieutenant-Colonel Shaughnessy came from Carolina. He spoke with a slow drawl and acted with lightning rapidity. He was not, after all, in command of one of Hodges' most daring spearheads, driving hundreds of miles into enemy territory in advance of the main forces, for nothing. Tried in battle, full of initiative and daring, he was one of the men who shortened the war and saved thousands of lives.

A Colonel, he was at the head of a force from Combat Command R of the Ninth Armoured Division (Fifth Corps) of the U.S. First Army. He had under him the Third Battalion of the 273rd Infantry Regiment, 69th Infantry Division, and detachments of tanks and mobile artillery taken from the Ninth Armoured Division. These together constituted his task force. By this time, incidentally, it is worth recording that the Ninth Armoured Division had been nicknamed by the Germans the 'Phantom Division' because it seemed to be everywhere there was action. Among Shaughnessy's junior officers was Lieutenant Kenny Dodson, the efficient young artillery officer who had commanded the shoot against Colditz. The first American squad actually to set foot in the Castle consisted of an Intelligence and Reconnaissance section of four men from H.Q. Company, Third Battalion, 273rd Infantry Regiment. They had entered the village in the early morning and were gradually driven up the hill to the Castle by American shell-fire. Seeing no guards they forced open the moat gateway and found themselves in the German Kommandantur courtyard. Two groups of men faced them. On one side were senior Allied officers led by Colonel Tod. On the other was a disconsolate body of German officers. The four young men promptly disarmed the Germans, and one of them, Private First Class Walter V. Burrows, of Pennsylvania, volunteered to escort them back to Shaughnessy's Headquarters. Private First Class Alan H. Murphy, Bronze Star Medal, of New York State, led the section. The other two were Privates First Class Francis A. Giegnas, Jr., of New Jersey, and Robert B. Miller, of Pennsylvania.

At the conference, held in the German Kommandantur, Shaughnessy accepted the surrender of the Castle and its garrison. The Commandant and Hauptmann Eggers, the Security officer, were arrested. Tod proposed that the P.O.W.s, other than those on special duties, should be kept within the Castle precincts until Tuesday the seventeenth. Shaughnessy agreed this was wise and warned that German suicide parties were still dotted all over the countryside. Tod offered the services of his organised squads to keep the water and electricity supply of Colditz functioning, to look after other essential town services, and to see that repairs were effected as quickly as possible. Shaughnessy accepted, and the British Technical Squads came into action.

Gordon Rolfe left the camp with a party within the hour, to take over the Colditz power station and start it running again. Dick set off with another party to look after the water pumping station. On the way he commandeered a powerful B.M.W. German Army motor-cycle which became 'his transport' until he boarded a plane for England. He found the pumping station had not suffered badly from the bombardment. Buildings had been damaged but the sturdy machinery was in working order. Debris alone had to be cleared and the pumps could be started again on power from the heavy oil engines. German staff were already back at the station when he arrived. The Teutonic passion for work and order could not be denied. Dick found they needed no goading and no supervision, although they did not know how, where or when their next pay packet would materialise. They cleared and cleaned and repaired. The pumps were working again by Sunday evening, supplying water to the town. Water pipes were burst and leaking everywhere. The task of repairing them was tackled by another squad of Royal Engineers.

In the Castle, Americans came and went and stories of the latter days went the rounds. Lieutenant Dodson confessed that the Castle was within an ace of being bombarded by his mobile artillery detachment with high explosive shells followed by phosphorus, when the task force approached Colditz. Standing orders were to flatten anything that showed resistance. Colditz showed resistance, and the best target in the town was the Castle. Dodson's artillery was fanned out and ranging on it when a spotter noticed a flag in one of the windows through his binoculars. It was a French flag. He scanned the Castle more closely and saw a Union Jack. He immediately telephoned Dodson who held his fire and sent word back to headquarters at Hohnbach, a village they had just captured, asking for confirmation as to the nature of the Castle. The answer came through: 'Do not repeat not shell Castle which contains P.O.W.'

The prison was, in fact, within an ace of being shelled. As far as can be ascertained Hohnbach received the order to preserve the Castle from Hodge's headquarters at about the same time as Dodson asked for confirmation. Be it noted that this occurred some twelve hours before Colonel Tod agreed with the German Commandant not to hang out flags. By then there was evidence indicating that the shelling was deliberately directed away from the Castle.

On Sunday afternoon, the glider was taken from its hiding place. The trap-door in the floor of the workshop was carefully enlarged and the glider parts were lowered into the big attic with the dormer windows. In this empty room the four builders assembled the glider. By five o'clock it was ready. They sealed the trap-door up to the workshop and then opened the main door of the lower attic. Dick experienced the pleasure of sitting in the cockpit and manipulating the controls. "It's a perfect little bird," he said as he waggled the rudder. "I believe I'd be as safe in this as in my old Matilda."

And Lulu Lawton commented sadly, "I'd have given a lot to see the Jerries' reaction when the bathful of concrete landed on the floor after falling sixty feet."

News of the existence of the glider had spread like wildfire. The camp had been advised that the glider would be on view and there was a queue already waiting that stretched to the bottom of the spiral staircase. When the door opened the crowd surged forward.

As there were thirteen hundred officers in the camp at the time, the queue continued late into the evening. An American girl, a newspaper correspondent—Lee Carson was her name—had found her way to Colditz and she was escorted to the attic by Duggie Bader. She took photographs. (The glider builders and the author would give much to be able to trace them.)

The glider reposed on its polished skid, a symphony in blue and white check; its wings glossy and taut; its controls sensitive, balanced, easy to the touch; a tropical bird, it looked as if it needed only a gentle breeze to float it easily off the ground. It filled the attic. Its total span from wing tip to wing tip was thirty-three feet. It was a beautiful piece of craftsmanship and astounded all who saw it. Men gasped with wonder and appreciation as they toured around it. The Americans asked,

"Where has it come from? How was it possible to build it under the Germans' noses?" They were told.

Germans, remaining in the camp under Allied orders, to keep it functioning, who saw it too, asked the same questions. The answer was, "You were our guards. You ought to know without being told."

Before the prisoners vacated the Castle the attic was locked up again. Both the glider and the secret workshop may still be there to this day. . . .

Monday the sixteenth was a dog day in which prisoners recovered from the celebrations of Sunday and began to regain their perspective, looking towards new horizons.

On Tuesday, they were allowed the freedom of Colditz, but warned not to venture into the surrounding country which was placed out of bounds. Three Frenchmen who disobeyed the order were recaptured by the Germans and disappeared.

Colonel Shaughnessy was busy, with British and French help, organising preparations for the evacuation of the prisoners. Dick Howe recalls two vivid impressions of that day. The first was that of the Weasel, the City Slicker and Mac (MacColm) holding open house in a villa near the Castle in which three beautiful blonde German Fräulein acted as their hostesses serving tea, coffee, drinks and meals throughout the day to all visitors. The second was that of the Distillery Monopoly Directors, Charlie Goonstein Van Rood, Bush Parker and Bag Dickenson, driving around the town in a huge Mercèdés Benz touring car.

The town was found to be full of slave workers of both sexes: Poles, French, Czechs, Russians, Rumanians, Yugoslavs, Hungarians and Jews.

On Wednesday, April the eighteenth, the evacuation began.

American trucks, driven by Negro drivers, carried the British contingent a hundred miles to the south-west.

Dick, on his B.M.W., acted as outrider to one of the columns. The convoy was widely spread out for safety, and on the move, the Negroes drove the trucks at full throttle all the time. The leading fifteen-hundredweight truck contained the American officer in charge and Hauptmann Püpcke, one of the German officers of Colditz. He knew the roads of the district. The going was dangerous at times, especially through the woods, where German *Sturmges-chütze* nests—S.S. stormtroopers—still lurked in ambush. Dick, at the behest of the American officer, had the nasty job of reconnoitring a road block which loomed ahead at one stage of the journey. He rode flat out up to it, weaving as he approached. He found it unmanned. Not once, through thirty miles of no-man's land, was the column shot at, though shadows flitted about amongst the trees in the surrounding woods. Strength in numbers seemed to be the explanation.

They arrived, in the late afternoon, at a captured airfield near Chemnitz, called Kaledar, were given a hot meal of American Army rations and bedded down on clean straw for the night.

Early next morning, as Dick stepped out of the hut where they had been sleeping he was accosted by the Major in charge of the airfield.

"I hear you boys are back from five years in prison?" he questioned.

"That's correct," said Dick.

"I guess you're keen to get back home then. I'll see what I can do." He hailed the leading crew of a flight of Dakotas that had just landed.

"Where're you going back to?" he shouted.

The leading officer replied, approaching,

"We're due for Rolle."

"No, you're not," said the Major, "you're going to England."

Suits me!" came the answer.

Within two hours they were boarding the planes. There must have been ten of them because they took the whole British contingent, thirty to a plane. Dick tried to take his B.M.W. with him—it was a beautiful machine. There was nothing doing, he had to leave it behind. He rode around the hutted camp at the edge of the airfield until he saw a G.I. coming out of a workshop. With a roar he rode up behind him, stopped and said,

"Hey! can you ride a motor-bike?"

"Yea."

"Well," said Dick dismounting, "you've got one."

He hurried off to join his plane and, looking back, saw the G.I., arms akimbo, slowly walking around the machine, with his eyes agog, like an art connoisseur who had just been presented with an old master out of the sky.

The weather was bad and the ceiling was practically zero. In Dick's plane were many of the 'Old Contemptibles' —men who had been in Colditz from the very early days: Guy German, Rupert Barry, Scarlet O'Hara, Cyril Lewthwaite, Padre Platt, Don Donaldson, Peter Storie Pugh, Stooge Wardle, Keith Milne and Jim Rogers. The plane cavorted about the sky. Everybody except Don Donaldson was sick. They landed to refuel at Rouen and then crossed the Channel amongst the clouds, almost dropping into the sea at times.

Jim Rogers, who was not as ill as some of the others, went forward to the cockpit and looked ahead into the blank wall of vapour. He asked the pilot,

"Are we anywhere near Dover?" The plane lurched and sank a hundred feet. The green spuming sea appeared just below them.

"Don't know!" was the reply, "I'm following the guy in front."

Jim scanned the clouds in front without seeing anything. He was rubbing his head ruefully where something hard had hit him when the aircraft bumped.

"Visibility yesterday was nil," said the pilot. "One of our planes flew head on into the cliffs. It's better to-day."

Jim went back to the others, seated facing each other on the floor, backs propped up against the bulwarks. They were looking green. The smell of sick was overpowering. Jim was terrified. After five years, to come to a sticky end in the Channel! He longed to see the cliffs of Dover but he did not want to meet them head on. He could see the crash coming. In a daze he heard his own voice,

"We're nearly home, boys. The pilot's terrific. Gives you confidence. He says he's sorry about the weather, but he wants you to see the cliffs of Dover. That's why he's flying low—so you don't miss them." He suddenly halted in his speech as he realised what he had said. Then another thought struck him. "About time I stopped this morale boosting," he said to himself. "The chaps'll have to look after themselves now."

Don Donaldson, the R.A.F. veteran, wedged in a corner near the tail, had been dozing peacefully. He looked up at Jim and then at the rows of green faces around him and said, "Tell 'em a story, Old Horse. They look as if they need cheering up. Tell 'em about the Mandarin's daughter you met in Hong Kong. They've got to get accustomed to having women folk around again."

---

* When Admiral Doenitz surrendered on May 2nd, after the death of Hitler, the Russians, by Allied agreement, occupied Königstein. A week later, the prisoners, including senior staff officers, Dutch, Belgian, French, British and American, were still confined in the Castle. Two Americans escaped to the American lines, forty miles away, and within hours a U.S. armed convoy entered the town and removed the whole prisoner contingent. Hopetoun and Haig were promptly flown to Britain in an ambulance plane. Both men recovered their health slowly.